THE ORIGIN OF A ROCK & ROLL FACE **WOOD**
RONNIE
WOOD

TERRY RAWLINGS

TERRY'S RAWLINGS' love of music dates back to the late 1970's when he was employed as a post boy by Decca Records.

His first literary break came courtesy of *Paul Weller* when he wrote his first booklet **'All Our Yesterdays'** (one of only two books ever published on 'The Jam' leader's short lived 'Riot Stories' imprint) in 1982 before establishing his career as a designer and art worker for bands signed to the Sire, Warner Brothers and Stiff record labels.

Terry came to prominence in 1994 with his highly controversial book **'Who Killed Christopher Robin? The Truth Behind The Murder Of Brian Jones'** - in which he uncovered the real and now widely accepted truth behind the fate of the Rolling Stones founder and original guitarist. Eventually much of his material formed the basis of the script for the major feature film 'Stoned' directed by veteran British film maker *Stephen Woolley*. Terry was the project consultant when it was filmed in 2005.

Following the success of 'Who Killed Christopher Robin' Terry teamed up with archivist and researcher *Keith Badman* to write **'Good Times, Bad Times: The Definitive Diary of the Rolling Stones 1960-1969'**. Terry and Keith pieced together the fascinating day-by-day rise to fame of the world's greatest rock & roll band, aided by the infamous *Tom Keylock*, the Stones minder and driver throughout the 1960's. Tom's first hand eyewitness accounts and personal photographs provided an exclusive insight into the band's secretive inner circle.

Following 'Good Times, Bad Times' Terry and Keith produced **'Quite Naturally - The Small Faces: A Day–by-Day Guide to the Career of a Pop Group'** repeating the successful format of the Stones book, and the tongue in cheek **'Empire Made; A Handy Parka Pocket Guide To all Things Mod'**.

Next up came the highly respected and acclaimed **'Rock On Wood'**, the first official biography of *Ronnie Wood*, published in April 1999.

The year 2000 saw the release of his best selling labour of love **'Mod - A Very British Phenomenon'**, a lush coffee table book covering the roots and continued rise of the most enduring of England's youth movements.

2003 saw the publication of **'Harmony in my Head'**, Terry's biography of *Steve Diggle*, the legendary *Buzzcocks'* guitarist which produced Steve's hilarious firsthand account of the Punk revolution of the 1970's and beyond.

Books on British fashion and the fashion industry followed including **'My Favourite Shirt: A History of Ben Sherman'** written with fellow author *Paolo Hewitt*, and **'A Century Celebrated: 100 years of Lee Cooper'**.

There was also the colourful and lavish **'British Beat'** an encyclopedic coffee table accompaniment to Omnibus' best selling 'Mod', and **'Sniffin' Glue'** a return to year zero, written and compiled with the fanzines originators *Mark Perry* and *Danny Baker*.

In addition Terry has contributed many articles to most of the major music magazines as well as over a dozen documentary and DVD releases.

Other activities include the setting up of London's very first gallery exclusively and solely dedicated to Rock Photography in Waterloo and (until his recent illness) he owned and managed 'Filthys', the successful live music venue in Twickenham south west London.

An updated version of 'Rock On Wood' will be released at The Vintage Festival at Goodwood in August 2010 in both paperback and e-book formats.

Currently in the pipeline is the forthcoming coffee table and e-book **'The British Invasion - The Pop Invasion of America'**, a re-assessed 'Who Killed Christopher Robin' (complete with unseen privately shot DVD material relating to the guitarist's mysterious death) and a 90 minute DVD release of the *Making The Modern Scene* benefit concert for Terry filmed at the 100 club in 2009, featuring Clash guitar hero *Mick Jones*, Sex Pistol *Glen Matlock*, Buzzcock *Steve Diggle* and Kink *Mick Avory*.

ACKNOWLEDGMENTS AND THANKS

TO ALL THOSE WHO HELPED WITH THE ORIGINAL... Ron, Jo, Art, Angie, Lizzie, Krissie, Barney, Ali, Kim, Tony, Nick Cowan, Rich and Sue Cunningham, Reg Pippet, Kenney Jones, Bob Garner, Eddie Phillips, Mandy and Steve Hume, Japp Hoetsman, Jack Jones, Dougal Butler, Sandy Sarjeant, Steve Marriott, John Gray, Marilyn, Kenny and Gary Millard, Mike Stax, Shirley Arnold, John Hellier, Phil Smee, Ian McLagan, Shel Talmy, Donovan, Jim McCarty, Keith Grant, Roman Saliki, Jimmy Page, Paul McEvoy, Paolo Hewitt, Lesley Benson and Keith Badman.

AND THANKS TO EVERY ONE WHO HELPED OUT AGAIN TEN YEARS LATER... Mainly Paul McEvoy and Eddie Piller, Dan, Rich, Berit and all at Acid Jazz, Mike Chapman, Paul Hallam...

Love to Geri, Molly, Nancy, Becca, Charlotte and Fiona.
And, of course, anyone I've mistakenly missed out.

PHOTOS - Thanks mainly to Lizzie Wood, Ron Wood, Art Wood, Tony Munroe, Ali McKenzie, Phil Smee, Kenny Pickett, Shirley Arnold, Reg Pippett, Angie Wood.

Any inconsistencies in name spellings are noted, and we apologise profusely to the people concerned...

ACID JAZZ

This edition published in Great Britain in 2010 by
ACID JAZZ BOOKS,
146 BETHNAL GREEN ROAD,
LONDON E2 6DG

AJX241B

© 2010 TERRY RAWLINGS

ISBN: 978-0-9523935-2-8

DESIGN & ARTWORK BY
PAUL McEVOY AT BOLD GRAPHIC DESIGN -
www.boldgraphicdesign.co.uk

PRINTED BY STERLING, LONDON EC3 -
www.sterlingfp.com

CONTENTS

AUTHOR'S PREFACE

When the chance came to re-write this book, I jumped at it. The first edition (in my opinion) ended up as an exercise in diplomacy and compromise between me, a pompous editor and the original publishers.

To cut a long story short, they basically wanted another run-of-the-mill Rolling Stones book, but Ronnie and I wanted one based solely on his early career. Now, while I'm a huge fan of the world's greatest rock 'n' roll band, I'm just as much a fan of all British R&B, 60s psychedelia, pop and rock.

It just so happens that Ronnie Wood was a key figure in some of the most outstanding English groups of that era and all those genres - The Birds; The Jeff Beck Group; The Creation and, of course, The Faces.

All four groups were expected to be criminally overlooked (with the exception of The Faces) in favour of a straightforward account of Ronnie's life with the Rolling Stones. Anyway, the publishers stood their ground and the first version of 'Rock On Wood' came out at the expense of some great stories from members of all the (aforementioned) bands concerned, and was the worse for it.

Happily, Acid Jazz have given me the chance to return to my original interviews and - without any interference - I can re-do the job. Therefore there may be the odd quote missing that was in the first edition, but that is to accommodate the new material (space is still a major consideration of all publishers).

The book you now get is the closest thing to my original vision. The greatest shock for me in re-writing this (and undoubtedly for Ronnie) some six years later is the horrific realisation that so many of the fantastic people that helped me, and gave of their time, are no longer with us.

It's also incomprehensible to believe that in that short space of time Ronnie has suffered at least five personal bereavements: the irreplaceable Kim Gardiner and Krissie Wood, his fantastic mum Lizzie, and most shocking of all, both his brothers, Ted and Art.

I therefore dedicate this second edition to All Five (how nuts is that?)

On a purely personal note, I would like to take this gifted opportunity to make a personal tribute to Art Wood - a man who I regarded as a father figure for fifteen or more years. He and his wife Angie became guardians to my daughters Molly and Nancy and treasured friends to me long before I thought about writing this book. We had so many wonderful times together and his loss is insurmountable to me and countless others who will miss him always.

Gawd bless ya Art!

TERRY RAWLINGS

It's 1.00 pm on 6th July 1997 and the Wood clan has good-naturedly gathered for Art Wood's 60th birthday party. Art, the oldest of the three Wood brothers, has chosen the Blues Club in West Kensington for his celebratory bash. Way back in the fifties, he'd been one of those musicians who'd helped bring R&B to an avid Britain and was one of the founders of the famous Ealing Club. The next youngest brother, Ted, was and still is well known on the Jazz circuit. The baby brother, Ronnie, is of course the lead guitarist with the Rolling Stones. So, it was either the Blues Club or Wembley Stadium.

Art has even managed to re-form his short-lived but cult-status band, Quiet Melon, for the night… well, re-vamp actually, since Rod Stewart couldn't make it and ex-Kinks drummer, Mick Avory, is sitting in for the original drummer Kenney Jones. Still, bass player, Kim Gardiner , one time Bird and one third of Ashton, Gardiner and Dyke, is there and Ronnie will arrive any moment. This will be the first time Kim and Ronnie have played together since their days in another cult favourite, The Creation, back in the late sixties. Of course, Ronnie had also been a member of the legendary Birds, alongside Kim, a band that self-destructed just like The Creation albeit in a quieter sort of way: everyone went on holiday one day and never came back.

Excitement flares in the club as Ronnie arrives, but these are his own family and friends standing up and craning their necks for a better view. People he's known all his life cluster around, needing him to remember when and where they were last together. He's grabbed and pulled from one side of the tiny club to another by nieces, nephews, aunts, uncles, cousins and relatives more times removed than Pickfords. Old musician mates - and the few obligatory hangers-on without whom no musician's party is every truly complete - shake his hand and slap his back. Ron good-naturedly works the crowd like a pro, careful to speak to each and every one of them, his laugh cackling above the excited hum and a band who've actually begun to play better since he arrived.

Ronnie is careful to remind each and every one that this is Art's night, not his. Which is not false modesty; family is all important, especially for the Wood brothers. If you scratch one, they all bleed and so, ultimately, will you.

The welcome isn't just for a member of the world's greatest rock 'n' roll band, nor a multi-millionaire who's partied with kings without ever losing the common touch. It's more for a life and soul of a party, for Ron is somebody who's partied… and partied… and partied. Fact is, people would want Ronnie to like them whatever he did in life. Although the other stuff probably does help, just a little. People want to feel that they're the centre of his universe for a few brief and sweet minutes. Ronnie Wood has something indefinable and everyone wants a piece.

Art, Ted and the other musicians roll their eyes indulgently as tempers suddenly flare. He's mine… no, he's mine… no, mine. For some, the mood has swung the other way. Krissie Wood, Ronnie's first wife, has commanded the stage and is colourfully explaining why her ex-husband is not such a wonderful guy, after all. The explanation dissolves into tears and she's led away to be comforted by Ronnie's present wife, Jo. You get the impression that Jo has done a great deal of comforting over the years. It always comes as a shock when a person discovers that they are not, after all, the centre of Ronnie's world.

For a moment, Ronnie's composure snaps. "Nice fucking speech, Kris!" He leaps on stage and barks a request to Quiet Melon's bemused guitar player, Ray Majors, who just happens to be Krissie's current and within seconds, Ronnie is breaking into a long riff on a borrowed guitar. A grinning Kim Gardiner answers back with his bass - he was always an innovative player, was Kim - and drummer Mick Avory takes a minute to recognise the tune. The mood in the club suddenly lightens. The rock scene's inimitable party-man has insured that the good times roll. Who the hell could ever refuse him?

Art orders another round of drinks, still smiling from the memory of Ronnie's almost anguished cry: "Give me a fuckin' guitar or I'm gonna fuckin' kill someone! Oh, and happy birthday". Music is the centre of Ronnie's world, and always will be. Everything else just gets in the way.

the author

TAPE REC

interviewing

♡ Romine

CHAPTER ONE

"MY MUM CAN OUT KNIT ANYONE ELSE'S MUM, SO THERE!"

1st June 1947. That bright Sunday, only one boy was born at Hillingdon Hospital. One baby boy amongst seven baby girls. Not exactly an omen, but still a novelty.

Boys were still the future breadwinners in those days - and too many men had been killed in the Second World War, which had only finished eighteen months before. So, a single boy baby was an event, to be admired and clucked over by all the other mothers. Except for the one who came back from the nursery with a worried expression on her young face, and called out: "Mrs Wood? Mrs Wood?" Lizzie Wood put up her hand. The young mother sat on Lizzie's bed. "I've just seen your little baby son." There was a long, maybe even pregnant, pause. "I must ask you, Mrs Wood - have you had something to do with a Jew?"

Lizzie Wood could laugh about it later, but at the time came close to hitting the woman with a bed-pan. True, traditional morality had been relaxed by the war, and the father's name on a birth certificate was often a triumph of expediency over truth. But the Woods were as a respectably devoted a couple as you could ever hope to find Lizzie had even been chaperoned when they first went out together. Yet, the inescapable truth was that her son did look a little, well, exotic.

Nothing so mundane as a standard, baby, squashed-button nose. Instead, the prominent family hooter and a mass of sticking-up black hair. A miniature version, in fact, of how he'd look fifty years later, give or take a wrinkle or two. Or twenty. Ronald Wood was born with a look that would spawn a thousand imitations.

Born as a bit of surprise, too, for as Lizzie used to explain, she'd 'shut up shop'. She and Arthur - her husband, not Jewish, but a water-gypsy - had already brought up two boys during the war and the bombing. If they knew one thing, it was that they didn't want to bring any other kids into such an inhospitable world.

Ronald David Wood had other ideas. And along with the family nose, he inherited the family luck and creativity.

Lizzie was born Mercy Leah Elizabeth Dyer in 1911, on a narrow-boat called 'The Orient' moored in Brentford Dock. Like her husband-to-be, Lizzie came from a long line of water-gypsies - the original boat-people - who'd worked the canals for generations. The Orient was a working craft, and she had family living the length of the Grand Union Canal.

Arthur Wood was born in 1908, at Number 40, Dock Road, Paddington, the son of a tug-boat skipper. He started work at fourteen, helping his father and grandfather transport timber from London to Manchester and by the mid-1920s, he was skipper of a tug called 'The Antelope'. And along with being an excellent waterman, Arthur - or 'Arch' to his mates - was an enthusiastic and gifted amateur musician. Albeit just a little eccentric - who else would put together a twenty-four piece harmonica big band or as he used to describe it, twenty-four musicians and a drummer?

Even in those days drummers bore the brunt of musicians' humour.

Not that Arthur took his musical career all that seriously himself. 'Booze, racetracks and women' was the band's motto - you just know that Big Bill Broonzy would have approved - and they could be found blowing up an inebriated storm next to the winning posts at Goodwood, Kempton Park even Royal Ascot. "Blaze Away" was their signature tune, and they did. And if they had a name, Lizzie Wood can't remember it: "Really, they only did it for a bit of a lark. They'd have a big day out at the races, or play at the Bricklayer's Arms pub in Yiewsley (the other side of the M4 from Heathrow), where they had a back room to rehearse in or the 'Crown' pub, where my parents sometimes went."

In fact, Lizzie father, Fred, was working with Arthur's father, Sylvester and both families would often meet at the Crown at weekends. Which was where Ronnie Woods' parents first met, and it was a leg of pork what done it!

It was the Whitsun Bank Holiday of 1932 and Arthur had won a darts tournament in the Crown. First prize a leg of pork. Arthur was still carrying it when he was introduced to Fred Dyer's twenty-one year old daughter, Lizzie. You don't spend your spare time playing the mouth organ at Royal Ascot without learning a thing or two about chivalry. Arthur, instantly smitten, offered her his prize, the gesture of a man who wanted to be taken seriously. As Fred, her mother Leah and younger sister Mary looked on, Lizzie accepted it. And after the pub closed, they all went back to the Dyers', where the leg of pork was cooked and eaten. Apparently, the crackling tasted particularly good.

Lizzie and Arthur began walking-out together at weekends. Initially, they were always accompanied by a chaperone - Lizzie's mother or an aunt - for the people who worked the canals were very strict: young couples were never left unsupervised. Until, that is, the man had been deemed to be as respectable as the girl herself. For Lizzie and Arthur this took about a month, after which they were allowed to begin courting on their own. This was the stage during which they decided if they really did want to get married, although usually the man had already made up his mind. In this case, so had Lizzie and they were married on Christmas Day, 1934. Arthur had his own river tug-boat by then, the Fastnet - and the couple moved into a comfortable two-up, two-down at Number 8, Whitethorn Avenue, Yiewsley. The two-up being bedrooms plus a small box-room, the two-down a kitchen, front room, small back room and a tiny kitchen. The lavatory was outside. This was widely considered pretty luxurious for Britain's working class in the 1930s, and some people in authority worried that such comfort might even spoil them. That said, Number 8 was solidly built and unlike a narrow boat, had stairs. And so Lizzie became the first Dyer for generations to decamp to dry land. She went to work as a polisher at the giant HMV plant in nearby Hayes, working from 7.30am to 7.00pm - but only until 12.00pm on Saturday - for the princely sum of 30 shillings and 7 pence and no sick pay. Or pension. This changed on 7th July 1935, when their first child, Arthur (Art), was born and Lizzie happily exchanged the conveyor-belt monotony at HMV for cotton nappies and wooden teething rings. Back in the 1930s, few women in their right minds preferred factory work to being a housewife. Four years later, the family would further rejoice when Edward (Ted) was born on 24th June 1939. A short-lived celebration, however, for three months later the Second World War began.

Canal work was a reserved occupation during the war. Men like Arthur Wood were exempted from being called-up because they were responsible for bringing supplies to and from London. Those canals became one of London's lifelines - a fact quickly realised by the Luftwaffe, who quite naturally tried very hard to bomb them and men like Arthur out of existence. So, on the one hand, Lizzie knew that at least she and her husband would be spending the war years together, unlike so many other thousands of couples. On the other, she also knew that Arthur faced almost daily bombing, until the closing stages of the war. Nor was it that much easier at home, for Yiewsley was both close to the canal system and London airport. Which meant that after the Blitz was over, the area would become an obvious target for flying-bombs, the VI rockets that Londoners nick-named doodlebugs, and later the V2s. This was because the VI sounded like a large bug, doodling almost absent-mindedly around, before deciding where to land - at which point the engine cut-off. That was the worst part, the few moments of silence while people on the ground automatically glanced upwards and wondered when and where the explosion would come. The V2 was even more sinister: because it flew faster than sound, you couldn't actually hear it until after it had exploded. Survivors must have felt that time had been brutally reversed.

Several doodlebugs hit Whitethorn Avenue. Another one destroyed the house opposite Arthur's mother-in-law. Worse, yet another destroyed the Black Bull pub in Falling Lane. The Englishman is a forgiving soul - but destroy his favourite pubs and you make an enemy for life.

The Wood family had spent many nights huddled together in the Anderson shelter in the back garden. These were corrugated iron structures sunk into the ground and then covered with anything up to three feet of earth. They were damp, cold and mostly only effective against small bombs and debris. And then the two boys, Art and Ted, came down with severe cases of whooping cough. Long nights in an Anderson shelter were not a good idea and the boys were too ill and too young to be evacuated out of London. So, one day Arthur and some mates from the Black Bull pub dug up the Anderson shelter and moved it into the small, back room next to the kitchen. The earth stayed outside.

Excuse me? Wasn't the earth the actual protection? An eighth of an inch of corrugated iron isn't going to stop a bad cold, let alone a bomb. But Arthur and his mates had thought of that, and built a wooden shell around the shelter, and another wooden roof on top of that. So it was a shelter-inside-a-shelter-inside-a-shelter, and to hell with the doodlebugs. Except shortly afterwards the Black Bull pub was destroyed by one, probably out of Nazi pique that the Wood family weren't being cold and miserable along with everyone else.

Instead, they were warm and miserable, crammed together in the shelter-inside-a-shelter-inside-a-shelter as bombs fell around them… like so many other families, knowing that the sound of the explosion that destroyed a home nearby was horribly preferable to the final, split second of light and noise that would herald their own deaths.

All of the Wood family, except the dog, that is. Chum was an Old English Sheepdog and far too large to fit comfortably into the shelter-inside etc, especially with two little boys suffering from whooping cough. So, Arthur built Chum his own shelter, out in the back garden where the original one used to be. It isn't that the English are eccentric. They're just practical in a way that often mystifies other nations.

Which explains how the young Art discovered he was an artist, as Ronnie also would many years later, which would lead him to become one of the world's most enigmatic and copied rock musicians. All thanks to doodlebugs and The Blitz.

Lizzie explains it best: "It was during the endless hours we spent in that shelter waiting for the all-clear that Art and Ted first learned to draw, because the shortage of metal or lead meant you couldn't buy any toys like a box of soldiers or cars and trains. The only thing that you could get hold of was paper pads and crayons. So that's what they got, that was their experience. I would take them down the shelter with their drawing books and try to take their minds off the bombings, which was very difficult, as you can imagine. But it would prove to be a very big part of all their lives. A part that has remained with them all, even to this day."

The war finally finished in 1945 and England faced up to the mammoth task of rebuilding. Ration books remained in place (cream books for parents and green ones for children), meaning the queues at shops still stretched around the block for even the most basic of household items. The memories are also still extremely vivid to Lizzie: "My Mother Leah would save up all her sweet rations and store them in a big yellow biscuit tin which she'd keep on top of her dresser. All the children in the street knew about it and they would ask her, "Have you got any sweets for us?" and she would hand them out. Everything came in two ounces. Two ounces of tea, two ounces of butter, ONE EGG? What you were expected to do with two ounces of anything amazed me. It was a terrible struggle, especially if you had children. It was heartbreaking to see them go without. But people did make the most of it and try and help each other out as much as they could, especially at Christmas or birthdays. Someone would make toys out of wood or make soft toys from fabrics, but mainly it was the drawing materials that they got because of the lack of resources. Arthur, their Dad, played a big part in developing the boys' imagination and their love of art. He was a very good critic. They used to sit and draw for ages and eventually bring their pictures up to him and say "Look Daddy, look what we've drawn," and he would say, "Now son, you wouldn't see a horse with legs like that would you?" or "You wouldn't ever see a dog with a tail like that" and so on, you see? Whereas I would say, "Draw me a nice picture" while I was getting the tea or something and they'd bring it back to me and I'd say, "Oh yes, that's lovely, now draw me something else." I didn't pick fault with it, whereas Arthur did, in order to encourage them, but they took notice of him, and it worked."

It was the classic way that parents encourage their kids, mother with unalloyed enthusiasm, father with practical advice. Probably to be much derided these days, even though it seems to have worked well for several thousand years. As witness the memories of Art Wood, now a successful commercial artist - and no mean musician himself: "Dad was honest with us, he would tell us, "No, that's wrong. That's the wrong shape for a horse's head," or "You don't see a rabbit with ears like that. Rabbit's ears are long, this long." so we learned by it. We didn't argue with him because we knew he was right. We'd then go away and make the rabbit's ears longer and then, sure enough, it looked like a rabbit! Dad didn't have any training in teaching, but he had a natural flair for drawing, which made us eager to please him, so we'd strive to get every picture right so he'd say, "That's much better," but he'd never say "That's excellent" or "That's good!" always "Much better." Whereas Mum would say, "That's lovely" whatever we did. Nothing was ever rotten with Mum, even the worst pictures were lovely. "That's nice Artie, now draw me a swan," she would say. So when little Ron was finally born, drawing and painting were already a firmly-established part of our family and our growing up."

Which was at 3.15pm, on the aforementioned 1st June 1947. Lizzie Wood was thirty-six and Arthur, thirty-nine. Neither expected any more children - "You shut up shop," Arthur had told her - and in those days, motherhood at thirty-six was considered a little on the old side. Little Ronnie Wood was taken home on his mother's actual birthday and his two elder brothers were waiting. It isn't sure what Art and Ted actually expected. Ten is an awkward age for boys - and stays that way for the next forty years or so - while seven isn't much easier. Both of them had known the warmth of a close-knit, loving family where all the attention was, quite naturally, focused on them. And while ten year-olds in 1947 were less sophisticated than today, Art was undoubtedly aware of the first stirrings of adolescence… one moment on the threshold of man's estate, the next expected to admire something that squeaked, puked and burbled. It was Mum's birthday, too.

Lizzie and the infant Ron were carried indoors by two ambulance men, followed by the midwife - no emergency, just the way the National Health Service worked in those far-off, caring, sharing days - and were met by Art and Ted shouting "Happy Birthday, Mum, Happy Birthday!" And as the stretcher paused to negotiate a bend in the stairs, the two boys piled it high with the presents and cards they'd made for Lizzie's birthday. Plus a much-prized Pyrex dish from Auntie Alma - in the late 1940s, ovenproof glassware was a rare luxury. So it was that the infant Ronnie arrived at the cot in his parents' bedroom as part of a mostly homemade triumphal procession. Never mind it was in Lizzie's honour and not his, a precedent had been set and ever since that day, Ronnie's been attending parties whenever he could.

Mother and son duly installed, it was time for the ten year-old Art, and seven year-old Ted, to be formerly introduced. Lizzie's mother, Leah, told the boys to come up one at a time and meet their new baby brother. As Lizzie remembers: "Art came storming in first, like he always does, walked round the bed, face white like a sheet, and just stared at Ronnie. "Well," I asked him, "What d'you think?" and with that, he just turned round and stomped off. Stomp, stomp, stomp, down the stairs, out through the kitchen and slam! out the back door."

Ted arrived next, except his face was bright red. Lizzie remembers him giving Ronnie exactly the same look as Art: embarrassment, shock and deep suspicion. But he did at least speak. "What do you think of your new baby brother?" asked Leah."Alright," Ted muttered, before stomping off to join Art in the back garden. But at least Art's increased older brother status merited promotion to the privacy of the box-room. Ted, on the other hand, suddenly found himself lumbered with a much smaller roommate who gurgled and smelled.

But it was a short-lived rejection according to Art, who remembers both Ted and himself adopting an almost over-protective attitude towards their new little brother. At least, outside the family, in the street. At home, it was understandably a little different and Art remembers asking his mother to take Ronnie back to the shop where she'd bought him. And no, Art wasn't really that unsophisticated. But it was far kinder than, say, suggesting the infant Ron should be abandoned to the wolves. Even if he had been, with Ronnie's luck the wolves would probably have brought him straight back. As it was, Art and Ted swiftly discovered the joys of babysitting: "Which you don't always want to do when you're young," Art remembers - and while the infant Ron might have been a nuisance, he was family. That meant everything to them, just as it does today.

And he was cute. Often unbearably so. Hence the request to take him back to the shop, when Ron was about two, and which was all to do with goldfish. Art and Ted had walked all the way to Uxbridge to buy them, and walked back with two innocent invertebrates swimming happily in a jam-jar.

Dogs and cats are fine, but there's nothing quite so pleasingly traditional as a boy and his fish. Loyalty, affection - albeit one-sided - and hours of harmless fun teaching it tricks, like "Open your mouth, close your mouth." These and other excited plans ran through Art and Ted's minds as they sat talking to their mother. But then their little brother toddled in. "Fish, Mummy, fish." The infant Ron pointed behind him, "Gone to sea." And Ted remembered with horror that he'd just heard the outside lavatory flush. To this day, Ronnie Wood's convinced he was only trying to liberate them. But at the time, it was just one more reminder that little brothers have to be watched like a hawk.

In turn, Ronnie adored his older brothers. Or in his own words: "I was a real pain in the ass, always tagging along everywhere like an eager little puppy. That's why, when I was older, they'd kick the crap out of me so often. They'd pin me to the floor and dangle a big gob of spit over my face, then somehow suck it back up just before it hit me."

Money for luxuries was still in short supply that close to the end of the war. Toys were carefully shared out amongst the three boys, which perhaps paradoxically would make Ron identify even more with his two elder brothers. After all, weren't they playing with the same tin soldiers and battered old football? Yet there was also a steady stream of drawing books and crayons to stimulate the youngsters' imaginations. Ron grew to inherit his older brothers' love of art, immersing himself in drawing and painting with results that greatly impressed the entire family. The two older brothers would sit at opposite ends of the small kitchen table, happily drawing away, as Ron would quietly edge his chair between them. At first, he'd content himself with merely glancing from one to another. But inevitably he'd begin jogging the table as he leaned to the left or the right for a better look. This led to complaints that he was being a fidget - a criticism that all older brothers feel safe to make about a younger sibling - and Lizzie would have to wedge her youngest son in the armchair with a tray to draw on. And there he'd sit, copying perfectly the pictures he'd watched being drawn by Art and Ted - until Ronnie began to develop his own style and interests, when he was about five.

"It was always Cowboys and Indians," Art remembers, "because Ronnie loved to draw horses and Indians. It was the thing that impressed his art teachers later on, these amazing pictures!"

Although one of Ronnie's earliest memories was of a bridge painted in the style of Van Gogh - whether pure coincidence, or taken from a book isn't known - but yes, horses were a speciality as was an early fascination for the Wild West.

"I loved to draw American Indians, I still do," Ronnie recalls. "I think it's because I've always thought I was part Indian, I mean I do realise I look like one. I've always wanted to trace my roots to see if I have any genuine Indian blood in me. But I'm a little scared of what I'd find if I dug too hard!"

Push him further, and he changes the subject or pours you another drink. Maybe it's to do with being a water-gypsy. If so, there's nothing to worry about: water gypsies were directly descended from Romanies - as opposed to travellers - and were horse-whisperers long before it became fashionable. Thousands of years ago, they were one of the many nomadic tribes who reached Europe from somewhere in Central Asia (there's a legend in Northern Afghanistan that one of their wandering tribes went on to become the English), and really did develop a near mystical understanding of and with the horse, most evident today in the Camargue. When Britain began building canals in the eighteenth century, it was natural for the Romanies to become involved in running them: they had the horses needed for towing barges, while the very life of moving from one town to another appealed to their wandering spirit. Music is one of the great Romany gifts to the world, particularly flamenco. Another of their great loves, partying, is more universal. Although it's also true that no-one parties quite like the Ron.

"I was brought up on tinned milk and the canals," remembers Ronnie. "It was a happy home life; we used to have parties with fifty people crammed into our tiny little semi-detached house… parties every weekend, with the music shrieking out."

The guiding spirit behind these parties was Arthur, the boys' dad. Arthur who loved to make music, with his harmonica band or anything else that came to hand, loved horses and loved people. Weekdays were for working, weekends were for playing music and for parties. And his sons grew up thinking it was all quite normal, never really asking themselves why so many of their friends seemed to spend more time at the Wood house than their own.

By 1950, Art Wood's own artistic abilities had taken him to Ealing School of Art, aged fourteen. In those days, art schools were seen as being both practical and purely creative. They produced as many typographers and illustrators as they did sculptors or painters, and gave all children from all backgrounds the chance to succeed… for art and its associated disciplines, like science or anything that requires a natural talent, cares little for social status, only originality and excellence. Or used to… nowadays, image and marketing appear to have taken over, at least in respect of art. Whatever, the fourteen year-old settled down to a regime of half academic and half art studies. At sixteen, he would begin specialising in a specific subject - the aforesaid typography or illustration, even fine art - secure in the knowledge that Ealing's contacts would always help find him a job, if he wanted one. It should have been a halcyon existence - and was, although not quite in the way the educational authorities envisaged.

Time for some social background.

More nonsense has been written about the fifties and sixties than any other recent era (I should know), all the more reprehensible because so many people really do remember them. Specifically, the fifties are often portrayed as a design-conscious decision to forget the Second World War and yet another brave attempt at an equally brave new world.

(No, don't lose heart or interest. The late fifties saw the birth of British rhythm and blues and subsequently, the world's greatest rock bands).

One problem is that eras don't work like that, nor is there any hard and fast cut-off between one decade and another. 'Fifties Man' - it was still too early for 'Fifties Person' - did not suddenly appear, any more than Neolithic Man had done…even if many of the early R&B bands did have a certain Neolithic look about them. Fifties England was full of people who'd grown up during the war, fought in it, or at the very least, survived it. And like most wars, WW2 had been a right old eye-opener. People had travelled and found themselves doing things they'd never have believed possible, legal or even moral. People had experienced immense tragedy and immense joy. And, let it be said, immense excitement. In a word, they'd been changed! And they knew it. Aside from anything else, the British Army dispensed over seventy million Benzedrine - amphetamine - tablets to soldiers during WW2. Which is not to say that the land fit for heroes was suddenly full of newly-demobbed speed freaks. Just that there were enough ex-servicemen who'd been wired by chemicals or natural adrenalin or both to make a difference. They'd learned to see things a little differently and reacted accordingly. True, there were those who just wanted to settle back into the old, probably forelock-tugging routine, with a nice cup of tea before sex with the wife, whether she noticed it or not. But there were also those men who were far more like the character of Joe Lampton in 'Room At The Top'. And those women who'd had independence forced upon them during the war, had found they liked it and had no intention of giving it back. Social subversives all of them, and nothing spreads so fast as a new idea. The population as a whole was growing edgy, which may partly explain why bedtime drinks like Horlicks and Bourn-vita promised that sound sleep which would lead to contentment, success and a new three-piece suite.

Another problem is that social historians tend to rely on then-contemporary movies, the media, advertising or government information films. But these usually only represent ideals, escapism, wishful thinking, propaganda or the desire to make money. All too often they follow trends, rather than lead them. All too often they represent a self-serving fixation with preserving the status quo… or returning to an imaginary time of peace and plenty that only ever existed in the imagination. Truth is, if you want to know what really happened, what people really thought and wanted, you have to look at their art, their literature and their music. G-Plan Furniture (named after the manufacturer, E. Gomme of High Wycombe, and not many people know that, or even care) led the way in the fifties: we had the Festival of Britain; drip-dry shirts; and an entire population suddenly discovered body odour. Like all other icons, these were merely someone's attempt to capture the public mood, either for profit or political capital. Which possibly explains why so much fifties design was quite so hideous, from furniture to housing.

Social mobility was also in the air. The Second World War had seen a great many officers promoted from the 'working class', whatever that was. Although according to the movies, Bryan Forbes or Richard Attenborough - playing the obligatory panicking Cockney - had to be comforted by John Mills or Jack Hawkins as the ship went down.

Women had worked in factories and on the land, had fought bravely in the Special Operations Executive. Few people wanted a return to the early forties.

The public mood was for change and continuing excitement, seen initially at those fringes of society which always provide a more accurate barometer than Mr and Mrs Joe Average… who anyway only ever exist as a commercial or political ideal. And the public, especially the London public, were avid for new ideas. London had always been one of Europe's more cosmopolitan cities, the result of Empire and a tradition of playing host to generation after generation of refugees. Naturally, London's art schools were at the forefront, which would result in Ronnie Wood enjoying a unique childhood.

Ealing School of Art had built up a reputation of being one of the best London had to offer. This might appear a little strange, for even today Ealing-the-suburb gives the impression that the pavement will be rolled up at 9.00pm sharp. Not the sort of art school that would eventually be able to boast alumni that includes Art, Ted and Ronnie Wood; David Bowie; Pete Townshend and Freddie Mercury. Except that Ealing Art School drew on all of West London, from Shepherd's

Bush out to Uxbridge and West Drayton. In terms of fine art, Ealing was the place you went to before, possibly, going on to do a post-grad at the Slade, Chelsea or the Royal College of Art. In terms of graphic design, Ealing graduates were assured of jobs in advertising or the media. That began to change in the early fifties. As Art Wood explains:

"Ealing was very unusual. It was constantly evolving at an alarming rate. It was a straight art school when I first went there in 1950. But it soon started to get this very musical feel to it. Everyone was getting very experimental, after all it was the 'beatnik' era. The sexy French look for girls, the beginnings of what would become Skiffle, it was all happening   so anyone who had even the remotest artistic or musical bent was just carried away!"

In other words, people began to go to Ealing as much for the music as the art. For new ideas, too… fifties students would discover Camus, Jack London, Sartre, Hank Janson and Mickey Spillane. Musical influences - aside from Juliette Greco - were predominantly American, Blue Grass, Trad Jazz and the Blues. Later, Chicago jazz, Buddy Holly and Elvis. Of course, Brits being Brits were no respecters of other people's traditions and quite happily mixed and matched - although there were some purists, most of whom vanished into the Folk music scene - until they got the result they wanted, adding their own particular spin. But all that was still in the future. All that the infant Ron knew was that his big brothers - for Ted followed Art to Ealing - would bring home the most amazing, motley group of friends that any child could hope to gawp at. By the time he was eight or nine, Ronnie knew exactly what he wanted out of life: sex.

"Art and Ted would always have their schoolmates over at our house." Ronnie recalls. "Artists, musicians and wild bohemians with shades, Teddy boys with drainpipe trousers, suede brothel creepers and big overcoats. They'd have all these nice looking 'chicks' with them and they'd lock themselves in the front room with all their instruments. We had a serving hatch in the wall between there and the kitchen and they would pass drinks through it. I was like a puppy scratching at the door from outside.

What went on in there is nobody's business, but I would see photographs of fifteen or sixteen people sprawled on the sofa. I knew that was the life for me. I wanted to emulate my brothers. I wanted to get into Ealing as soon as possible, mainly because I fancied their art school girlfriends."

Ronnie had left St. Stephens Primary at the age of seven, moving to the tiny St. Mathews Secondary, which was attached to the parish church in Yiewsley High Street. Here, those early lessons around the kitchen table bore fruit and he was asked to paint a frieze along the entire length of the school's entrance corridor. The painting, depicting the Biblical scene of St. Francis and the animals, greeted parents and visitors on the next school open-day. Lizzie remembers it as the most wonderful picture she'd ever seen: "It was a lovely day because all the teachers were telling us how good he was and how proud they were, which was more than could be said of the other two at that time!"

Which isn't to say that the young Art and Ted were running riot, although they did enjoy far more freedom than their friends. But as the boys finally realised years later, their parents hadn't been weak, merely thoughtful. Arthur in particular believed in allowing his sons to think for themselves, with a bit of sensible advice and guidance thrown in from time to time: "That didn't make him weak, or suggest he didn't care. Because our Dad did care, he cared a lot. Dad was just very loose with us." Small wonder that the Wood household became such a magnet for all of Art and Ted's friends - although the endless supply of food probably had something to do with it. Sometimes, Lizzie Wood felt she spent her entire time in the kitchen, making sandwiches, beans on toast or boiling eggs for starving teenagers, with a bored young Ronnie serving up through the specially-built hatch, which also allowed Lizzie to keep an eye on things. If the noise became too loud, or - every parent's real nightmare - stopped altogether, she'd quietly peep in, just in case. The one memory she carries to this day is watching entranced as four or five beautiful girls, wearing roses in their hair, laughed and danced together.

Sometimes, Ronnie would manage to sneak in and for a little while, become part of his adored older brothers' private lives. He learned to sit quietly and say nothing, merging into the background like a smiling mannequin until someone wanted another sandwich or a cup of tea and he'd be sent back to the kitchen. Years later, people would still be remarking how the adult Ronnie always managed to merge into the background…especially when something has gone wrong. Like Macavity the Cat, he was never there - as Keith Richard was to complain ruefully in 1977, referring amongst other episodes to Ronnie's affair with Margaret Trudeau, wife of the then Canadian Prime Minster, variously and inaccurately laid at the loins of Mick Jagger or Keith Richard himself.

The front room was actually supposed to be Art and Ted's rehearsal room, for both had inherited their father's love of music. Art's instincts led to skiffle, blues and thence R&B, while Ted was a jazz man through and through. So Ronnie's earliest musical influences were eclectic, to say the least. Then from the age of four, which is the earliest he can remember making music with his brothers (or more to the point, making one hell of a noise), Ted's drum-kit was played with mad abandon by the three boys whenever their parents were out. These sessions inevitably resulted in massive arguments between Art and Ted - teenage musicians can be so sensitive - leading to fists flying and much rolling about on the floor. According to Ronnie, he was convinced that one of them would end up killing the other, which so upset him he developed a nervous stutter. But either peace broke out, or he learned not to take the free-for-alls so seriously, for the stutter wore off by the time he was f-f-f-f-five.

The rehearsal room was meant to be just that, for only music could justify turning over the family living room to the two older boys. Naturally, Art and Ted had other ideas, namely, sneaking girls in the back door, and if a beady eye wasn't watching through the hatch, upstairs. At which point, Art remembers, his father would usually shout out: "Where do you think you are - on your father's yacht?" Point being that neither Arthur nor Lizzie ever allowed adolescent fumbling to get out of hand. They gave their boys freedom, but never enough to make a serious mistake. At least, not until they were old enough to take responsibility for their actions.

But the biggest bar to Art and Ted's love life was little brother. As he freely admits, Ronnie learned both art and music from his elder siblings. It seemed only natural to learn about girls as well. Not everyone agreed with him. It's difficult to be amorous, even as a teenager, with a grinning child quietly lurking in the shadows and on those rare occasions when both parents were out, Ronnie would be given a few coppers and sent to the shops. Strangely, he never seems to have understood that the actual purchase was less important than the time taken in making it. Besides, his place was at home, by his brothers' side. To this day, all the brothers are convinced Ronnie could make it to and from the local shop in under two minutes - Ronnie with a sense of pride, the other two with remembered frustration.

The family dynamic changed forever in 1955, when Art received his call-up papers. Two years' National Service beckoned, with the dubious distinction that Art was the nation's very last A1 conscript. The family dreaded a foreign posting, but in the event number 23267647, Private Wood, A, reported to the Army barracks in Devizes where he was issued with the regulation pick-axe handle, and pledged to defend his country and the Dorset coast against... well, against anyone put off by an unloaded pick-axe handle, really. "Still no sign of the dreaded Jap invaders," Art would announce on his visits home, and Yiewsley would breathe a sigh of relief and sleep soundly in their beds.

Ronnie was eight years old and bereft. "I was so close to my brothers. I was like a little lost sheep without Art. Ted too was lost without him. In fact, when Art came home on leave towards the end of his Army career, Ted would happily donate his girlfriend to Art and vice-versa." Quite what the girls thought about the arrangement isn't recorded.

Even so, it couldn't have been a total waste of time at Devizes, for Art managed to found his own skiffle band, the Blue Kats.

In 1958, Ronnie passed the all-important eleven-plus exam and went to the highly-respected Ruislip Manor Grammar School. He'd originally been enrolled in St Martin's for his secondary education, but good as it was, the school couldn't offer a final qualification in art. However, Mr Reesey - the school's sainted headmaster - realised that Ronnie would be wasting his time if he couldn't carry on painting. A transfer was arranged and Ronnie was enrolled in Ruislip's three-year art course. If all went to plan, he'd later follow his brothers to Ealing Art School.

Within a month of starting at Ruislip Grammar, Ronnie won an open art competition, the presentation made by Victor Sylvester, the famous band-leader. This was to be Ronnie's first and last brush with light music and his first taste of fame. He began entering the 'Painting Of The Week' competition, set each week by artist Adrian Hill on the Wednesday night BBC show, Sketch Club.

"He won it seven weeks in a row," Art recalls. "He would get home from school, gulp down his tea and switch on the TV. Every bleedin' week it would be "Yes, once again the winner this week is Ronnie Wood.""

Schoolboys can be quite bitchy when one of their number achieves fame. This didn't happen with Ronnie, who still remembers the schoolyard acclaim he received with immense and touching pride, while typically playing down the cause: "Yeah, well, I got a couple of pictures shown."

Not so easy to play down was his appearance as Adrian Hill's special guest on Sketch Club, when it was staged live at St Alban's Town Hall. Or the subsequent articles in the local newspapers, which were "really encouraging to a young artist." Growing up as the youngest of three brothers does teach one the value of modesty.

Actually, it's often been observed that the youngest brother in many families tends to go one of two ways: either effectively gives up, knowing he'll never be able to compete... or becomes determined to excel, but quietly. Perhaps it all depends on how much love and encouragement he receives from his elder siblings, not just his parents.

Tony Munroe was another new pupil at Ruislip Grammar. He and Ronnie discovered to their amazement that they were almost neighbours - going to different primary schools had managed to keep them apart, even though their parents knew each other. Now, it was natural to travel to and from school together, ten miles each way and in Tony's words, the two boys "quickly became best mates on a number of levels."

Especially art and music.

Ruislip Grammar was one of those schools where teachers tirelessly encourage their pupils. It had its own choir, which staged regular recitals and entered most local competitions. The art department was equally committed and altogether, the school provided a perfect environment for children with an artistic gift or a competitive appetite. The atmosphere suited both Ronnie and Tony's hard working attitude to their work: they wanted to learn, they wanted to succeed and Ronnie at least desperately wanted to go to Ealing Art School.

Soon, Tony's painting of a country scene became the winning entry of another TV art show, ITV's 'Tuesday Rendezvous'. Remember that at this time, Ronnie more or less had the BBC sewn up via 'Sketch Club'. That success earned Tony an article in the local newspaper - titled, with crashing unoriginality, 'A Rendezvous With Tony.'

Then another article - 'An Artistic Family,' the headline writer now pulling out all the stops - featured all three Wood brothers, for by now Art and Ted had a growing reputation as musicians. The article also mentioned that Ronnie had two paintings on show at a local CND exhibition (nothing to do with politics, artists will show anywhere); his record breaking run on 'Sketch Club'; and that he'd just come second in a competition for a fire prevention poster. The winner? Another local lad, one Tony Munroe.

"And that," Tony reflects, "was the start of our competitive rivalry. Although we always pretended not to be. If Ronnie went out with a girlfriend, I went out with her mate. If I entered a painting competition, so would Ron. We both felt we had to keep doing better by going one step further than the other. Ronnie, I remember, was never satisfied with what he'd achieved, and that continued right through from the art to the music. It's what would go on to give the group that edge later on."

The group being the now legendary Birds, which was to become one of Britain's top live R&B bands... and from which Tony was ultimately fired - by his best friend, Ronnie Wood.

CHAPTER TWO
"ALL MY ANCESTORS LIVED ON BOATS."

The baby Ron had been born into a music-mad family. The infant Ron grew up in a music-mad house. His brother, Ted, had made him a drum out of the shell of an old banjo body when he was five - if only to keep Ronnie away from Ted's own drum-kit. Art and Ted later clubbed together and bought him a guitar when Ronnie was ten. From Art he learned the blues, from Ted he learned jazz. There was never any doubt that one day he'd play in a band. Aside from anything else, both Art and Ted had their own bands; his father, Arthur had his own band.

"I was always fooling around with the instruments that Art and Ted kept stored in the backroom," Ronnie remembers. "Trumpets, banjo's, kazoos, drums and, of course, washboards. But I knew the guitar was for me. When I saw someone playing, I got an itch to pick one up and believe me, I saw some great guitarists play with my brothers, especially Jim Willis and Lawrence Sheaf, and they helped me learn how to play. Jim showed me the fundamentals by writing out all the chords and finger techniques, while Lawrence showed me how to play all the great 'Big Bill Broonzy' stuff. My first guitar was actually given to me by a guy named Chalkie White, but he took it back when he went into the Army. I was about ten years old then. Art and Ted felt bad about it, so they chipped together and bought me a replacement, so I suppose that was my very first guitar." In fact, Jim Willis spent hours painstakingly inking in finger positions on the guitar's neck, making allowances for the fact that the boy Ron didn't have the hand-reach of an adult. Talk to Ronnie Wood about Jim and Lawrence today and you get the impression they were a combination of Eric Clapton and Segovia… he still sees them in his mind's eye as he did when a child. But they undoubtedly were two young men who generously gave him a great deal of their time. It's one thing to be encouraged by your family - what else are families for? It's quite another to be encouraged by your big brothers' mates. That really makes you feel important.

Art was very much into Fats Domino at the time and taught Ronnie "Blue Monday" and "I'm Walking". But the record that made the greatest impact did so for tragic reasons. One day, the brothers' cousin, Rex, arrived at the house in a state of great excitement. "You have to hear this," he told Lizzy, and put "Blueberry Hill" on the turntable. "I've bought it for Ronnie." Who loved it and immediately began learning the song.

The next day, February 14th, St Valentine's Day, Rex was killed in a car accident. He was just sixteen. It was the first time that Ronnie had been brought face to face with death. It wasn't to be the last, for his first girlfriend would also die in a car accident.

Yet Ronnie always seemed to be relatively untouched by tragedy. It isn't lack of feeling, only the total conviction that whatever happened, however bad things seemed, somehow he'd survive. "I remember feeling that way as a little kid," Ronnie will tell you, "which is one reason why I never grew up worrying about money - I always knew that I'd be okay, I always felt emotionally secure. I guess it's to do with growing up in such a secure family."

More than likely, but it also had something to do with Ronnie always having his music. He can pour all his emotions into his guitar playing and to a lesser extent, into his painting. Threaten to take those outlets away from him and the security might well begin to crumble.

If Art was teaching Ronnie the finer points of the blues, Ted was teaching him about jazz. In fact, Tony Monroe always thought that Ted was the greater musical influence, for two reasons. Firstly, because Art went into the Army for two years, when Ronnie was only eight, then left home altogether to marry his girlfriend Doreen in 1960, when Ronnie was thirteen. Still at least Ronnie got to inherit the box-room, much to Ted's relief. Secondly, despite the age gap Art and Ronnie were effectively in competition with each other. Both loved and played rhythm and blues and no matter how great the affection, Ronnie at least wanted to go all the way, his own way. "Ted was teaching me all about the music of Louis Armstrong, Bix Beiderbecke and Jelly Roll Morton." Ronnie recalls. "He was, and still is, a real jazz purist. He's got all those old 78s and jazz albums, which he's kept in perfect condition in boxes. Meanwhile, Art had crossed over to R&B with his band The Artwood Combo.

Ted took me to my first live show which was Duke Ellington supported by Chris Barber at the Walthamstow Town Hall in 1959. I remember, in particular, Barber's drummer Carlo Little, who played a leopard-skin drum kit, a remnant from his days with Screaming Lord Sutch!"

It's often forgotten that Sutch was once a serious musician - well, -ish - who'd been at the forefront of the British rock 'n' roll movement that would help revolutionise British music forever. He probably deserved to be a real Lord for that alone.

Nor was Ronnie a stranger to performing live. Back in the fifties many cinemas would feature live groups during the intermission. It was the days of the double feature show - well, three if you include the inevitable, smug travel documentary, presumably intended to make the British public regretful that on the whole they could only afford to holiday at home. Live music was an added attraction that also gave the audience time to buy their light refreshments. These mainly consisted of Wall's ice creams, nasty watered-down orange squash that came in square plastic containers and everyone's favourite projectile, monkey-nuts.

Traditionally, the live music used to be supplied by an organist or piano player. If it was a cinema lucky enough to have an organist, moviegoers were treated to the spectacle of a huge organ, rising magisterially out of the orchestra pit like a reverse Titanic. It was a short-lived phase because such an irresistible and slow moving target only encouraged people to throw things at the organist, like monkey-nuts for instance, horrible to eat, but easy to aim.

Anyway, a medley of 'all-time favourites' would then follow, invariably sounding like a homage to the silent days of film and one which never sat very well with Hollywood's latest offering. This was in the days before the Hammond organ helped kick R&B into the music stratosphere, before then organs were something people mostly associated with church, the Blackpool Tower and early Walt Disney cartoons.

Eventually, things changed and the once mighty organ (and the poor organists) was replaced by actual live groups, albeit of the mostly acoustic variety.

Art Wood played many interval gigs at the Regal in Uxbridge, often with his Art Wood Combo. Ted followed suit, with his band The Original London Skiffle Group. Of course, when Art went into the Army, the music mantle of Bringing Up Ronnie had fallen onto Ted's shoulders. On this particular night in 1957, with the O.L.S.G. scheduled to knock 'em in the Regal aisles, word came that one of Ted's musicians was ill. But luckily Ronnie was free that night. Actually, Ronnie was free most nights - hardly surprising, since he was not yet ten. So it came to pass that Ronnie Wood's first live gig was playing washboard for the O. L. S. G. They had to push him on, he was so scared. But once he'd got into the rhythm of it all, good authority has it they had to pull him off. The two films, by the way film and trivia fans were "The Tommy Steele Story" and "Tommy The Toreador".

The O.L.S.G played the current Lonnie Donnegan favourites, "Rock Island Line" "Gambling Man" and "Putting On The Style", which given Ronnie's future career, were apt. Meanwhile, Elvis Presley had a Number One with "All Shook Up". Which was just as it should be.

Given Ronnie's background, and given that Tony Munroe was also music-crazy - Everly Brothers and Buddy Holly - it was inevitable that the two boys would form a group. "Our starting point was, of all things, classical," Tony recollects. "In fact, Ronnie and me would sing tenor baritone duets together. Our school was renowned throughout the south of England because it had a seven part choir, which helped us both later on in our performance, singing-wise. We were originally going to form an acapella group using just voices instead of instruments, because we couldn't play any good enough! We came second in a competition around this time in 1962. It was choir singing. We sang as a duet, a song-cum-hymn called 'We Be The King's Men Hale And Hearty'."

You can almost hear a displaced cinema organist sniggering quietly in the background.

The two boys began practising guitar whenever they could and soon entered a local talent contest in Ruislip. They sang "St Louis Woman", which was Ronnie's choice, and then an Everly Brothers number, both playing acoustic guitars. Unfortunately, there was another group who'd modelled themselves on Shane Fenton and the Fentones. Not only that, but they had Fender electric guitars and wonder of wonders, their own amps. To make matters worse, the group - neither Tony nor Ronnie can remember the name, perhaps understandably or intentionally - also moved on stage like the Shadows. The group won hands down. Tony remembers looking at Ronnie as they both realised: "Uh-oh, so that's the next step, so let's go electric."

Nowadays, Tony Munroe runs a thriving sheet-metal business in Yorkshire. He's the very model of a successful businessman. Until recently widowed, he was happily married to one of those Yorkshire women who effortlessly combine a no-nonsense approach to life with an-incredible warmth, and a slightly wicked sense of humour.

She was also a superb cook, and made just about the greatest steak pie in the world.

Despite such a tragic set back, life is still good for Tony Munroe, but get him talking about the early days, and not just the about The Birds - of which much more later - but about the days when he first began learning his musical trade, and you know the rejected hurt and confusion is still there. This is a man who never really said his goodbyes to rock and roll, probably because he was never allowed the time: one moment rhythm guitarist with one of Britain's greatest, up-and-coming cult R&B bands, the next job-hunting. Oh he was a God for a while, but as with The Birds, more later.

So how does it happen? What is it, aside from talent - sadly, never necessary to succeed in anything - that enables one person to make the grade, and forces another to rethink their life? Remember what Tony said: "Ronnie was never satisfied with what he'd achieved, and that continued right through from the art to the music."

And that was the difference. Tony Munroe was, musically speaking, always more easily satisfied than Ronnie Wood. Not that he didn't love music as much as Ronnie, nor that he didn't want to succeed as much, it's just that he didn't see music in quite the same way Ronnie did. It's simply the fact music wasn't his mistress, nor his obsession, in life.

He lacked that streak of wildness which, when successfully harnessed, leads on to single-minded greatness. If not, to destruction. Or maybe he just wasn't secure or desperate enough to take the risk. But other people were, and those that did would reject anyone unable or unwilling to make the full musical commitment. It would be a tough lesson to learn, especially when he discovered that when pushed, Ronnie would always choose music before friendship. How could Ronnie do otherwise? He'd discovered very early on music was his calling.

But that rejection was still some way in the future. During the early sixties, Ronnie and Tony continued juggling their respective musical and artistic pursuits for a further two years at Ruislip Grammar School. At sixteen they would take the 'O' Levels necessary to land a place at Ealing School of Art - at this point, music was only an absorbing sideline, and Ronnie for one was pouring all his creative energies into painting. Too much so, for he neglected all the other standard subjects like biology, chemistry, metal and woodwork. He was eventually caught cheating in his history exam after the particular dates he needed were discovered written up the length of his arm! Meanwhile, his musical education continued apace. In 1962, Art was singing with the great Alexis Korner's Blues Incorporated (featuring harp player Chris Barber and drummer Charlie Watts), while planning his first, serious assault on the world of R&B with his own Artwood Combo and ultimately the Artwoods which featured Hammond player Jon Lord and drummer Keef Hartley. Art was also taking Ronnie to the Railway Arms at Harrow and the Crawdaddy Club in Richmond where bands like The Yardbirds and The Rolling Stones were just starting out on their own musical journey. "These clubs were springing up everywhere trying to cater for the huge demand for R&B" Art recalls, "It was the new thing and these clubs would be packed to the seams, but they weren't solely R&B clubs, R&B would only happen on certain nights." Art was quick to spot the massive potential in running an exclusive R&B-only nightspot. In fact, it was Art who first discovered the little beatnik drinking club, complete with old fishing-nets and glass floats, beneath the ABC Tearoom opposite Ealing Broadway tube station. It was this little underground cellar that was to become the famed Ealing Club. Both club and band names tended to be prosaic in those days, maybe to disguise the insanity within or maybe it was to allow legends to quietly develop; for example, it was here that Brian Jones would first introduce himself to Mick Jagger and Keith Richard.

Not that the little club was always known by such a pedestrian handle, it was originally known as the The Moist Hoist, a slightly obscene-sounding name which actually referred to a practical necessity.

It was the water what done it. Specifically, the condensation that poured down the walls and dripped incessantly from the ceiling when the club was full, threatening to electrocute musicians and audience alike. The answer was a tarpaulin, erected over the stage, which gave the place a certain coy ambience - even if it did play hell with the acoustics. Some R&B fans were wrongly convinced that the tarpaulin was their mocking comment on the obligatory fishnets' plastic crabs, and all manner of seafaring paraphernalia that decorated beatnick hangouts and coffee bars at the time. Nevertheless, it really was a case of, out with the old and in with the new, for British Rhythm and Blues was the new sound and the fans loved its hatred of anything twee, folksy or wholesome.

R&B, a mix of blues, blue grass and jazz; there's even a little bit of dance band music in there, swinging, good dance band music that is. Do not think Victor Sylvester. Think Big Bill Broonzy and Duke Ellington. In the early fifties, a sanitised, watered down version of R&B surfaced with banal lyrics and simple rhythms, they called it rock 'n' roll now I don't mean the likes of Elvis, Little Richard or Chuck Berry, more your Bobby Vee, Del Shannon and Frankie Avalon. What the Brits did via Skiffle was take rock 'n' roll back to its R&B routes, apply some new arrangements and stamp their own identity on it.

Then they exported the whole lot back to a white America who took some time to realise that this thing had been started by black American musicians in the first place... Which is one reason why so many great black American musicians began making what was almost a pilgrimage to Britain during the sixties: to jam with the bands that had kept their music alive. Changed it almost out of all recognition too, the Limey rascals - but it was still nice for men like Muddy Waters and Howlin Wolf to be lionised by bands who were top of the charts both sides of the Atlantic. The visiting musicians' concerts were invariably sold out, too.

Ronnie eventually managed to get two 'O' Levels, in geography and English Literature. But it was the 'A' Level pass in Art, taken two years early, which got him into Ealing Art School, along with Tony Monroe - the only two Ruislip pupils who managed to pull it off that year - and once again, Ronnie made the local paper. He'd achieved his dream, was about to follow in Art and Ted's footsteps - and the girls at Ealing were every bit as attractive as he remembered from his nipper hood. But there was far more to it than that. First, Ronnie was well aware of the opportunities a college education offered. As he says a little sourly - and not totally accurately - today: "Working class kids like me weren't expected to get any further education. We were supposed to leave school at sixteen and go straight to work in a factory. College was largely to do with the upper class. I don't know if my parents thought it was a curse or a blessing that all three of their kids went to college rather than punch the clock." While that might be his 'emotional' truth, as the Americans say, it actually isn't accurate. Ever since the mid nineteenth century, art and grammar schools had been one of the few ways a working class child could make it into politer society. The others being the music-hall, emigration and the Armed Forces... which possibly explains the reputation touring British rock bands earned back in the sixties: great acts, but they went through hotels like an invading army. However, the main problem with art and grammar schools was that working class kids were expected to start contributing to the family income almost as soon as their eyes opened. They weren't held back by a dislike for the arts or learning, but mainly because the whole family needed to eat.

But Ronnie's parents were always determined that all their sons would have every chance in life. And if society and the educational system expected certain standards from him, Ronnie Wood was equally demanding. It was an unpleasant shock to discover that Ealing School of Art had changed dramatically since his brothers' time. He went there expecting that art would be taken seriously. Not just because it was his hoped-for future profession, but simply because it deserved to be. Ronnie found the Ealing of 1963 a place of pretentious chaos.

Ealing Art School - the original name - had been founded in 1876. Over the generations it built up an enviable reputation of being one of London's premier colleges for fine art and associated technical subjects. Come the sixties, and that all changed - along with the name - under the direction of Dr Orman Pickard. In the words of a recent retrospective booklet, " In 1956 the facilities at Ealing were said to be the best in the country, but its outlook on art education and teaching methods had become old fashioned in the light of the exciting changes that were taking place in the art world."

In other words, a bunch of second-rate academics were looking to make a name for themselves. Actually, this was part of the widespread belief that teachers and critics were just as - if not more - important as the artists themselves. An amusing little theory, originally French, adopted enthusiastically by the Americans, which would ultimately lead to 'positioning'… which expresses the belief that the artwork is to be judged by how well it expresses the all important 'concept'. Naturally, academics and critics are best able to judge this concept, so any angry artist handing over a pencil, paint brush or piece of charcoal and saying, "Show me" will be justly derided. Ealing School of Art's contribution to the new enlightenment would be the Ground Course, instigated by Roy Ascott, which "combined science and behaviourism with artistic practice, required the student to go through a period of acting out a different personality, in direct contrast to the student's usual one. The purpose of this 'experiment' was to enable the students to realise their own potential." For example, Pete Townshend - who was at Ealing a few years before Ronnie Wood - had been required to assume a physical disability, using only a handmade trolley to manoeuvre around.

Puh-leeeze. That faint sucking sound the more perceptive could hear, by the way, was academia disappearing up its collective backside. Although it does have to be said that Pete Towshend's 'experiment' would have helped considerably in his later, drug addled days with the Who, when he was so drunk or stoned that the little trolley would have been a godsend. Moonie could have made good use of it too.

Not surprisingly, many students at Ealing turned to music. Okay, the general air of anarchy helped, but music also offered an essential discipline and sense of excellence. Not everyone can have prizes. You can fake art, especially when it's anything anyone says it is, but you can't fake the ability to play the drums, come up with a riff, sing in tune or indeed, be truly original. Or you couldn't before the industry discovered that it was easier to manufacture and sell the whole thing to the pre-teen market that knows no different.

By and large, music has always been more approachable than art, especially in Britain during the sixties. Music and the movies/theatre were the people's first art form. (Anyone putting a hand up for football should remember that more people visited museums during that era than physically watch the glorious game). Nowadays all that's changed of course, and this has nothing to do with Ronnie Wood, it's merely one of those comments writers like to make at the expense of a quietly sobbing editor.

Of course, the academics loved the idea that art-schools had become a breeding ground for rock and pop musicians; since it gave the impression they - the academics - were at the forefront of popular culture. It wasn't until the late 1970s that Malcolm McLaren, fresh from failing with the New York Dolls, successfully called the academic bluff, and initially launched the Sex Pistols via the art school circuit. What could the professors do? Say that the Pistols sounded god awful, and possibly miss out on a cultural happening? Or give them the artistic seal of approval? No contest, really: academics have a well-honed instinct for survival. The real irony would come when the Pistols began to believe their own publicity and later learned the truth of the old maxim: never trust a hippie.

Ealing Technical College has now become Thames Valley University, having served its apprenticeships as Ealing College of Higher Education and the Polytechnic of West London. The art school side had been closed down in the late seventies. Well, it was uneconomical and took up too much space. But you can always do a BA in Design and Media Management. All those artists and musicians will always need someone to rip them off.

When Ronnie Wood and Tony Munroe arrived at Ealing in 1963, they were disgusted by what they found. To Ronnie, in particular, it must have seemed like middle-class masturbation. His family remembers him coming home in the evening and complaining, "They weren't doing serious art." If this sounds a little po-faced, remember that all of Ronnie's musical heroes took their profession extremely seriously and technique was just as important as the idea behind a composition. In fact, how could anyone ever hope to express themselves musically without being able to play an instrument properly? Shouldn't the same apply to art? Especially as one of the new students was looking to a career in art to pay back his parents for the sacrifices they made and the faith they'd shown in him?

As it was, everything and anything at Ealing was open to artistic appreciation and expression. Shows with names such as 'Auto Destructive' and 'Flash Art' were put on, to a background of white noise or electric guitar feedback. Most of the students seemed to have given up any hope of becoming a professional artist, in Ronnie's terms. In fact, most of the students seemed to be forming or auditioning for the next most popular band to come out of the place, "Almost everyone I knew in Ealing went on to be a professional musician." Ronnie recalls. "Even Art and Ted could have gone all the way, they were certainly good enough, but as Art says, he knew when to hang up his rocking boots!"

If you can't beat 'em, join 'em. And Ronnie had been around bands all his life. "We knew we had to get a band together. It was very obvious to us. I used to see Keith Moon around Ealing, he wasn't a student, but he lived nearby. I could see the fun he was having with Pete Townshend and those guys in the early days of The Who. He was a maniac even then, but the creativity impressed me. I also watched a girl named Linda Keith around school a lot. She was a student and really gorgeous and I was told she was going out with Keith Richard. I knew he was in the Rolling Stones. I'd seen their earliest publicity shots and I was really excited by them, especially those pictures of them standing by the Thames with their long straggly hair blowing in the wind. I looked up to them because they were a few years older than me. I'd seen them individually playing around the same club circuit as my brothers, with the likes of Alexis Korner. I thought "girls look at them differently. They want to go out with them." I simply realised that I'd do a lot better for myself, both socially and financially, by drawing people to gigs than drawing people on canvas!"

And so the deed was done. At least, the deed was decided to be done.

The realisation would take a little longer. "We had two real problems with forming a band at Ealing," Tony remembers. "One was, who the fuck was going to be in it? And the other, what would we play? We realised very early on that our personal musical tastes were a bit at odds with each other. As I said, Ron was still very much influenced by his brothers, Ted in particular, because Art was that much older and had moved out to get married, so that left Ted at home, turning Ron on to Jazz more and more. Art had just about got The Artwoods up and running who were still a bit jazzy too, so that was Ron's stable influence. But I was a rocker, Chuck Berry and Buddy Holly, so we didn't really know the answer, because there was just the two of us."

They found the answer a few weeks later, at a gig by a local band called The Renegades. Actually, The Renegades were due to disband and the gig - at the nearby West Drayton US Air-Force base - was to prove their last. "We didn't have a clue who they were," admits Tony, "we were told by friends at Ealing Art School to check them out. We got talking to them after the gig and that's when we found out all was not well within. We wanted a bass player and drummer so that was when it all sort of fell together. We left that night with their rhythm section. We got talking to their bass player, Kim Gardner, after the gig and he let slip that he thought the group weren't going anywhere. So we grabbed the chance and asked him to join Ron and me. Kim was so obviously the leader, so when he came on board so did Bob Langham, the drummer and Robin Scrimshaw, their harp player."

In fact, both Ronnie and Tony originally wanted Ali McKenzie, the Renegades' singer. They'd have wanted him even more if they'd realised that he owned the Renegades' PA system. As it was, they were knocked out by his stage performance - Ali was a natural-born showman. But Ali, in the words of Kim Gardiner "was feeling all deserted and left out, so he played hard to get. Of course, when Ronnie and Tony realised Ali owned the PA system, he became even more important."

This, after all, was the time when people were invited to join bands just because they owned an amp, a PA system was like owning the crown jewels, only owning a van was thought of as more important. So much so that even if the player who owned or had access to a van didn't shape up musically, they would often end up being kept on as either the road manager or in some cases, even managers. Even when a band got successful enough to afford its own van and equipment, seldom was this bond broken.

There has been the odd exception to the rule, however. For example, keyboard player Jimmy Winston had been invited to join the Small Faces a band who were forming at around the same time as The Birds in East London. Jimmy owned a van but that never stopped the group unceremoniously sacking him without so much as a by-your-leave.

A fact he never quite understood, nor for that matter, even knew about, until he showed up at a gig one night and found his replacement, one Ian McLagan, already performing with the band on stage. The fact that they could afford their own van by then wasn't lost on Jimmy who eventually sued the band, but not until 1969 (what kept him?), long after the Small Faces had achieved massive success, but ironically when the band could least afford it. Still, that's another story.

In one of those strange but true coincidences that crop up in Ronnie Wood's life, Kim Gardiner, Ali McKenzie and Bob Langham all lived in or close to Whitethorn Avenue - they're going to have to put blue plaques up there one day - and all were pure local boys, except Kim who'd moved from his native North Wales when he was nine. Kim had originally formed the Renegades with Ali when they were both attending St Martin's Secondary Modern; they were a typical after-school session band of thirteen and fourteen year-olds, playing mostly Shadows instrumentals and a few covers of rare American R&B records. These were mostly learned from listening to the records on, or to be more precise, pilfered from, the PX jukebox at the US Air Force base in West Drayton. It's a point worth making that the American bases in Britain, possibly without meaning to, played a definite part in developing British R&B. Maybe West Drayton should have a blue plaque as well.

The first solo Kim ever learned, Nivram, came from watching his hero, Jet Harris of The Shadows. "I tried to look like Jet," Kim admits, "and our lead guitar player, when Ronnie heard us for the first and last time, had glasses like Hank Marvin. I remember we played James Ray's "If You've Got To Make A Fool Of Somebody", which I played for Ronnie and it knocked him out. He never forgot it; in fact, he recorded it himself years later, on his first solo album."

Ronnie called the first band meeting together for the following night, when he informed the new recruits they would now go forth as 'The Rhythm & Blues Bohemians'. The rehearsals began in earnest, often taking place either in the back room at Ronnie's, whenever Ted wasn't around, or on a Wednesday night at the local Community Centre or, strangely enough, in the front window of the Rainbow Record Shop on Yiewsley High Street every Sunday morning. The owner thought it would be good publicity, as did the band.

A month later, the Rhythm and Blues Bohemians felt confident enough to perform live and threw open the Community Centre doors to a surprisingly-large invited audience of around 300 friends and family. "We weren't very good", remembers Tony. "Only Kim and me had amps so the PA went through Kim's along with the bass and Ronnie and me both put our guitars through mine. Robin was singing and playing Harp, which he wasn't very good at, and the whole thing sounded crap!"

It did, however, grab the attention of The Hillingdon Mirror, who ran an article under the heading "Taking A Cue From Brothers", which once again focused on all three brothers Wood. Kicking off with Ted and a report on his imminent trip to Zurich with The Colin Kingswell's Jazz Bandits, the article went on to report that Art's group, The Artwoods, had recently turned semi-pro. The final column space, however, was devoted to youngest brother Ronnie and The Bohemians' pledge to "Avoid any Beatles music!" and their promise to "Stay true to Rhythm & Blues".

They were already talking a good game, yet despite such obvious determination and the fact that their families and friends loved them, it was fairly obvious that The Bohemians were destined to become a short-lived affair. Their lack of any real equipment, and the need for a confident lead singer, meant that their public exposure would be limited to the occasional gig in the Community Centre, and every Sunday morning in the window of the Rainbow Record Shop.

"It clearly wasn't going to go any further", Kim confirmed, "and this is with no disrespect to Robin, but he was never meant to be a member. He was just a mate who came along and sang because no one else wanted to. He was tall, about six foot fuckin' six, and we thought he looked like Long John Baldry. So we thought if he stood up front we would look really cool, but he didn't and we never did!"

It seemed that the answer to the Bohemians' problems lay with Ali McKenzie. But he was remaining defiantly stubborn, while acutely aware of the band's dilemma. "He would even watch us rehearse," Kim said, "but he'd decided to keep his options open, hoping for a better offer."

That better offer never came and Kim nagged continuously at his best friend. But the clincher came when Ali met a new girlfriend called Carol who - surprise, surprise - lived in Whitethorn Avenue. It was at that point Ali consigned himself to the inevitable and joined the band. Incidentally, he also (eventually) married Carol.
Robin politely stepped aside, and in time honoured tradition stayed on as the band's roadie, ironically lugging the Ali-supplied PA to rehearsals, often in the back room of Ronnie's house - the one which had once housed the dug-up air-raid shelter.

The new line-up now read Ali McKenzie, lead vocals; Ronnie Wood, lead guitar, harmonica and vocals; Tony Munroe, rhythm guitar and vocals; Kim Gardiner, bass; and Bob Langham, drums. Say again? Ronnie Wood playing harp? Since when?

Well, since the day before, actually. Lizzie tells the story: "Ronnie picked everything up so fast, just like with his painting. He came home one night and he said "look mum, look what I've got" and he'd bought a mouth organ, a harmonica. He'd given a pound for it. I said "what did you buy that for? You can't play it!" and he said "I will". He took it upstairs to his bedroom on something like a Wednesday and started blowing it until he fell asleep with it, and in the morning he came down and said "I've cracked it!" and that very night he was playing it on stage with the band."

Art confirms the story - as a musician, not a brother. "He stayed up all night practically and the next night, people were going 'great harp player!' and he'd only had it one bleedin' day!"

At this point they decided to drop the vaguely beatnik sounding Bohemians name and at Ronnie's suggestion, decided to call themselves The Thunderbirds, named after the Chuck Berry song, "Jaguar And The Thunderbird".

Local gigs followed, and The Thunderbirds won a Beat competition that netted the group a permanent residency back at the local Community Centre every Saturday night. Naturally, the band renamed their new venue The Nest.

Art Wood believes that this was The Thunderbirds' major step-up. They now had the security of a regular gig, and the chance to develop their own sound. And not before time, because their individual preferences were all very different. Ronnie and Tony had become avid Yardbirds fans, in particular Eric Clapton. Actually, it was next to impossible to find any R&B musician in England who wasn't an Eric Clapton fan. However, neither Ronnie not Tony could agree about the Rolling Stones. Put bluntly, Tony thought the Stones were a wishy-washy group who'd be nothing without Mick Jagger, while Ronnie thought they were the greatest thing since booze and fags.

Ali agreed with Ronnie that the Stones did indeed have tremendous charisma, but argued that they were merely pale imitators when compared to his own personal heroes, Sam Cooke and Marvin Gaye. Kim was still rating Jet Harris over Bill Wyman and as for Bob, well he didn't seem to particularly care either way.

Soon all the local newspapers began publishing little stories about the band, like where they were playing and what competitions they'd entered. As witness the headline:
WHEN THE THUNDERBIRDS FEATHER THE NEST - NOW MODS AND ROCKERS RECKON THE DRAYTON SOUND

The same article went on to talk about the 'West Drayton Beat' and reminded readers that the Beatles had also started as rank outsiders. It got their ages wrong, too.

The Nest generated the Thunderbirds the first real money they ever earned, due to them being allowed to charge people at the door and keep the takings. It was an essential financial arrangement for the band for the band's instruments left a great deal to be desired. Ronnie, for example, was playing an old beat-up electric guitar, which he rented for a few pounds a week from Terry Marshall, owner of the Rainbow Record Shop. Terry was an early Thunderbirds fan, even to the point of allowing the band to use both shop and various items of equipment for rehearsals, on the understanding that nothing was 'borrowed' for a gig.

But, with a bit of cash coming in, they could at last start to up grade. The first big change came when Tony's father bought him (on the understanding he eventually paid him back) a Vox amp costing £130; this at a time when the average wage was less than £15 a week.

"Our family circumstances were different," Tony now says. "My parents were better-off than the others and maybe that's where the competition started with Ronnie. Who was the best painter, who was the best basketball player, who was the most popular person - albeit we were great friends, or at least I thought we were, there was always this underlying rivalry. I never gave the fact we were better off much thought, but I was made to feel aware of it so I made a point of never using it to my advantage over the others.

"I'll give you a classic example. When my Dad brought me that amp, I didn't think twice before giving it to Ronnie because he was the lead guitarist. I said to him, "Here, you have this and I'll make do with the old one," which was a tiny, fifteen-amp thing. It made a world of difference to his playing, because it was the first time he could hear himself clearly, it was our first proper amp to go through."

Tony's father helped out with the transport problem, too. None of the band was yet old enough to drive, so he made them two large wheelbarrows so they could take the drums and amps from rehearsals to local gigs. If they ever played further afield, Tony's father or a friend old enough to drive would take them. Pretty soon the band and their wheelbarrows became a familiar sight around Yiewsley and West Drayton. As undignified as it may have been, the wheelbarrows did at least make it easier and cheaper to get onto Eel Pie Island.

Like the Chiselhurst Caves in south London, Eel Pie Island in the middle of the Thames in Richmond was to become one of London's most unusual and legendary music venues of the sixties. The island was reached by a single narrow bridge, which bands had to manhandle their equipment across in order to reach the venue. That was until an enterprising chap realised that the bridge was just wide enough to drive a Mini-Moke car across. Once he realised that, he set himself up as the Eel Pie shuttle, ferrying groups and their equipment back and forth. It was, as they say, a nice little earner but not one that The Birds had any use for. No sir, The Birds had two bloody big wheelbarrows so they could afford to ignore such examples of young enterprise and do it themselves.

Eel Pie Island in particular became known as the R&B venue - Art Wood remembers fans of all ages flocking in at the weekend. "That was one of the differences between now and then; there was no age limit to liking a particular type of music. I don't mean that everyone liked everything, but it wasn't strange to see kids, adults and even grandparents at the same gig. They'd be in their own little cliques of course, but they were all there, all enjoying themselves."

Fact was, although the pre-teen and the teenager had been discovered and promoted in America, mostly as a way of selling anything from trainer bras to counselling, in the UK children were mostly seen as being trainee adults. You can argue either way, but one indisputable fact remains: children growing up in the fifties and early sixties were expected to be extremely responsible, and to know how to take care of themselves from a comparatively early age. Also, that the great social divides based on age hadn't totally kicked in yet. The sixties 'yoof' culture, as oxymoronic as it is meaningless, wasn't seen as quite the marketing invention it was to later become.

Within a matter of months, the Thunderbirds' tough, home-grown brand of rhythm and blues had earned the band a large and very loyal following.

"Ronnie and I saw The Stones during this period," Ali remembers, "and they were obviously a big influence on any young R&B band at the time. Their sheer charisma and charismatic quality, or whatever it was, they had it. But I can't honestly say they influenced the group at that point particularly, because, although we played the same sort of stuff, our roots in music were far more diverse to what we actually performed. Sam Cooke was my all-time favourite, alongside Marvin Gaye and later Dionne Warwick. Ron and Tony were into The Yardbirds. They were their favourites and Kim? Well fuck knows what Kim was into! But we were all into different things. So we took all these influences, Motown, R&B and rock 'n' roll and added our own extra ingredients. We were, after all, white English kids. There's no way we could have been just a Motown band, and sounded just one dimensional like that, we just added our sound to this mish-mash."

Ronnie remembers it differently. He was alone when he first saw the Stones... or if anyone else was there, like family or his own band, he can't remember them: "The first time I saw the Stones live was at the Richmond Jazz Festival in 1964. They were playing inside a tent that was bopping up and down, looking like an elephant with its big ass rocking and rolling from side to side. From the outside you could tell something good was happening in there. I went in and stood at the back, like this awkward kid totally intrigued by it all. I remember I was the last one to leave. Walking out, I kept on turning to watch the Stones haul their gear off-stage - and almost broke my leg by tripping over a tent peg and rope.

"Then I went again to see them at the Windsor Cavern, when they were still wearing those dog-tooth uniforms. They were working pretty hard, doing about two shows a day. There was a long line of people zigzagging up the road, waiting to get in. I assumed the Stones were already backstage. Instead, this putrid orange van pulls up, packed with amps and human cattle. The driver, it must have been Ian Stewart, gets out and walks to the back door of the van and opens it. Five guys come pouring out like water over a broken dam and fall into the gutter, all in their wrinkled uniforms and sprawling in the dirt. And yes, I knew I belonged in that band. I've always been a believer in fate. I just counted on it happening, thought I'd be patient because it would fall in my lap some day. I just had to wait it out."

It was going to be a long wait. But worth it.

Another musically-significant event in the life of young Ron during 1964 occurred when Ted left the family home to marry his long-term girlfriend, Gill. This meant that Ronnie could move into more spacious quarters - leaving the now famous box-room empty. Ah, but not for long, as Art needed homes for his band. Drummer, Keef Hartley, was billeted out with Art's mother-in-law, in his wife's old bedroom, while keyboard player, Jon Lord, found himself the happy occupier of the Wood box-room   £4.00 a week full board, washing and ironing included. This made Jon Lord the latest successor in a long line of musicians to teach Ronnie the finer points of their profession.

For Tony Munroe, the individual influences were what made the Thunderbirds, soon to be Birds, unique. "The two guitar set-up set us apart from a lot of groups. Ronnie and I were the R&B side of the group, whereas Kim was real rock 'n' roll and Ali was into Motown. Ronnie and me were very 'arty-farty art school', so we were up on all the very rare R&B records like St. Louis Woman, Muddy Waters and all that sort of stuff. R&B was relatively innovative at that time, so we were considered very cool, and we were."

Life was good for Ronnie. The band was beginning to develop its own sound. They had a regular gig and an ever-increasing group of regular fans. He was part of a musical and cultural explosion that would eventually influence so many people who were born too late for the sixties. It was truly bliss to be alive.

What could possibly go wrong?

The answer came on Sunday 31st May 1964, the day before Ronnie's seventeenth birthday. Only a week before the local paper had carried a front-page photo of a pretty, sixteen year-old brunette called Stephanie de Court, photographed taking part in a 'Twist & Shake' session at the Nest. A week later, the same newspaper carried the same picture only this time it reported she was dead, killed in a car crash.

Ronnie had been dating her for over a year.

"She was my first true love," Ronnie freely admits. "I'd met her at Ruislip Grammar. I never fumbled with her though; I was too awkward with girls then, sweaty palms and everything. I mean I simply idolised her. She would let me walk her home from school, carry her books and all that and that was enough for me. I would run home from her house completely elated, clicking my heels in the air. The great thing was that she would come to The Nest to see us play, and even when we started to play other towns, she would drive up with a bunch of friends."

"He was madly in love with Stephanie" Tony remembers. "He would have married her for sure. He was that in love. He was in a world of his own when he was with her."

That world was shattered on that fateful Sunday. Stephanie had been killed the evening before with three friends while travelling to a barbecue party in Henley-On-Thames. Apparently they'd become lost, then had been hit head-on by a drunken pilot going home from Heathrow. The Thunderbirds had been playing to a packed house in Reading at the time, and Ronnie had been anxiously scouring the audience for her all night.

"My father woke me up with the news. The subtle guy that he was: "Wake up Ronnie. C'mon. Stephanie's been killed. Come downstairs and see her uncle." I was in a daze walking down the stairs and into the living room. There was her uncle who said, "I'm afraid that Stephanie died in a car crash last night." "Ah" I thought, that's why she never turned up."

Stephanie's uncle also had with him the after-shave she'd bought for Ronnie's birthday, for she'd been expected to tea that same Sunday.

Tony Munroe heard about the accident by a phone call from Robin Scrimshaw, and they rushed round to console Ronnie by taking him to the local pub. "It was the first time any of us had experienced death" Tony said. "We hadn't ever been in that situation before because we were all just kids, and here was someone who was not only dead, but she was also our age. We didn't think about the other driver who died though, we were trying to cheer Ron up which was obviously impossible. We weren't even old enough to drink legally and Robin, who was the tightest bloke around, gave Ron a pound for his birthday, which was a miracle in itself! But what sticks in my mind the most was Ronnie. He just sat there for ages, then looked up and said: "After all the money I've spent on her!" That was his reaction."

Black humour used as an emotional release? Or one of those things that you say without knowing why, and then wishing to God you hadn't - probably because you can't quite come to terms with what happened? One of those comments you remember years later and groan aloud with remembered embarrassment and remorse - usually when you're sitting with a bunch of strangers on the train. Or perhaps in that one throw-away comment - albeit caught by Tony Munroe who's still wondering what he meant - Ronnie showed the 'been there, done that, time to move on,' side to his nature that would characterise his professional career until he finally found his musical home with the Stones.

Of course, he went to the funeral and cremation, together with Tony and Diane Salmon who'd been Stephanie's best friend; she had also been seeing Tony himself two best friends going out with two best friends for the very last time. Ronnie looked dapper in a new black jacket, tailored with a hint of Regency flair, white shirt, black tie, dark trousers and the square-toed shoes with two raised seams on the uppers. The three friends were quiet, still stunned. For Ronnie, it was all a little unreal there'd be no grave to visit, nowhere to bring flowers. And the ceremony wasn't really about his Stephanie, but about the girl who'd also belonged to her family and other friends.

A few days later he dressed more casually and went on his own to see where Stephanie had been killed: "I went to look at the spot and tried to picture her, the tyre marks were still there, the skid marks and everything. It happened on a strip called 'The Henley Fairmile'. I just had the morbid need to go to be in the same place she had been. There and then, after I'd seen it, I put it out of my head."

CHAPTER THREE
"FUCKING BIG IN CHESHIRE!"

The Thunderbirds had reached a stage in their existence when they hovered uncertainly between local-boys-having-fun and semi-professional musicians. On the one hand, they were developing a unique sound and an incredibly strong rapport with audiences. On the other, they were still trundling their equipment around in wheelbarrows, or being driven to distant gigs by Tony's father and a family friend. Aside from being impractical, it was just so bloody embarrassing.

Enter Leo de Klerk, a South African-born impresario who owned a string of nightclubs - including the 'Cavern' clubs in Windsor and Reading. Leo was very typical of the type of pop businessman who began appearing in the sixties. He was young, in his early thirties when he met the Thunderbirds - always well dressed and charming. In addition to his nightclubs, Leo was also a bit-part actor specialising in the smooth, 'heavy' type of role - he was also a bodybuilder - and would later appear in TV series' like 'The Professionals'.

But Leo was also a fake. Oh, he owned various nightclubs, acted whenever he could, and was a genuine body-builder, but he was never South African; instead a South London Cockney whose assumed name oscillated between 'de Clerck' and 'de Klerk' (and the not very hard-sounding Lionel, his real first name)   presumably depending on whether he wanted the Flemish/Huegenot or Dutch/Boer spelling. He ran his mini-empire with the help of two large West London brothers, Colin and Tony Farrell, who were also avid body-builders. Leo wasn't a gangster, but he was sharp with a good eye for the main chance.

The real gangsters would appear later.

Leo had visited The Nest at the suggestion of a friend he was meeting nearby. According to Tony Munroe, Leo had been instantly impressed by the chemistry between the Thunderbirds and their audience. "Everyone had their own thing going on stage, their own little show if you like. Kim, who was a 'nutter', had this quiet air of madness about him, he was a loon, you knew he could erupt at any time, he would be in a world of his own just pounding out this thunderous rhythm. He was one of the best natural bass players around, amazing bass player.

"Ali was a born showman, he would take over the whole stage - if we let him. He had a star presence that was undeniable; I reckon he was probably the most underrated front man of his generation. That would leave me and Ronnie standing either side trying to out do each other with this competitive thing we had going between us, guitar battles at every gig, it really was electric. So Leo, being an entrepreneur and with his club background, could see here was a group he could put into his own clubs and save money while making money. He certainly knew a good thing when he saw it and he grabbed it."

Leo had made up his mind, he was so blown away that very first time that no sooner had the band downed their instruments, he asked to meet the band's leader, fully expecting an audience with Ali. So it came as something of a surprise when a few minutes later he found himself shaking hands with Ronnie Wood. In those days, lead guitarists - no matter how good weren't seen as the leader of a band. That role was always reserved for the singer, or lead vocalist or "LV" as musos like to abbreviate it.

Right there and then, Leo made Ronnie an offer that he simply could not refuse.

Basically, Leo would manage the Thunderbirds on a professional basis and pay them each £10.00 a week - that's about £250 in today's money, He'd also provide them with transport and pay for petrol and maintenance, he would even hire them a road manager to drive them from gig to gig. Later, there'd be a clothes-allowance and in time, record deals and foreign tours. Effectively Leo took a bunch of sixteen and seventeen year-olds up to a very high place and offered them the world.

It all sounded too good to be true; unfortunately it was. No one did their sums. No one realised that the Thunderbirds would be costing Leo at least £250 a week each in wages and expenses. Say £1,200 per week in modern money, plus road expenses and transport, which came in the shape of a light blue, second-hand Commer van.

It all added up to the fact that in order to make his investment profitable, the Thunderbirds would have to play an awful lot of gigs, unless or until they became wildly popular. But even if they did, they'd still be stuck on £10.00 a week.

But it was a career opportunity for which most aspiring young bands would have sold their families into slavery, let alone themselves. Which of course is exactly what the Thunderbirds did. The scene was set; on the one hand a bunch of naive, but ambitious musicians, on the other, the archetypal smooth operator. Remember, Leo de Klerk/Clerck had no idea how big the Thunderbirds could or would become. He wasn't exactly taking a chance - the band would repay his investment and then some, merely by appearing at his own clubs - so, at least it was generous slavery. The only problem was that the deal never took into account the fact that bands and teenagers often grow up, or rather mature and then begin asking awkward questions, like "What's really in this for us/me?" Leo began losing the Thunderbirds the moment he signed them.

For the present, all Ronnie Wood knew was that the band had only been together a matter of months and here was the chance of regular work and a steady wage. Ronnie already knew what he wanted to do for the rest of his life. It only took one glance across at the stage to confirm it; the sight of his band mates loading the gear into their wheelbarrows was all the encouragement he needed. How on earth could you expect to be taken seriously as musicians when you looked like the guest band on 'Gardiner's Question Time?' Where do I sign?

"I knew there and then" Ronnie recalls, "I knew what choice I had to make. I knew I wanted to be a musician first and an artist second. My brothers would eventually choose art, but they'd still made good money out of music. The Artwoods had even played in Poland. The moment we started to make any fucking kind of money at The Nest, I knew the windfalls were soon to follow. I knew they would come in time. I mean, look at Elvis, he only had to wait a few years to sell a few million records, but Van Gogh sold only one painting during his whole life. The choice was easy. The rest of the band thought so, too."

The choice may have been obvious to Ronnie, but whether Lizzie and Arthur would see it quite as plainly was going to prove a whole different matter.

"I had mixed feelings really." Lizzie ruefully remembers. "I wanted him to get on with his music, but I didn't want him to stop doing his art, but I knew his heart was in his music. He was so good I was very torn in-between. A lot of people would have given their right arm to be at art school and he hadn't been there for even a year. I went to talk it over with the Headmaster and that was the worst part - explaining why Ronnie wanted to leave and why I was supporting his decision. They didn't want him to go. They kept on telling me all these reasons why he should stay. They said "he's got it in him to do well" and they "didn't want to lose him". I had to simply tell them the truth as I saw it. He had his mind made up and he had to go with his heart, not his art."

Lizzie duly signed her son out of Ealing Art School and went home, a deeply worried woman. She stopped off at the local bakers, looking so concerned that the sympathetic staff asked what was wrong. Lizzie told them the saga of her youngest son who'd chosen music over a proper career something you certainly can't do in a modern supermarket, not unless you feel like pouring your heart out to the disinterested spotty pothead on the cheese counter.

"The shop was called Clinches and as luck would have it, the woman who owned it was in there that day, she had a daughter who went to school with Ron, and I'll never forget what she said to me. She turned to me and said, "Mrs. Wood, don't you worry about Ronnie too much. You let him take his choice and he'll be alright"."

The comment helped, but Art Wood still remembers how worried Lizzie remained. "Mum was very upset about Ron, she really felt she'd helped to ruin his career and she was frightened he'd fail. Ted and me were into our music but we didn't drop out of school to do it. There was never a choice for us, but Ron was giving up what looked like a real secure future to go off with that bunch of Herberts, The Thunderbirds. I was sure it didn't look like the right choice and Mum did too, she felt responsible. I came up with the compromise by getting Ron a little job with my brother-in-law Robert Colewell who had a sign writers' company called 'Signcraft', and that calmed everything down for a while."

It was also around this time that Ronnie met the girl who would eventually become his first wife.

Krissie Findlay was born on 11th February 1948, in Malta, where her father was stationed with the Royal Navy. Her mother was part Italian and Swedish, her father pure Scots - an exotic mix that gave Krissie her captivating features: ash-blond hair, blue eyes and high cheekbones. Not that Ron was studying such things; no, the first thing he noticed was her bra.

"The first real memory I have of him is seeing him and Kim (Gardiner) in the audience at the Crawdaddy club, because they both had really long hair. The club had fluorescent blue lights, and I had a black blouse on with a white bra underneath so the fluorescent light lit up the white bra and all I can remember is Ronnie looking at my tits with this incredible great smile, and me thinking, "who is this man?" I just remember thinking what beautiful teeth he had 'cos it was fluorescent, and what a cheeky grin. Ronnie isn't what you'd consider handsome, but he was the most incredibly unusual looking guy I'd ever seen, and I was instantly intrigued. Not exactly attracted sexually, but he did have an incredible impact on me. I just thought "yeah!" I had no idea they were musicians until I saw Ronnie on stage with Eric later that evening."

Krissie was sixteen, a year younger than Ronnie, but considerably more adult. As with many Service brats, her father's various home and foreign postings had given her a maturity way beyond her years. Constant travel, the need to be able to make new friends on a regular basis, and the traditional self-reliance of Service families had given her an outgoing and vivacious personality. Very much part of the Ealing/West London social scene, whose central core of revellers included Pete Townsend, Richard 'Barney' Barnes, and Eric Clapton, who just so happened to be Krissie's boyfriend since meeting him at the tender young age of fourteen.

"I know I was comparatively young when I lost my virginity to Eric - but some girls do grow up faster than others. Eric was sixteen when we first met, very sweet and thoughtful. He was my first love."

In those days the Crawdaddy Club was at the Richmond Athletic Ground. Krissie was naturally in the audience that night in early March 1964 when the Yardbirds' lead singer, Keith Relf - doubly impaired by severe asthma and only having one lung - was unsurprisingly taken ill in the smoky club. Clapton asked the packed audience if anyone could play harmonica, and Ronnie, goaded on by Kim, hesitantly volunteered his services.

And having done so, he more than held his own with musicians he'd long considered his mentors. In fact, as Art remembers: "That was a real confidence boost for Ronnie. After that there was no holding him back, now more than ever he knew what he wanted to be."

The next time Krissie saw Ronnie was in April 1964 when he was playing with the Thunderbirds at Harrow Technical College: "Pete and Barney had given me free tickets and I went with a friend of mine, Suzy (Cunningham). I recognised Ronnie, but I remember standing in the audience thinking I really, really like him but he's copying Eric, which of course he wasn't."

Which was as far as it went, since Krissie was still going out with Eric Clapton, and Ronnie with Stephanie de Court, so the question of any stronger attraction was purely academic... or a least filed away in Krissie's mind for future consideration, and why not?

By early June, everything had changed. Stephanie had been killed in a car crash, and Krissie's relationship with Eric Clapton was beginning to run its course, as first loves inevitably do. The Thunderbirds had turned professional and were about to shorten their name to The Birds to avoid confusion with the considerably more famous Chris Farlowe and the Thunderbirds. They were also playing the occasional gig at the Station Hotel in Richmond. Krissie and Suzy Cunningham went along one Saturday night and once again found themselves watching Ronnie perform on stage. That same night, Leo de Klerk decided to invite a few of the local gig-goers to an after show party in order to meet the band. Neither girl needed much persuading.

"Originally I was going to go for Kim, because that was the way Suzy and me planned it, like teenage girls do. But it didn't work out like that, because Suzy and Kim vanished into the garden and I saw Ronnie standing there by the fireplace. So we had a slow dance together and then we kissed, and then that was it, I knew I was in love. We spent every day together after that; we became inseparable which was very young to have such an intense relationship. I was living at home, he was living with his Mum and Dad, and he used to come to my place and we used to sit round the kitchen table and Ronnie would paint and I'd try and paint, because that was Ronnie's other passion. But our backgrounds were very different - I'd been bought up in a very proper, middle-class family, quite strict in its own way, and Ronnie was from this gypsy background... very free and easy, anything goes. He always lived for the now. When you were with him, he could make you feel like the most special person in the world."

Shortly after Krissie and Ronnie began dating, he quit his job as an apprentice sign-writer. He'd been earning £4.00 a week, but Leo's plans for the group to go full-time and begin touring made a day-job impossible. Perhaps equally important, sign-writing had proved creatively stifling, or 'totally fucking boring," as Ronnie succinctly sums it up today, and even life threatening.

"My swan song was painting ads at the local football ground," Ronnie recalls with a shudder. "It had this steeply sloping corrugated iron roof over the stand that you could read from the other side of the field. It felt like fucking Everest and I was scared shitless going up there every day with a fucking paint pot!" But then, that's what apprentices were meant to do, really: take risks and get scared shitless, and so learn their place in the scheme of things. Mind you, Ronnie did have the added distraction of a bikini-clad Krissie sunbathing on the centre-spot.

"That little job did give Ron a bit of security and a bit more money," Art offers, "for as long as it lasted. Plus it was a bit 'arty' which kept his hand in and enabled him to do his thing with the group too. But the main thing was it had made Mum feel better. At least he kept it up until he turned pro."

That sign-writing job would prove to be the first and last time Ronnie ever worked outside the music industry. If he couldn't make any money by playing, he was prepared to starve. Or at least, go round to his Mum's for his tea. Luckily, Krissie also understood musicians and was prepared to support him in his dream. She knew how good he was and sensed he could be even greater, so she embarked on a series of jobs varying from temp work in a solicitors office, to selling clothes for the up and coming fashion queen, Zandra Rhodes. All of which helped supplement Ronnie's wages from The Birds. They were kids, it was all an adventure they were part of the new world the sixties were promising. They became an inseparable partnership, Ronnie already exhibiting his life-long need to have a strong and supportive woman in his life. But two's company, etc and Tony Munroe for one was just a little miffed. He felt that his and Ronnie's working partnership was threatened by the new love in Ronnie's life."

"I didn't like her - I felt she was a stuck up snob and basically a hanger-on. Ronnie used to fall in love whenever he went out with a bird, one two three he was in love completely, totally gone. I remember one time Ronnie was absolute fucking livid because he thought Krissie had gone back with Clapton for a night. So I said to Ron rather hopefully, "Why don't you fucking dump her?" But he was so in love, he'd forgive her anything. It was a shame I didn't get on with Krissie, but I couldn't tolerate her, I found her totally boring, such a stuck up little prissie. I could never communicate with her; she was always in another world. One Saturday lunch time we were playing in The Marquee and Ron and Krissie were in the changing room, and they were both in a stupor because Ron had been on uppers during the night and they had both taken downers and they were both well falling asleep all over the place. For fucks sake, I mean we're in the Marquee, you know in the changing room! She was always there, she'd turn up everywhere we'd go, whether it was a lunch-time or a recording session, God it drove me mad."

When Ronnie and the rest of the band turned professional in June 1964 he was still a minor; this meant any commercial contract had to be signed on his behalf by his parents. "Leo (De Clerk) had come round our house one night," Lizzie recalls, "and gave me all these forms to fill in which I'd never seen or heard of, and he'd said "I must sign here and here", well, I didn't know. He went on and on for so long about what he thought he was going to do and what he wanted the boys to do, then when at last I went to sign the form he said "No, I couldn't use a biro pen", it had to be in ink from a fountain pen which I had to get from my neighbour Mr Pearce, who advised me to be careful, and to read the small print, which got me worried all over again."

But she signed, if only because Ronnie had set his heart on turning professional. Besides, Leo was so very well dressed and charming. He was South African, too, which somehow made him all the more believable. It wasn't as if he was a South London wide boy now was it?

Leo wasted little time in securing the parents' signatures of a further three Birds: Ali, Kim and Tony. But it was at the fourth he failed. "Bob wouldn't turn pro." Tony explains. "He had this extremely overpowering Mother who wouldn't let him turn professional. She thought we would all turn into 'druggies'!"

Bob's mother was right.

If the sixties did anything, they democratised drug use. Cocaine had once been a common pick-me-up in the States, but Coca-Cola had long changed its original formula. In the UK, from the twenties onwards, cocaine had been predominantly an upper-class drug, and one unlikely to be found outside London or the Home Counties. Heroin was known about, but again the vast majority of registered addicts - less than a thousand - were in London. In the early sixties, both drugs were used mainly by artists and musicians, probably with some justification. No. With a great deal of justification, along with marijuana - popularity increasing following the wave of West Indian immigration in the fifties, and increasing links with American musicians - and opium for the truly exotic. The working-class, R&B drug of choice was to be Amphetamine or speed until the others filtered down. But initially, speed was mod and speed was also part of the American truck-driving culture which so impressed British youth. For whatever reason, British youth and especially R&B enthusiasts were inexplicably obsessed by large trucks and even bigger trains. "They fucking loved trains" Ronnie opines and he's right; songs about trains and train references were mandatory during the early R&B boom. "The Train Kept A-Rollin", "Ridin' On The L+N", "Smokestack Lighting", "Crawling Up a Hill", the list is endless. Skiffle music was just the same if not worse, just watch any episode of the BBC pop programme, 'The Six-Five Special and you'll get enough train references to last you a lifetime. It's enough to give rise to the suspicion that there was something of a train-spotterish aspect to this fascination (if nothing else, it might explain why mods wore what were quite frankly Anoraks (US Army issue Parkas) and collected shiny head-lamps)! Couple this with the intensely romantic way Britons saw the Wild West - wide open spaces, freedom to move, man - natural in a people who live on a very small island and it starts to make a bit more sense. If anyone represented the dreams of freedom and a new life that characterised Britain from the fifties on, it was John Wayne carving out a whole new continent. So it was, incidentally, that until the sixties really arrived and helped make Britons feel good about their own country, emigration to countries like Australia and Canada continued apace. "Both me and Ronnie loved the Wild West." Ali remembers "Well we all did, Ronnie even named his first son Jessie after the outlaw and I called my son Jay after Jay Silver heels who played Tonto in the Lone Ranger."

Strange but true; still, Wild West themed offspring were a long way off in 1964 and in the meantime, The Thunderbirds had a drummer problem to sort out. Now given the way they were originally formed, it seemed only natural to steal one.

On 20th June 1964, two days after Christine Keeler had been released from prison and a week after 300,000 screaming fans had greeted the Beatles in Adelaide, the Thunderbirds entered the 'Battle Of The Bands' competition at the Uxbridge Blues Festival. The competition was a complete sell out, with over 400 people crammed into the West Drayton Woman's Institute Hall (each competitor got a jar of home-made jam or a bean-bag frog. No. But they should have), and half as many turned away at the door. The Thunderbirds swept into first place and collected the trophy plus twenty pounds in prize money, leaving The Hustlers as runners up and the Confederates and The Rhythmics being left to share out a £15 consolation prize.

The Uxbridge Weekly Post would run an article announcing "The Town's Biggest Swing Night Ever", and printed quotes from teenagers who declared The Thunderbirds were 'fab', 'wonderful' and "Yes! We want more of this!" Today, Uxbridge; tomorrow, the world.

The band also left the competition with a new drummer from The Dissatisfied. Which they definitely were when they saw Pete Hockens, one of the most naturally-gifted and versatile drummers on the circuit, vanishing fame-ward with Ronnie Wood and Co.

Which leads us to a spot of trivia, the Dissatisfied's lead guitar player, Jim Cregan, eventually joined Rod Stewart's band in time for his 1974 'Atlantic Crossing' album and tour, coincidentally and effectively replacing Ronnie Wood, and thus finally achieving his own fifteen-minutes of fame.

Pete Hocking was twenty, and some three to four years older than the rest of the group. Ali was eighteen, Ron and Tony seventeen and Kim, who instantly renamed the drummer Pete Hockey Stick, a mere sixteen.

"He hated being called that," Kim remembered "He changed it eventually to McDaniels, because he said it sounded 'bluesier'." Which it didn't. But what do drummers know?

Pete brought with him a little more than age and experience. He also brought his step-mother - not literally, she mostly stayed in West London - a liberally-minded woman who had some sort of deal with a local pharmacist.

"She used to get what we called purple hearts in those days," Tony Munroe recalls. "She got those great big sweet jars full of them. We couldn't talk openly about pills or purple hearts so we used code words, it made it all the more secretive; we called pills 'shoes'. We'd say, "Got any shoes on you?" and people used to look at us like we were fucking stupid. "How many shoes you got?" that sort of thing. And then Pete went on to heavier stuff when we were in the group. I didn't, I stayed on purple hearts. Although I did take black bombers, you know those great big shiny things?"

Whatever they think now, at the time none of the band found it strange that Pete's step-mum would have been so helpful. Actually, enthusiastic gratitude are the two words that spring inexorably to mind. It was the start of the mass drug-taking culture, and kids in general were already searching out those Over-The-Counter medicines that contained all manner of interesting ingredients. "You could still buy benzedine inhalers." Kim recalled. "Dr J Collis Browne's cure-all had a morphine base; a cough and cold proprietary product called Romilar gave the most amazing hallucinations; and everyone claimed to have a cold that needed instant relief worked like a charm."

The band's next few years were to be fuelled by a diet of music, booze, drugs and when they could get it, sex. Ronnie had already fallen in love with music. The remaining three would come a close second.

With Pete and his sweet-jar of goodies safely on board, the band could turn its mind to the next most pressing problem: that inevitable name change. "Chris Farlowe and his own Thunderbirds had gone from strength to strength," Ronnie says "they were one of the scene's highest profile R&B groups, so we could hardly accuse him of copying us, even if we had the name first." So the band plumped for the slightly more subtle 'The Birds', and Ronnie proudly painted it on the side of the not-quite-new Commer van.

And so began a three-year odyssey that would see The Birds become one of Britain's best-known live R&B bands who never quite made it. They never got a record in the Top Ten, not even the Top Twenty. Yet they brought R&B, great R&B to the yearning masses from John O'Groats to Land's End. And in the process, had themselves one hell of a time.

"We were the biggest thing since sliced bread in Salisbury" according to Tony, "We used to get mobbed with girls actually wanting a piece of your hair - they'd actually rip it out or rip your clothes. It was our own little bit off Beatle-mania. Birds mania in Salisbury - now there's one that should have made the headlines. We were also pretty big in the West Country, up in Derby, Altrincham and Cheshire - we were fucking big in Cheshire!"

CHAPTER FOUR
"A SCRUFFY LOOKING LOT TO SAY THE LEAST."

The van became legend, too.

It was rarely, if ever, washed and certainly never repainted. In time, even the band's name became barely distinguishable from the graffiti that fans - mostly female - wrote on the sides.

"We lived in that fucking van. Five days a week!" Ali fondly remembers. "Bed and breakfast 'half a crown'. All five of us in the same bed, and that was after travelling all night to get there! It was okay when we played locally or in Leo's clubs like the Zambezi in Hounslow, but it started to get a bit rough when we got a big following, then we had to really travel and we travelled a fucking lot. There was only one motorway back then, the M1, so if, for instance, we had to play in South Wales, we would have to go via Ross-On-Wye, all the way round. It would take forever to get anywhere. Six, seven, eight hours, maybe even longer. We'd get twenty quid and have to drive all the way back. Break down, spend the night in the van and nearly freeze to death!"

What more could a bunch of teenage boys, plus an adult, stoned drummer, ask for? Nowadays, quite a lot, but in those days it was bliss to be merely young and alive and playing music.

Psychotherapist and gallery owner - and one-time avid Bird-watcher - Lindsay Grant remembers the band well from this period. "I used to go down to the 100 Club when I was a student and they were absolutely fantastic." Lindsay's normally ultra-calm demeanour suddenly becomes far more animated and for a moment you're looking at a nineteen year-old mod. "But they also had a real tension on stage - you could see that the guy who played rhythm guitar (Tony Munroe) often upset the other band members. He was always going off on his own, or trying to dominate everyone. And I remember Ronnie crouching down and playing his guitar around his ankles! The funny thing was I also had a part-time job at a nearby garage. The Birds used to come and get petrol there, it was before self-service, and I used to fill up their van, it was a truly disgusting van, covered in graffiti... and I'd look into the cab and all you could see was a mass of long hair and two or three pairs of bloodshot eyes staring back at you! In my opinion, they were the band that got thousands of people hooked on R&B and really interested in good music. We never grew out of it."

"We lived on sausages, egg and chips for three years," is Tony's clearest memory. "Leo got us an agency which got us bookings as far away as Scotland. We received our £10 a week and were now professional. I'll give you an idea of one typical week. On a Friday night we played Cleethorpes, in Lincoln, supporting Julie Driscoll and the Steampacket with Rod Stewart and Brian Auger. On Saturday we played with The Who on the west pier in Blackpool that was after sleeping in the van and driving on these little country lanes. Then on the Sunday we played in Salisbury, completely the other end of the country! Then it would be two nights playing at Leo's clubs in and around Windsor and back up to the north by Wednesday. It didn't matter what the weather was like. Snow, sleet, or rain, it was a weird experience! We did one show in Scotland where we were on at 9 o'clock, then we had a midnight gig seventy miles away followed by a three o'clock performance one hundred miles further on. We had to live, crap and piss in that bleedin' van! We made a hole in the floor that we would piss through. It was like 'can't stop, got too far to go, piss through the hole.' The whole van was covered in lipstick where girls would scrawl messages to us, or scratch our names and theirs into the paint work."

Kim also remembers the graffiti: "We all had our own little groups of girl fans. It would be KIM is FAB! or I LOVE ALI! Ronnie, I'm sure, would creep out in the night and scratch his own name on it!"

However, not all fans were quite so loving. Britain was still very parochial and local boys in particular resented outsiders - especially long-haired ones from London - attracting and seducing their girlfriends with their music and stage-presence whenever they could. Except for Ronnie, who was still touchingly faithful to Krissie waiting at home for him in London.

The rest of the band - especially Ali - seemed hell-bent on screwing their way around the country, and found the presence of a non-combatant in their midst just a little annoying. So it was most of the band came to be occupied by two major concerns: how to avoid being attacked by jealous men-folk, and how to get Ronnie laid. Kim, however, followed his own sexual agenda where being beaten up was an occupational hazard, like the time he was nearly killed in sleepy Herne Bay.

Not exactly one of the country's most renowned fleshpots, is Herne Bay. This particular Saturday night was no exception, and the band was faced with yet another boring drive home. Until Kim convinced them that a girl he'd just met was throwing an all-night party and they were all invited. Truth being that the party was Kim's invention: he simply needed a lift, which meant using the van, and the band would have to come, too.

The other insignificant fact Kim chose to keep from his band mates was that the girl was fifteen, therefore under-age. But her parents were away for the weekend, so in Kim's book, her age didn't matter. After all, he was only just seventeen himself.

The house was in darkness when the van creaked to a halt outside. Kim leaped out with the girl and disappeared inside, leaving the rest of the band with the distinct impression that they'd been conned. But, that's life on the road for you and they settled down to wait, sniggering that Kim never took very long anyway.

In this case, five minutes would have been too long, for out of nowhere, five cold and damp fishermen appeared: the girl's two brothers and their three, Bluto-like friends who eyed the van suspiciously as they filed past into the house.

Four musicians looked at each other and shared a single, collective thought: oh, fuck, Kim's had it, let's get out of here. Only Colin Farrel, driver and gate-money collector, demurred. He had strict orders from Leo: keep the little bastards out of trouble, and not to lose any - there were gigs lined up for the rest of the year. Colin started the engine, looked in the rear-view mirror to say a last goodbye to his teeth and climbed out of the van.

Meanwhile, five fishermen were staring at a trail of clothing, Hollywood style, along the hall. They listened for a moment. Faint giggles floated down the stairs.

You have to feel sorry for Kim, even if the girl had been underage. One moment the world is a beautiful place. The next, five large bearded men smelling of fish are charging up the stairs hell-bent on beating the crap out of him. Or whoever was in bed with little sister. Give him credit, Kim had the door locked and barricaded with a chest of drawers within fifteen seconds. Another thirty seconds to dress, then over to the window. Uh-oh: no drainpipe. And then the door caved in.

"They punched me all the way downstairs," Kim recalls painfully. "Then they got me outside and they were bouncing me back and forth off the fence, hitting me every time I bounced back."

Enter Colin Farrel, who hit two of the fishermen on the head with a couple of well-aimed flowerpots, which allowed Kim a second or two respite, enough to bolt for the safety of the van's open door: "All I could hear was these fucking huge blokes shouting 'kill the bastards!'"

Pairs of rescuing hands scurfed Kim aboard and the van roared off just as a house brick smashed through the passenger window, showering front seat and its occupants with glass.

Once a safe distance had been established, Ronnie leaned forward and put a lit joint between Kim's battered lips. There wasn't very much else anyone could do for him, really. Kim had a broken nose, fractured cheekbone and broken ribs. It was going to be a long and painful ride back to London and a hospital, and he might as well smile at least part of the way.

As Tony Monroe says, "Kim would have his mad hour and would always get us into trouble. He was always quiet on stage but socially, particularly when we were travelling around, if there was going to be any bloody trouble, Kim would have started it one way or another. It was almost as if he was going loopy every now and then, particularly with the boredom of travelling, I mean it was extremely boring all the time, you know the M4 finished at Maidenhead and the M1 finished at the Blue Boar and if you were travelling north from those, then it would be bloody tedious. And we used to do these silly things, and Kim always used to instigate it. Like, he'd tell whoever was driving to slow down and stop, then stick his head out the window and ask total strangers if they knew where Frederick Street was. And they'd say, "No, we can't help," you know how polite Brits are, and Kim would say, "Well, you go down there, turn left, second right…" And I used to think that one day he'd pick on a real nutter who'd do us all over. Or his other favourite was to stop and ask: "Is this the way?" And they'd be looking back all confused like, and he'd repeat it, sounding really worried… and they'd get all concerned… and then he'd say, "Well, you see, we've lost it, we've lost our way," and you could see the light dawn on their faces, and you'd never believe the kind of language outwardly respectable people use when they're pissed off. But it wasn't only Kim doing stuff like that, or mooning out of the windows, it was Ron and me as well. Pete was usually well out of it, and Ali was too straight and worried about his hair. He was a maniac on stage, but he never drank, hardly ever did drugs."

The drugs of choice were hash and speed, often taken simply because travelling was so very boring. At times it felt like they were living their entire lives in the van, peeing on the move out of the hole in the floor like wolves marking out their territory. Always rushing from one gig to another, often playing two, or even three, separate venues between 7.00 pm and three the following morning.

The little matter of Ronnie's reluctance to screw around was settled in the Altrincham Hotel, near Manchester. One of The Birds' groupies was determined, in her own picturesque phrase, "to get Ronnie" and foolishly promised Kim and Tony that if they set it up for her, they could come and cat-call in the morning. Groupies do like their triumphs witnessed, and it was going to be such a jolly jape. The band shared rooms on tour - Tony with Ali, Kim with Ron, Pete with the hapless roadie - and Kim faithfully promised that the girl would have Ron and the room to herself. The suspicion remains that she was either criminally naive, or driving on empty. Whatever, she duly made her way to Ronnie's room. Ronnie was just back from the gig and by all accounts needed very little persuading to entertain. So, she locked the door and things took their inevitable course, as things always will when there's a chance of embarrassment on the Richter scale… in this case, sounds of hysterical laughter, followed by three musicians bursting out of the walk-in closet. Still, at least they'd waited fifteen minutes. So as far as both Ronnie and the girl were concerned, it wasn't a total fiasco although his colleagues were fascinated by the fact that Ronnie had kept his socks on. Red socks. Either he'd been making a sartorial statement, or he'd been very, very keen. Either way, he carried on regardless.

Meanwhile, the fights continued. Actually, England has always been a fairly - and even happily - violent country. That Golden Time of sweetness and light only ever existed in people's nostalgic imagination, the fact is that everyone in England has always been prone to violence as a way of settling arguments, conquering the world or simply having fun. As A G McDonnell pointed out in 'England, Their England,' this strange nation of mixed Celtic, Roman, Viking, Saxon and Norman ancestry - plus countless other tribes and nations who'd arrived for a pillaging weekend and stayed - became a country of essentially good-natured, albeit violent, drunken poets.

Or drunken mods in The Birds' case. Mod began life as a London street-level fashion statement. Small pockets were first spotted in Soho, Stoke Newington, Shepherd's Bush, Mile End and Bermondsey, apparently oblivious of each other's existence. As Ronnie points out: "Each part of London had its own little mod scene. There was The Birds and Artwoods in Yiewsley - even Art was riding a scooter - the Who in West London and the Small Faces in the East, who were the first band to dress the same as the audience. For them it was natural, not like other bands who deliberately copied whatever the audience was wearing - and their dance steps, too."

Mod roots lay in an appreciation of the ultra-cool, white American jazz look. Of course, being English, mods looked beyond the obvious and realised that white American jazz had its roots firmly in Black American music. Which was just as well, because few mods actually liked jazz, so they embraced Black Soul and idolised heroes like Otis Redding, Sam and Dave, and Curtis Mayfield.

"The Small Faces were the first real, home-grown mod band." Ronnie says. "They looked fantastic and were one of my all-time favourite bands. The Who on the other hand on the advice of their managers, adopted a mod look and later added a pop art feel, the same as the Mark Four, who would become The Creation. However, The Birds fell somewhere inbetween: the mods loved the hard, R&B sound, but didn't like the band's slightly feminine look. Overall, the favourite mod groups were the Stones (Charlie Watts definitely mod, and the band looked hard), The Action, the Yardbirds, the Artwoods and FleetWood Mac Part One. All these were an acceptable, White-faced alternative to American Black Rhythm and Blues. They hated the Beatles."

Mod was also a working-class reaction against authority, their rebellion expressed by looking far smarter, harder and cleaner than their so-called betters. The first part made possible by hire-purchase, for mods could now buy their tailored clothes on the never-never. It was an amphetamine-fuelled, clothes and music obsessed, intensely narcissistic movement and in the beginning, predominantly male. Mods had no time for sex and given the amount of speed they took, wouldn't have been very good at it, anyway. mod wasn't violent to begin with: no one wanted to ruin their clothes. Then the media rapidly got hold of the story. Within a matter of weeks, mod was handed lock, stock and barrel to the High Street as a watered-down and pre-packed version of the real thing - and what can only be described as style wars broke out in early 1964. The movement's elitist originators countered the mass-market merchandising by constantly evolving, to which they were prone anyway, as a speed-inspired lifestyle gave them the attention-span of a gnat on a bad day. They buzzed from venue to venue, shop to shop on their glittering, Italian scooters, which for a period had to be as dressy as their owners. Scooter accessories came and went at the same alarming rate as the latest thing in shirts. Mods' entire lives had been dedicated to making a specific sartorial statement, which the High Street now wanted to control.

The new pretenders, who never understood what mod was really about but liked the music, the drugs and the clothes, competed to be Mod-er Than Thou. English tribalism asserted itself and the inevitable violence broke out. This is a point little understood by current historians, who always presume that the mods only had one enemy: rockers. In fact, would-be mods always tended to fight more with each other than anyone else, until the media seized upon one small incident. The subsequent publicity resulted in the notorious seaside riots between mods and rockers, where a rollicking good time was had by all. But there's always someone who takes things a little too far, in this case a hybrid mod probably concerned about getting his clothes dirty. He solved the problem by carrying a sawn-off shotgun beneath a triple-vented jacket that cost more than his boss made in a month, and using said shotgun on a hapless rocker before they'd even exchanged ritual insults. At this point, the original mods went underground and would stay there, cocooned in their memories and quietly comparing jacket patterns, until 1967 when many re-emerged as Hippies and everything was all so beautiful, like crushed-velvet butterflies fluttering into the sunlight. Crushed being the operative word, because by now the original hybrid mods had their own identity and were waiting for them in the guise of Suede Heads, later to become Skin Heads. R&B had been replaced by Jamaican Ska and Blue Beat, and the violence had moved from the seaside to football stadiums. The drugs stayed, but were partly replaced by booze, especially Watney's Red Barrel and double diamond beer. These hybrid mods had also become fiercely nationalistic: American parkas had been replaced by the English Crombie, hush puppy boots by Oxford brogues and in some cases, even the bowler hat made a bizarre appearance, red or white handkerchiefs were ironed and placed strategically in top pockets and a rolled up umbrella was the 'de rigeur' accessory so long as it had a stiletto-sharp tip that is.

They were also looking for new prey.

Paradoxically, the Suede Heads never realised that many of the Hippies they beat up had started the whole thing off in the first place. That said, even if they had it wouldn't have mattered: Hippies of whatever background were an affront to their sense of style. Revolutions are notorious for consuming their young. This one consumed its parents.

There is such a thing as bad publicity and by mid 1964, many mod-popular bands were in the awkward position of having to publicly distance themselves from their fans. The industry was determined to maintain a nicer-than-nice image, which meant wholesale tsk-tsking at such barbaric behaviour. Only the Small Faces remained true to their roots and later would be heard bemoaning the fact that their audiences weren't as violent, or as much fun, as they used to be. Diplomacy was never The Small Faces' strongest suit.

In April 1964, the Rolling Stones had even found themselves stranded on stage during a riot at the Mad Mod Ball, held at Wembley's Empire Hall. Rival gangs of amphetamine-crazed mods battled it out with each other, resulting in over thirty arrests. Naturally, the government denied that a drug problem existed, while the pharmaceutical companies said if one did, it was nothing to do with them. This, despite the fact that so many amphetamine tablets being sold were stamped with the makers' initials, like SKF for Smith Kline and French who made Drinamyl. It wasn't that the drug companies were deliberately getting people hooked, merely that the extra security needed to stop theft from warehouses and production lines would have been too expensive. As Pete McDaniel's step-mother - a sympathetic woman if ever there was one - had proved, it was so easy to get all manner of adult sweeties.

Inevitably, violence broke out during many of The Birds' live gigs, helped by Leo, or Lionel's, habit of booking the band into various seaside venues favoured by marauding mods on Bank Holiday weekends. "I remember we played the Aquarium in Brighton and just as we were packing the gear away, all these mods arrived on their scooters and for no reason started attacking the van," remembers Tony ruefully.

"There was no reason for it; they were just looking for trouble. I laid out the first one and then they all turned on us. Luckily we had Colin (Farrell) with us who was an out-and-out nutter and Ali had a go as well. The rest of them always did a runner - Kim and Ronnie and Pete were never anywhere to be seen. I got my shirt ripped right off my back, and then the knives came out - flick knives, and we had to do a runner ourselves, that fucking van was like a magnet for trouble you couldn't miss the thing, we eventually got an anonymous one."

And so it went on, from one seaside town to another and one encounter after another. On one occasion, Kim was once again on the receiving end, but it had nothing to do with under-age girls. He was stabbed by a sharpened umbrella outside the venue and had to be taken to hospital by Tony and Ali for stitches and tetanus injections. Once again, Ronnie was sensibly doing his Macavity impression.

But The Birds raved on, becoming as wild, if not wilder, than their audiences. Tony Munroe - who firmly believes: "No-one who was ever a Bird should ever be ashamed of what we did" - remembers playing at the Nottingham Boat Club, which had two clubhouses and two stages. As luck would have it, the Artwoods were playing on the other stage, the first and only time the two bands played the same venue together. The evening started light-heartedly enough with both bands swapping personnel - Jon Lord playing with The Birds, Tony Munroe with the Artwoods, then Pete swapping for Keef Hartley. However, this harmless revelry eventually degenerated and spiralled downwards, and pretty soon both groups' vans were roaring back to London full of musicians and selected girl fans. They stopped at a service station on the M1, where a mini-orgy broke out in a secluded area of the car park. The air was suddenly full of flying clothes and even, Tony swears, a flying tampon that had been extracted by one of the Artwoods with his teeth. "Crude, but very rock 'n' roll." The party continued until dawn back at Pete McDaniel's flat, with the tampon-less fan - by now recognised as being several sandwiches short of a picnic - being dumped naked and stoned into the bath while her equally naked companions grappled with various band members.

Despite such obvious road-life perks, there were some sexual pursuits that can lead to some very unpleasant surprises as The Birds minus Pete discovered one evening.

The four Birds had left a pub in Barnes and were walking back across Hammersmith Bridge when suddenly a taxi pulled up with two of the most beautiful and stylishly dressed women in the back. The girls beckoned them over and all four got in, they drove to a flat in Earls Court. It looked to be a promising evening, especially when the lads found themselves confronted with a room-full of equally gorgeous looking women.

This was the stuff of fantasy and Kim and Ali lost no time in disappearing off with the first two mystery women. Tony and Ronnie began chatting up two others in the living room, albeit with a growing sense of unease. Nothing you could actually put your finger on - nor, as it turned out, that you would want to - but all was definitely not kosher.

Perhaps it was the lack of any feminine fripperies in the flat, as Ronnie remembers: "It was all blokes stuff, fucking car manuals and tins of beer."

Five minutes later, Ali came back into the living room looking pale, disgruntled and deeply shocked. He looked at his mates and simply said: "They're all fucking geezers."

Minutes later, Kim - not quite as fast a worker as Ali - also reappeared, but being Kim he was laughing like a drain as he collapsed on the sofa. "Fucking hell," he gasped, "I've just had a handful of dick!"

The band made for the door as fast as they could, hotly pursued by a couple of abusive transvestites in various states of undress. Luckily, the fully dressed TVs found it hard to negotiate the stairs in their over-sized heels and the semi-dressed ones thought twice about chasing the band down the road. After all, what would the neighbours have thought?

A flat full of incredibly well-dressed and attractive women in Earls Court with a penchant for long haired and pretty-looking musicians? "All part of life on the road."

As Ali remembers:" I suppose we did look a bit feminine, Ronnie had started his Cleopatra stage and I had longer hair than any of the trannies. "We used to go to the weirdest parties - not so much round our area, but when we were playing away. Kim would always suss out the parties, he used to get himself invited to hundreds. I remember one particular one he dragged me to. It was at Oxford University after we'd played and this huge gay bloke tried it on with me, he grabbed hold of my arm and was trying to drag me away to fuck me. I'm only a little fella and this bloke wasn't going to take 'no' for an answer. He was pissed and drugged up, Kim was nowhere to be seen, nor was Ron, it was very worrying I can tell you. Luckily, Colin spotted what was going on as I was being frog-marched out, he got hold of him and diced him down. He saved our arses literally, on so many occasions. He really had his work cut out, did Colin. Then he'd get us invited to parties that were at the other end of the scale. Places where the mums and dads were supervising their daughters. Mums, dads, aunties and uncles they'd all be there, even fucking old granny sitting in the corner, and we'd have gone there thinking it was a going to be a rave up and we'd end up drinking fucking cups of tea while they had a glass of sherry. The mums would always try and feed us because we were all so skinny."

There's no denying the Birds enjoyed a varied and colourful social life; however, the constant rounds of gigging and partying was beginning to encroach on their professional one. They had been together for months and yet they'd never tried to record a thing. Their next obvious and most pressing step was to try to capture their sound on vinyl and in turn, promote themselves to the media, and so gain record company interest.

Leo was only too happy to help out. He paid for an acetate (today's demo tape) of a Ronnie Wood composition, "You're On My Mind", a steaming slice of powerful, British R&B driven along at high speed by Ronnie's wailing harmonica and Kim's thundering bass lines. It also features a series of agonising breaks, which flip the song on its head and change its direction at several key points. It's without a doubt a song that showed a maturity in Ronnie's song writing and arranging that was far beyond his years.

The demo was also responsible in securing the band an appearance on ITV's weekly "Battle Of The Bands" programme, "Ready Steady Win!" A spin-off programme from the hugely popular "Ready Steady Go!"

"Ready Steady Win!" was a straightforward knock-out contest, which offered a first place prize of £1,000 worth of musical instruments. It was held on 24th June 1964 at the Associated-Rediffusion television studios in Wembley Park Drive, London.

The band's big break looked a certainty.

Ten million viewers tuned in to see The Birds open the show, performing "You'll Be Mine", which compère, Keith Fordyce (looking more like a vaguely disapproving headmaster than ever), described as "a lively start!"

Unfortunately, the panel of judges, which included chart-star Adam Faith and 'Evening Standard' journalist, Maureen Cleave, didn't agree and The Birds finished a demoralised fifth out of the six competing acts.

"I've fucking hated Adam Faith to this very day!" Ronnie will tell you, "and that bloody Maureen Cleave, she fucking hated us, Bitch!"

The show's eventual winners were mod favourites The Bo Street Runners, (A band who incidentally, fact fans, later gave the young drummer Mick Fleetwood his first chance to professionally bash out a beat) who performed a frantic version of their self-titled theme tune, "Bo Street Runner".

In addition to the £1,000 worth of musical instruments, The Runners were also presented with a one-off single deal with Decca Records. All The Birds could do was watch the presentation enviously, whilst consoling each other with the fact, that at least they didn't come last. Even so, fifth out of six?

The Birds had every right to be deeply disappointed. A show like "Ready Steady Win!" was not the place for an up-and-coming band to fall flat on its face.

"Ready Steady Go!" was "the" music show, and anything associated with it was watched avidly. In fact, it's testament to the ground-breaking brilliance of those shows that bands like the Bo Street Runners and The Birds were even on them in the first place. Even as late as 1964, British R&B was still being considered as nothing more than a fad by most of the mainstream music show makers. The mainstream disc jockeys thought so too; unless someone sounded and looked like Cliff Richard or indeed, Adam Faith, there weren't too many TV outlets available. On the whole, the staple diet of popular music consumption in England in the early sixties was either pop, rock 'n' roll (The Billy Fury variety) classical, or jazz.

Bands that looked and sounded dangerous were not to be encouraged; why, even the Rolling Stones wore nice houndstooth jackets for their debut TV appearance. Why couldn't they all be like The Beatles or that nice Herman and his Hermits, for gosh' sake? Now, there was a good role model. Of course, the Rolling Stones soon became an exception, but by then it was generally felt that one bunch of nutters was enough until The Who and The Pretty Things showed up that is.

Even then, an enormous amount of industry publicity insisted that the more extreme bands were all deeply caring and responsible people, and rarely, very rarely prone to the occasional spot of high jinks. This approach probably explains why groups like John Mayall's Blues Breakers (one of the most influential R&B groups on either side of the Atlantic), never appeared on Top of the Pops. Remember, if you never made it to TOTP, you didn't really exist. Yes, The Birds were quite right to feel down.

Leo De Clerk expressed his and the band's disappointment in the local press, but promised The Birds would still 'fly higher', adding, "I still have faith in the boys, they really have something and I know they will get to the top!" The Hillingdon Mirror, meanwhile, was less complimentary and delighted in declaring "Beat Birds Beaten" and quoted Maureen Cleave as saying "I hated their long hair!"

Still, at least The Birds were starting to get noticed.

This was proved on 19th August 1964 when they took part in another TV programme called "The ABC Of Britain". "ABC" was a highly-rated Friday night variety show made by the BBC and The Birds' appearance generated a one word mention in the TV listings on the day Great Train Robber, Charlie Wilson, escaped from prison. Three women were also found guilty of indecency for wearing topless dresses and the latest Beatles' release, "A Hard Day's Night", went to number one. It must have seemed to the band that you had to be either a criminal, supremely gifted, or female and naked to make any sort of impression on the general public.

Undeterred, The Birds continued their round of club dates and in October 1964, secured a Monday night residency at the prestigious "100 Club", based at 100 Oxford Street in London. One of their regular support bands was a group called The Tridents who featured a certain Jeff Beck, a young guitar player who never liked playing second fiddle to anyone, least of all a band that in his view needed two guitar players to do what he did single-handed.

A less-insular group that landed the support slot was the aforementioned Pretty Things, whose drummer, Viv Prince, always liked to sit in with other groups. Given that he was a) usually stoned out of his mind, and b) one of the truly great lunatics of the time, thus he got to play with most bands, including The Birds.

Meanwhile Leo, armed with copies of the by now well-worn acetate of "You're On My Mind", capitalised on The Birds' brief, bleak TV exposures and managed to arrange a meeting with Decca's legendary Dick Rowe. Rowe was still head of the label's A&R department, despite being more famous for turning down the Beatles than eventually signing the Rolling Stones (and then only because a merciful George Harrison had recommended them). Thankfully, he passed The Birds onto his assistant, Franklin Boyd, an A+R man who obviously had his ear pressed closer to the ground than the hapless Rowe because The Birds impressed him enough to land a deal.

The band entered Decca's recording studios for the first time in October 1964 to record their first single as professional musicians, a polished version of "You're On My Mind".

It was an experience that by all accounts most of the group hated. They preferred to play live, and naively viewed the record-making process as a tedious chore, especially Ali who needed an audience in order to perform, and Kim who'd have preferred to party any day of the week.

Ronnie, on the other hand, had the benefit of his musical family background and therefore more of an insight than the others into how the music business really worked. He understood the importance and the necessity in recreating the band's live sound in a studio environment. Ronnie loved it and from that moment on, the recording studio felt like a second home.

The B-side was a treatment of "You Don't Love Me" which owed a great deal to both the Pretty Things and the Stones. Actually, both tracks are a perfect example of how British R&B groups at that time could take the original sound from the States and somehow strip it down and bully it into something new and very exciting. It also has to be said, into something very British!

The record was released in November to wild acclaim in West Drayton, Salisbury and of course, Cheshire but, er- nowhere else. It simply wasn't mass-market enough - there was some industry doubt as to whether it was even a pop record at all - and it got very little airtime, either. Britain didn't have the radio-station musical variety enjoyed by Americans and if the record company wasn't totally behind a new release, forget it.

"You couldn't help feeling that most executives at Decca were waiting patiently for the R&B fad to fade away" stated Kim, "It was old establishment; they wanted the Bachelors, or a new Vera Lynn, they only tolerated the Stones because they sold records."

"That was the problem with the music industry in the early sixties." Tony adds: "Everyone knew that musical tastes had changed, and that evolution if not revolution was in the air. But I don't think the majority of the industry itself was equipped to handle it. Or, more to the point, wanted to... for every Andrew Oldham, George Martin or Glyn Johns, there were a hundred confused or uninterested agents, producers and engineers."

Ronnie puts it in a little better perspective, "We were part of the most exciting time for music ever, and The Goons, Ted Heath or fucking Toppo Giggio were given the respect and considered the big stars at Decca, bands like The Birds were thought of as a five-minute wonder, I think they even secretly thought that about the Stones".

Naturally, it was a situation ripe for the hustler selling re-assurance and specialist knowledge. Still, if you think the sixties bands were interesting, they had nothing on sixties managers, promoters and musical con-artists, who burst onto the music industry like pirates boarding a rich, fat, stately Spanish galleon.

True, despite Decca's stuffy image they did manage to sign some of the most famous names in British musical history. But after the post-Dick Rowe debacle, Decca would sign anything if it were warm and breathing. In time, Decca would become the embarrassment of the music industry when it replaced acts like the Rolling Stones, Ten Years After and John Mayall with such shining stars as Woolly Rhino, Isla St Clair and Father Abraham and The Smurfs. Finally, Jonathan King complete with a rainbow Afro a-go-go wig was brought in to save the company from itself, and within a year effortlessly delivered the coup de grace. So, maybe Ronnie has a point.

Still, at least The Birds had a record out. Getting a record out meant you were really professional, that your fellow musicians would start taking you seriously. It also impressed club owners and agents, and venues throughout the land would soon begin advertising the imminent arrival of Decca's Newest Recording Sensation.

Getting a record out also meant that the band were eligible to audition for BBC radio and their two audition reports from 1965 survive and make interesting reading.

The first, recorded on Friday, 12th February, was heard by the Talent Selection Group, who on Monday, 15th February reported: The Birds - Leader: Ronald Wood - performed "I Ain't Got You"; "Bring it to Jerome"; and "Leaving Here".

A good selection so far as the band were concerned, but, all things considered, it was probably not the best of times to have auditioned for the BBC as a scan of the day's news items reported that America had just bombed the crap out of North Vietnam, thus raising the spectre of another world war. By strange coincidence, the Righteous Brothers' "You've Lost That Loving Feeling" had just reached Number One and cigarette commercials had just been banned from television.

So it was that a hard drinking, heavy smoking, pill-popping and extremely aggressive group of long hairs turned up to play some American-based Rhythm & Blues. It's certainly reflected in the report.

Seven people sat on that Talent Selection Group. Comments ranged from: "A scruffy looking lot to say the least" and "Their numbers were very monotonous, and lacking in entertainment value", to "Ordinary and not of broadcasting standard." Then there was "Ordinary" again and "Ponderous, unoriginal styling". "A difficult medium to deal with and this group is not outstanding enough" was another and so was "Musically and rhythmically unexciting." The Selection Group finished up with, "A rather dreary R&B group, who are vocally unexciting." One Roger Fusey, by the way, gave The Birds an unenthusiastic pass. His was the only one. But also noted: "A scruffy-looking lot to say the least."

This is a little strange, because Ali for one was addicted to clothes and Ronnie was developing his own style of Art School/Regency/Mod. Maybe they'd just had a bad flair day. Maybe they'd just come back from touring. Or maybe, just maybe, there was no one around to say: "Look, lads, this is the BBC and they're, oh, you know, kinda proper, and stuffy."

Ali for one takes great exception at the scruffy jibe; he was after all, notorious for arriving at the start of a tour with enough clothes to dress the entire band. "He'd always be the last one to be picked up" Ronnie remembers, "He would insist on hanging everything, fresh from the dry cleaners, all along the inside of the van." And as The Birds trundled on their merry way to Scotland, Cornwall, Wales or Cheshire, Ali's voice could be heard imploring his mates to "mind me fucking trousers" and "lean off me effing shirts".

Certainly The Birds' publicity photos show an original and immaculately-dressed group.

"We customised a lot of stuff," Ali points out. "Those famous checked belts couldn't be bought, we made them ourselves, using that checked metallic tape used to decorate scooters, "Go-faster" tape it used to be called; Ronnie covered his guitar with it." How appropriate! The Birds were no strangers to speed.

In April 1965, The Birds released their second single, a cover of a slightly obscure, Eddie Holland, Tamla-Motown number, called "Leaving Here". Originally, the song had followed that winning Motown formula that could be relied on to transform even the most boring run-of-the-mill composition into something quite special.

However, in the hands of The Birds' full-on, twin guitar assault, "Leaving Here" became the band's personal property. It even looked set to inch its way up the charts, purely on its own merits, especially as they had enough fans to guarantee a Top Fifty entry. The 'B' side was "Next In Line", a second composition by Ronnie Wood.

Years later, avid Birds fan and sometime roadie, Lemmy would take The Birds' version of "Leaving Here" a stage further and score a hit for his own band, Motorhead.

"Leaving Here" also led to The Birds' infamous appearance on ITV's 'Thank Your Lucky Stars' where they were lowered onto the stage with wires, and yanked off the same way.

For Ali, the downside of such an entrance (besides the embarrassment) meant the ruination of the band's stage clothes. Brand new hand-made shirts, dark blue with light blue collars and cuffs, from Star Clothes. "They ripped them apart to fit the wires."

"That wasn't all, Pete's wires got twisted round and he landed backwards on top of his kit, and couldn't turn round to face the audience, and Kim was dumped in the audience. He landed in some old lady's lap, before being swung back onto the stage and ended up dangling, suspended a few inches off the floor."

"It was all down to this little cunt of a job's worth," Kim remembered with a shudder, "You know, an old bastard with a brown coat and a clip-board, been in the union for fucking hundreds of years and suddenly he's a special effects man. Ronnie was left hanging too; its funny now, but at the time it was terrible, at the end he forgot the song fades out, so we were yanked off while we're still fucking supposed to be playing."

It was as much vaudeville as R&B, and why not, since the music-hall/vaudeville tradition was so important? A point often missed is that the British bands of the late fifties and early sixties were composed of musicians who also loved to perform on stage. Everyone, or nearly everyone, wanted to try their hand at acting. The Beatles for example did many sketches early on in their careers and the audiences lapped it up.

In early 1965, Krissie's parents moved to the Midlands. The family had originally bought a flat at The Laurels, in Edge Hill Road, Ealing and the plan was to sell it. But Krissie, exerting her formidable independence, refused point-blank to leave London and more importantly, Ronnie.

After some discussion, it was agreed that she could stay on in the flat until the family were settled. When that time came, the flat would have to be sold and Krissie either join her parents, or find somewhere new to live. So it was with a certain, understandable, trepidation and nervousness that the Findlay's left London, only to have at least one of their many fears instantly justified. By the time they'd hit the motorway, Ronnie had moved in.

Krissie was still seventeen when she discovered she was pregnant. The sixties might have been swinging, but illegitimacy still carried a terrible social stigma. Seventeen is an age when everything seems either terribly simple, or unbelievably complicated. Possible consequences aren't always carefully weighed up. Krissie only knew that bringing a baby into their world might well be the end of Ronnie's career with The Birds, or worse still, the end of their own relationship.

"I kept it all to myself and never told Ronnie. We were so poor we could hardly afford to keep ourselves, let alone a baby living as we did. I couldn't tell my parents, either. Everyone I really loved would have wanted me to keep the baby, but none more so than Ronnie. But I knew - or thought I knew - that if we'd had a baby at that time it would have been the end of everything. We were too young to cope. Nowadays it must seem mad, because kids seem to think nothing of being a young, single mum in their teens. Plus there isn't the same sort of shame attached to it any more. What made it even more difficult was that I'd been brought up a Catholic to believe abortion was wrong."

Krissie and Ronnie had recently become friendly with another young couple, a singer called Rod Stewart and his girlfriend, Jenny Rowlands. Jenny was the daughter of Rod's manager, John and Rod had just released his first solo single, "Good Morning Little Schoolgirl". Ronnie and Krissie had been regulars at Rod and his band's (The Soul Agents) Thursday night residency at the Marquee Club in Wardour Street and the four had become firm friends. Ronnie looked up to Rod, who although only a couple of years older, seemed vastly more experienced. Krissie felt the same way about Jenny, so it was natural that she turned to her older friend for advice.

Not to help her make a decision, though; Krissie had already made up her mind. All she needed was an address. Jenny supplied it.

"The doctor was in a real back-street on the south side of the Thames, just by London Bridge. I thought it was going to be terribly quick and simple. But it all went wrong."

In 1965 abortions were as medically safe as one could afford. Krissie couldn't afford very much and a couple of days later she was rushed to hospital where she nearly died from complications and an infection.

Ronnie was away touring with The Birds. Krissie left a message with Lizzie to say that she was going to visit her family and then another one to say she was going on holiday to Malta, when in actual fact she'd been sent there to recuperate."My parents tried to break us up, which was why I was sent to stay with family friends. They liked Ronnie, really loved him, but they didn't think he was right for me. They hoped I'd forget him in Malta."

While Krissie was away, her parents arranged for the sale of the flat in Edge Hill Road. This had always been the plan, but now there was the possibility that without the flat, Krissie would come and live with them for a while.

Krissie instead returned to England and to Number Eight, Whitethorn Avenue, to be reunited with her lover in his own family home. They only stayed there for a few months, Ronnie sharing a bedroom with John Lord, who'd been promoted from the box-room so that Krissie could move in.

"Ronnie used to creep in in the early morning for a snuggle," Krissie laughs, "Until one time we both fell asleep and his Dad caught us when he got up for work. He came in to ask if I wanted a cup of tea, which was when I first heard his famous line: "Where do you think you are, then - on yer father's yacht?" We were both really scared, but then he said: "I suppose I better bring two cups up, then." He was such a lovely man."

Even so, the two made plans to get a flat together. Krissie began working in the Chelsea Kitchen in Kings Road in order to earn an income, while Ronnie and the band continued to gain momentum.

While all this was turmoil was happening in Ronnie and Krissie's private life, The Birds were flying high with "Leaving Here". Four girls had even set up the official Bird's Fan Club, based in Hillingdon, Middlesex, who sent out thousands of postcards specially prepared by Leo and the Harold Davison Agency, now enthusiastically booking the band nationwide. All the signs were good. "This is the one that's going to do it, boys," Leo enthused, especially after the Harold Davison Agency reported live interest in the band from all over Europe.

Even Decca printed up thousands upon thousands of little pink stickers that announced: 'The Birds Are Leaving Here,' and included the record's catalogue number. The band happily stuck their little pink stickers on any available surface, including equipment belonging to other groups. Occasionally, voices were even raised in protest.

Ronnie was so sure that the song would be a hit that he had his first guitar custom made at Marshalls' of Ealing: a solid Telecaster body fitted with a Danelectro, twelve-string neck and finished in lime-green which he named a Danecaster. Tony answered the fan letters. Kim got drunk. Pete got stoned and Ali got a new suit. The record was selling well and everyone was happy... for a month.

CHAPTER FIVE
"ALL I REALLY WANT TO DO."

In April 1965, a flurry of angry letters began arriving at The Birds' fan club.

It seemed that the single that hundreds of fans thought they'd ordered, wasn't the one they finally received. Instead, they'd been given a jingly-jangly cover version of a Bob Dylan song.

The American Byrds had landed, spelt with a 'y' but pronounced 'serious trouble' for the British group, and were racing past "Leaving Here" in the charts with a song called "Mr Tambourine Man".

"All the fans were saying that they ordered The Birds' latest record from the local shop," Ronnie remembers, "and they were complaining that they'd been given some fucking folksy rubbish instead."

Ah, it may well have been folksy rubbish so far as the majority of British R&B fans were concerned, but by mid June, "Mr Tambourine Man" (already an American number one) was sitting on top of the British pile and still selling. "Leaving Here" on the other hand had simply left.

Columbia records, the American band's label launched the biggest campaign that Britain had seen in years. The Byrds were billed as America's answer to the Beatles, and never mind that they'd hit big with a cover song, they were under the protective wing of ex-Beatles press officer, Derek Taylor. They'd also been invited to England in August by celebrated show biz impresarios, Mervyn Conn and Joe Collins, father of Joan and Jackie.

Neither Conn nor Collins were really rock promoters, but between them they had more than enough industry connections to be taken seriously in almost anything they turned their hands to. They (like most of the UK), had been caught up in the massive hyping of The Byrds by the American media, desperate to regain the rock 'n' roll crown after years of British rule. It wasn't just pride - money was at stake, too.

It also nearly never happened. In the sixties, British and American bands played either side of the pond on a strict one-for-one basis. Visiting US performers could only play in the UK if a British act could be found to replace them back home, and vice versa.

Panic had set in the Byrds camp on the eve of their arrival when it was announced that a suitable British band hadn't been found to accommodate the Union ruling. The trip looked like it would have to be scrapped. It was the worse possible news the Americans could have heard, for it meant the band stood to lose out on a lucrative tour that coincided with both their US and UK number ones.

However, at the eleventh hour The Dave Clark Five nobly volunteered their services and a 'five-for-five' deal was struck. It was an exchange that saw Clark and Co take their Tottenham sound stateside and rival even The Beatles in US popularity.

Funnily enough, the same thing wasn't to be repeated in the UK.

Excitement mounted as touchdown approached. As usual, journalists were caught up in the frenzied anticipation as much as any impressionable fan. Headlines proclaimed:
"BYRDS BIGGEST CRAZE SINCE BEATLES!"and "BYRDS AMERICA'S BIGGEST GROUP EVER!"
Even the jingoistic New Musical Express predicted, "BYRD MANIA".

Mervyn Conn started a massive poster campaign that simply announced: 'The Byrds Is Coming,' stealing the (ungrammatical) idea from the 1964 poster campaign that promoted the Hitchcock film of the same name, but then spelt with an "i". Paradoxically, that same movie had once given the British Birds a small amount of publicity.

Conn's posters literally covered London. The Birds took one look and threw their little pink stickers in the back of the van. Then Leo struck back on 2nd August: "It was in the early hours, on a Monday morning," Ronnie recalls. "We'd just finished a gig up North and I'd only just got to bed. Leo called and told me to get up and get myself down to the airport, which was only a few miles away. When I got there at eight o'clock the place was full of screaming girls. It was like those scenes for The Beatles. I think all the band were there and everyone was moaning about having had no sleep and being knackered. Everyone except Leo, who was fuming and saying that he was going to 'teach them fucking Yanks a lesson".

Leo then produced no less than seven legal writs, all of which claimed infringement on The Birds registered name and sued for damages and loss of earnings.

It was a cold day in August when the American Byrds landed at Heathrow. Derek Taylor should have warned them about the British weather and to pack something warm. Instead, they sloped off the plane jet lagged, pale and shivering in their thin, Californian finery. Through Immigration, through Customs, and into the Arrivals Hall, where they were greeted by hundreds of shrieking girls, and a group of pissed-off British R&B musicians armed with writs.

"It was Leo and the Farrell brothers who actually served the writs," Kim remembers. "One for each Byrd, and obviously two for luck. They shoved them in their hands and the cameras were going crazy. We sort of shuffled around and looked at our feet for a bit, then sloped off and waited for the pubs to open."

In fact, the other two writs had been served on Mervyn Conn and Joe Collins: welcome to the rock world, nothing like the Royal Variety Performance, is it?

When Byrds' leader, Roger McGuinn, was asked for his reactions, he squinted through his grannie glasses and dreamily quoted a Bob Dylan lyric: "I don't want to compete with you, all I really want to do is be friends with you." Which, all things considered, was a bit limp.

The other limp thing was the actual legal action itself. There's no doubt Leo believed he was in the right, and all he was doing was taking care of business, carrying out a bit of damage limitation, so to speak. "He was completely serious when serving the writs" Ronnie says convinced, "But then (as we'll see), Leo never did get the best legal advice."

As it was, Columbia's legal department swatted the writs aside as if they were so many arthritic flies. Nonetheless, the airport episode did make the papers - well, the West London Weekly Post (Uxbridge edition), and two paragraphs in the Daily Mirror.

It did merit a short mention on BBC TV News At Six too.

Mervyn Conn was shown looking utterly appalled, and claimed that "It was just a nasty publicity stunt, and not a very good one at that." The general consensus was that The Byrds were the next big thing and the British public would love them. Right? Wrong!

British audiences weren't ready for The Byrds at all. But then to be fair, The Byrds were equally unprepared for a British audience. An audience spoilt for choice and getting increasingly harder to please. "They underestimated the English crowds" was how Kim saw it, "They were the kings of Hollywood, but it's a little harsher in East Acton."

If the visiting Americans found the Brits a hard and critical crowd to please, then heaven knows what they made of this country's infamous two-faced press. It must certainly have come as something of a shock. Lauded one minute, rubbished the next. "They were seen as five permanently-stoned, pampered, petulant and overly-privileged Hollywood brats." was how Kim summed it up. "They all looked like they'd modelled their entire image on Brian Jones." So it was that the Byrds learnt a valuable lesson about the English press. Everywhere the band went, they found themselves confronted by the same journalists that only days before had brilliantly built them up to near God-like status, only to take great delight in tearing them down again.

As usual, it all began good naturedly enough, with a series of successful press conferences, an audience with The Beatles (courtesy of Taylor), and televised trips to Carnaby Street boutiques. It all started going downhill when the band starred in their very own "Ready, Steady Go" showcase special. For some inexplicable reason, they failed to deliver their expertly-recorded trademark sound live.

This was followed by a string of equally disastrous live dates in wholly unsuitable venues, including mod clubs like the Flamingo. It was in these small, intimate club settings that the Byrds' standoffish and ultra-cool demeanour annoyed audiences most. These sorts of clubs were popular with a hard-core clientele who were used to their acts being sweaty and hard working, they wanted, nay, expected to be thoroughly and fully entertained. They weren't used to a band who right from their opening note came across both distant and aloof.

At the Pontiac Club in Putney, for instance, the Byrds were heckled all through their first set and not only by British Birds fans. The situation deteriorated so badly that the only cheer of the night came when DJ Rick Gunnel announced that instead of a second set by The Byrds, 'gramophone' (sic) records would be played until (mod fave) Geno Washington and the Ram Jam Band arrived and took over.

In the Byrds' defence, it must have been yet another shock to play venues like the Flamingo and be confronted by a staunchly mod audience whose only between song request was to inconsiderately yell for the Californian hippies to fuck off home.

Still, the ill-fated tour limped painfully on, with Mervyn Conn heaping more and more misery on the band by adding extra dates in an ill-fated attempt to win back the British public, regain that loving feeling and most importantly, get some of his money back.

"FANS SO COOL OVER TOO COOL BYRDS" screamed a Melody Maker headline and underneath reported the comments of a girl picked at random from the audience: "The Byrds were dull, very, very dull." The article didn't mention if she was a British Birds fan.

By this point The Byrds really were regretting not packing something warm, as the first of them, bass player Chris Hillman, collapsed in the dressing room with an asthma-related chest infection. He was closely followed by McGuinn who collapsed with a temperature of 103C and finally drummer, Michael Clark (who incidentally really did get the job because he looked like Brian Jones), went down with the 'flu. Gigs were cancelled and the press speculated that The Byrds had simply had enough.

Another kick was delivered to the comatose five piece by no less a respected scribe than the NME's Keith Altham, who wrote snootily that, "The Byrds were simply pretenders to The Beatles crown."

That was bad enough, but surely the final and most devastating put-down came from none other than Derek Taylor himself. Taylor gave an interview to the same paper and in a most uncharacteristic manner turned on his charges and said, "Take them out of Hollywood, put them in the real world and they couldn't handle it."

It was all a trifle harsh, especially considering that Mervyn Conn had expected them to play thirteen gigs in six days, flu or no flu, and then he moaned that he was used to working with much harder clients.

Eventually, the ill and dejected Byrds flew home to the sun, vowing never to return! Well, not until the time was right that is.

McGuinn, and bass player Chris Hillman, brought a different Byrds line-up back to the UK in 1967, but the classic original line up would never again set foot on British soil.

Tony Monroe is convinced that the whole American Byrds fiasco hastened the demise of the British Birds. "In 1965 we were one of the few professional groups that never needed to go abroad. We never had the time we were working three, four, five nights a week in this country, week in week out; we didn't have to go to Holland or Germany like practically every other group did. By 1965, we had one of the biggest followings in this country with huge fan bases all over the country. There'd be twenty of them sleeping in our rooms, even in my parent's front room.

"I'll tell you what I think happened, "Leaving Here" went straight in at Number Forty Five, with hardly any airplay and no backhanders, taking place because it honestly didn't need them. Then the American Byrds single came out and it was a completely different sound and it was a really good song; ok, it was a Dylan song, but if you're going to do a cover, Dylan was a safe bet. We were getting hundreds of fan letters a week complaining that record shops were only stocking the American single and our fans were buying it in the hundreds. Of course it was such a great song, that once people got it home they kept it.

"Once that started to happen, sales of our one automatically dropped off and that fucked it all up. Then of course because our sales dropped, Decca lost interest, even though they knew what was happening. We were little fish in a big pond and they never supported us, unlike the American Byrds' label, who went all out for them. It was a classic catch 22 situation, people couldn't buy The Birds because the shops stocked The Byrds and a hell of a lot of records were ordered in those days, and each order was logged in as a sale. So, by the time our fans went back to re-order "Leaving Here" you couldn't get it anymore as Decca had stopped pressing it.

"One other thing which didn't help, was the fact there were no picture covers to tell each group apart; it was either a blue label, or an orange one. Naturally if you can't buy something it wont sell, and poor sales as far as your label is concerned constitutes a flop, it doesn't matter why! Sales figures are all that count. I still reckon to this day that The Byrds knew there was an English Birds.

"You don't call yourselves the Byrds with a "Y" unless you have a reason. They'd probably say it's because Dylan had a "Y" in his name or some nonsense, but I reckon they knew all about us. They must have heard of The Yardbirds, and Chris Farlowe and his Thunderbirds. They were total anglophiles for fuck sake; the whole Brian Jones look and the Beatles guitars. It really ruined us with Decca, because Decca were very fickle with their groups. They couldn't handle opposition; their attitude was, groups are ten a penny, if one don't work out, sign up another it doesn't matter they'll be gone in eight months.

They didn't like hassle, they wanted an easy ride. In fact, they killed loads of groups off because of their attitude, not just us. Anyway that's my story and I'm sticking to it."

Fantasy? Maybe, maybe not. As said, the American music industry was desperate to regain the rock 'n' roll / pop crown. As far as America was concerned, British pop had ruled the world for too long - unfortunately, any US group wanting worldwide acceptance still felt they had to establish good UK credentials. Hendrix had proved that. They all wanted to be accepted by the Brits and be seen to embrace the English style, hence Beatles-style instruments, boots and haircuts.

The Byrds certainly had a look that was quintessentially British, so Tony could just have a point. One thing's for sure, The Byrds never forgot that first English experience; instead, they immortalized it in the song "Eight Miles High". "For years, everyone assumed the track was a blatant reference to drugs," says Ronnie, "but it's really about their trip to England, that first time. Flying over London, "Eight miles high, and when you touch down, you'll find its stranger than known."

So, lets just take a minute to put all this into some sort of perspective. As Ronnie quite rightly pointed out, "Eight Miles High" wasn't about drugs after all. By the same token, "Lucy In The Sky With Diamonds" we now know had nothing to do with LSD; "Perfect Day" nothing whatsoever to do with heroin; "White Lines" is about road-markings, not cocaine; and 'Purple Haze' was simply a colour fashion statement. So the artists that recorded songs like these were simply misunderstood by a thrill-seeking media. "Canned Heat were obviously going against the grain and being dangerously subversive for recording "Amphetamine Annie," as was Hoyt Axton for "The Pusher". Occasionally, a band slips one past the industry and media goalkeepers and scores like with the blatantly obvious "Here Comes The Nice", The Small Faces' anthem to their friendly, neighbourhood pusher. Such moments bring gladness to the hearts of the more cynical amongst us.

Anyway I digress, but before we finally leave the The Byrds incident I feel it's only fair to put across a case for our American cousins, and point out that the group's hatred for England wasn't totally xenophobic after all.

England's inclement weather is always a shock to the Americans, but even by our standards the climate The Byrds found themselves struggling with was a doozy. 1965 had one of the wettest summers on record, and was the major contribution in nearly all the band coming down with flu. The band's other understandable bugbear was this country's either missing or inexplicably-placed street signs (something that's been pissing us Brits off for years). "Signs in the street that say where you're going, are somewhere being their own" Roger lamented.

Mod clubs had been an eye opener too and the line: "In places small faces abound" was a reference to DJs continually playing the diminutive mod band's records at every venue where The Byrds suffered. However, the most telling line of all was a reference made at the expense of the British Birds: "No where is there warmth to be found from those afraid of losing their ground."

In 1997 Ronnie Wood met Roger McGuinn (who'd spent some time as Jim McGuinn, following a typical Californian religious experience, before reverting to his original first name) and happily remembers baiting him.

"Yeah, I saw Jim McGuinn and I was saying to him, "Oi Jim, do you remember when you lot first came to England?" and he was like, "Yeah, why?" and I'm going, "well how was it?" and he said, "Okay, why?" and I said, "well when you got off the plane, was there a guy at the airport serving you with a writ?" and he said, "'Yeah, and he managed it too." Then he stopped and looked at me and said, "Was that you?" and I said, "well, yeah, and no it wasn't me personally, it was our manager, he would do anything for publicity, so he sued you lot." and Jim said, "You bastards! We had the worst time ever in England because of you lot!" and I went, "Yeah! Fucking Great!"

Upon their return to the States, The Byrds released the song "All I Really Want To Do" which featured the same quoted Dylan lyrics McGuinn had spoken to journalists at Heathrow. It became CBS's fastest-selling single in the UK.

This second Dylan cover was released in August, the same month that Ronnie and The Birds were back auditioning for the BBC. This time only four anonymous judges sat on the Talent Selection Group.

One of the panel remarked that the band had made, "A marked improvement from their last audition. An R&B group providing a good sound, all being adequate instrumentally and vocally. The lead singer has a good, rough R&B type voice and his performance is now up to standard."

A good start, but then its goes rapidly downhill with comments like, "Most unattractive lead voice." Not to mention, "Poor equipment giving guitar distortion of the worst quality, uninspired arrangements causing a bad attack of Listener's Monotony." And there's more, "A very dreary R&B group, guitars badly distorted."

It was another bitter disappointment and setback for the band: "It felt like no one was really out there fighting for us," claimed Kim. "No-one did it for The Birds. In fact, there was only one DJ who regularly mentioned the band in his column and that was Jimmy Saville; he'd actually come down and heard us live and liked us." It's a point often forgotten, that for all his clowning around, Jimmy Saville was one of only a handful of DJs who both knew and really cared about early British R&B music and musicians. But even he could never quite fix it for The Birds.

The band tried to stay positive despite their second BBC airplay rejection, quite an achievement considering that in October they recorded their third and last single for Decca, "No Good Without You, Baby". This was an attempt to further develop the formula sound of "Leaving Here" by taking and recording an obscure American soul number in The Birds' own aggressive style.

It had looked like working with "Leaving Here" and the band were convinced they were on to a winner. It was backed by another original, the Wood/Munroe "How Can It Be", a double-tracked crescendo of pent-up angst which is possibly the best recorded example of just how powerful The Birds' sound could be.

Still, without that all important airplay, it flopped.

A measure of public taste at the time can be gauged by the record holding the number one spot at the beginning of the month - Ken Dodds' "Tears". There again, Ian Brady and Myra Hindley had just been charged with what became known as The Murders On The Moors, so perhaps that song represented the nation's outpouring of grief for their victims?

On an up-beat note, The Beatles received their MBEs from the Queen at Buck House, and The Rolling Stones ended the month as the number one act on both sides of the Atlantic with "Get Off Of My Cloud".

Despite having had two and a half successive flop singles, a near perfect no-chart show profile and complete lack of radio exposure, The Birds continued to work solidly. In fact, if anything their heavy workload increased during the latter part of the year.

It was so unaffected that the band even landed a respectable slot above Geno Washington And The Ram Jam Band (but below Ted Heath And His Music) at the Glad Rag Ball (sensibly retitled from the original Mad Mod Ball), at the Empire Pool, Wembley in November. The gig was headlined by the Hurdy Gurdy Man himself, Donovan, who within a few short months (July 1966) would gain world-wide notoriety as the first high-profile British pop musician to be busted for drugs.

Naturally, fans of Donovan wondered why it had taken so long. "Sunshine Superman" was a hymn of praise to LSD, "Mellow Yellow" the same for marijuana - and God only knows what Donovan was taking when he kept seeing that mountain coming and going. The real irony being that one of the charities benefiting from the Glad Rag Ball was Lady Hoare's Thalidomide Appeal - druggies raising money for one of the greatest drug-tragedies of the day.

Still somewhat miffed, The Birds reminded the programme readers not to "Confuse us with the Byrds" and added that they, "Put their trust in God and their manager." Pete McDaniels went on to say that his interests included, "Drums and Hindustani Wog Dancing" - nice one, Pete.

The main supporting bands at Wembley were The Kinks, The Hollies and The Who, which effectively established The Birds as one of the top ten live acts in Britain. So, who needed a record in the charts anyway? Well Ronnie did. He could imagine growing old with the band, still playing the same faded venues - but big in Cheshire - until his gnarled fingers could play no more.

McCavity was nothing if not an ambitious cat.

Incidentally, a final twist to the "Byrds" versus "Birds" scenario occurred in 1993 when ex-Byrd drummer, Michael Clark, walked into ex-Bird Kim Gardiner's bar, "The Cat and Fiddle" on Sunset Boulevard, wanting to track down his old High School sweetheart. He was at an age when men do that sort of thing, hoping to re-discover their youth. Michael had heard his old-flame was working at the bar, and asked to speak to the owner: "Hi, I'm Michael Clark from the Byrds," he said modestly, "and I'm looking for Paula." "Are you?" replied Kim. "That's a fucking coincidence - I'm Kim Gardiner from The Birds and I'm married to her."

It would have been nice if the two men had then got drunk together. In reality, Michael Clark made his excuses and left - and who could blame him?

Those bloody British Birds were still buggering up his life.

CHAPTER SIX
"STIGGY-POO WASN'T FUSSY."

Ali always liked Leo De Klerk and to this day, thinks that The Birds were wrong to fire him. But as Ali could have used a second van just to carry his dry-cleaning, and Leo paid the band a clothing allowance, Ali would feel that, wouldn't he? Actually, the truth is a little more complex. Leo looked after the boys very well, but they were his boys and they did what he said. This was fine by Ali, who liked being looked after, but not so fine with the rest of the band who felt they should be making some of the decisions. All except Pete McDaniels, by now so permanently spaced out that he found it hard to decide whether it was light night or dark day. Specifically, Ronnie, Tony and Kim thought they should be making more money. But at the same time, career tensions were beginning to surface, particularly between Tony and Ron. Not that Tony noticed them at first, although he did think Ronnie should have given him a lot more credit for his creative input on songs they developed together. He remembers Jon Lord - still lodging chez Wood - pulling Ronnie to one side, in a brotherly sort of way, and telling him as much:

"I think that was a catalyst with Ron, after that he saw me as a threat. I'll always remember coming back from a gig one night, after we'd sacked Leo, and there was this heated conversation going on, like there always is when you're still all fired up, the adrenaline's still pumping and it takes a hell of a long time to unwind. And suddenly Ron, who's been saying fuck-all, turns to me and says: "You'll be good at whatever you do, but you're not going to do it in music." It was like bells being struck, and I thought oh, all right, I know where this is going."

Of course, Ronnie's remark might have had something to do with Tony's increasing habit of snapping back at interviewers that he wasn't simply a rhythm guitarist, but a second lead. There was no question that the two boyhood friends were becoming increasingly disgruntled with each other.

The problem was partly one of ambition. Ronnie came from a professional music background and knew exactly where he wanted his career to go. The others, represented by Tony Munroe, were reasonably happy to carry on the way they were, although more money would be nice. So in that sense, the trouble with Leo encapsulated all the tensions, all the niggling doubts and disagreements that had built up within the band over the past three years.

It all came to a head on 31st December 1965. The band had been playing a New Year's Eve gig at the Starlight Ballroom in Sudbury, but at the end of the night neither Leo nor the Farrel brothers were there to collect Leo's share of the door money. Big mistake. Peter Lindsay, the Starlight's manager, handed over a large amount of cash to Tony Monroe, asking him to give it to "your boss."

"I couldn't believe it," Tony remembers, "I mean, I was looking at nearly a thousand quid! And we were costing Leo, what? Maybe a couple of hundred a week, tops? We were working flat out and had to be earning Leo a fucking fortune. I called the rest of the band over and showed them. Ali wasn't too worried, said maybe we should ask for a raise. I don't think Pete cared. Ronnie and Kim were the two most pissed off, I mean really pissed off. We felt so stupid, like we were little kids who'd found out a really bad secret, and that secret was we were being fucking ripped off by this big bad adult?

The fact that Peter Lindsay called Leo our 'boss' didn't help, either."

When Leo realised his oversight and showed up to collect the takings, he was met by a quietly-amused Lindsay who said knowingly, "Sorry Leo, you weren't here so I've given the money to the guitar player, Tony." Lindsay also said laughingly, "I think you had better up their wages mate or they'll be giving you the sack."

Leo rushed straight round to Tony's house and arrived at around two-thirty in the morning, accompanied by Colin

Farrel. After a few minutes of banging, Tony's mother eventually opened the door. Leo was as polite as usual - and just as insistent. Could he see Tony? It was really terribly important. Tony's mother was equally firm and said "No, he couldn't. Tony wasn't in, and even if he was, have you no idea of the time?"

Leo and Colin Farrel left, apologising.

Tony sat in his bedroom, clutching a large amount of cash and wondering what the hell the band was going to do next. No such misgivings affected Ronnie. He'd gone home and to bed, secure in the knowledge that whatever happened would be for the best. Kim knew that whatever Tony and Ronnie decided would be okay by him. Pete had nodded off wondering what year it was. And Ali was dreaming fitfully about a new shirt that was missing its buttons.

Leo was naturally piqued, but was generously inclined to overlook this single act of mutiny. After all, he had just announced to the press that: "The Birds are flying high into '66 with a proposed tour of Ireland and Scandinavia and another single release at the end of January."

Leo had decided the band could keep the money from the Starlight gig, after all it wasn't worth rocking the boat over. No, Leo was in it for the long haul - there'd be other pay-days, bigger and better ones and Leo intended to make the most of them, after all its not as if he didn't work for it.

The Birds' appearance at The Glad Rag Ball had raised their profile sufficiently enough for Leo to wrangle them a part in the cult-classic B Movie, "The Deadly Bees".

This was a limp sci-fi thriller starring Suzannah Leigh as an exhausted pop singer seeking rest and relaxation on a remote island somewhere off the British coast. Unfortunately, the brochure never mentioned that the island was inhabited by a swarm of deadly, killer bees (Michael Caine was to reprise the plot line in The Swarm, which was another stinker) and various homicidal maniacs. The Birds were intended to represent mod as they lip-synched to "That's All That I Need You For", another Ronnie/Munroe composition and one of three new songs recorded on 12th January 1966.

Despite a script by Robert Bloch ('Psycho') and director Freddie Francis' best efforts, the movie was under-funded and it showed. The Birds went to the film studio on 14th January, directly from an all-night gig, still sweaty, unshaven and exhausted for real.

"I think we were there for a morning," Tony remembers. "Didn't even last until lunch-time, and that was it. We got fifty quid between us, even though Ronnie and me had written the song specially. We couldn't wait to get home to bed."

Even so, they successfully managed to project their sharp mod aggression and cool, despite being plastered by heavy pan make-up.

By rights The Birds' brilliant performance in "The Deadly Bees" should have been a turning point for the band, but the movie was a disaster and it sunk without trace, which was pretty much the same fate suffered by The Birds' fourth single.

The band recorded "What Hit Me?" another Wood/Munroe composition on 18th March with all the high hopes and good intentions of it being the hit record that Leo had so proudly announced two months beforehand.

It wasn't. The record was never even released. Mainly because Decca cold-heartedly decided to drop the band, rather than risk going another bloody fifteen rounds with CBS and the American Byrds.

Naturally, all of which The Birds saw as being Leo's fault. His response was to take his young charges and introduce them to a brand new record label called Reaction, which fortunately formed that very same month and was looking for acts.

We'll come back to that one later.

Now, this next sequence is affected by selective memory loss. The former Birds can remember what happened, but not exactly in what order, or who was ultimately responsible for getting the band involved with one of London's most infamous crime families.

It all began one night in March 1966. The band had just played a club in Catford, south London, and were packing away their equipment, when a tall, dark stranger approached them. In fact, a powerful-looking man in his mid thirties, well dressed and with a certain air about him, who said how much he'd enjoyed the gig.

They got talking. One of The Birds mentioned they were having management problems. "How sad," said their new friend, "how shocking." Had the band thought about taking on a new manager? The band was thinking about little else. Well, maybe their new friend could help. Funnily enough, he'd been a fan of The Birds for some time, ever since he'd seen them at another club in Bromley. Interestingly enough, their new friend had an involvement with several clubs himself, and had been thinking of getting more closely involved in the music scene for some time. He also had a very good solicitor in Mayfair. Phone numbers were exchanged and a suggestion made, that maybe they should all meet up in a few days' time. Mayfair's a long, long way from West Drayton, but in the right direction.

The band said yes, why not?

There was no great mystery as to why Charlie and Eddie, the Richardson brothers, would want to take over The Birds. They did indeed have interests in many clubs, and knew how many fans the band brought in. Besides, it was the sixties and even traditional villains were branching out, although the Richardson's were far from traditional. If the Kray twins epitomised the public face of villainy in the sixties, the Richardson brothers represented a far more skilful and imaginative approach to criminal activity. Based in Bermondsey and Rotherhithe, they followed a tradition of organised crime that was old when the East End was nothing more than a stew-pot of pickpockets, muggers and diseased whores.

Whereas the Krays were criminals who went into business, the Richardson's were primarily businessmen who went into crime.

It was the Richardson's, for example, who developed the long-firm fraud to near-poetic flights of fancy, but always those that made money. They relied as much on intelligence as they did on muscle - although they were never short of the latter. Frankie Fraser, he of the gold-plated pliers and an interest in amateur dentistry, worked for the Richardson's, and the man was truly fearsome. Not very tall, but with a brooding stillness about him that made even strangers look the other way. There again, anyone else who'd spent so much time in solitary confinement would probably also look pretty damn thoughtful.

The Richardson's had firmly avoided the celebrity circuit, unlike the Krays whose egos would prove as fatal as their actual crimes; just because they supplied rent-boys to the gentry, didn't mean they belonged, the upstarts. That was the Krays' biggest crime: not knowing their place. Although shooting people in front of witnesses didn't help very much, either. The great myth, of course, was that the Krays only ever harmed their own.... unless the word 'own' refers to anyone who had something the Krays wanted. Gangster chic may be fashionable fun for some, but the downside can be terror for many.

At least one of The Birds had to have known that their new friend - and soon, new friends - were a little 'heavy', as they say. On the other hand, so was Leo and the boys, and the band had spent the past two years playing the club circuit, where few if any club owners or managers were known for their shy, retiring natures. Besides, along with jazz, R&B is the music of outlaws. Back in the twenties and thirties, many musicians had been launched and supported by various American gangsters. Jelly Roll Morton, for example, had been given a lucrative slice of a numbers and prostitution racket. Duke Ellington was offered - although never accepted - bootlegging action in New York during Prohibition. Owney 'The Killer' Madden owned the Cotton Club, Al Capone the Arrowhead and for a while, Bugsy Seigel had Las Vegas. The savage beasts had long appreciated music's charms, and all musicians really want to do is to play. Musicians also appreciate the protection that villains can provide; after Frank Sinatra's son had been kidnapped and then rescued, Frank sent him to England in 1964 to avoid the publicity surrounding the subsequent trial. It was no coincidence that Frank junior stayed with Charlie Kray, Ronnie and Reggie's older and vastly more sensible, brother.

In fact, the normally shy and retiring Richardson brothers had achieved certain notoriety in the beginning of March. For a while, London was talking about little else - except the missing World Cup, the twelve-inch high, solid gold Jules Rimet trophy, stolen from its display case in Westminster (which does have some relevance here, because Pete McDaniels was actually almost arrested for the theft).

He'd been walking to a Birds gig at the 100 Club from his flat in Westbourne Grove when he'd been stopped by an increasingly frantic police force (The World Cup itself was only a few months away), on the grounds that here was a suspicious-looking character carrying a big leather hold-all that chinked suggestively. As indeed it did: Pete was taking his cymbals and stands to work. Of course, those were more innocent times, when a thief could be expected to walk the streets of London carrying a solid gold statuette that had been stolen several days previously, and given that the bag had the word Ludwig written on its side (obviously the German for 'swag'), was the final clincher.

Matters weren't helped when Pete refused to let the arresting police look inside. How could he? Pete was carrying the band's supply of blues, shoes, and black bombers. Pete had more drugs on him than the average chemists. Luckily, the police were only interested in the Jules Rimet trophy. Threatened with arrest, Pete eventually and nervously agreed to open his bag, they took one look, saw the collection of crash cymbals, and high hat and realised they weren't gold but brass. Pete quickly re-zipped the bag and made a relieved and hasty exit.

The trophy was eventually found (sports fans), by a dog-named Pickles hidden under a bush in South London on 27th March.

Anyway, still in March of that year, back to the 8th, to be exact and Eddie Richardson and Mad Frankie Fraser had been shot at Mr Smith's nightclub in Catford. It was a bungled protection-racket takeover that had gone badly wrong and both ended up being taken to Bromley hospital under police armed guard. This means that it was either Charlie or one of his associates who had originally approached the band that night in Catford. Certainly none of The Birds remember their original contact being bullet-riddled.

At the very first meeting The Birds had with their new found friends, the band handed over their contracts with Leo to an individual introduced to them as their solicitor. In exchange, the Richardson's suggested that all future live engagements could be handled by their good mate, Roy Tempest, whose agency offices were in Wardour Street, Soho. This would obviously mean leaving the Harold Davison Agency - assuming the contracts with Leo could be legally broken.

Somehow, The Birds were left in no doubt that the contracts would be legally broken. If not, something else would be. For the next month - April - they kept their contact with Leo to the bare minimum, and their new friends to themselves. Meanwhile, news articles in both the NME and Melody Maker reported that The Birds would indeed be signing with the Reaction label, in order to release a fifth single (technically their fourth) "Say Those Magic Words" once again a Wood/Munroe original. Reaction, of course, was the label set up by Robert Stigwood in order to help The Who's managers exclude record producer, Shel Talmy, from any royalties.

Then came a more formal meeting at the Richardson's plush Park Lane headquarters in May, to which Leo was invited. There was a large, impressive, polished wood table in a large, impressive room. The Birds sat on one side, opposite their new friends who, needless to say, were also large and impressive. At the far end sat Leo de Klerk and his solicitor, flanked by the Farrel brothers. To a casual onlooker it might have looked like a trial, with Leo as the accused.

"The contract's illegal," the Richardson's solicitor began. "The boys are under age."
"No it's not," Leo said, a trifle smugly, "I got their parents to sign. Every one of them."
How right Lizzie had been to worry about the small print.
"It's still fucking illegal."
"Oh yeah? Why?"
"Because you forgot the education clause," the Richardson's solicitor explained gently. "You have to provide a certain number of hours' tuition every week in the case of minors. You didn't. So what have you got to say about that?"

Leo looked at his own, increasingly nervous, solicitor, who'd drawn up the original, flawed contracts, and spat out: "You cunt!" Then got up, pushed back his chair and stormed out, leaving his copies of the contracts on the table. The Farrells followed, leaving behind the now-terrified solicitor watching as his original work was torn to shreds before his eyes.

That night there was a party at a large, impressive house in Bromley south east London's version of the stockbroker belt, where all upwardly mobile south east London villains aspired to live before moving on to Chiselhurst.

Large, impressive drinks were shoved into The Birds' hands as their cigarettes were lit with sold-gold lighters. Brightly-dressed women with beehives and curves tut-tutted at how thin the boys were, and force-fed them with salmon and roast beef. Meaty hands clasped The Birds' shoulders and large, impressive promises were made. Phrases like, "Alright, my son?" and "Now we'll get you a proper record deal," filled the air. The future looked good. In a few weeks they'd sign new contracts. They felt that they'd grown up. The Birds went home to West Drayton secure in the knowledge that their luck had finally changed.

But they were still just a little concerned about Leo. Not to worry - their new friends, who were interested in assuming the managerial role, had already thought of that. A company was formed called 'Popgressive', with the Richardson's solicitor appointed as Chairman. The new deal was loyally reported, as normal, by the west London newspapers, one headline announcing: "BREAK-AWAYS IN BEAT STREET" and went on to say that The Birds had flown away from their manager to warble their pop tunes on their own.

The interviews were given by Tony Munroe, who'd apparently appointed himself the band's spokesman and business advisor - yet another source of friction with Ronnie. Tony was quoted as saying: "We broke away about a week ago because of a certain unrest which has been going on for some time." The article added, straight faced, that to protect themselves against any possibilities of legal action, the group have their own protection in the form of a company called Popgressive. Of course, Tony never realised how prophetic that statement was, nor did he realise that in reality, the groups' dynamics had changed well beyond their control.

The article stated that the day-to-day running of The Birds was taken care of by Ronnie and Kim. It also mentioned that Leo de Clerck - giving yet another spelling of his assumed name, had taken back the group's van. Quite what he'd do with a clapped out, scratched and lipstick-smeared elderly Commer, complete with a hole in the floor that stank of piss, is anyone's guess. One can only hope that whatever he did with it was mercifully swift and with full R&B honours... although legend has it that for years the van could still be seen on moonless nights, roaming the hedge-rows and lanes of Cheshire, as a voice called out, "Is this the way?" before collapsing into helpless giggles.

Bizarrely enough, Leo would go on to play a bit-part role as a villainous manager in an episode of Britain's second-rate version of Starsky and Hutch, The Professionals. He still has connections with clubs in the Windsor area and in 1983, gained some small revenge when he barred an inebriated Ronnie and Mick Jagger from entering one of his establishments. Apparently he was heard to gleefully say, "I've waited years to get one over on that fucking Ronnie Wood."

For Leo knew what others had only suspected. While Tony Munroe had become The Birds' spokesman in getting rid of Leo, the move had actually been orchestrated by Ronnie and Kim. Fact was Leo had never given them a hit record. Worse still, his publicity stunt with the American Byrds had made The (real) Birds look unprofessional and down right silly.

The Birds' transport problem was solved at a meeting held at Kim's parents' house between Ronnie, Kim, his father and the Richardson's.

Kim laughs about the memory now. "We did it at my house because my Dad had got concerned about who we'd got involved with. He wanted to secretly record the meeting because we hadn't signed any contracts yet. We hid a tape-recorder under the table, covered with a table-cloth and taped the whole conversation with the Torture Boys. That was taking a proper fucking risk because tape recorders were huge great things in those days. They used the old reel-to-reel tapes that eventually ran off the spool once the tape was used up. There was no way to disguise that and Ronnie and I were giggling and kicking each other under the table, going 'this is fucking great!' I wish I had that fucking tape now!" Sadly, Kim lost all his personal memorabilia when his parents' home caught fire in 1996.

The meeting ended with enough cash handed over to purchase a new, long-wheel base Ford Transit minibus, worth about £20,000 today, incidentally just like the one Art Wood had bought for his band. The rest of The Birds never did discover how Ronnie and Kim had come up with the money, "They never would say," Tony complains, still perplexed to this day, but one thing became abundantly clear: He who pays for the transport, calls the tune. Now, more than ever, Ronnie and Kim were firmly in the driving seat.

The band now had a new agent too, Roy Tempest; new personal management, Popgressive; new record label, Stigwood's Reaction; and a new van, Ford.

Ronnie and Krissie even had a new home: a small flat in Benbow Road, Shepherd's Bush, partly financed by Krissie's new job working for a solicitor. They could even allow themselves the occasional luxury of eating at a nearby Mexican restaurant, where they both tasted steak and (bitter) chocolate sauce for the very first time. Mostly though, they made do with instant curry from a packet, a culinary delight brought from the local corner shop, which Ronnie had nicknamed R Sole Spam's.

Life was good again, what could possibly go wrong?

Robert Stigwood was an enterprising, gay Australian who'd come to London in 1957. Initially he'd worked as a clerical assistant in the social services, before setting up his own theatrical agency. By March 1966 he had his own label, Reaction, which was licensed to Polydor, formed solely to release The Who's single, 'Substitute'. He also controlled Cream and The Bee Gees.

To this day, some of The Birds are convinced that Kim was the major attraction for Stigwood. For his part, Kim still remembers that, "Stiggy-poo was always trying to grab my knob."

"He might well have succeeded," Tony Munroe commented a tad cynically. "Kim was mad enough to try anything once, and he was always over at Stigwood's apartment."

Kim's later hatred of the BeeGees, however, can be put down to personal taste, and not jealousy.

It was also during this particular period that Ronnie first met Jimmy Page - or to be totally accurate, Jimmy Page's guitar. The musician came later. As Kim remembers it: "We'd really lost our way musically by that point, we even started doing fucking Beach Boy covers. Jimmy was a top session man then. He was working in the studio next door one day, but he'd had gone out and left his guitar behind. It was a truly fucking amazing thing, some sort of weird Japanese make with this fucking great sound, and Ronnie went in and pinched it for the track we were recording. He's half-way through a solo when Jimmy Page comes back looking for it. Ronnie was really fucking embarrassed, but covered it up by dead-panning and saying "Oh, is this yours" "Sorry, I had no idea." Jimmy was all right about it though, I remember he told us he was thinking about joining the Yardbirds which was a fucking good gig to get. I remember Ronnie being well pissed-off because we loved the Yardbirds. Ronnie went out the next day and bought the very same guitar." A few years later, Jimmy Page would 'borrow' Krissie, then Ronnie's wife, for a year. That's the problem with rock musicians - they're always misplacing things.

Recording sessions for Reaction finally began in June 1966.

'Say Those Magic Words' was finished on the 5th; 'Daddy, Daddy' on the 15th; and a cover of a French song entitled, 'The Doll Who Said No' on the 20th. Great song, but pretentious title - as far as The Birds were concerned so they re-titled it "Good Times." The memory is still painful for Tony Munroe: "It was fabulous! We got the demo disc from France and had it translated. It was a really beautiful song - very unusual and very original. Ronnie and I thought it was fabulous. Ali said it was our finest moment. We wanted it to be the next single, and even said so in the Melody Maker (who listed the release date as 29th July), but Stigwood was still sticking with "Magic Words". He called the shots, deciding what was and wasn't to be released and that one wasn't. Instead, he would have us in recording and re-recording stuff that we thought he wanted as the next single; he would get excited over a number and we'd think, "Oh, so this is going to be the next release, then," but nothing ever was and it went on like this for months."

What none of the band realised was that Stigwood was distracted, locked as he was into a major legal drama of his own making with record producer Shel Talmy and Decca. It was not a good time to be around him. But Stigwood was expert at hiding the truth from his clients. And colleagues. And friends. He was also nurturing the fledgling Cream then known simply as "Eric Clapton, Jack Bruce and Ginger Baker" who played their first gig on 30th July.

What Stigwood did do, for some inexplicable reason, just possibly contractual, was re-name the band Birds Birds and for more logical reasons, market them as London's first gangster group. He produced a three-page, fold-out promotional brochure for which the band had their hair cut short (except for Ronnie who stuck with his Cleo look) and had them pose for photos wearing double-breasted suits complete with carnations. They all carried sub-machine guns and stood in front of a Roaring Twenties limousine, complete with gangster-friendly running boards and spare wheel. Stigwood either knew about the bands link with the Richardson's, or he really did have exceptional foresight, for within six months, Hollywood-inspired gangster chic would be all the rage.

Interestingly enough, within a few months The Artwoods would do the same.

In 1967 they re-named themselves The St Valentine's Day Massacre in a lame attempt to re-establish themselves and cash in on the Bonnie and Clyde craze then sweeping London. "It was a bloody stupid idea," Art freely admits, "but everyone went gangster mad after that film came out, and we saw Georgie Fame was getting away with it. I think even the BeeGees dressed up in all that gear. We were running out of steam and it was suggested we needed a gimmick and we stupidly went along with it. We even released a single, or it might have been an EP, with all these sort of 1920's Broadway style numbers like "Brother Can You Spare A Dime". We put it out under the new name, and bizarrely enough we did promotion for it by doing personal appearances with the actress Faye Dunaway who played Bonnie in the film. I have no idea how that one came about but I remember doing one in a Carnaby Street shop window. Whatever fans we had left were walking past saying "Look it's the Artwoods and they're dressed up as fucking gangsters" which was a sad way for such a good band to go out; we broke up pretty soon after that."

Krissie had changed jobs yet again, and was now working as the receptionist for manager Don Arden at his Carnaby Street office, witnessing first hand some of the problems another band was having: the Small Faces, who despite a hit with "All or Nothing" seemed to be permanently broke.

It was Krissie who introduced Ronnie to Small Faces' singer, Steve Marriot. "I loved Steve and I wanted the two of them to get to know each other because I felt both Steve and Ronnie were very similar. They both had the same childlike humour, very silly, disruptive like naughty schoolboys always laughing and having a smoke. Not that they didn't moan as well. The Small Faces were terrible moaners, they were always going on about what a terrible time they were having with Don. I didn't know what was really going on, because I wasn't privy to anything to do with money, or contracts, but they were always in the office needing money for one thing or another and it got to be quite bad. I remember the language was always very colourful, especially from Steve and Mac, yet they all looked like butter wouldn't melt in their mouths.

"It was funny, but I had no idea The Birds ever had any problems, whether it was to do with money or anything else. I knew we didn't have much money personally, but Ronnie always kept everything like that from me.

"I naively thought Ronnie could possibly help Steve out with any problems the Small Faces were having because on the surface, it looked to me as if The Birds were problem free. I also knew how much Ronnie loved the Small Faces, so I told him what a miserable time they were having. I remember one time Don Arden had stopped taking their calls for some reason, so all of them blocked up every line on the switchboard; they all rung from different phones so that no one else could get through and Don would have to talk to them.

"He was really angry and came and shouted at me as if it was my fault. Towards the end, the Small Faces got really scared about Don because they probably pushed him a little bit too far. I heard a rumour that soon after the Small Faces had left and moved out of the house in London up to that cottage in Marlow, a car pulled up and someone shot at the house. I remember telling Ronnie about it, and saying how lucky we were not to have those sort of problems. And he just laughed his head off."

Ronnie and Steve remained close friends right up to Steve's tragic death in a house-fire in 1990. In fact, I visited him at that very house a few times and pride of place in the kitchen hung a big print of Keith Richards painted by Ronnie. Steve would always point it out to guests, and good-naturedly ask, "Have you seen Ronnie Wood's tracings."

Stigwood might not have been refusing to take phone calls from The Birds, nor for that matter was he shooting at them. He was, however, still managing to alienate himself, just as much as Arden was from the Small Faces. Ronnie, for example, was less than enamoured with the new Birds Birds name, and the rest of the band were equally unimpressed by the way

Stigwood was trying to re-package and resell them.

The little three-page brochure, which stated that the Robert Stigwood Organisation now had sole representation rights for Birds Birds (as opposed to Popgressive or The Birds themselves) gloats lovingly that: "Birds Birds is paradoxically one of those rare groups elevated to 'hit parade' status without ever having had a Top Twenty record. The group members describe their music as aggressive, scientific wildness and regimented excitement, and see each performance as an environment in which the senses and music are integrated and in which the audience is hypnotically made to respond. They believe in basing their performance on a combination of art, science and music and personify the science of life rather than that of destruction."

Just the sort of quasi-intellectual bullshit that had helped drive Ronnie away from Ealing School of Art. But Stigwood's pretentious spiel gets even worse.

"That Birds Birds is a happy group and this is exemplified by the fact that there have been no personnel changes since the band was formed as 'The Birds' in 1964. At that time, Tony, Ron, Ali, Kim and Pete had no group experience and just decided to play together as an enjoyable experience. Little did they foresee that Birds Birds would ultimately resolve their futures and that they would be acclaimed as one of the major Ballroom and club attractions in Great Britain. This is a group of musicians influenced by no external musical strains, but willing to adapt any suitable melodies or to create their own where none exist. Here is a group unafraid to use a discord where it is meaningful - five musicians eager to perform for sheer fun and the satisfaction of achievement."

Inaccurate, misleading, and above all, indescribably mimsy.

It is also a truth, universally acknowledged, that the first sign of serious trouble with any organisation is often heralded by fulsome publicity. It's as if the public relations people use bullshit to disguise their own lack of belief, instead of trying to fool some of the people long enough to make a profit.

One thing Stigwood did get right was his description and prediction for Ronnie, when he wrote: "Ron Wood (Guitar/Harmonica/Vocals) lives for his music. With him, playing is more than a way of earning money. He is one of our finest guitarists and harmonica players who excels in the Blues. At nineteen, Ron can be assured of an outstanding musical career ahead." Spot on, Rob.

After much deliberation on Stigwood's part, "Say Those Magic Words" was finally released in September, making it the Reaction label's fifth single release. This came after two flops in a row.

"She Can Build A Mountain" by Paul Dean and The Soul Savages and Oscar's "Club Of Lights". Not that Stigwood was overly worried; he had only set the label up as a vehicle for The Who and aside from Cream, he never exercised strict quality control. He just wanted the label ticking over.

"Say Those Magic Words" was yet another cover version, this time of a McCoy's album track. As usual, Ronnie and Tony were relegated to the B-side with their composition "Daddy, Daddy", which the band described as a far-reaching, experimental example of auto-destructive Modernism. In hindsight, Kim thinks of "Daddy Daddy" as "A bit of a racket, really, but typical of a lot of British stuff in 1966; we were the punks of our day."

Once again, The Birds/Birds Birds were spared any chart irritation, and spent all their free time practising in the Regent Sound studios planning a national tour and waiting for Stigwood to show up. He rarely if ever did.

It slowly began to dawn on the band that Stigwood's long-term interests lay elsewhere. Rumour had it that overloaded Beatles' boss, Brian Epstein, was on the look out for a partner in his NEMS organisation, and Stiggie-poo was going all out to impress.

Allegedly, Stigwood, in a calculated move, invited American soul stars, The Four Tops to London and arranged a date for them at Epstein's Saville Row Theatre. It was brilliant bait and one that easily lured and snared Epstein, especially as Epstein was already impressed by Stigwood's enterprise and foresight. Of course, it helped that Epstein had his own eyes set firmly on a piece of the Cream's action. Naturally, by the end of the night Stigwood walked away with the offer of a job he had always known he'd get.

At the same time, certain other allegations began to surface about the Richardson brothers. Nothing too serious - something about large-scale fraud, armed robbery and nailing a police informer to the floor with masonry nails. Still, it was enough to make the band worry just a little. Even more so when they read about mock trials held by criminals in a large, impressive boardroom furnished with a large, impressive table - at an equally impressive Mayfair address.

The very same room, in fact, where Leo de Clerk had been given, some would say, his lucky break. Things got even stranger when the band tried calling their new friends and were met by either silence at the end of the line, or no one answering at all. The solicitor supposedly running Popgressive seemed to have vanished, and no one at any of the addresses they had visited seemed to have heard of such a company.

The Richardson's seemed to have disappeared from The Birds' life just as mysteriously as they had entered it.

Ronnie and Krissie had been forced to leave Benbow Road when they could no longer afford the rent. They moved to a cheaper flat in Edans Court, close to the Uxbridge Road, their fourth address in a little over a year.

By now The Birds as a group were totally directionless.

They were also manager-less, riding around in a Transit van bought with money borrowed from real gangsters and playing the same old venues night after night. Frustrated and demoralised, they unsurprisingly began to turn on each other.

Actually, they specifically turned on Tony, due to the fact that aside from the escalating musical differences between Ronnie and himself, Tony had recently assumed responsibility for the Birds' business affairs. That same three-page brochure produced by Stigwood had also pointed that out with its declaration that, "Tony helps with the group's administration."

The band basically needed someone to blame, and Tony had inadvertently put himself up for offer.

"He was trying to run the show," as Kim put it, "Plus he was getting really argumentative and stroppy, and getting on everyone's nerves. Everyone was just going: "Shut up Tony, just fucking shut up!" He became a real nightmare."

Or, as Ali more subtly says: "He got really gobby."

Tony, on the other hand, blames the falling out on the simple fact that he was doing the job everyone else refused to do and yet they resented him for it. "I was the most vociferous member of the group and for that reason I ended up doing most of the organising because basically no-one else could be arsed or interested - particularly Ronnie.

"Anything that involved organising went right over his head. He didn't give a shit as long as he got to play. I mean, he was such a natural musician he just wanted to play and that meant the logistics of running a group - bearing in mind we were practically managing ourselves - were way above him. You simply could not, and he would not, get involved in that at all.

"I thought I was the catalyst of the group. I'd do all the shit jobs and keep things together and often sit in as mediator if people were falling out. No one else cared.

"I also think one of the reasons I was pushed out was because once Leo was out of the way, suddenly we were splitting a lot more money from gigs. They started thinking: "Well we've proved we can survive and do alright without Leo, so why can't we do without Tony too!"

"Obviously it was a lot more attractive splitting everything four ways instead of five. We were young and impulsive and it should have been handled differently, but that's the way it went. I eventually became friends with Ali and Kim, but I haven't spoken to Ronnie to this day."

Tony's had years to analyse exactly why the great divide came about, but there's just a couple of sour ingredients he may well have overlooked.

Certainly, Krissie had never forgiven Tony for initially telling Ronnie that he thought she was just another hanger-on when they had first met. Nor had she forgotten how Tony had spoken out and implied she was double-dating both Ronnie and Eric Clapton back in those early days.

She was also defiantly still somewhat miffed about Tony's recommendation that Ronnie should "Fucking dump her" too. However in hindsight, probably one of the most significant factors in Tony's ostracism from the group was the fact that in addition to Krissie disliking Tony, she also hated his girlfriend. Ronnie for the most part seemed oblivious to Krissie's simmering situation and on the surface, he quite commendably appeared to steer well clear of the backbiting and bickering.

"It's always been the same," is Ronnie's appraisal, "Girls get in the way when they get involved with bands, it's always "Oh, don't say that about my husband." It was the same vibes with the Faces, Jan Jones hated Sandy McLagen, Krissie hated Dee Harrington (Rod Stewart's girlfriend) and they all fucking hated Ronnie Lane's missus.

"In The Birds' days it was Krissie against Tony's bird. Whoever the girls were, they always got in the way and they'd set their husbands up against each other, or off in the wrong direction, or the worst one become their managers, and that would ultimately finish off any band - it's a fact. That probably explains why we ended up being called "The Bird's Birds" towards the end, because we were all bossed around by the birds - The Birds' birds bossed The Birds around."

The conflict finally came to a head with the band's last weary tangle with mod violence. They'd been playing at an east London club and after the gig, the usual jealousy for the band surfaced. The Birds were now being road-managed by ex-Thunderbird, Robin Scrimshaw, who'd had the good sense to be away that night, leaving the driving and humping duties to another old school friend, Roger Jeggo. Actually, Jeggo had really gone along for the ride and was totally unprepared for a violent stage invasion. One minute the audience was cheering good-naturedly, the next it turned into a horde of pill-crazed mods intent on beating The Birds to a pulp. Jeggo bravely decided to intervene. Tony went to help him, as the rest of the band were hurriedly unplugging.

"I was the only one who went to help him, and the boys didn't like it, claiming I'd jeopardised the equipment. By the time the police arrived, Roger was in a terrible mess, all his teeth were hanging out and he needed stitches. I turned to the others and said: "You bastards! You ran away again!" I got Roger to hospital and stayed with him all the night while they sewed him up."

All this within a few months of Time Magazine writing: "Dominated by its youth, London has burst into bloom. It swings, it is the scene." Any suspicion that American journalists then resident in London were huddled together in Chelsea, Kensington, Hampstead and not the east end, was probably well-founded.

The following day, Tony set off for what was usually the weekly band meeting held at Ronnie's and Krissie's flat at Eden Court. When he arrived, he was casually informed by Krissie that the rest of the band had actually all gone to see Stigwood.

Tony hadn't been told of any such change of plans, and still annoyed by the previous night's events, was now understandably livid. However, he'd been up half the night slumped in a chair in the hospital's A&E department and he was tired. "I thought it wiser to give the meeting a miss rather than risk another scene." so Tony decided to go home instead and catch up on some much-needed sleep.

A few hours later, Tony was woken by a call from Stigwood himself telling him that he'd been sacked - but not to worry, the band might change their minds and if they didn't, Stigwood had another group Tony could join. "I was completely brain-shot and I asked Stigwood who was the instigator and who had done all the talking, but he wouldn't tell me because he apparently tried to talk them out of it, but they'd been quite adamant. So eventually Kim and Ali came round to tell me personally."

A devastated Tony, tears streaming down his face, leaped at the pair and screamed out in frustration and pain. "You are supposed to be my mates, why are you doing this?" "What have I done?" and more to the point, "why wasn't Ronnie there?"

The one glimmer of hope in Tony's mind was that Ronnie and Pete were staying neutral, or even better, didn't even agree. Yes that was it, it would all be cleared up tomorrow. Ok it was a mess but it was nothing that couldn't be sorted out, Ronnie would sort it out wouldn't he?

"Well, er, no, not exactly," Kim explained. "You see it was all Ronnie's idea in the first place." Et tu, Ron, et tu.

A shell-shocked Tony kicked around, licking his wounds for a couple of weeks before eventually summoning up the strength to take up Stigwood on his offer of joining his latest infatuation, a new band called The Gods featuring a promising young guitar player called Mick Taylor.

"It was like starting all over again," Tony recollects. "I was a lot older than the others in the band, they were just kids starting out and we were playing the same old shit-holes The Birds played two years ago.

"It was so demoralising, my heart wasn't in it; it felt like such a backwards step that I couldn't do it. I was also totally embittered by the whole thing. I had lost my friends, I felt betrayed, the loss was enormous. It was such a painful experience that in the end it became so much to cope with, I just gave it all up and tried to adapt to Civvie Street. It was like coming out the army.

"I worked on a building site, got married and didn't listen to music for years. But what still hurts is Ronnie's actions. We'd been like brothers and it disappeared overnight. I'd known him for seven years and we'd learnt to write songs together. We'd taught each other things on the guitar, gone to school with each other, shared conflicting girlfriends together. We had so many things in common; we were both musicians and artists. There'd always been rivalry, but it had been a healthy rivalry, or so I thought, but that was replaced by animosity.

"Say Those Magic Words" turned out to be "fuck off, you're sacked"."

Stigwood infiltrated NEMS in December and the band - now a four-piece and calling themselves The Birds again - recorded yet more songs to add to their growing unreleased record mountain. One of Stigwood's parting shots, acting on Kim's confidential advice, was to hire Tornados and session drummer Clem Cattini for these recording sessions, sessions that would prove to be the band's last.

One of the tracks recorded was a song called "Granny Rides Again" - a solo Ronnie composition - and the benched Pete, probably assuming or sensing he was next in line for the chop, one day simply stopped going to the studio.

Which was the last anyone saw or heard of him... except for one very strange meeting two years later. Tony Munroe was coming out of a sports centre in west London, after playing a basket-ball match alongside Robin Scrimshaw - who'd finally discovered a use for his height.

"I noticed this figure sitting opposite on a bench who looked really familiar, so I walked over and found myself staring at Pete. I was so happy to see him, until I realised he looked really down-and-out, like a tramp. I went up to him and said: "Pete, it's me, Tony! How are you? What are you doing?" But he just stared up at me blankly and said "My name's not Pete, and I don't know who you are." I thought he was joking at first and said, "Don't be daft, of course you know who I am!" But no, he just got up, stared at me and shuffled off. I stood there dumfounded watching him until he disappeared out of sight, wondering had I really seen him. It was like encountering a fucking ghost. It was so weird and spooky, but it was Pete, without a shadow of a doubt - you don't spend three solid years with a bloke without knowing him."

With Tony gone, there was no one to find work for a band that was now effectively a three-piece combo. There was no one to liaise with an agent, no one to tell the band where to be and when.

Stigwood was too busy getting his feet under the table at NEMS to worry about a band that already had the smell of yesterday's men about them. Ron and Kim were soon reading the writing on the wall. They realised too the nature of the business and resignedly saw the inevitable approaching.

It wasn't to be the slow death of a thousand cuts, but the death of a thousand unreturned phone calls. Not that anyone thought to tell Ali.

Ali still kept on showing up at Regent Sound four nights a week.

"I thought it was a bit odd. I was up there most nights, overdubbing vocals, always on me own, overdubbing, overdubbing, and overdubbing the overdubs. It was Christmas by then and I thought maybe everyone was out doing their shopping."

Eventually even Ali realised that 1967 was going to be a Birdless year. He went to the studio one last time on Christmas Eve and spent a half-hearted half hour overdubbing a vocal that had been niggling him and after finally nailing it, hung up his head-phones, grabbed his coat and walked out. As the door closed behind him, he pinned a note to it that read: "GONE FISHING, ALI."

CHAPTER SEVEN
"I NEVER WANTED TO MENTION JEFF'S SPOTS."

So, where had Ronnie and Kim been while Ali was over-dubbing himself into a stupor? Simple: they'd been working with elder-brother Art and Artwood's keyboard player, Jon Lord, plus Fairies' drummer, John (Twink) Adler in a new group provisionally titled, The Art Birds. Ronnie and Art had both realised that their respective bands were no longer contenders, and decided to pool the best of their resources. Think of it as being a not-so-super "Super Group". There would be no room for Ali, for Art would obviously be Lead Vocalist, as he had been with his own band, therefore it was kinder to not tell him anything about it.

Not that Ron and Kim didn't feel a little bit guilty.

After all, they did leave him on his own in a recording studio, laying down vocals for a record that would never be released by a group that had ceased to exist.

In 1975 by way of making amends, Ronnie coaxed Ali to come and record a demo at his home studio in Richmond. Ronnie even put together a none-too-shabby studio band for him, comprising of himself, Kenney Jones on drums, Ronnie Lane on bass and Mick Jagger on rhythm guitar.

Of course, nothing ever came of it. In fact, Ali is still waiting to hear the tapes but by now assumes they were taken some years to a deserted crossroads during a full moon. And there they were buried with a stake through the centre spool.

The Art Birds rehearsed quite a bit during early 1967 and according to Ronnie, had all the potential to have taken flight. They certainly had all the necessary ingredients: talent, experience and individual reputations.

Unfortunately, there was a slight age disparity... not one that affected musical differences, appreciation or even ability, but one that concerned creature comforts.

Art was the eldest and was learning to enjoy a comfortable home life with his wife, Doreen. Ronnie and Kim on the other hand were ten years younger and talking excitedly about touring Germany and Poland, countries that Art already knew well.

One day he went on his own to look at the filthy Ford Transit van that would be his new touring home for several weeks on end and shuddered: "Fuck that for a game of soldiers!"

Art eventually went to work with brother Ted's graphic design company, yet he's never completely hang up his rocking boots - Art Wood's Quiet Melon was still to come and even today, he still plays and produces - but for the time being at least, he's got no thoughts of stardom.

Art had been at the forefront of the R&B boom in Britain, had played with Alexis Korner and Cyril Davis, fostered the careers of Keef Hartley and Jon Lord and had been instrumental in turning the Moist Hoist drinking den into the famous Ealing Club. If anyone had deserved chart success, it was Art. He didn't get it, and he knew when it was time to go home, but he has no regrets; in fact, he has nothing but pride. "Me and Ted were always happy that at least one of us made it and lets face it, Ronnie made it big enough for all three."

The Art Birds minus Art renamed themselves Santa Barbara Machine Head.

"We wanted to have a West Coast progressive sounding name," Ronnie remembers, "Like Iron Butterfly or Big Brother and the Holding Company - a hard sounding name."

SBMH did in fact record three tracks, all written by Jon Lord who was still living in the box-room chez Arthur and Lizzie Wood. The songs were "Porcupine Juice" "Albert" and "Rubber Monkey", three songs that can legitimately lay claim to being the embryonic strains of heavy rock.

Certainly it was enough for Jon Lord to go off, grow a moustache, reinvent himself and help form Deep Purple, the world's first classically influenced and extremely loud, rock behemoth.

Ah, but at whose expense? "Incidentally," Ronnie is quick to point out, "He went off whilst still owing my mum £4.00 for a week's rent and without collecting clean washing." These rock stars eh?

It was around this time that Ronnie, Krissie and Kim went to Blaises' nightclub in South Kensington in order to catch one of Jimi Hendrix's early London gigs with The Experience. There, they ran into Jeff Beck who was the guest of Hendrix's manager, ex-Animal's bass player, Chas Chandler. News had just broken that Beck had been sacked from The Yardbirds. Or, as Yardbirds manager Simon Napier Bell spelt it out in Melody Maker: "Due to Jeff's ill-health on two American tours, it has become obvious that he is not up to intensive touring. Reluctantly, The Yardbirds will carry on as a four-piece."

This, only weeks before Beck was about to embark on the most exhaustive period of concentrated live work in his career!

The truth was, Beck's grandstanding and hypochondria had driven The Yardbirds to distraction and provided the excuse they needed to sack him.

That said, it wasn't all one sided.

Beck mentioned that he was thinking of starting his own group. The next day he got a call from Ronnie asking for a job. If The Birds and Art Birds and Santa Barbara Machine Head weren't even cold yet, they were now.

"I'd known Jeff since his Trident days and obviously from watching The Yardbirds, so I felt confident enough to ring him up and offer my services along with Kim's of course".

Just like that.

Actually, Ronnie had also been present at the Marquee Club when Beck had auditioned for The Yardbirds. Art Wood had already booked the club to audition for drummers, following the departure of Artwood's first drummer, Reg Dunnage, who'd taken the decidedly un-rock 'n' roll route to respectability and got a job at Heathrow airport.

Art charitably allowed The Yardbirds to double up auditions and look for a guitar-player to replace Clapton, who'd left because The Yardbirds weren't playing pure Blues. "He objected to the commercial success of "For Your Love", Art remembers, "There's no trains in it."

Seeing this nervous and very spotty young bloke sitting all by himself with a guitar between his knees, Art went up to him to offer a few words of encouragement.

"I remember he was the first one there, he was literally shaking, he was so scared. He said he'd come to audition for The Yardbirds, but didn't think he was good enough. There was a line of other guitar-players waiting outside the club, but no drummers for me, and it was meant to be our fucking audition! I told him, "Don't worry, it'll be fine, just do your best, son, and you'll be all right." Which he was, because they didn't bother to audition anyone else after him - they sent everyone else home.

"Incidentally, we did get our drummer, Keef Hartley, who'd originally replaced Ringo Starr in Rory Storm and The Hurricanes, so we were pleased with that."

If then it had been just a little galling for Ronnie to see a former support band guitar player join the group that next to The Rolling Stones were his idols, he never let on. Now, aside from the delicate problem of who would be lead guitarist, Ronnie relished the opportunity of working with him. Beck was high profile and therefore Ronnie's next logical step.

It also suited his and Kim's firm resolve to maintain their musical partnership - Kim had replaced Tony as Ron's creative sparring partner long before Tony Munroe had even realised, let alone been sacked.

So it was that both Ronnie and Kim began early 1967 by dropping in on Jeff's first audition/rehearsal sessions at a studio in Goodge Street. Beck's first choice of a rhythm section had been the ill-advised pairing of ex-Pretty Thing, but still full time madman, Viv Prince on drums, and the one time mean and moody-looking ex-Shadows bass player, Jet Harris.

It hadn't worked: Viv just wasn't user-friendly and Jet was mostly drunk - just another rock 'n' roll tragedy, but this time involving a man who was arguably one of the greatest bass guitarists Britain had produced. A well-publicised affair with the bottle had already cost him two very successful careers and earned him the tag of being unemployable; which makes one wonder why Beck had ever considered him in the first instance. Unless Beck was desperate, a bad judge of character - or just didn't want people around who might outshine him.

Kim, for one, was shattered to hear how far his hero had fallen. As Ronnie remembers: "It upset Kim because he started out modelling himself on Jet, and now he was like shot to pieces. I think he'd turned up a couple of times to rehearsals, but was obviously so out of the game it was a waste of time. That was a great shame; he was a bit like Brian Jones was at the end."

Harris had stopped showing up for rehearsals and the next time he was heard of, he'd been involved in a near-fatal car crash alongside singer, Billie Davis, whom he'd been having an affair with. "That pretty much finished him off for good," Kim says, "He disappeared into near obscurity after that. He became one of those guys that only showed up if Cliff Richard was in the news and they'd do a 'where are they now' bit, and it would always be somewhere fucking horrible."

Ronnie always joked that if only he'd hung around long enough, Jet Harris could have joined the Faces, where his behaviour would have been understood and even positively encouraged.

Viv Prince was next to go, replaced briefly by Beck's old Tridents' band mate, Ray Cook.

Beck's major asset at this point was in his choice of vocalist, Rod Stewart, who at twenty-two years of age was already a veteran of the British rock circuit.

Rod and Ronnie already knew each other originally meeting in October 1965 on the day when Rod had performed his debut solo single, "Good Morning Little Schoolgirl" live on "Ready Steady Go!".

They hadn't met in the actual studio as such, but later that evening when he'd been accosted by the enthusiastic eighteen year-old Ronnie in a pub. It was to be the start of a life-long friendship and a shared hair style.

Beck had moved from Balham, south London to Sutton in mid-January, following the final split from his wife, Patricia.

"He had this big penthouse place," Ronnie remembers, "So we started going over there to rehearse, me and Kim. Or Jeff would sometimes come and see us, driving his Stingray with a fucking huge Afghan Hound in the back. The neighbours loved it. I thought we were sounding great but after a while, Jeff was trying to ask politely for Kim to leave. He was sort of saying "Er, would you mind not playing bass?" In the end, Jeff said to me, "I don't think Kim's going to cut it on bass, would you tell him?" And I said, "yeah, but I like Kim, he's me mate, I don't want to throw him out." And Jeff said, 'well, I'm not going to throw him out, he's still going to be a friend, but he's not going to work in this project - do you think he could live with that?" So I had to say to Kim, "Look, this is how Jeff wants it." I said, "I'm really sorry, I don't quite understand it, or why, but he wants you not to play bass, he wants to try someone else." That was bad enough, but what was a lot worse than that was it turned out to be me.

"Kim was great about it and said, "Oh, no, that's cool, you've got my blessing, you go on ahead and I'll go and do something else."

"He did really! He was really fair about it, he didn't get all mean and moody and say "Oh, fuck you I've been thrown out."

"The good thing for me was I had reached saturation point on the guitar at that point, I was sort of losing interest in it. Then when Jeff said, "would you consider playing bass?" I thought yeah, why not? It didn't cross my mind at the time that maybe Jeff wanted to be the only guitar player."

Why would it? Ronnie was still moving through his life almost as if he was in a dream, convinced that ultimately, everything would happen for the best in the best of all possible worlds. Like Voltaire's Candide, Ronnie always possessed that awful innocence which can destroy far wiser and even more cynical people who get too close.

Rehearsals for Beck's new band now moved to Studio 19 in Soho's Gerard Street. There was only one problem: Ronnie didn't own a bass guitar and hadn't got the money to buy one. He also wasn't about to sell one of his beloved guitars to buy one. There was only one thing to do, steal one.

"I nicked one from Sound City on Wardour Street, right by the big Durex sign. Me and Kim had stood on the corner for about two hours, pretending to say good night, but sizing up a bass. I chose a Fender Jazz not because I liked them, but because it was nearest the door.

"So I went and grabbed it off the wall and run like mad up a Chinese alley. A few years later, when I was with the Faces and had made a few bob, I went back in and the same guys were still working there and I said, "Hello, I'm the bloke who nicked your bass years ago and I'm here to pay for it" and they were delighted because bass guitars were so much dearer by then!"

February 1967 began interestingly. The Musician's Union banned the Rolling Stones from singing "Let's Spend The Night Together" on the Eamon Andrews Show. On the other hand, the films "Alfie" and "Georgy Girl", which both featured a high degree of nights spent together, did well at New York's Golden Globe Awards. Petula Clark's "This Is My Song" was fighting it out with The Monkees' "I'm A Believer" for the top spot, and Melody Maker announced the arrival of Jeff Beck's new group.

It reported that the newly-formed four piece were booked as support to Roy Orbison on a nationwide tour which also featured The Ryan Twins and Small Faces.

Ronnie was also quoted as saying: "I don't mind playing bass with Jeff. He's a very good blues guitarist and I expect we will be playing blues with a difference."

How right he was.

Now the Small Faces had (deservedly so) built a reputation for themselves as complete troublemakers whilst on the road, but Beck's new (but only fifty per cent) manager, Peter Grant, and record producer, Mickie Most, were desperate to launch Beck on the road to pop (not R&B) stardom, and the Small Faces were the perfect pre-teen crowd pullers to get him noticed.

They even had the song that would appeal. "Hi-Ho Silver Lining" was due to be released on 10th March. It all made solid, commercial sense.

The tour kicked of at the Finsbury Park Astoria on 3rd March 1968. True, Jeff Beck's band was under-rehearsed. On the other hand, who could have foreseen that their amplifiers would break down mid set?

Steve Marriott for one, as he'd happily sabotaged them in the first instance. Why? Well, it was all a bit of a laugh, really. Later on during the tour, Marriott would 'borrow' Orbison's guitar and re-tune it to an even higher pitch than the falsetto-prone crooner was used too. This had the side-splitting effect of forcing Orbison to reach for notes previously thought impossible except for castrati.

Orbison, handicapped by poor eyesight, never realised why the Small Faces were being so friendly before each performance. But he did spend a great deal of time on stage squinting mournfully into the wings, where his new best friends were collapsed in hysterics.

Krissie Wood's memories of Ronnie's early days with Jeff Beck are still clear: "I remember the first rehearsals with Jeff and it was in a dingy underground studio in Soho's Gerard Street, but I remember it very clearly because I liked it, it had a really nice feel about it. Jimmy Page walked in at one point and everybody played together. But it wasn't pointless jamming, everybody just wanted to play together and it was a lovely atmosphere. The show at the Finsbury Park Astoria was totally different, that was truly weird. They all had to wear yellow suits which I found really extraordinary because none of the bands dressed up in uniforms anymore. They started off and all of a sudden the power went off, thanks to Steve Marriott who was larking about backstage. It left Rod and Ronnie looking really silly standing there in these yellow suits and black collars, that didn't quite fit. Jeff was quite moody that night too, maybe for good reason I suppose. I always hated them doing "Hi-Ho Silver Lining" the song was okay but with a vocalist like Rod in the band, why have Jeff singing it?"

According to Krissie, the switch to bass caused no problem for Ronnie. Although she maintains her suspicions about why Jeff wanted it done: "Ronnie loved playing bass, he was a great bass player. But I don't think Jeff was being very honest about why he wouldn't let Ronnie play guitar. Okay, Ron is a guitarist and played bass like a guitarist, so the sound was really unique. But at the same time, Jeff seemed unable to let him pick up a guitar. I'm not saying Ronnie was a better player because he obviously isn't as good as Jeff, that goes without saying. But I did feel it was either insecurity, or a little bit of jealousy even."

Jeff Beck's debut had not been a success. Words like "unmitigated" and "disaster" sprung to the minds and typewriters of the music press who unanimously savaged them, singling out Beck personally - in the way that British journalists have made their very own.

"Jeff seemed to have difficulty even playing a good solo." ran one review, "Jeff sounded diabolical, it's hard to believe he's a guitarist praised to the heavens." sneered another, but the clincher was the one that ran, "Gimmick and stack of noise".

Beck immediately quit the tour and was replaced by PP Arnold, former backing singer for Ike and Tina Turner, and Marriott's then current squeeze. So, Steve was alright then.

"A lot of reasons contributed to me calling off the tour," Beck told one his detractors, Melody Maker, the following week. Sounding a tad desperate to find an excuse, he went on: "All these things seemed to come to a head on opening night. It's not worth appearing on a bill starring such names as Roy Orbison and Small Faces. Frankly, I would never tour with such artists again. I'd rather top a ballroom tour."

Which all things considered, was a bit unfair on Roy Orbison.

The trouble was, so many people were unable to resist being unkind to Jeff Beck. He took himself extremely seriously, unlike Ronnie or Steve Marriott. They took the music seriously, but life still had to retain an element of fun. Which is perhaps why they were viewed as never quite growing up. Nor was Beck ever comfortable with musicians that had a bit of stage presence. His insecurities only allowed for one star per group and it had to be him. Allowances were made for Rod Stewart, but only so long as he suffered from an almost debilitating stage fright, that would soon change once he found his confidence.

The first to suffer at the hands of Jeff's unpredictable behind the scenes wrath was drummer Roy   Cook, who was also made the official scapegoat for the Finsbury Park Debut Disaster. He was unceremoniously sacked, even though he'd been assured that his position was a permanent one, to the extent of being urged to buy a brand-new, £400 drum kit, say at least £2,000 at today's prices.

"Roy has had such a raw deal," said Roy's mother, Winifred, "Now he faces a very grim future with no job and a very heavy debt incurred by a new drum kit, which he was told he would need for the new group. I can't understand why Jeff should do this to Roy, we've known him a long time and Jeff was a friend of the family."

Don't put your son on the stage, Mrs Cook.

Ronnie's new rhythm section partner was Micky Waller, an old friend of Rod's from his Soul Agents days, who'd also previously drummed with Georgie Fame and Brian Auger's Trinity.

"I feel I'm entitled to one mistake," Beck was quoted as saying in Melody Maker, once again being asked about the Finsbury Park fiasco. "People who like music and know I've got Rod Stewart and Micky Waller with me will know I have a good group now. I challenge any group to compete with us in a group battle!"

No mention of Ronnie Wood?

Praising Micky Waller turned out to be a little premature. In two and half years, the Jeff Beck group went through six drummers - Viv Prince, Roger Cook, Micky Waller (twice), Rod Coombs and Aynsley Dunbar. And by the end of March 1967, Waller quit, for the first time to join The Walker Brothers (none of whom were actually related). He replaced Gary Leeds (Walker) who'd somewhat bizarrely left to form his own band and gone to Japan.

Waller was replaced by Rod Coombs - once again, another friend of Rod's. If it seems that Rod was becoming something of a foreman, he was, but only with the best of motives, which he insists were the identical ones that had led him to join Jeff Beck in the first instance.

"I thought I'd better help him out" Rod offers, "I mean, for a guitar player like Jeff to come out with a song as lame as "Hi-Ho, Silver Lining" was a crime. I didn't want it to be over before it really begun, so I suggested a few good players."

Rod also brought in ex-Shotgun Express Dave Ambrose on bass, a surprise move that enabled Ronnie to take up second guitar. In early April, the new five-man line up were summoned to plush offices at 155 Oxford Street, where they were told by Peter Grant that he had bought out Simon Napier Bell's fifty per cent share in Jeff Beck. He also told the band that together with Mickie Most, they had set up RAK Management; and a new agency deal with NEMS was currently in the offing.

The future looked bright Grant assured them, and all the band agreed, there was only one other thing, from now on, all members of the band (aside from Jeff of course) would have to negotiate their own wages separately. Luckily for Rod, he had his own manager to do this for him. The others didn't, and it was made clear that Grant regarded them as nothing more than hired help.

"It was like the Oxford Street Mafia up there," Ronnie says, "with the Andrew Oldhams, your Peter Grants and your Mickey Mosts - all those wheelers and dealers. They used to have Mickie Most on one side of the office and Peter Grant on the other and I'd go in with Rod and they'd say, "No, no, not you, we just want to see Rod," and they'd wave you out of the room so they could talk money.

"Then they'd call you and say, "Oh, you can come in now, Ronnie" and Rod would come out and I'd go in; that's how it used to be. Divide and rule and they were just bullying Jeff all the time, isolating him, which was a fucking shame."

In time, those early wide-boy managers and agents would give way to the Alan Kleins of this world, along with grey suited accountants who were rumoured to be Mafia connected. Most of these rumours were put about by themselves, but for a while it worked. Finally, these people would in turn be replaced by the record label executives and music industry organisation people who talk nothing but market research and believe consumer focus groups can best choose the best songs. People, for example, who decide the play list for BBC Radio One: men and women terrified by premature stomach and bottom droop and obsessed with the youth market; easy marks for the record industry and probably the main reason why Radio One haemorrhages listeners.

Say what you like about the managers and agents of the sixties - people like Don Arden, Tito Burns and even Peter Grant - but at least they were colourful and mostly enjoyed the music for its own sake, as opposed to music as merely a point of sale.

Or a somewhat desperate attempt to persuade the world that one is still really young at heart. The other point is that those sixties British agents, who thought they were world-players, were so often totally outclassed by Americans like Alan Klein and Stan Polley. The latter, for example, ripped off the Apple band, Badfinger, so badly that the band's principal songwriters were driven to commit suicide.

Klein (along with Yoko Ono, of course) is widely blamed for effectively finishing off The Beatles - he's also known to be a rather expensive thorn in the side of the Rolling Stones since the late sixties. Compared to those two beauties, men like Simon Napier Bell, Andrew Loog Oldham and Tony Calder were mere small-minded chancers, albeit with bucket loads of charm and flair.

Beck's new five-piece band, now billed as The Jeff Beck Group as opposed to simply Jeff Beck, opened at the Marquee on 11th April 1967. With a two guitar line-up, just like The Birds, the group set about restoring Jeff Beck's slightly tarnished reputation.

Art had gone along to support his little brother, taking Jon Lord with him. Both men thought "it sounded great," Art still enthuses, "with Ronnie and Jeff playing, they used to be great for each other. Ronnie would go dah-dah and Jeff would go wah-wah and then they'd both go bah! and the crowd loved it, you know it was really exciting guitar battles. Afterwards, Jon Lord went up to Jeff and said it was the best band he'd ever seen."

Great for the crowd! Great for Ronnie! Alas apparently not so great for Beck. According to Ronnie: "Jeff fucking hated it. I thought it was too good to be true; he wanted to be the only guitarist in the band. So Dave Ambrose had to go and I was back on bass.

"Jeff's management treated me and the rest of the guys like second-class citizens both musically and financially, even Rod. People would just come and go. Not that Rod seemed to mind - but then again, he was happy being around anyone that breathed, seeing as how his last job had been a fucking gravedigger! Still, not surprisingly, Rod was pretty shrewd when it came to money. Come to think of it, everyone did a lot better than me. I was crap at negotiating money and fighting my corner. I just used to struggle on the best I could. We were all made to feel dispensable, so you didn't rock the boat."

Sure enough, the next to go was drummer Rod Coombes, replaced by Aynsley Dunbar, ex-Mojo and John Mayall's Bluesbreakers, who could be thought to know a thing or two about percussion and the blues. Indeed, Dunbar stayed for four full months.

"That's how it used to be," Ronnie says ruefully, "It was all them cunts up in Oxford Street going, "The band will be much more popular, sell more records if you get this guy in and that guy out," but all it did was fuck everyone off - the band and the fans. When they asked me to play bass again, I just went, "OK you want me to play bass, I'll play bass, it's your fucking band, mate"."

Ronnie was making the princely sum of £15 a week, a fraction of what he'd been making with The Birds, but as he saw it "There seemed to be few options as good as Jeff at the time so I just got on with it."

The great British wedding-reception favourite, "Hi-Ho Silver Lining" had been released on 24th March with Rod Stewart on backing vocals.

It eventually had a fourteen-week run in the charts, coincidentally peaking at number fourteen and the band appeared twice on Top of the Pops, the first time on 27th April.

Actually, not all the band appeared on the show, it was just Jeff Beck. Ronnie, Rod and Micky Waller had to stand watching from behind the cameras as Jeff in close-up mimed his way through an excruciatingly bad sing-along song as unrepresentative of his style and talent as it is possible to imagine. Even though it was his first official non-appearance on Top of the Pops, Ronnie was more than happy to sit and cringe out of shot, as was Rod - especially as The Who were also appearing that week.

They had their pride, and even Jeff Beck could see the absurdity of the situation. "I quit The Yardbirds to concentrate on playing the guitar, which was why I had a really great vocalist like Rod Stewart fronting the band, and a great rhythm section in Ronnie and Micky with me. You have to remember that around this time, Cream had released "I Feel Free" and Hendrix had "Purple Haze" and all I had was "Hi-Ho-Silver fucking Lining".

Ronnie also remembers how much Beck hated the song. "When they played live gigs, we would wind Jeff up. Rod used to announce to the crowd "And now our guitarist is going to sing our hit, 'Hi-Ho, Hi-Ho!'" At which point Jeff would shout across the stage: "No, I fucking ain't, fuck off!" So much for Mickie Most's dream of bubble-gum pop stardom."

It was obvious that the Oxford Street Mafia had planned to take the Jeff Beck premium brand downmarket for short-term profits. The more money Beck made personally, the larger Peter Grant's own percentage. Which meant that the other band members - except for Rod - who it transpired was on a retainer, were paid on a gig-by-gig basis.

Jeff Beck himself was the money-making solo star, and the rest of the group simply had to learn their place.

It was a time of deep frustration for Rod Stewart, who felt more than a little bit responsible for the players he'd personally brought to the fold. "There was this guy (Roy Cook) who got sacked just after he'd bought these drums on hire-purchase. Then after the Finsbury Astoria nonsense, nothing happened for a while until Aynsley Dunbar came in as drummer, beautiful drummer, really got the band together. Unfortunately for us, he was a blues purist, so he soon left because he didn't think we were playing real Blues.

"One night we did a gig at the Saville and Ronnie and me came on dressed in flowers and kaftans, it was the time of flower power and we were only taking the piss, but Aynsley took it really seriously and quit that night. So we got Micky Waller back and he and Ronnie played great together, but then Beck started recording tracks without crediting us, like "Tally Man" and the group's anthem, "Rock My Plimsoul". On crap like "Love Is Blue" he didn't even use us at all, and we'd all have to stand in the wings while Beck did it with session guys and then we'd have to do it live on stage. If you ever see those first two Beck albums, you won't see a picture of the band on them, only Beck by himself.

"I guess he got his ego inflated by Mickie Most and Peter Grant, but having said that, he was usually okay with me. Aside from the crap going out as singles, the problems were mostly to do with the money.   None of us, except for Beck, ever earned a great deal.

"That was where the real problems lay, that and all the line-up changes of course. It was like a revolving fucking door. Like the time after the second American tour, when Beck decided to sack both Ronnie and Micky! They were only one of the best rhythm sections going at the time. The band was never the same after that".

Actually, Rod got it wrong; Dunbar didn't leave the band until August. But being faced by two freaked-out hippies on stage really had made his mind up. Dunbar left to form his own true-Blues band, The Retaliation, followed by Aynsley Dunbar's Blue Whale - both went on to absolutely nowhere.

Finally, faced with the reality of true-Blues authenticity, which at the time usually meant starving near to death, Dunbar returned once again to the pop world in 1973 wearing stack-heeled boots and a fair bit of slap as one of Ziggy Stardust's backing band, the brilliant Spiders From Mars. As John Lee Hooker so memorably said: "How, How, How, How?"

On 11th May 1967, The Jeff Beck Group appeared for the second time on Top of the Pops promoting "Hi-Ho Silver Lining" or rather, Jeff Beck did again. Once again, he featured as a solo artist whilst his band mates took up their usual position behind the camera. Not that they were bothered in the slightest; in fact, both Ron and Rod were doubly embarrassed because that particular show included Jimi Hendrix, who was there to effortlessly push "The Wind Cries Mary".

A better gig occurred on 2nd July 1967 when the band supported Cream at the Saville theatre. Also present were John Mayall's Blues Breakers and Jimmy Powell and the Dimensions.

In a way, this was a bit like a school reunion: Eric Clapton and Jack Bruce of Cream had served their apprenticeship with John Mayall, as had Beck's drummer, Aynsley Dunbar. While Mayall's current drummer was none other than Micky Waller, Rod Stewart had played harmonica with Jimmy Powell and both Jeff Beck and Eric Clapton had played with the Yardbirds; meanwhile Krissie had dated Clapton before Ron and also, oh you get the picture!

The music world is a truly promiscuous place, both on and off stage. Of course what no one could possibly have known was that Mayall's then lead guitarist, Mick Taylor (late of The Gods, which had briefly featured ex-Bird Tony Munroe), would be replaced by Ronnie Wood as lead guitarist in the Rolling Stones some eight years later.

It was at this gig that Ronnie first met George Harrison (well, at the after show party at the Speakeasy) who was to become a life-long friend to Ronnie and Krissie. So much so, that when in the early seventies Krissie began an affair with the quiet Beatle, it was ok, because Patti Harrison did the same with Ronnie.

In fact, the two guitarists would even greet each other when their paths crossed with a cheery, "How's my wife?" exchange, to which the other would reply "Fine, how's mine?"

The next night, Krissie and Ronnie went to the Speakeasy - a celebration party was being held for America's latest answer to The Beatles, The Monkees, who'd just finished playing three sell-out nights at Wembley.

Socially, Ronnie had arrived! He was now down as part of a guest list that included all four Beatles and their Beatles wives, Brian Jones, Dusty Springfield, Lulu and Eric Clapton. Mick Jagger and Keith Richards would have been there too had they not been spending the night in gaol following the infamous Redlands drug bust - which was why The Monkees had performed that night's gig wearing black armbands.

On 7th July, Jeff Beck released the single "Tally Man" which didn't credit Ronnie Wood, even though - along with the rest of the band - he played on both the 'A' and 'B' sides. The 24th August saw yet another solo appearance by Jeff Beck on Top Of The Pops. Ronnie went along, if only for the free performers' bar, and once again met Jimi Hendrix. The two got along well, even though Hendrix had yet to see him play a note, either mimed or otherwise.

By now, Ronnie was beginning to get the message and following a handful of gigs played over the next few months, he finally took a leaf out of Beck's own book and went AWOL. It was October 1967, and Ronnie had just sat in as a guitarist with The Crazy World Of Arthur Brown for a BBC Radio One session, later broadcast on the 8th.

"I can't remember exactly why I went, or for that matter where," Ronnie ponders, "Maybe I went on holiday - I don't remember having a row or anything. Even though I wasn't happy with the way it was going, I still would have stuck it out for Rod."

He's probably right, because aside from this small blip in the memory banks, the high point of Ronnie's year came that summer.

The Jeff Beck Group played a festival called The Summer Of Love held at Woburn Abbey, which was arranged by kind permission of His Grace, The Duke of Bedford. The Small Faces were also on the bill, but they had to cut short their set when the marquee they were playing in mysteriously burned down.

"I don't think I played with Jeff much after that, I was on the look out for something else."

If Ronnie was feeling a little undervalued at that point it's not surprising, but what really hastened his departure from Beck was the arrival of a group from America called Vanilla Fudge. Jeff Beck saw them at the Astoria on 4th October and was deeply impressed by the rhythm section of bassist, Tim Bogert and drummer, Carmen Appice.

In fact, word filtered back to Ronnie of how impressed Beck really was.

"That was it really," Ronnie reflects, "I heard he was sniffing around, and had his eye on them, and I just instinctively knew he wanted to get them in the band. So I just thought fuck it, I'm not hanging around to get sacked. It wasn't as if we were doing much, anyway. I mean Jeff only used to show up for a gig if he felt like it, and that wasn't very fucking often. We must have cancelled more gigs than we actually fucking played!"

Rick Cunningham, a life-long friend of Ronnie, remembers turning up to a concert and going backstage before the gig to see Ronnie, Rod and Micky Waller tucking in to the hospitality food and drink. "They were getting extremely drunk, Jeff was nowhere to be seen so I asked where he was and why they weren't getting ready for the gig. Ronnie said, "he hasn't shown up... again."

Cunningham couldn't believe it. "The place was packed and the fans had started chanting for Beck. I said to Ron, "What are you going to do?" and he turned round and said, "Fuck him, It ain't my name on the front.""

By September 1967 Ronnie was more than a little disillusioned and restless. He saw only too clearly that his role within the Beck group was a thankless one and about as secure as a Robert Maxwell pension plan.

"I'd spent a year with Jeff Beck and I was still fucking struggling." He recalls, "I realised I was simply treading water with Jeff and what I needed was something a little bit more permanent and not to have to keep watching over my shoulder." Ronnie also needed a sense of direction; Krissie was still temping and they were constantly short of money.

Still, he wasn't too worried. Something would turn up - something always did.

Specifically, Kim Gardiner in a large grey Jaguar saloon clutching a suitcase full of money.

CHAPTER EIGHT
"I CREATED ON AND OFF FOR A YEAR."

Flashback to January 1967.

When Kim Gardiner had been let go (before he'd actually got started) by Ronnie via Jeff Beck, he'd asked his old friend Robert Stigwood for advice.

As Tony Ashton of Ashton, Gardiner and Dyke remembers, "Kim always played up to Stigwood because he knew Stigwood fancied him rotten. He used to get whatever he wanted just by leading him on. It was maybe a bit out of order, but you couldn't help laughing or even wondering, which Kim loved; he loved to wind everyone up and keep them guessing."

Stigwood had already helped Ronnie and Kim out by clearing up the debt still owed by The Birds - he even bought the van off of them and gave it to The Bee Gees who incidentally never did discover that it had originally been financed by one of London's most feared criminal families.

Stigwood introduced Kim to Arthur Howes' agency, the most powerful booking organisation in London at the time. Howes had been one of the first to take a chance on The Beatles back in 1962, despite their first performances for him (as support to chart-topper Frank Ifield), which apparently left audiences lukewarm.

Howes was renowned as a shrewd judge of talent, and had recognised the Fab's huge potential, so much so he secured an option to promote further Beatles' shows, despite their virtual unknown status, as and when he chose.

The deal paid off handsomely within a few short months and Howes found himself with a major financial grip on Beatlemania. In 1966, Howes teamed up with record producer Shel Talmy and formed Planet Records.

This was one of the first small independent labels whose priority was the Pop-Art, demi-mod sensation, The Creation - then at their gimmicky height following two massive European hit singles "Making Time" and the Number One (and a much later irritation by Boney 'M'), "Painter Man".

It's often forgotten, like the band itself, that Boney 'M' were a German group and that covering "Painter Man" was testimony to the massive popularity of The Creation in the fatherland. The band went largely unnoticed in Britain, and that was mainly down to one slight problem - The Creation were both totally neurotic, and terminally paranoid about each other.

Every now and then, two of them would gang up on a third, with the fourth keeping well out of it, and fire him. Or one of them would quit before he could be fired. Or they'd just fire each other en masse. Which was really okay, because then they would happily reform since there wasn't anyone officially left in the band to say who could or couldn't join.

On the other hand, The Creation were one of the most innovative and exciting bands Britain ever produced, with The Who for one copying their anarchistic stage act... except for The Creation it wasn't an act, but all too frighteningly real.

Let me try and explain. After the two aforementioned brilliant singles, drummer Jack Jones was fired by bass player, Bob Garner, in favour of an unknown Liverpool drummer and friend of his called Dave Preston. He was then embarrassingly rehired less than three weeks later by lead vocalist, Kenny Pickett, who then effectively fired himself and was replaced by Kim Gardiner.

"That was strange," recalls Jones, "Kenny had got total paranoia at that point and he'd got it into his head that we were going to fire him, which was rubbish, anyway he confronted us all with it one day and said "I know you lot want to get rid of me, so I'm fucking leaving." So he did, but I swear no one wanted him to. The next thing I knew was someone said he'd heard that Kim Gardiner from The Birds was looking for a job, I think it came via the Arthur Howes Agency. None of us had heard that The Birds had finished, we just assumed they'd fired him so a meeting was set up."

Which was as organised as The Creation ever got, inasmuch as the rest of the band showed up at the agency on 10th February 1967 to find Kim sitting in reception with Eddie Philips, who told them Kim would be at rehearsals the next day. Just like that.

That was okay for Bob Garner at least, because Kim showed up with Ronnie Wood and for a wild moment he wondered about firing Eddie and getting Ronnie in his place. No one had left or been fired for at least a week and the band was getting restless.

"It so happened I was actually thinking of going;" Eddie reflects, "I was starting to get real flak from my wife at the time - she'd started to give me the big ultimatum "me or the band."

However, Ronnie knew nothing of the internal wrangling of The Creation so his motives for tagging along were totally honourable: "I'd always thought Eddie Phillips looked really cool and of course I'd heard how great a guitar player he was. I'd also heard he played with a violin bow and fucking hacksaws, which was way ahead of Jimmy Page, so I went along with Kim to watch."

By all accounts it turned out to be a very weird rehearsal, even by The Creation's unorthodox standards. Bob Garner switched to lead vocals, in order to accommodate Kim's more versatile bass playing and John Dalton (who had been the bass player with the group in their earlier "Mark Four" incarnation) sat in on guitar in place of an absent Eddie Phillips.

Just as the band was plugging in, the recently self-fired Kenny Pickett arrived... "He was in a right ol' strop," recalls Kim, "storming about, calling everyone cunts, and what not! I didn't actually know who he was, because The Creation mostly played on the Continent, so we'd never met before.

"So I'm standing there, and Ronnie's sitting on the amps watching all this, and I turn to Jack (Jones - drummer, recently re-hired) and said, "Who's that bloke?" and he goes, "Oh, that's the singer," and I'm like, "I thought Bob was the singer," and Jack says, "ah well, he is now, but he was the bass player," and then I look over to John (Dalton - original bass player) and say, "well, who's he?" and Jack goes, "he was the bass player too"... and I said, "What the fuck! How many fucking bass players does this band need!" And Ronnie just cracked up."

"I don't know why I missed that rehearsal" says Eddie, "and that's probably why I don't honestly remember how Kim came to be in the group." It's true what Kim said - we never knew each other at all, which was pretty amazing considering how similar we all were. Kim had the look that fit right in.

"Having said that, we were very aware of each other, we knew The Birds had a good reputation and were well respected. I don't know how Kim got an audition, but we knew who he was and we knew he was a tremendous player. There are two kinds of bass player; the one who simply plays along with the songs and the one who'll work out a line that complements the song. Kim was always coming up with those lines. The other thing about Kim was the fact that you could never be down while he was around, he was always up. I hear the same thing said of Ronnie and it's true; they were always together and always laughing and joking, they never had their girlfriends with them; they would turn up laughing in Kim's big old Jag, just two mates from West Drayton."

The Creation's fragile, ever changing alliances may have helped give them that hard-edged brilliance which so illuminated their live performances, but they also destroyed the band's stability. Kim could see that the group was ultimately doomed to implode, but with nothing else in the offing... and since "the fucking wages were good," Kim got Creative.

His first jaunt with The Creation came the following week. Eddie had returned to the fold and the band, together with Ronnie, set off for Portsmouth.

"We had this regular gig called "The Isle Of Wight Beat Cruise" explained Eddie "we would drive down to Portsmouth, board this boat and play all night sailing round and round the Island. Ronnie would come down in the van with us; we had a long trailer attached to the back and it was weighed down with all our gear, great big Marshall stacks, the drums and the stage gear. It was so heavy the back of it would scrape along the road making a horrible screeching noise. Ronnie would help us get it all on board, but he never got up and played - he would watch from the side. Which is kind of weird because he was so much a part of that scene, he had the whole look sorted out.

The following month The Creation gave the Rolling Stones a serious run for their money when they were invited along as the opening act on a short tour of Germany, beginning on 29th March. "The Stones were quite cute at picking the right support act for the right places, even back then," reasoned Kim. "They knew The Creation were a big draw in Germany; they were very on the ball - they still do it today. Acid was quite new then and I remember we had our drinks spiked on the very first show... we did the whole show on acid, which was absolutely brilliant."

So, with a stable line up and electrifying stage act, manager Tony Stratton-Smith's dogged determination and Shel Talmy's masterful production expertise, The Creation (despite themselves) almost looked as if they would be around for a little while yet. According to Ronnie at any rate, "they had all the ingredients needed to become a world-class act."

Sadly, it wasn't to be; by late 1967 the incessant back-biting, paranoia and ridiculous personal differences had all but totally decimated the band, to the point that their pioneering lead guitarist, Eddie Philips (aided by his wife's threat of divorce), suddenly quit. "It was in somewhere like Munich," Eddie lamented, "I'd had a huge row with my wife on the phone and I just thought fuck this, it ain't worth it. I told the band I was going home which was the wrong thing to have done, but my head was done in. I simply couldn't reconcile the two loves in my life. So I upped and left them to it and I remember sitting in the airport with my red Gibson and my amp thinking this is not a good move."

The unknown Tony Ollard was hastily drafted in to replace Eddie and the band soldiered on and fulfilled the remainder of their European dates.

"It was a major blow when Eddie went " Kim explained, "The worst thing about it apart from trying to replace such a unique guitar player was the fact we had a single due out in January 1968 and naturally, Eddie was the guitarist on it and Tony couldn't cut it live. Then to top it off, Bob decided he wanted to go back to Warrington, because Kenny was back on the scene - it was ridiculous. Eddie going home to try and save his marriage was a fucking waste of time too, he'd got that ultimatum from his missus: me or the band, and when he went home she left him anyway."

Eddie takes up the sorry tale: "I thought about going back but I wasn't up to it emotionally, so I went and played bass for PP Arnold" (a move Ronnie could identify with) "... it meant I could take a bit of a back seat, plus it was something different."

So, with Bob homeward bound, Tony not wanted and Eddie busying himself with four strings rather than six, The Creation were down to two men. "It was just the rhythm section left," Kim correctly pointed out, "It was literally me and the fucking drummer! That was when Jack said sod this, why should we give it all up! There's still a lot of money to be made off The Creation name in Germany alone - let's put another line up together." Luckily he was still friendly with Kenny Picket because they'd stayed in touch and he talked him into agreeing to give it one more go around the block. "I immediately went round and found Ron and he was skint and pissed off with the Jeff Beck situation, so I said, "Do you want to make some real easy fucking money and fast? Come on, let's milk this," we had tours lined up in Holland, Spain, and of course, Germany and Ronnie only had a few gigs pencilled in with Jeff Beck at the end of the year, I'll tell you he didn't need much persuading."

Ronnie and Krissie were now living in a tiny flat above the "Little Pink Pig" estate agents in Lower Sloane Street, together with Peanuts and Butch the goldfish, and Beano the cat. Perry Press who owned the Little Pink Pig displayed an uncharacteristic side to his profession by allowing them to live there rent-free... which was a blessing since Jeff Beck's management were extremely careful when it came to money matters, or as Ronnie puts it "they were extremely tight fisted."

Luckily, Krissie was still bringing home a steady wage and had taken on yet another job, this time selling poster art on Harvey Goldsmith's 'Big O' poster stand in Kensington Market.

Ever helpful, Ronnie made sure she was never late for work. First, he tried putting smelly socks under Krissie's nose hoping to wake her up. Unfortunately, Krissie was as big a sleeper as Ronnie was an insomniac, so that trick failed. Next, he hung a big brass alarm clock from a hook in the ceiling, just above the centre of the bed, and just out of reach. This meant Krissie would have to get up in order to turn it off.

This never worked either and the incessant din drove Ronnie mad, not enough to get up and deal with it mind you, no; he'd hit it with a big stick he kept by the side of the bed. Krissie would eventually wake up to see the still ringing clock swinging happily from side to side.

They were poor but happy - even so, a little more money was always welcome.

It was into this scene that Kim Gardiner suddenly arrived one mid-October morning, with the suitcase stuffed with cash. "The Creation basically lived in Germany eight months of the year," Kim explains, "so we didn't have to pay British tax. But we did come back to do TV and the odd gig. triple gigs sometimes, it was a bit like The Birds - we'd do a matinee at 5.00pm, make the next town and set up by eight, and the last one by eleven. We made a lot of money; I would come back to England just to spend it! But I couldn't spend it all, I would stay in Bridal Suites at hotels, and still couldn't fucking spend it. I made £13,000 just in gig money. Jack Jones used to be an accountant, so he just split the cash four ways."

Kim took Ronnie and Krissie out in his new Jaguar to explain The Creation set-up. And, harking back to his earlier acid experiences with the Stones, offered to impart more than just his slightly superior knowledge of the drug. "Ronnie was learning to drive at the time, so I let him drive my jag on acid. He was driving and tripping and suddenly he can't find the steering wheel. He tried to pass this big truck, and I'm seeing all these red flashes, and suddenly he goes, "The Steering wheel's gone! It's fucking gone!" and he can't really drive anyway, but he's laughing his head off and the truck's getting closer and closer. Just then he cuts in front of it, and the truck hits us and we spin around and around like a merry-go-round. And we're both grinning at each other, tripping in a car spinning out of control, and screaming Whaaaaaaa!"

Fucked the car right up.

Suitcases full of cash. New Jaguars. Multi-coloured driving lessons. What ambitious professional musician wouldn't jump at the chance to join?

One of the few commitments left concerning Jeff Beck was a BBC Radio One session with DJ John Peel on Top Gear. The band were also to be the featured stars on the David Simmonds Show also on Radio One. Aside from John Peel, the only real buzz Ronnie had got from playing with the Jeff Beck Group for the past four months was his first date outside the UK: at Ghent, in Belgium on 13th October. There, Ronnie learned that Beck had fleshed out the band with pianist Nicky Hopkins and singer Madeleine Bell (another Mickie Most inspiration) for the purpose of recording a new single entitled "Love is Blue" in December. The recording session and single were news to Ronnie… as was the unofficial discovery that Jeff planned to play bass himself. He could sense the "Not Wanted On Voyage" label was about to be tied around his neck. Bearing in mind that Ronnie and Jeff had been friends since 1965, Jeff's behaviour was a little cavalier, to say the least.

Ronnie began 1968 as a full-time member of The Creation (Mark IV - who's counting?) and a part-time member of the Jeff Beck Group.

He flitted between both bands during January and February, playing a handful of gigs to promote the new single, which he doesn't actually play on - while rehearsing with The Creation. Ironically, "Love Is Blue" only reached number twenty three, beaten out of the Top Twenty by Frenchman Paul Mauriat's version of the same song - which also made it into the US charts. Beck was reduced to making slighting remarks about the record in the weekly music press: "We rushed into the studio and the whole thing was finished in a couple of days," he told Disc and Music Echo, "and the fantastic thing is I really like the melody." Excuse me? Rushed into the studio? Which just happened to have been pre-booked at least a month earlier?

No-one had forced Beck to go along with Mickie Most's dreams of bubble-gum pop stardom. The least Beck could have done was put on a brave face about a record that left many critics and fans totally bemused. Instead, he went on to announce that he'd changed the band's name to Jeff Beck's Million Dollar Bash. Given how little Ronnie and most of the band were earning, the name was a tad insensitive. Nor did it ever catch on.

Even Rod Stewart was beginning to become disillusioned with Beck and his management. In the true musical tradition of making a bad situation worse, Stewart signed an ill-fated solo deal with Andrew Loog Oldham's Immediate Records and produced the single "Little Miss Understood" which died of general neglect.

In March, Ronnie told Rod he was leaving Beck to concentrate on the more lucrative opportunities offered by The Creation's European bookings. He didn't bother to tell Beck himself; after all, Beck had hardly been communicative over the past year.

The first item on Ronnie's new musical menu was an April tour with The Creation to Germany and Spain. The flavour of a Creation tour is best illustrated by the recollections of Roman Salicki, a Polish refugee who'd been a top fashion photographer in London during the mid sixties. He'd originally learned his trade with Michael Cooper, famous for his work with The Rolling Stones and Sergeant Pepper album cover.

By 1967, Salicki was burned out and bumming around the South of France, where he ran into Shel Talmy. The two men got on well, so much so that Talmy persuaded Salicki to come and work as his personal assistant.

"One of the band's he (Talmy) was recording was The Creation and Shel asked me take them out on the road, which meant Germany. At that time I didn't even have a British passport, all I had was this British Travel Document. At that time the Wall was still up, the Iron Curtain was still drawn, and we'd have to travel through East Germany to get to Berlin. Being slightly crazy anyway, I said "what the hell, what can they do to me?" So we packed up this van with the band, a roadie, all the equipment and me and took a ship to Germany.

"Everything was fine for a while, but with The Creation you never knew what they'd get up to next. And driving through East Germany was especially scary, because they had watchtowers and tanks all up and down the autobahn. We had to go through Checkpoint Charlie when we left West Berlin - me, the roadie and five long-haired idiots stoned out of their minds, not giving a damn about anything even when they were straight.

"The American guards said, "Listen, guys, we don't advise you to go through. If you do, it's at your own risk." So we did and crossed over to the Eastern checkpoint where there were all these stony-faced guards. And the band were making faces at them, and making all these disparaging remarks, but after we'd been grilled for about an hour and a half, they finally let us go. As we went through, the boys stuck their naked arses against the van windows, which somewhat worried me.

"We eventually got back into West Germany, checked into a hotel and the first thing the boys wanted to do was go out and get drunk. Which was nothing new, because they were absolutely stoned and drunk out of their minds every night. They'd bust up hotel rooms, insult people, anything to make my life miserable.

"I seemed to have spent the entire time placating hotel managers, cops, club owners, border guards and generally, keeping the band out of prison. Especially Ronnie and Kim - I was sure I was only going to come back with Jack and Kenny, leaving the other two banged up in some gaol, probably in the East.

"The only time I had any peace was when the band went on stage. They were very professional; they did the job they were supposed to do and they did it well. It was really like a Beatles scene: total sold-out chaos at the concerts, people stacked up against each other, and the boys playing with the audience. It got to the point where I'd be up on stage trying to pull the girls away, except one time Kim Gardiner put his boot in my back and pushed me into the audience, but that was okay because I was an honorary band-member, so I wasn't mauled too badly.

"The best part of that tour was going to Spain. The weather was great, and the guys had plenty of girls to take care of them. We met an old friend of mine in Madrid, a model called Norma Perriman, who was married to one of Los Bravos, who were away on tour. Norma and Kenny hit it off, which meant the band could go to her place after a gig... which was just as well, because they were running out of hotel rooms to trash.

"I finally got back to London totally exhausted. I enjoyed the band, they were a great bunch of guys, but there comes a point where you say 'I don't want any more of this. I want to go home'."

In May, Ronnie was one of the many musicians asked to play on Jeff Beck's ground-breaking album, "Truth". It finally looked as if Mickie Most had learned his lesson, for the album was unashamedly AOR. The same month also saw the release of The Creation's new single, "Midway Down", recorded in January, with Ronnie playing lead guitar.

Talmy's own label, Planet, had folded in the aftermath of the Great Payola Scandal in late 1966. He'd moved his operation to Polydor who allowed the band to record whenever the opportunity arose, but without any real commitment. The Creation had laid down six tracks, the first of which, "Midway Down", ironically turned out to be the band's swansong. Written by a little-known German composer, the song tells of the many attractions the traditional circus sideshow had to offer and obviously owes a great deal to The Beatles track "For The Benefit of Mister Kite".

Even so, it was a priceless slice of sixties psychedelia, with the lines "Ten foot giant find it tough to lift a feather" and "Three foot midget hopes he won't be small for ever."

The song descends into a la-la-la sing-along in the finest pub tradition. It was backed by the group composition, "The Girls Are Naked" - a closer approximation to the Eddie Philips sound on early Creation recordings - and released simultaneously in Britain and Germany.

These were excellent, well structured pop songs, every bit as instant as anything the band's contemporaries were producing. But without any real record company to push it, the single sank without trace, even though the Eddie Philips reprise earned respectful airplay on German radio. Always important, respectability in Germany - but it won't pay the rent in England, where the indifference continued.

Still, a further two releases were lined up for German consumption only: a cover of "Bony Maroni" backed by "Mercy, Mercy, Mercy" and "For All That I Am" backed by the group composition, "Uncle Bert" - credited to Garwood Picton, an amalgamation of all their surnames. "For All That I Am" was probably the band's finest hour, with Ronnie's full-on Fuzz guitar shaping the song, while "Uncle Bert" perfectly showcased Ronnie and Kim's schoolboy humour at its sniggering best and was undoubtedly the original blueprint for Pete Townshend's "Uncle Ernie".

"Uncle Bert with his trouser hanging down
I spied him lurking deep on Hampstead Heath
White mac stained and opened down the front
He has a soggy carrot in his hand
A dog name Rover bit his trouser leg
This exposed his rotten wooden peg
The dog ran off with splinters in his teeth
And Uncle's leg went rolling down the hill".

A drunken, sing-a-long Cockney knees-up chorus closes the song, complete with the band opening bottles and clinking glasses in the studio, doors opening and slamming shut, wild cheering and yelling as Jack Jones taps out a rhythm on an empty beer-bottle.

Another song written and recorded at these sessions was "The Girls Are Naked" - a number inspired by a sign above a shadowy Soho doorway that the band saw one night en route to playing the Marquee club on Wardour Street. Underneath was another smaller sign that read "And They Dance". The recording demonstrates perfectly how at ease Ronnie and Kim were with each other's playing, beginning with a mighty Kim Gardiner bass line that builds the song up for an excellent lead guitar intro. Unfortunately, as good as these releases were, it really was a case of too little too late.

The trouble with The Creation was best explained by a somewhat embittered Shel Talmy: "They (the original line-up) hated each other. They couldn't put aside their personal enmities for the good of the band, or the good of themselves. So instead of becoming extremely rich superstars, they've all become very working/middle class nobodies. Not Ronnie Wood or Kim Gardiner, of course - but Kenny basically did nothing, he drove Led Zeppelin around, and I heard Eddie ended up driving a bus, which is like a criminal waste of a talent! What a waste! Bob, I have no idea what happened to Bob. It was like he was born with three chips on his shoulder. A totally disruptive personality, I think is the nicest thing I can say about him. Jack was cool, fine with the whole thing, and of course when Ronnie Wood and Kim came in that was great, but it was already over.

Bob thought he deserved, quote unquote, to have more notice than he did. Certainly more than Kenny or Eddie, which was wrong - he wasn't even in the same league. Maybe it's a Northern thing, because people from the North, like Warrington, have this fucking attitude!"

Shel Talmy still talks of The Creation as being the greatest of all bands from that era, and this from a man who knew a thing or two: "I was still determined to push The Creation, even after the original line up broke-up in 1966, just as they were about to explode in England. They managed to carry on and regained the lost ground very quickly with Kim (Gardiner).

"England had lagged behind when it came to The Creation, which was fine because I had my eyes firmly set on the States; that was their obvious market, they could have gone on for thirty years because they were as good as The Kinks or The Who, maybe even The Stones. The main players couldn't even stand to be in the same country as each other, never mind the same band. Ronnie (Wood) was a good choice but I always felt he was brought in by Kim when it was too late. Kenny had a presence; he had a real attitude - he really looked the part and for a little while, he was the lead singer.

"He was the first one to my knowledge to initiate Action-Art painting live on stage - and of course they almost burned a theatre down in Germany, because they would ignite the paintings afterwards using aerosol spray paint cans like little flame-throwers. That got them some great publicity - this was before Jimi Hendrix had set fire to anything and it got them the number one record in Germany. Unfortunately, Eddie was the main ingredient, there were very few guitar players around who played as well as Eddie could. Ronnie was good, but he wasn't anywhere near Eddie, who was certainly a more interesting player. I never gave up hope of getting him back in the group, and this is no disrespect to Ronnie, because Ronnie is a wonderful guitarist. It just wasn't The Creation without Eddie.

"I still went across to New York in order to get them a big American deal, hoping it would reunite them. And I got it - a five album deal with United Artists worth millions of dollars, but when I got back there wasn't really a band in any shape or form... there wasn't a band at all. Here I was with this huge fucking deal and it was all over.

"The original guys were all to blame because each and every one of them contributed to the gradual erosion of the band. What a fucking waste! Those guys were the biggest regret of my career when I think of what they could have been; and they would have been, too!"

On 20th May 1968, a now dying Creation left for a short tour of Germany and Holland. Ronnie's place in the Jeff Beck Group was taken by Junior Woods from the band Tomorrow, a group only notable due to guitarist Steve Howe going on to join Yes. What proved to be The Creation's last gig was performed at the John Lewis Store theatre in Oxford Street in early June. Although according to Jack Jones' diary, the band did play one more time. Unfortunately, no can remember where or anything at all about it.

Kenny Picket died on 10th January 1997 - shortly before he was to be interviewed for the first edition of this book. Luckily, Mike Stax, editor of the brilliant Ugly Things, the magazine specialising in obscure R&B and Garage Bands, has allowed exclusive use of an earlier interview where Picket remembered Ronnie in The Creation's line up and had this to say:

"I think Ron was with the band on and off for about nine months. It was well after The Birds. He was our lead guitarist, a good lad, good fun, yeah. He wasn't a particularly good guitarist, but he turned the band round in a different direction, leaning more towards BB King, R&B, that sort of stuff, because that's what Ronnie was into. So we almost reverted back to when The Creation was The Mark Four doing cover versions and stuff. It was full circle, which felt really weird, like I'd come back in at the very beginning. Ron was still with Jeff Beck at the time, but I don't think it was happening, so Ronnie came on board - but he left us when he got the chance to go to America with Beck. But that was fine, because The

Creation was just about dying by then. That last band was a good band, but it wasn't The Creation as people knew The Creation to be."

On the Friday he died, Kenny Pickett had just played with a friend's band at his local pub in North London. After leaving the stage, he went to the bar and ordered a pint. Someone walked up behind him and tapped Picket on the shoulder to congratulate him on his performance. Whereupon The Creation's former lead singer fell to the floor, dead.

According to close friends, Kenny was going through a particularly ugly separation from his astrologer wife at the time and was under a lot of stress. Following three autopsies the authorities were still unable to determine the exact cause of death. Pickett had managed to remain an enigma right to the very end.

As for the others, Eddie and Bob still play very occasionally as The Creation and in keeping with tradition, they don't invite Jack who now runs a newsagents in North London. Tragically, Kim passed away in 2002 after losing his battle with cancer.

On 14th June 1968, the Jeff Beck Group began an eight-week tour of the States, without Junior Woods. Ronnie was back, the lure of America had proved too strong for him: goodbye Creation, hello New York. Especially, hello Bill Graham's famed Fillmore East, where the band was to support The Grateful Dead.

That June was an interesting time to cross the Atlantic: Bobby Kennedy had been shot dead nine days earlier and Martin Luther King the previous month. Pierre Trudeau had just become Liberal Prime Minister in Canada, with a landslide majority (which a few years later would inexorably lead to a major political crisis featuring Trudeau's young, star-struck wife and Ronnie himself).

Change was in the air, except perhaps in Britain where Cliff Richard had won the Eurovision Song Contest with "Congratulations", which had also gone to Number One in the UK charts. One of the more interesting facets of the UK charts is the way a novelty song - sung by little blue cartoon characters, say, or a frog - will so often reach the Number One spot. Not that "Congratulations" fell into that category, of course. And Sir Cliff's career has been anything but a novelty. Actually, to go from Espresso Bongo to the Centre Court at Wimbledon in only forty short years is nothing short of a miracle.

"I only went back with Beck because I wanted to go to America," Ronnie admitted.

Or as Kim also said: "Ronnie joined The Creation to get him into Europe and re-joined Beck to get to America. In the same way I joined The Creation for the experience of Europe and I then formed Ashton, Gardiner and Dyke to reach the States. It had always been our dream, our goal, right from The Birds days. America was our aim, it was more important then money."

Originally, and at Tony Stratton-Smith's suggestion, AG&D was to be called "Charisma" but as Tony Ashton later said, "We didn't even know what charisma meant, let alone spell it, so we just used our surnames, the way Clapton, Bruce, and Baker did before they became Cream, and later you had Crosby, Still, Nash & Young. So Tony took the name for his own record company, and that's how you got Charisma Records."

What is hard to appreciate now is that for many kids growing up in the fifties and sixties, America was a true cultural icon. It wasn't just the money, and the real hamburgers, hot dogs and steak for everyone, Flinstones-style, but the sense of excitement and freedom America promised. For London kids in particular, whose earliest playgrounds had been bomb-sites surrounded by rusty corrugated iron and who could remember rationing and NHS concentrated orange juice in medicine bottles, the idea of wide-open spaces where the deer and the buffalo roamed seemed like heaven. Pink grapefruit juice, beach parties where bikini-clad girls cavorted on real sand, not pebbles. Teenagers owned convertible cars, or even hot-rods, as opposed to a jacked-up Ford Zephyr (which granted looked vaguely American), Route 66 and the far-off wail of a train... all this was the stuff of dreams. The music was good, too.

It's questionable whether Ronnie's departure from The Creation even registered with either Jack Jones or Kenny Picket, for they too had become fed up with being the 'nearly' band... with or without Ronnie, The Creation would have ended anyway - it's just a shame that such a great band finished not with a big bang, but a tired whimper in an Oxford Street department store.

If there'd ever been any doubt how Jeff and his management viewed the rest of the band, that first tour to America quickly confirmed it: with contempt.

While Jeff and Peter Grant stayed at the Hilton, Ronnie, Rod, Mickey Waller and Nicky Hopkins were crammed into one room in the down-market Goreham hotel several blocks away; they were also kept extremely short of money.

"We were so desperate, one time we had to go down to the automat and steal eggs," Ronnie admits. "The Goreham wasn't too bad in theory, it was a real rock and roll hotel, all the bands used to stay there - Cream, Sly and the Family Stone and Hendrix - but they had their own rooms, and we were all together. Still, the place had real energy - in fact, Rod and I passed by there a few years ago and they still had the same staff."

"Ronnie was happy to get to America," Krissie remembers, "but he was really unhappy at the way they were being treated. He didn't even have enough money to phone home, so he had to write letters all the time."

The band played the Fillmore East for the first time on 14th June. It was a resounding success - so many encores were demanded and given, that The Grateful Dead had to cut short their set (an unheard of thing). Beck and Peter Grant went back to the Hilton, and the rest of the band to their one room at the Goreham.

It should have been a resounding personal triumph for Beck, for The Yardbirds had played a last low-key gig at the Fillmore on the 5th, and here he was the toast of New York.

Oh, but there was a spectre at the feast, specifically a certain Jimmy Page who'd stayed on in the states after the Yardbirds' last American tour. Page had been invited along by manager Peter Grant and every night Beck played, he stood in the wings, gauging the audience reaction to the way the band played. He was also staying at the same hotels as Beck. Beck could tell himself that his old mate had simply come to support him, but deep down, his old paranoia began working overtime.

As Rod Stewart remembers: "Aggravation and unfriendliness developed very early with that band. Especially as Jeff would stay at a top-class hotel and the others would be at Hotel Third-On-The-Bill round the corner."

Beck's paranoia would, as often happened, prove to be justified. Page had been flown out not to support, but to emulate him... although it could be argued that Beck had taken his own stage act from the Yardbirds and modelled his playing in part on Eric Clapton. All the same, you have to admire Peter Grant's chutzpah, if not his ethics. There he was, launching Beck in America with one hand, while nurturing Page and Led Zeppelin with the other. Peter Green's judgement would turn out to be correct, however: Jeff Beck was doomed to be remembered for "Hi-Ho, Silver Lining", while Led Zeppelin would become rock gods.

To make matters worse, following the Fillmore East shows, Beck was asked to play a benefit gig at The Reality House Rehabilitation Centre on Staten Island, asked by Jimi Hendrix himself.

"Jeff said, "do you fancy doing a gig with Jimi Hendrix?" and we said yeah!" Ronnie reminisces. "When we were playing, Jimi came up and played with us, and he started bossing Jeff about. Jimi was the first person who ever gave me any credibility in that band. He'd stop the music and say: "Jeff, why don't you shut up and give the bass player a chance?" And Jeff's face just sort of crumpled up. Jimi give me solos, at Statten Island and later at the Scene Club (the Daytop Music Festival), he used to recognise my guitar playing through the bass. When we got back to England he even gave me a dog! But Jeff really hated me getting that kind of recognition. I mean, here was Jimi, the world's greatest fucking guitarist, telling Jeff to shut the fuck up and let the bass player have a go!"

In fact, Hendrix showed up every night of the band's five-night residency at the Scene Club, jamming with them on each occasion and giving greater and greater prominence to Ronnie's bass playing. To make matters worse, New York was hit by a week-long torrential downpour and the humidity played hell with Beck's spots.

Beck began to withdraw into himself once more; he had always been extremely sensitive about his complexion and going on stage looking like a hormonal teenager made him overly self conscious. Mind you, having Jimmy Page taking notes from the wings every night and Jimi Hendrix turning up and insisting that the bass player be given solos, did nothing for his peace of mind either.

Even when the tour became a sell-out success and the band the darlings of the American music media, Beck's misgivings grew and grew. Especially so when that very success helped Rod Stewart get his solo deal with Mercury Records. (He'd been seen at the Shrine Auditorium in Los Angeles by producer Lou Reizener who brokered the deal.)

True, Peter Grant did ensure that Beck's album, Truth, was rush-released in the States. But that hardly helped with Beck's nagging suspicions that some band members had their own fans. One reason, perhaps, why the album cover only mentioned Jeff Beck. You had to read the sleeve notes to discover that he was supported by the same band who'd helped that first tour become such a success. The album entered the charts at number 163 and quickly rose to fifteenth place by October, when the band was sent back to America in order to promote it, this time with tour manager Richard Cole, who would go on to become tour manager for - yes, you guessed it, Led Zeppelin. Ironically, Cole would appoint an assistant roadie and driver called Kenny Pickett.

The first tour, however, lasted until 24th August. Ronnie returned home to find an offer waiting: would he like to join Jimmy Page and Chris Dreja in a group to be called The New Yardbirds, with a ten-day tour of Scandinavia. The original Yardbirds had broken up in July; both Page and Grant were eager to try out the ideas gleaned from watching the Jeff Back Band. Ronnie declined. That Scandinavian tour, plus the next Beck band tour to America would have meant that he'd be away from home for well over six months, and he was badly missing Krissie.

Besides, for all his misgivings about Jeff Beck and Beck's management, the band was one of the hottest in America and staying put gave Ronnie the chance to really make his name in the Land of the Free.

Chris Dreja would eventually leave The New Yardbirds and become a photographer. The band hired John Paul Jones as bass player in Ronnie's place, and Robert Plant as lead vocalist. Ronnie Wood had turned down the chance to join the band that would go on to sell over forty million records, world wide.

On the other hand, he did go on to become a Rolling Stone. Which was all he'd ever wanted.

When the Jeff Beck Band returned from that second American tour, they played a 'welcome-home' gig at London's psychedelic hot-spot, the Middle Earth Club in Chalk Farm: Rhythm & Blues meets the Hobbit, unthinkable only a year or so before. Beck was confident enough to refuse a follow-up series of American dates that Peter Grant had provisionally booked over Christmas. No problem - Grant simply sent Jimmy Page and The New Yardbirds instead.

Of course, they weren't called The New Yardbirds any more, courtesy of a remark made by Keith Moon. "You'll go down in the States like a lead Zeppelin," he joked, and the name stuck. The rest, as they say, was history.

Beck wasn't worried about his old mate taking over the tour. Why, he'd even heard that Page was actually employing the same stage antics as former Creation lead guitarist, Eddie Phillips - using a violin bow, for example - and look what happened to him: ding ding.

Besides, Beck was busy buying himself a new house, in true rock-star fashion; a secluded mansion in the heart of the countryside, into which he would move with current girlfriend, Truth cover star, fashionable model, and one day, friend to cats, Celia Hammond.

Ronnie and Krissie were also on the move again, this time to the Gloucester Place flat belonging to Ten Years After guitarist, Alvin Lee, who was off with his band to improve their own American profile.

"We got notice to quit the earlier flat for some reason," Krissie recollects. "Kim (Gardiner) knew Alvin's girlfriend, Lorraine, very well, so really it was Kim who got everything sorted. It took a lot of the pressure off. Ronnie was due to go back to America with Jeff soon, and once again, we wouldn't have to worry about rent money. We scraped together what money we had and planned a big party for my 21st birthday in February, a few days before the band was due to fly out. Everyone was going to be there."

Even given that Ronnie's always been a free-spender, and touring can be expensive if you will keep on buying drinks for everyone, the lesson was plain. Jeff Beck was living the rock-star lifestyle, while Ronnie was relying on handouts. Nor were the rest of the band much better off, except for Rod Stewart whose manager had shrewdly negotiated a separate contract and in any event, was due to issue his first solo album.

So Ronnie and Krissie moved into Gloucester Place, looking like a Romany Dr Doolittle and a pagan, blonde high priestess - for they took with them a small menagerie and Krissie had embraced New Age fashion with a vengeance - especially beaded headbands, belts, flowing silks and scarves. It was a look Ronnie loved. So much so, that due to his fashionably slim frame he would raid Krissie's wardrobe in order to supplement his own. "They would fight over who was to wear which jacket or scarf!" friend Susie Cunningham laughed.

"Krissie and me both had these big Afghan overcoats," she admits with a blush, "we used to do the rounds - Kensington Market, Biba, Mary Quant - because the coats were big enough to hide masses of clothes. I mean, I'm ashamed to admit it, but we shoplifted in all of them. We would come out of the changing room wearing six pairs of silk and satin trousers and all these bright coloured, velvet jackets.

"I'd go round for Krissie and Ronnie would be wearing them! I know Krissie says that The Faces' flamboyant style all stems from this period. She would also say she made a lot of hers and Ronnie's clothes, but honestly, back then she couldn't sew a fucking button on, bless her!

"Everything was nicked, because that was what you did! It was all a great laugh. But they did have the most awful, screaming rows over who was going to wear what."

Back to the menagerie. In addition to the goldfish, Krissie and Ronnie bought a parrot called Sadie, who really could fly on LSD, although usually into the nearest wall; various cats who remained stubbornly drug-free; and now they were the proud owners of the dog that came courtesy of Jimi Hendrix - a Basset Hound puppy called Loopy.

Krissie was still working on Harvey Goldsmith's poster stall in Kensington Market, when one day Ronnie arrived after having visited Hendrix. "I'll never forget it" says Krissie, "He had this long velvet coat and the puppy's head was just poking above his collar. Jimi was going back and forth to America so often he couldn't look after it properly. So he'd asked Ronnie if he'd like it, and Ronnie being a soft-touch and loving animals said yes, even though we already had a parrot, cats and everything else to look after, and were just about managing to feed ourselves. I remember Ronnie standing there, saying "Can we keep it, Kris? Can we?" I knew he'd already made up his mind anyway. Jimi had called the puppy Ethel, but Ronnie re-named it Loopy because he said he couldn't see himself standing in the park shouting "Ethel! Ethel! Come here, Ethel!" Nor could I for that matter."

The band reunited on 14th January for a single gig at the Marquee Club, before starting sessions for the follow-up album to Truth, and their third American tour. Chris Welch in Melody Maker described the gig as "a little rough", but went on to say that "the band was happily different and unpretentious, and once they developed a head of steam, could blow many a group off stage." Following which Beck, displaying his customary loyalty and tact, stated that the whole band "are lazy bastards" except for himself, naturally. He also blamed the rustiness on the long Christmas lay-off: "You'll never find the Jeff Beck Band rehearsing." It hadn't seemed to have occurred to him that if true, this was as much a comment on his leadership and Peter Grant's management, as on the musicians in the band.

In early February, the band played one more gig, a relatively low-key affair as much for practice as anything else, at the Tally Ho Pub at Tolworth - one of those vast booze 'n music establishments far removed from ancient timbers, thatched roofs and warm beer. Something more like the roadhouse bars of North America.

A day or so later, the band entered the Kingsway Recording Studios to begin sessions for the album to be called "Beck-Ola", produced by the ubiquitous Mickie Most.

A tad early for post-modern irony, the name merely sounded naff. Which was as it should be, because the record itself was destined to be one of those truly awful albums that only the most convinced fan needs. Cover versions of "Jail House Rock" and "All Shook Up" showed not just a complete lack of imagination, but a level of laziness that beggars belief. The other group-penned tracks were given such throw away titles as "Hangman's Knee", "Rice Pudding" and "Spanish Boots", which strongly suggested they were all written in the studio with one eye on the clock. The only half-decent numbers were the Nicky Hopkins original "Girl From Mill Valley" and the Beck, Wood, and Stewart track "Plynth (Water Down The Drain)" a forerunner to The Faces song, "Plynth (Stranger Than Fiction)".

It couldn't have escaped Ronnie's attention that for Beck to release such a lacklustre alum so soon after the appalling "Hi, Ho Silver Lining" was nothing short of disastrous and could easily have sent Beck to the end of the pier cabaret circuit, a fate that had befallen many.

It was a fact not lost on the ambitious Stewart either, a man who still holds a somewhat tainted view of the whole Jeff Beck saga. He spoke about it in a retrospective conversation with Pete Frame and said, "It was a great band to sing with, but I couldn't stand all the aggravation and unfriendliness that developed. It was getting too ridiculous for words near the end; we were trying to hide from each other all the time. Do you know that in the two and a half years I was with Beck, I never once looked him in the eye… I always looked at his shirt or something like that."

Beck's views were equally disparaging, particularly about the friendship between Ronnie and Rod. "Before the friendship between Rod and Ronnie cemented, everything was great and we were all over the moon about what was happening. Then they started acting like a couple of girls together and I couldn't handle that idiot kind of girlie humour. We were all self-destructing then and I didn't want to go on much longer with those silly vibes."

Beck also defended the album and said "Beck-Ola" was the first heavy metal album to ever be recorded. The true title of the album was in fact "Cosa Nostra Beck Ola" which when translated means "our cause." However, the record label hated it, so that was hidden away on the rear of the album sleeve. The "Beck Ola" part was apparently a nickname Beck was given by Peter Grant. "He called me that after the old Rockola jukeboxes," Beck admits, "the Cosa Nostra part was a Mickie Most suggestion, he thought it had a sinister overtone to it, which of course it didn't. He said it suited the band's music."

The album's sleeve also bore a message presumably written by Beck, which reads "Today with all the hard competition in the music business it's almost impossible to come up with anything totally original, so we haven't." Which pretty much summed up the whole sorry episode.

"The writing was clearly on the wall after that," Ronnie says, "I knew it was just about over and so did Rod."

Krissie's 21st birthday was on 11th February and by all accounts, it was a good party, despite only half as many of Ronnie and Krissie's rock musician A listers showing up as had originally promised. Oh, and Ronnie receiving a downer of a phone call.

The party was in full swing when the phone rang. Not the neighbours complaining about the noise, but Peter Grant wanting to speak to Ronnie: "We won't be needing you for the American tour," Grant said casually. "You and Micky Waller have been sacked."

As Beck later explained to the music press, he'd noticed that Ronnie and Micky's playing had deteriorated over the last couple of gigs. Hang on - hadn't he called the entire band "lazy bastards?" So what about Rod and keyboard player Nicky Hopkins? What indeed. It later emerged that Hopkins disliked Micky Waller intensely and according to the drummer, Hopkins could be an arch-trouble maker at times.

"That was the reason I was fired," Waller insists today, "they also didn't like Ronnie and Rod teaming up. I wasn't surprised I was dropped, but I was surprised he sacked Ronnie."

Krissie remembers that night very clearly: "Ronnie was standing talking to Rod after the phone call, except he was so shocked he hardly could talk - especially so soon after turning down Jimmy Page's offer to join Led Zeppelin; I think Micky is right, Jeff didn't like Ronnie's friendship with Rod."

Ronnie's own theory backs this up. "I still feel now as I did then, total disbelief. But I just smiled when I got the news and thought, "Thanks very much for Krissie's present, Jeff." But firing both Micky and me on the same day? I remember saying to Micky, "You're a great drummer, and we're a good rhythm section, I don't give a fuck if they fire me, but if they've got rid of us both, something's seriously wrong."

"Actually, I think it was more Jeff's management, although Rod reckoned it was down to Jeff that I got the sack, and it was Nicky Hopkins who got rid of Micky.

"Jeff never liked Rod and me together because he couldn't understand our sense of humour, he always felt left out, and thought we were always taking the piss out of him because he had these hideous yellow spots. We weren't at all, but he was paranoid.

"Well, not all the time anyway. I mean, he always thought we were talking about him behind his back, so the Oxford Street Mafia got rid of me. All Grant and Most liked doing was wheeling and dealing and keeping Jeff happy. "You can just see them saying, "Okay, Jeff, let's get another rhythm section, Jeff, anything you fucking want, Jeff, you're the fucking star." But it didn't work and they had to come crawling back a few weeks later, going "Oh, Ronnie, ple-e-e-ase, we need you, please can you come back?" Cunts!"

Micky Waller was a little less-bothered by Beck or Hopkins or the Oxford Street boys: "I couldn't have cared less. I'd already played with a lot better musicians and a lot better bands than Beck, I'd only joined so I could tour the States. I've never missed Beck to this day, he was too weird. I do remember Ronnie was very upset, but I always thought Krissie was upset a whole lot more. She liked Ronnie playing with that band, she always liked high-profile musicians; she was a bit of a groupie really."

Ronnie's replacement was an unknown bass player from New Zealand called Douglas Blake, whose only claim to fame was that he played with gloves on. Maybe he came from the North Island and felt the cold. Maybe he was just pretentious. But at least he was an unknown, and therefore, no possible threat to Beck.

Micky Waller's replacement was Tony Newman from Sounds Incorporated who could play pretty well and wasn't disliked by Nicky Hopkins. But the new line-up obviously needed to rehearse, so Beck's first five US dates were cancelled. This would give the band a full week to practice before picking up the tour in Boston.

Meanwhile, a somewhat disillusioned Ronnie managed to pick up a couple of sessions with the new Apple Records signing, The Ivey's - a band that went on to become Badfinger. Say what you will, the boy's been hired and fired by the best. Ronnie did toy with the idea of joining up with Micky Waller, who'd wasted no time in forming a power trio called The Silver Meteors with American and former Blue Cheer guitarist, Leigh Stevens.

"Leigh had moved from L.A. to live in England," Micky explains, "and we'd become good mates when I'd gone to California. So one night I took him and his girlfriend, Liz, over to meet Krissie and Ron. They got on really well and we all spent a lot of time hanging out together. Ronnie was out of work, but he never asked to join and I didn't think to ask. I eventually got Pete Sears in on bass and later on a singer called Harry Reynolds."

Rock musicians seem to have their own, unique way of getting together in a band: they sniff around each other, like stray dogs, one waiting to be asked to join, the other waiting to be asked if so-and-so can join. Or perhaps 'kids in a playground' is a better analogy, since stray dogs rarely play such mind games.

Micky Waller also took Ronnie and Krissie to see Ronnie Lane at a cottage the Small Faces' bassist had just rented: "I picked them up in my Mini one day and we went up to see him just for something to do. Lane was rehearsing up there with Kenney Jones and Ian McLagan. Steve Marriott had recently left and had said some nasty things about them in the press. Ronnie was pissed off about Beck and they were all pissed off with Marriott who'd gone off and formed Humble Pie, so Ronnie was in a similar position to them. They were all sort of directionless."

Lane for one was totally unaware quite how fateful that meeting would be: "I didn't really know Ronnie. I'd seen him around Steve Marriott's now and then - he always had this big smile on his face, and I always remembered him as The Smiling Head." Ronnie knew that Marriott had ignominiously left his three old band mates stating publicly that he, "wanted to play with real musicians who played real music," which Ronnie thought was a little mean. He was also intrigued to learn that Lane, McLagan and Jones were determined to stay together, moreover thinking of it a fresh start - they'd even joked about calling the new group Slim Chance.

"When Steve (Marriott) left," Lane remembered shortly before his death, "I thought the hardest thing in the world would be to assemble a group of guys who would get on well together musically and socially. So why break up a friendship with the others, that had grown really strong after working together for five years? We decided to stick with each other and hunt around for a guitar player."

That day, courtesy of Micky Waller, the three remaining Small Faces found one. Only they didn't know it yet.

As it was, Ronnie returned to London with the comforting knowledge that at least he wasn't the only one starting afresh. Over the next few days, he was equally comforted by a series of postcards from Rod Stewart in America, saying how miserable the band was without him and that Beck had already fallen out with Ronnie's replacement.

The real icing on the cake came a few days later, with the news that after only one try-out gig in Virginia, Blake had been sacked. This resulted in yet more shows being cancelled, including Boston. With a contracted tour stretching into April, Beck and Grant were facing the mother of all lawsuits: they'd have to pay dear for the privilege of losing their own appearance money.

Grant called Ronnie again.

"That was great, I dictated my own terms, I'll never forget it. They were really fucked and the tour was on the line. So I said, "I want two fucking grand a gig." You could hear him swallowing on the other end of the phone."

Grant and Beck had no choice. Ronnie knew the repertoire and perhaps more importantly, he knew how to play with Beck. Ronnie was known and he already had his own group of fans (one other reason, perhaps, why Beck had come to treat him so shabbily). Still there was nothing for it - Ronnie and his demands would have to be endured.

He flew out on the first available flight and joined the tour party for two shows at the Psychedelia Ballroom in Chicago, on 14th and 15th March 1969. He wasn't exactly welcomed with open arms. The management were openly resentful.

"Vibes were decidedly hostile," Rod Stewart remembers, "and Ronnie was well pissed-off with it - you could tell he was just using the group as filler while he looked for another band."

Even so, the tour was a commercial success - and Ronnie managed to meet up with his wandering landlord, Alvin Lee, when the band played alongside Ten Years After and the Moody Blues at the Shrine auditorium in Los Angeles.

Then came the infamous San Diego Pop Festival in April, and a line-up that included fellow playing Brits, Savoy Brown and the legendary John Mayall's Bluesbreakers. Ronnie and the rest of the group watched in horror the chaos caused by massive overcrowding; fights broke out, police helicopters buzzing angrily overhead, and police on horseback tried to corral the crowd.

Beck took the mini-riot personally and cancelled the rest of the tour, promising to return yet again in May and so make amends to various angry promoters and disappointed fans. He was later quoted as saying that the cancellation was necessary in order to concentrate on developing material for a new album. Tour insiders put it down mainly to the escalating ill-feeling between Beck and Ronnie - whose £2,000 per gig, say £8,000 in today's money, came directly out of Beck's own cut - plus Beck's knee-jerk reaction to a typical American riot.

When "Beck-Ola" was finally released (June 1969 in America, December in Britain), the five original tracks (only seven in all) credited Ronnie Wood and Nicky Hopkins four times; Rod Stewart three times; and Jeff Beck and Tony Newman (the drummer) once.

In other words, Beck hadn't contributed a great deal in words or music. Arrangements and brilliant guitar-work, yes, but always with Mickie Most having the final say. Which suggests another reason why Beck and Grant were prepared to pay Ronnie £2,000 a gig: they were playing his songs. Incidentally, this would be the first time that Ronnie and Rod

Stewart wrote together, a partnership that would stand them in good stead in the not-too-distant future.

Back in London, the band trouped into the Kingsway Recording Studios again, slightly handicapped by a Swedish film crew shooting a documentary about the genius of Mickie Most.

A studio full of serious-minded Swedes gave Ronnie the excuse to duck out of recording and spend time jamming with Lane, McLagan and Jones again. There was no real discussion about Ronnie joining the other three, only the occasional 'what if,' or 'one day, who knows?' Musicians do that sort of thing very well.

"We jammed together and we weren't very good," Ronnie Lane was to later recall. "Ronnie was all right, not brilliant, but we thought why not? We never expected him to turn out as good as he is now. He'd been mainly playing bass, so his guitar playing had lapsed a bit and to be honest, we wondered if he was the man for the job."

Ronnie played live with Beck on 25th April, when the band headlined at the Lyceum Ballroom in London. On 2nd May, the band returned to the States still with Ronnie, to make good their promise to play all cancelled gigs.

This was the fourth time the band had gone to the States in less than a year and Krissie was feeling lonely. Still, the extra money Ronnie was earning slightly made up for it - and it certainly helped her feel more secure. They'd made a deal with each other whereby the first big money Ronnie made, he would buy a Revox reel-to-reel tape recorder, and then put down a deposit on a house.

Ronnie and Krissie had been together for four years and Krissie was very comfortable with their secure and loving partnership. She was also more than happy with her role as the loyal woman who went out to work in order to help her lover's career take off. Behind every successful man, etc, etc.

Not for her was the worry of Ronnie's continuing high profile driving a wedge between them. Which it has to be said is an age-old problem that's faced many a couple at some time or another: everything is wonderful and romantic when they're both struggling, but when fame and fortune arrives for one of them, everything changes. Not quite Good-bye, Baby, and Amen, but close.

This transition has made many partnerships wobble. But Krissie, whose childhood had taught her independence, reacted slightly differently. The closest she could get to Ronnie's whirlwind existence, except on the rare occasions he was home, was to meet their mutual friends at clubs like the Speakeasy - which she could now afford to visit often, since for the first time Ronnie's wage packet matched his profile. Krissie knew Ronnie's accelerating success was now due more to his talent than her financial support, but she was genuinely happy for him.

Krissie was a regular face about town, flitting from one party or club to another.

There was always someone on the London club scene who'd either just seen Ronnie on tour, or had even played on the same bill. The well wishers and good-natured gossip would help fill in the gaps between his letters and it enabled Krissie to bask in Ronnie's reflective glory.

She was now part of an elite social circle where Ronnie was fast becoming a major player and it felt good. She mixed with stars like The Beatles and their Beatle wives, The Rolling Stones and The Who all of whom now accepted Ronnie unquestionably and by association, Krissie too - and to all intents and purposes, she deserved to be. After all, Krissie had grown up with people like Pete Townshend and other Ealing Art School alumni like Richard Barnes, who'd re-named Towshend's group The High Numbers The Who. She'd even known Jeff Beck when he was in the lowly support band to The Birds and if that wasn't proof enough, well how about Jimi Hendrix giving them a dog. Yes, Krissie was one of the beautiful people all right.

One evening towards the end of May, Krissie and long-time friend, Susie Cunningham, arrived at the Speakeasy, and were sitting alone at a table when a familiar figure walked up.

"Hi - do you remember me?" Which was a slightly silly question, under the circumstances. Krissie looked up at Eric Clapton. "Of course I do." After all, a woman rarely forgets the man to whom she lost her virginity.

Clapton stayed and chatted. Susie went home alone. Krissie went home with her first lover.

"It was a spur of the moment thing," Krissie was to say many years later. "But to this day, I don't know why I did it. I had no reason to believe that Ronnie had ever been unfaithful to me. Maybe it was just this thing of the first real boyfriend, someone who was there at the right time. Except it was the wrong time, I suppose. But what you have to understand is how different things were in those days. Everyone was just sort of floating around, feeling that freedom. It was all that mattered."

Only years later would Krissie and her friends realise that monogamy isn't a type of wood, or a board game. 1967 had been the Summer of Love, and people had swallowed the hippy myth hook, line and sinker. If it felt good, do it. Spontaneity was god. As of course was Clapton, according to that year's London graffiti. So who could blame the girl?

The cynical might suspect that most people were more interested in sex for its own sake than as a political, religious or spray-painted statement. That all the high ideals were mainly an excuse, often self-delusion, for getting one's rocks off. Which of course they were - when was it ever any different?

That said, little digressions are always best kept to one's self and Krissie had the good sense never to tell Ronnie. Unfortunately for Krissie, that little episode established a pattern that would eventually go on to destroy her's and Ronnie's relationship.

CHAPTER NINE

"I WOULD HAVE KEPT THE BAND TOGETHER JUST TO PLAY WOODSTOCK."

With all contractual dates covered, the Jeff Beck Group returned home in early May with a clean slate. Joe Cocker and the Grease Band had supported them for four nights at the Fillmore East, and by the Nice for the remainder of the tour. It was looking like (in America at least) they could do no wrong.

The band played a sold out home-coming party at the Marquee, which also celebrated the America-only release of the single "Plynth (Water Down The Drain)" written by Hopkins, Stewart and Wood and it was here that Mickie Most enlisted their help in boosting the American profile of another one of his acts.

Singer songwriter Donovan had done well on the British and European circuits; however, Americans tended to see him as a pale imitation of Bob Dylan.

Most was trying to harden up Donovan's image by pushing for a more 'rockier' approach. It was a route Donovan was more than happy to follow, having momentarily tired of his own whimsical, lightweight pop profile.

Eager to reach America's growing Adult Orientated Rock market, he jumped at the chance of joining up with Beck. "It was totally Mickie's Most's idea," Donovan charitably remembers. "And it turned into the most extraordinary session I ever did."

Donovan duly reported to Advision Studios, where he was surprised to find that drummer, Micky Waller, had taken the session-player's shilling, instead of Tony Newman. Actually, any student of the era knows that Micky Waller turned up absolutely everywhere, mainly because he was simply the best drummer for hire. Which made Beck and Grant sacking him all the more suspicious.

"He (Waller) was giving the skins a fair old wallop of a drum groove, and it suited the song perfectly," Donovan says today, still the archetypal hippy. "I said, "Hey, Micky, How ya' doin'? Ya heard the song, then?" And he replied; "Haven't heard a bloody thing." And I said, "But that's the drum pattern for the song," And Micky said, "Well, you're all right, then."

"Nicky Hopkins was the next to show, a thin and waif-like character. He asked me to sing the song while he read a Silver Surfer comic book. There were only two chords, and Nicky got my funky groove down and he liked the jazz, and never said another word after that, the whole session." Of course, Donovan had no way of knowing that Hopkins had been instrumental in ousting the easy-going Waller from the Beck band touring line-up. Or any of the other politics that had so bedevilled the group's existence.

"Woody arrived next with Rod Stewart. It was the first time I'd ever met Ron. Mickie Most had laid on these little snacks and fine wines, but they both looked hungover from the night before. I thought it was funny how a lot of great guitar players had taken on the bass part in bands over the years - there's always too many pickers to go around. I remember Beck's guitar was locked in the van, so Most rented him one, and Jeff asked for any old Fender. When Jeff cut into a riff for the intro, it just left me breathless.

"Then the whole band just followed on two phrases and the arrangement and it was all there. Madeleine Bell and Lesley Duncan sang back-up vocals and the whole thing came together as easy as that. I wrote most of the song on the spot and the whole thing was done in six hours."

The absolute cool of Ron Wood moved the song along - powerful but controlled madness. The final track was christened Goo-Goo Barabajagal, which summed up the song's on-the-spot spontaneity perfectly. Beck was less impressed and said in an interview with the New Musical Express, "Let's be fair, a song with a title like that isn't something you sit at home playing for six weeks."

True - but it was a quirky little masterpiece, dominated by Ronnie's fluid bass lines and Micky Waller's voodoo drumming. "I recorded another three tracks with Woody, one called the "Stromberg Twins" which was about carburettors, hot rod cars and two Jewish twin girl fans that Ronnie knew. Jeff was into hot-rods and I guess the song was about him. The other tracks were "Trudi (Bed With Me)" and "Home-sickness".

"Ronnie was this artful dodger character, always was, always will be. He epitomises that street-grin of British rock. His playing is superb. He's able to change from rhythm to lead in the classic style that Brian Jones taught to Keith Richards."

Goo-Goo Barabajagal was a unique and extremely successful example of a mixing of musical styles and performers - the Hippy Troubadour meets Guitar Hero Rock Star. It was also one of Most's inspired projects as a producer.

The unanswered question is why Beck and Donovan never recorded a follow-up, as this one record was to prove both their last flirtations with the hit singles chart. The other slight mystery is that according to the record's label copy, Tony Newman played drums. So, either Donovan was totally mistaken, or Micky Waller's playing was later wiped.

Donovan remains adamant it was Waller that played on the track and that the whole experience with Beck whetted his appetite to experiment with a heavier sound. He decided to form a band, and set about recruiting likely or suitable collaborators.

His first port of call was the three remaining Small Faces, still holed up in Ronnie Lane's cottage. "I thought here was a ready made band without a record deal or a front man, it looked perfect."

So Donovan set off to Lane's with high hopes; he would ask them to become his backing band.

The point about Donovan is that he really was and is a genuinely nice man; naïve yes, but nice nonetheless - far too nice to have ever become involved with three strutting little mods from the East End. Unfortunately for Donovan, they must have felt the same way. It's at this point the story takes on an almost fairy tale-like quality. Picture if you will the foppishly dressed Hippy minstrel strolling dreamily up to the idyllic country cottage that contained the little people. Only these little people weren't jolly faced munchkins busily chopping wood. Oh no, these were three totally embittered, industry weary ex-mods from London's East End.

All three sat in a stunned silence as Donovan outlined his plan and put forward his kind and well-meant offer. It was, after all, the solution to their present directionless, wasn't it? All three thought not, and Donovan scurried from the little cottage with laughter ringing in his ears. It had been Ronnie Lane who'd finally broken the silence when he'd so succinctly put it: "Fuck off mate!" And with that, Donovan resumed his solo career.

Apollo 10 splashed down safely in the Pacific on 26th May, the same month that the Fab Four had fittingly released "Get Back" - a title that also summed up Ronnie's mood. He knew it was only a matter of time before he'd once again be deemed as surplus to requirements by Beck and his management.

He was also getting tired of playing bass. What isn't always realised is that behind that street-urchin grin, Ronnie can be single-minded to the point of ruthlessness when it comes to his own career, especially when he could combine an interesting career move by helping out family, namely his older brother, Art.

Life had not been good to Art recently. Basically, he was bored. It hadn't been quite as easy to settle down in a normal job as he'd hoped. The music was still calling him. Art explained, "The Artwoods had long since broken up, yet for some unfathomable reason, Fontana had kept an option open on me which eventually I thought I'd exercise.

"They gave me free rein of a studio and said "Come up with some new stuff." The trouble was I didn't have a band anymore, so I asked Ron if he'd help out. Naturally, he said yes and he also said he thought little Ronnie Lane might help out too. He said yes and then the other Little Faces said well, we've got nothing to do either so we'll come along as well. So that's what they did, bless them.

"I remember Ronnie Lane turning up on his bicycle and hanging his clips on the studio hat-stand. Rod Stewart turned up with Ronnie and we made up these songs on the spot: "Engine 4444" and "Diamond Joe".

"More bleedin' songs about trains! Rod and me did this call and response vocal and Ronnie made up the tune. It was very close to how The Faces ended up sounding - obviously because it was the same players, but they didn't know they were going to be a band at that point, if you know what I mean. All that came out of it was to show up how much better a singer Rod was than me, which was not a good idea when you're doing your own demos. It was like: "That's very nice Art - but who's the other bloke singing? He's good, you're crap".

"We recorded another two songs, one called "Right Around The Thumb" and another one called "Two Steps To Mother" - bloody silly titles. I called the group Art Wood's Quiet Melon and took the demos to Fontana and sure enough, they hated them. They said it was uncommercial and unreleasable rubbish and you can't have any more studio time. I said, "Charming! Well I've done my bit, it's not my fault you hate them.""

What Ronnie and Rod Stewart had realised while helping Art was how fed-up with the Jeff Beck situation they really were. Quiet Melon provided some much-needed light relief, as well as helping Ronnie cement his relationship with the three remaining Small Faces. Whether Lane, McLagan and Jones knew it, Ronnie was now intent on pulling them all together in a new group.

There was no record deal in the offing, but Quiet Melon had all got on (and played) well together; well enough to agree to look for some live work. Easier said than done - they could only find one agent throughout London who was remotely interested in putting them on his books.

Rufus Manning managed to find them work at the Oxford and Cambridge May Balls. They were originally meant to support former Ike'ette (and former girlfriend of Steve Marriott), PP Arnold, with Kim Gardiner standing in for an absent Ronnie Lane, but for some reason Arnold pulled out at the last minute.

"We were on two hundred quid for the night," Art reminisces, "which was good money. We played for three-quarters of an hour, doing mainly standards plus a few of our own songs, a lot of blues numbers, and then came off stage, ready for a beer... which actually meant everyone having more than a few drinks and throwing these strawberry pies at each other. Then the promoter came up and said that PP Arnold wasn't going to play, and would we mind going back on for another £250? We were back up there in seconds. Afterwards, Kenney came up to me and said, "Thanks, Art, that's the first time me fruit bowl's going to be full in weeks!".".

That initial camaraderie survived into the Faces, becoming one of their biggest on-stage assets. However, the Quiet Melon experiment soon petered out; ironically, the very same week the New Musical Express printed the official announcement of the band's formation. Press ads were scrapped and business cards went un-issued.

"I suddenly thought, sod this for a living!" Art admits, "I packed it in and went to join Ted in his graphic design business, which he ran in conjunction with his part-time jazz career. He ended up doing quite a long stint as singer/drummer with the Temperance Seven."

Today, Art can still be coaxed out to play the occasional set - just try stopping him - with a revamped Quiet Melon Two, which also features ex-Kinks drummer, Mick Avory. Ted sadly passed away in 2003 after returning full-time to music as the drummer in Bob Kerr's Whoopee Band.

So Ronnie appeared on two single releases that year. The first was the aforementioned "Plynth (Water Down The Drain)" backed by the inexplicable cover version of "Jail House Rock" and "Goo Goo Barabajagal". "Plynth" was a US-only release, which despite the Beck group's live success in the States, failed to chart. This prompted Nicky Hopkins to throw an artistic tantrum and leave the band. He relocated to California, where he would carve out a respectable career as a session musician before joining the Quicksilver Messenger Service... which was a group, not a courier company. He too passed away in 1993.

"Goo Goo Barabajagal" fared a lot better. Released on both sides of the Atlantic, it reached number twelve in the UK - two places higher than "Hi-Ho Silver Lining" and number 36 in the US. None of which worried Ronnie one jot, he had already effectively moved on. He was now spending a great deal of his time in the company of Lane, Mclagan, and Jones and had all but dismissed Beck from his future plans. Almost, but not quite; there was still a little matter of another US tour - and £2,000 a gig, was not to be sniffed at.

On 7th June, Melody Maker printed the rumour that: "Ron Wood is joining the Small Faces, as a replacement for Steve Marriott. No definite date has been set, but Ron has been rehearsing with the group recently."

The rumour was partly right: Ron had indeed joined up with the remnants of the Small Faces, every Sunday morning in fact, to play a kick-about game of football in Marple Hill Park, on the banks of the Thames, calling themselves the Richmond Spasmodicals.

"I don't know who started it," says fellow team-mate, Rick Cunningham, (still married to Krissie Wood's life-long friend, Susie), "but it began with just a few people turning up for a laugh on a Sunday morning before going to the pub at lunch-time. It became almost ritualistic and the local kids joined in; sometimes there would be about twenty of us divided into two teams! It wasn't real football, of course.

"I think Kenney Jones turned up twice; he wasn't into football. I remember the first day that Rod Stewart turned up because Woody and Mac were always saying to him, "why don't you come down, it'll be a laugh", but he never would, even though Rod loves his football. Then one day he did, he turned up fully kitted out, a brand new strip, new boots the lot.

"Everyone else played in jeans and a tee shirt and he pulls up in his little yellow sports car wearing a full football kit; he even had shin pads. He came across from the car park, which was about a hundred and fifty to two hundred yards away from the field, and he's bouncing up and down, doing physical jerks, you know the whole warm up bit.

"Someone booted the ball over to him and he went to kick it back and tripped right over it, spraining his ankle. It was his first touch of the ball; it was hysterical! Everyone cracked up laughing as he limped off back to his car and drove off.

"It couldn't have happened to a better person really, he was all Jack the Lad, the only one who could actually play football, because none of us could. When we saw him later down the pub everyone tried to be really sympathetic, but they couldn't stop sniggering and once again he just roared off home, he never showed up after that."

In June the news that Brian Jones had been rather ungraciously fired from The Rolling Stones made the headlines. Mick Jagger and Keith Richards had drawn up a short-list of possible replacements which, thanks to the rumours of a split with Beck, included Ronnie Wood. Not that he ever found out until a long, long time later.

"I was round at my mum's one afternoon and there was this phone call apparently from Mick asking what I was doing. I thought it was a wind-up, an impostor doing an impersonation, which isn't as ridiculous as it seems. People have been doing impersonations of him forever. So I thought I'm not going to get caught out here, so I said sorry mate I'm busy, and the voice on the other end said "Oh well then, we'll see you around". I mean, I had no idea Mick ran the Stones that way, but of course it was him, fuck it!"

In the meantime, Jeff Beck managed to coax together the remaining members of his Group. It was tour time again and America was calling. Actually, this trip to the States was more of a goodwill gesture to the various promoters Beck had repeatedly let down on previous visits.

At the first gig in Central Park, Beck played the Star Spangled Banner some six weeks before Jimi Hendrix was to immortalise his version at Woodstock. This was followed by the obligatory appearance at The Fillmore East, where according to Ronnie the Group finally began to break up.

"Tony Newman was becoming increasingly annoyed about his salary; he'd have been even more upset if he'd known how much I was making. He was beginning to talk insurrection and mutiny."

The real crunch, however, came not from Newman but from a phone-call from former-Yardbird roadie Bruce Wayne, who was now working for Beck favourites Vanilla Fudge. It transpired that their guitar player, Vinnie Martell, had been taken ill just as the band were due to record a lucrative advertising jingle. Wayne asked Beck to step in.

He did, and the subsequent Beck version of "Things Go Better With Coke" was played across America throughout the rest of the year.

The significant thing about that was, Beck had finally got his chance to play with the Fudge's rhythm section, Tim Bogert and Carmine Appice.

Never one to miss an opportunity, Beck talked to the pair about forming a new group together. The first time Beck met Bogert and Appice had been at the London Astoria back in October 1968, and it was his enthusiasm for the Americans even then that led to Ronnie quitting and teaming up with The Creation. "I thought back then, fuck this, I'm not hanging around to get sacked and now I was watching as history started to repeat itself."

Except things were never that simple with Beck, as Rod Stewart attests. "It was all being done under our noses, which was bad. The original idea was that Jeff wanted me to join him and the Vanilla Fudge guys, Carmine and Bogert. We were having these awkward meetings throughout the tour, and it made the atmosphere unbearable. Christ, it could have been an immaculate group, a world class group but there was too many differences. They were hard workers and wanted to work seven nights a week, which Jeff didn't want to know about. Jeff said, "we've got to rehearse in England, because I'm not doing it in the States." Then of course they said, "we're in the US and we're not going to England." It was a stand-off basically and no one was giving in and all this was happening in front of Ronnie. I knew he wasn't going to hang about for all that."

On the other hand, to be fair to Beck, he must have heard the rumours of Ronnie joining the Small Faces which, given the money he was paying him, it might well have seemed a little ungrateful. Especially as Ronnie never confronted him about anything he was unhappy about. Then again, Beck never asked either. Perhaps the deeper truth was that in Beck's mind, he'd always intended the group to be a collective of coming and going players. A rolling roster of talent whose only function was to highlight his own undoubted talent.

Beck stayed on in the US with his new fudge friends while the rest of the group flew home for a week's break. Ronnie arrived home to find that Fleet Street was still having a feeding frenzy on the rotting corpse of Brian Jones' reputation.

Everyone, from chauffeur to school friend, was crawling out of the woodwork, offering exclusive stories about Jones' debauched life. Ronnie was intrigued that one man could still so dominate the headlines, little realising that his own time to be dissected by the media was not that far distant. He also felt a great sadness for Jones, and not just because the Stones were his favourite band.

"It's all fantasy situations, all hindsight, but I always used to think that if only I'd known Brian when he was going through all his troubles. Maybe I could have helped him. Mind you, I used to think the same thing about Elvis too - that all I'd have had to do was get him away from all those bodyguards and doctors, that all he really needed was a mate! I suppose that's what you do with heroes, isn't it? Of course, on today's scene I don't think there's anyone worth saving! Except mates left over from the old days; musicians who've paid their fucking dues."

Ronnie also arrived home in time to be approached a second time by the Rolling Stones, this time the call came while he was actually rehearsing with the three Small Faces. The difference this time was he never even got the message.

"We were down at the Stones' practice studio in Bermondsey Street, which was a little street of warehouses near London Bridge," Ronnie winces, "It was Mick again and he was apparently asking if I was still busy. I would have said, "Is sixty seconds too late to show up?" I found out years later that they actually got Ronnie Lane on the phone; who was fully aware of the fact that the Stones were looking for a new guitar player.

"So he answered and said, "Yes, he is! He's quite happy where he is thank you!" I honestly never found out about it until years later when Brian's replacement, Mick Taylor, was about to leave and they wanted someone to replace him! The funny thing is that I coincidentally bumped into Mick and Charlie on the way to the memorial gig they did for Brian. It was just before I re-joined Beck for that last US tour. I was walking around the edge of Hyde Park and they were coming out of their hotel on the other side of the road. I shouted out "Have a good gig" totally ignorant of the fact that it could've been me up there with them."

It seems Ronnie Wood was going to join the Small Faces whether he wanted to or not. Yet, given that Ronnie Lane - by his own admission - was an extremely determined and very shrewd character, he'd have been unlikely to have said "no" to Jagger on Ronnie's behalf unless Ronnie had indicated some sort commitment to them. Or at least, unless Lane, McLagan and Jones thought he had.

So the would-be Stone and the rest of the Beck Group flew back to America to rejoin their leader and perform at the Baltimore Jazz Festival as the somewhat reluctant support act for Led Zeppelin. They were also booked to play the Flushing Meadow Singer Bowl backing up none other than headliners, Vanilla Fudge.

What these ironic engagements did to someone with Beck's fragile psyche is anyone's guess, but by all accounts he carried out his duties admirably.

The tour was planned to end at Woodstock, a three-day open-air extravaganza that according to its promoters, promised to be the music event of the decade. No one in Beck's band knew very much about Woodstock, but the suspicion shared amongst them was that it was going to be huge. The main reason for the tour was to keep on promoting the album "Cosa Nostra - Beck-Ola" which much to Ronnie and (more importantly), Beck's delight had climbed to number fifteen in the US charts.

Ron knew that if Beck appeared at an event the size of Woodstock, it could very easily push it all the way to the top. It was the first time he felt a real sense of excitement come over the band.

"Things looked really good for the group in America on that tour; I even thought spirits were improving. We were selling a lot of albums and building up a strong fan base and just for a minute, I thought it had every chance of going further. We were in the charts at a position that guaranteed The Jeff Beck Group got respectable billing at Woodstock - which you need when there's about a thousand bands playing."

Alas, Ronnie found his new-found optimism was to be short lived. As the tour wound its weary way west, the band's old antagonism towards Beck began afresh.

Things came to a head when they reached Woodstock. Sure enough, the posters and advance publicity listed The Jeff Beck Group prominently alongside the likes of Crosby, Still and Nash, Ten Years After, ex-Artwoods drummer, The Keef Hartley Band (who incidentally took the hippie ethic a tad too far and insisted on no publicity... "just playing for the people man". He also asked to be excused from the event's subsequent movie and soundtrack. Consequently, he now spends his days trying to convince people he was actually there) and headliner, Jimi Hendrix.

Still, there was unrest in the camp.

"It was a few days before Woodstock and we were all sitting round the hotel pool," Ronnie explains. "We had Woodstock on the cards and Tony Newman started a new uprising. It didn't really have anything to do with Jeff, he kept out of it; it was basically Tony against the management, he was calling them all cunts. He was like a union shop steward, getting us all together and saying, "We're not being treated fair, we should get together and fuck that lot off... tell them that we're not going to work unless they give us more money, the cunts." Well, they weren't going to give me any more money - I was already on fucking two grand.

"I didn't know how much Rod was on, and that was all part of the trouble; everyone was on a different deal. It was dog eat dog; everyone looking after themselves. So Tony was trying to lead an uprising, a one man uprising, he was like a slave driver - he wouldn't let it drop. He kept on saying, "Let's make a fucking stand", we had all started to realise just how big Woodstock would be, and he was trying to hold it to ransom, saying "I'm not fucking doing it, how about you Rod? How about you Ron?"

"It was getting really uncomfortable because I was really looking forward to playing it. I knew a lot of the bands that were playing and we were going to be amongst them - who wouldn't have wanted to play it? I had the feeling it was going to be huge; bigger than anything that'd gone before, so I kept out of the way. Then we hear that Tony had gone to the management and said none of us were doing the gig unless we all got more money. So that was the end of it! Nothing else happened after that, the management must have told him to fuck off, so he did. We never heard another thing about it - we were off.

"It was a fucking shame, I would've loved to have kept the band together just to have played Woodstock, but no one said anything; we all just let it slip away. That's how bad the vibes had got - so bad that no one tried to save the situation. The band couldn't have lasted a couple of more hours, let alone days. So we packed up and came home."

Logically speaking, the attitude of manager Peter Grant made absolutely no sense. Until you remember that Beck was heavily courting Vanilla Fudge's rhythm section, and Grant could see far greater potential with Led Zeppelin.

He had far too much invested in those projects alone than to worry about what he saw as a mutinous drummer and a ransom-demanding bass player. What he thought of the singer we don't know, but whatever it was, it wasn't enough to give in to what amounted to unreasonable demands. He had America to conquer and besides, Beck could always pick up another backing band.

"It was weird the way it ended because we never actually broke up, there was no announcement or anything." says Rod Stewart today. "We came back from the American tour and went our separate ways; no one said it was over. I knew Woody had as good as left, but he never came out and said it. I didn't know what I was going to do and I never knew what Jeff was going to do because we never spoke to each other. He'd never asked me if I was going to leave, or go with Woody and I never asked him what he was going to do. so we just drifted apart. Next thing I heard was that Vanilla Fudge had come to England."

A fair summing up, but back in 1970, Rod Stewart had a slightly different slant on things, and had this to say. "Woody and me had all the ideas behind the two albums. We wrote most of the songs, Hopkins as well and Tony Newman. Beck would just come in and put the guitar track on afterwards. He used to call it playing "evergreens", meaning it was the same pattern every time. I'm sure it's why he hasn't got anything together now, because he hasn't got anyone to turn to. Beck's the sort of person who can't take anything on his own shoulders.

"I owe to him exactly what he owed to The Yardbirds. I think he's a great guitarist, better than Jimmy Page or Eric Clapton. You know, he was huge in America, really immense. We'd play on bills with The Moody Blues and Ten Years After and the whole audience would only want Beck. Yet they wouldn't recognise that success in Britain. I think that's why he's so bitter. I suppose having a huge chip on his shoulder didn't endear him to anyone, but not only did he never get recognition in his own country, but even when he was this incredible force abroad, nobody even mentioned it."

It's possible that Stewart was worried at the time that he'd added to both Beck's bitterness and the group's premature demise, by never opening up to the guitar player as a friend, or even as a band member. You'll notice that he certainly doesn't describe their working relationship as being on an equal footing. He ironically talks about Beck in an isolated manner, as if he was a separate entity - aloof and distant. Exactly how the rest of The Faces will come to view him within a few short years.

Curiously, Ronnie emerges as a team player, one of the lads who surely wouldn't do anything to merely feather his own nest; which to all intents and purposes is true.

It's certainly a view producer Shel Talmy holds to this very day.

"I don't think Ronnie ever really thought about any band as a long-term affair, not even the Stones, because even there he wasn't a full member for years. I remember he lived very much for the moment - that's how he manages to give his all in every situation, because it's for the now; not yesterday, not tomorrow, but now. It was the same in those days with The Jeff Beck Group; he would have been there as long as he was wanted, and he would have gone when he wasn't. He would have been just as happy to be back playing lead guitar, with Kim Gardiner on bass, with The Creation."

Beck eventually did get together with Bogert and Appice, but not until years later and not before he'd tried their patience to breaking point with his endless deliberations - forcing them to form their own new group, Cactus. In fact, Beck carried on going about his business in the usual haphazard way for months after his return from America. He tried out several ill-conceived rehearsal groups with the very same disregard and foresight he'd shown when trying to form the very first incarnation of The Jeff Beck Group.

Line-ups included Ace Kefford, brought in as a lead singer, when he was only known as the short-tempered drug-addled former bass player with The Move. He continued his maddening habit of agreeing to gigs, only to cancel them at the last minute and even travelled to Detroit to record a bizarrely-conceived album by Mickie Most. A whole album of Motown covers with, of all people, drummer Cozy Powell - a musician not known for his subtlety, as was demonstrated when Beck and Powell arrived at the studios in Detroit.

"You want the Motown sound?" asked bass-player James Jamerson, when he saw Beck's roadies replacing Kenny Benjamin's modest drum set up with Cozy Powell's shop's worth of kit. "Yes" replied Powell. "Too bad, man. You just took it out."

Ultimately, the finished album was considered so thoroughly wretched by all parties concerned, that it was deemed unfit for public consumption. It was never released.

Still, Mickie Most got something out of it, the singer Suzy Quatro, who he discovered singing in a Detroit bar.

By the autumn of 1970, Beck was seriously considering a Yarbirds reunion, only to be told by their former singer, Keith Relf, that he wasn't in the slightest bit interested.

All this confusion had left the way clear for Led Zeppelin and Jimmy Page to clean up in America. That last tour was the end of Beck's career as a concert headliner. One of Britain's most original musical talents had been consumed by mismanagement and his own ego. Or, as Elton John (then comparatively unknown) said after also trying out with Beck in the summer of that year, "We had rehearsals that went just fine, but if I'd have stayed I would have ended up being known as Jeff Beck's pianist."

Beck returned to England set on promoting the eventual September UK release of the Beck-Ola Cosa Nostra album with a series of press and radio interviews which, as usual, he used as teasers to outline his future plans. During each interview he let it be known that Ronnie Wood no longer featured in his scheme of things, but he hoped to keep Rod, which was news to Rod. He also hinted that two 'name' faces had been chosen as replacements for Ronnie and Tony Newman.

"It'll be big news when it comes together" he chirped "but both replacements are under contract at the moment, so they've got to be careful. Ronnie says he's leaving because he wants to play lead instead of bass, and I wish him the best of luck. There's no bad vibes or anything, like there is with most groups." Which was also news to Ron.

Assuming that the two big names were Bogert and Appice, about the only thing Beck got right was Ronnie wanting to play lead guitar.

CHAPTER TEN
"WE NEED A FUCKING REFEREE."

Throughout September 1969, Ronnie rehearsed every day with the Small Faces in their Bermondsey bunker, thrashing out a handful of hastily compiled new songs and various old soul covers.

Ronnie thought they sounded tight, but they lacked what he described as "a proper vocalist, none of us had a lead vocalist's voice, so the songs would trail off into an improvised jam session, until the rehearsals became almost strictly instrumental run-throughs. You have to remember, Steve Marriott is a hard act to follow.

"We were all too scared to sing, Marriott had one of the best soul voices ever and he was almost impossible to replace. All groups need an identity, and that identity usually stems from the lead singer. I'm not a lead singer, nor was Ronnie Lane. A group needs a sound that is instantly recognisable and that usually stems from the lead singer.

"Take Mick Jagger, for example, he isn't technically a great singer, but you know from his voice that you're listening to a Stones record. Dylan isn't a great singer, but you know right away who you're listening to. We were getting nowhere, so I eventually called Rod and craftily said, come down and see who I'm playing with now!"

As Rod Stewart remembers it, "Ronnie was always hinting that I should come and have a go, he'd say 'Oh the lads are pretty good, but there's no one to sing." To which I'd reply, "Oh, yeah, shame innit!"

Rod had already started work on his first solo album, "An Old Raincoat Won't Let You Down" with American producer, Lou Reizener, who'd signed him for a mere £1,500... which just happened to be the exact price of the aforementioned little yellow sports car which he'd hankered after for months.

"He would have signed for however much the car was," Kenney Jones later commented. "That's how his mind worked then. If the car had been six hundred quid, that's what he would of asked for."

That album, which also featured Ronnie back on lead guitar, would be released in America as the more prosaically titled "Rod Stewart Album".

This was to a set a pattern for any number of British artistes being forced to re-title their albums for the fear that the American public would misconstrue any slang or humour other than their own. And they have a point, as anyone who'd ever asked to buy fags in New York, will testify.

Americans are still convinced that Dick Van Dyke does a perfect Cockney accent and Mickey Dolenz of the Monkees once wrote a song, inspired by Alf Garnett in Till Death Do Us Part, called "Randy Scouse Git". It was banned by the BBC and Dolenz later admitted he had absolutely no idea what it meant. Dolenz eventually re-titled it "Alternative Title."

Its not just music either. The film "The Madness of King George III" had to be re-titled for the US to simply "The Madness of King George" for fear of American audiences wondering why they never got to see Parts I and II.

Anyway, Rod eventually gave in to Ronnie's badgering and decided to visit him and his three new chums at their rehearsals. He arrived giving the impression that he was just passing by, and was certainly not interested in rehearsing with a band he already partly knew from their brief Quiet Melon stint.

Stewart could be forgiven for being a little wary of having any involvement with the three Faces, remembering how the Small Faces had sabotaged the Jeff Beck Group's debut gig on 3rd March at the Finsbury Park Astoria.

YOUNG RONNIE WITH HIS BROTHERS... ART ON THE LEFT, TED ON THE RIGHT. LAWRENCE SHEAF LURKING IN BACKGROUND

THE RONALD WOOD SHOW

YOUNG TELEVISON ART CHAMP

RONNIE AND BUSTER

KIM GARDINER'S FIRST OUTFIT 'THE RENEGADES'

EARLY BIRDS

PHIL, ALI, RONNIE, TONY

THE VAN! COURTESY OF LEO

KIM, ALI, RONNIE

City Hall, Salisbury
ANOTHER FABULOUS
BIG BEAT DANCE
FLYING INTO SALISBURY
SATURDAY
24th JULY
THE BIRDS
PLUS
THE TROGGS
Admission 6/-   Popites 5/- (before 8.30)
7.45 - 11.45 p.m.   Refreshments

LONDON ZOO AVIARY

THE BIRDS

Personal Management : "LEO"
Bookings—
HAROLD DAVISON AGENCY LTD.
22 Newman St., London, W.I.
THE BIRDS FAN CLUB
18 Evelyns Close, Hillingdon,
Middlesex.

PHIL, RONNIE, KIM, ALI, TONY

Make **DECCA** Your Choice!

THE BIRDS
Leaving Here
Decca

"Seven Single"

TONY MUNROE
IN THE THUNDERBIRDS

THE BIRDS
NO GOOD WITHOUT YOU BABY · HOW CAN
IT BE · LEAVING HERE · NEXT IN LINE
DECCA

THE BIRDS BIRDS... GANGSTER CHIC! PROTO SUEDEHEAD TONY, KIM, RONNIE, PHIL, ALI

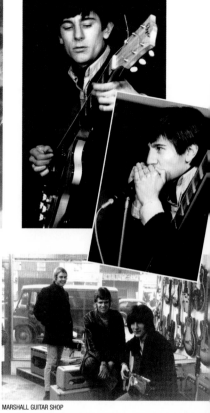

DECCA PHOTO SHOOT AT
WOOLWICH ARSENAL

MARSHALL GUITAR SHOP

LEFT - APPEARING IN 'THE DEADLY BEES'

THE NEW 'RICHARDSON'S' VAN!

DECCA PHOTO SHOOT - BOMBED OUT CHURCH AT WOOLWICH ARSENAL

KIM THINKING ABOUT THE NEW VAN

READY STEADY WIN!

READY STEADY WIN!

Rediffusion, London invites you to come along to the Beat Contest at the Wembley
Television Studios Wembley Park Drive on Tuesday, 23rd June, from 8.00-9.00 p.m.
Doors will be open at 7.30 p.m.   No admittance under 13 years of age   No chewing
gum or smoking, please.

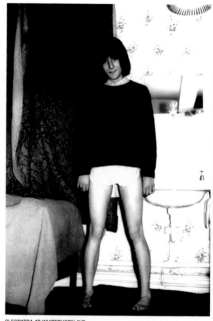

PHOTOSHOOT, SOHO SQUARE

CLEOPATRA AT WHITETHORN AVE

THE ROAD CREW

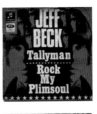

THE ARTWOODS HOP A BUS - ART WOOD FAR RIGHT... HOLD TIGHT!

BASS DUTIES FOR BECK AT THE FILLMORE

RON & JEFF
GETTING DOWN

THE JEFF BECK GROUP - ROD STEWART, JEFF BECK, AYNSLEY DUNBAR AND RONNIE

ROD, RONNIE, MICKY WALLER AND JEFF

THE CREATION - JACK JONES, KENNY PICKETT, RONNIE, KIM GARDINER

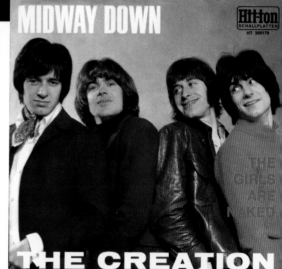

ART WOOD'S QUIET MELON - KENNEY JONES, ART WOOD, KIM GARDINER, ROD STEWART, IAN MCLAGAN, RONNIE

FACES SMALL

WITH ROD STEWART
RON WOOD/IAN McLAGEN
RONNY LANE/KENNY JONES

MUSIC HALL

THEATRE
TUESDAY
FEB. 9th

268 TREMONT STREET, BOSTON

SAVOY
PLUS THE GREASE BAND

Tickets $6, $5, $4 at High Ticket Agency, Tyson Ticket Agency, Out of Town News Agency, Boston U., M.I.T., Harvard, Music Hall Box Office
Mail Orders: Payable to PACIFIC PRESENTATIONS, c/o Music Hall Theatre, 268 Tremont St., Boston

PACIFIC

THE FACES - IAN MCLAGAN, RONNIE WOOD, RONNIE LANE, ROD STEWART, KENNEY JONES

FACES
FIRST SINGLE 'FLYING'
FIRST ALBUM 'FIRST STEP'
on Warner Reprise of course

Rod Stewart

Kenny Jones

Ron Wood

Ian McLagan

Ronnie Lane

the first step

"The First Step" is Small Faces' debut for Warner Bros. The second step is their current smashing cross-country tour. Small Faces, with miracle ingredients Ronnie Lane, Ronnie Wood, Rod Stewart, Kenny Jones and Ian McLagan. On Warner Bros., where they belong.

ROD STEWART
RONNIE WOOD
RONNIE LANE
IAN McLAGAN
KENNY JONES

RONNIE WOOD WITH STEVE MARRIOTT - THE 'MISSING LINK' BETWEEN THE SMALL FACES AND THE FACES

RONNIE LANE

THE FACES, STRIKING A FAMILIAR POSE

RON WOOD &
RONNIE LANE
MAHONEY'S LAST STAND

RONNIE AND KENNEY JONES

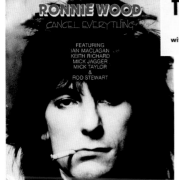
RONNIE WOOD
CANCEL EVERYTHING
FEATURING
IAN MACLAGAN
KEITH RICHARD
MICK JAGGER
MICK TAYLOR
&
ROD STEWART

NORTH EAST LONDON POLYTECHNIC
(Waltham Forest Precinct)
FOREST ROAD, WALTHAMSTOW, E.17
FRIDAY, DECEMBER 4th
THE FACES
with Rod Stewart
+
Little Free Rock
with African Drumm
Moonchild Lights   Bar
10/- Advance 12/6 Door

Stay With Me

RONNIE AT HOME AT THE WICK

CINDY INCIDENTALLY
Words and Music by ROD STEWART and RONNIE WOOD

Recorded on
Warner Bros. K 16247
by
THE FACES

WARNER BROS. MUSIC LTD.
sole selling agents:
MUSIC SALES LTD., 78 Newman Street, London W.1.
20p

You Can Make Me Dance, Sing Or Anything

(Even Take The Dog For A Walk, Mend A Fuse, Fold Away The Ironing Board, Or Any Other Domestic Shortcomings)

Words & Music by ROD STEWART, RONNIE WOOD, KEN JONES, IAN McLAGAN & TETSU YAMAUCHI

Recorded by THE FACES on Warner Bros. Records

WARNER BROS MUSIC LTD. & ISLAND MUSIC LTD.
sole selling agents:
MUSIC SALES LTD., 78 Newman Street, London, W.1.
25p

WESTFIELD COLLEGE
KIDDERPORE AVENUE, N.W.3
Telephone: 435 6593

Tubes: Finchley Road and Golders Green
Saturday, January 30th, 8 p.m.

FACES
with ROD STEWART
plus
Admission 12/-   Bar   Lights

STAY WITH ME
Words and Music by R. WOOD and R. STEWART

Recorded on Warner Bros. K 16136 by

FACES

KINNEY MUSIC LTD.
sole selling agents:
MUSIC SALES LTD., 78 Newman Street, London, W1.
20p

BORSTAL BOYS
faces
OOH LA LA

FACES
Cindy Incidentally
Skewiff

the SMALL FACES
Flying
Three Button Hand Me Down

FACES
Maybe I'm Amazed
Oh Lord I'm Browned Off

You Can Make Me Dance,
Sing Or Anything
faces
As Long As
You Tell Him

FACES
POOL HALL
RICHARD
I WISH IT WOULD RAIN
(18th ff Trumpet)

ROD
STEWART
AND FACES
MUNICIPAL AUDITORIUM
NASHVILLE, TENNESSEE
SEPT. 26 · 1975
8:00 P.M.

STEVE ROBINSON in association with NORTH WEST PROMOTIONS LTD

BUXTON
FESTIVAL THIS WEEK

AT BOOTH FARM NEAR BUXTON. DERBYSHIRE

5TH JULY FRIDAY 4.30 p.m. till midnight approx.	6TH JULY SATURDAY 12.30 p.m. till midnight approx.
MOTT THE HOOPLE	**THE FACES** AND ROD STEWART
MAN	SPECIAL GUEST STARS **HUMBLE PIE**
J.S.D BAND	CHAPMAN/WHITNEY STREETWALKERS
HORSLIPS	TRAP...
WALLY	BADG...
GUEST STARS	CHOPPE... STRIDER NATIONA...
LINDISFARNE	SPECIAL A... **NEW Y...** D.J. BOB H...

SAT. ONLY TICKET	2 DAY TICKET	Plenty of tickets available on gate Sat only £3.00 2 day £4.25	The festival site... continuous bus ser... site and car parks (8... 3rd July. Large marq... tion. 3 acre shoppi... buses and trains to... (Special coach trips fro...
£3.00	£3.75 advance price		

Special coach trips and tickets available from Edwards and Edwards Theatre...
2 day £8.50 (leaves Kings Cross Friday 5th July 12.30 p.m.) Saturday only £7...
9.30 a.m.) These prices include ticket and return coach trip.

TICKETS CALL AT
ABERDEEN Virgin Records, 411/413 George Street
AYLESBURY Harlequin Records, 31 Friars Square
...

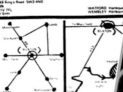

LIVE AT BUXTON

faces
POOR HALL RICHARD
I wish it would rain

faces
cindy incidentally

Had Me
A Real Good Time
FACES
Rea...

WEELEY
MUSIC FESTIVAL '71
HALL FARM WEELEY BANK HOLIDAY
WEEKEND Fri. Aug. 27th commencing 6 p.m.
and Sunday Aug. 29th. Tickets £1.90 in advance
(£2.50 at the gate) available with S.a.e. from
R.T. TICKET AGENCY, 16, ALBANY GARDENS
EAST, CLACTON-ON-SEA, ESSEX.
Phone Clacton 22728.

STAGE PASS

THE FACES WITH RONNIE LANE'S DOG MOLLY... TAKING AN EVIDENT SHINE TO MAC!

SHIRLEY ARNOLD'S LEAVING PARTY - NERVOUS RONNIE LANE PICTURED WITH MICK JAGGER, CHARLIE WATTS AND MICK TAYLOR

THE FACES WITH RONNIE LANE'S REPLACEMENT - TETSU, FAR LEFT BELOW - AND FAR RIGHT ABOVE

THIS VOUCHER IS WORTH 50 PENCE OFF WHEN YOU PURCHASE ONE OF THE FACES ALBUMS FROM ANY DEALER LISTED ON BACK

KEEF AND RON...

WITH THE ROLLING STONES - MIAMI STADIUM SOUNDCHECK

ART, RONNIE, SHIRLEY ARNOLD & DOREEN WOOD

WAITING FOR THE MAN...

RON AND PREGNANT KRISSIE

TED WOOD, JO WOOD AND RONNIE

JERRY HALL, MICK JAGGER AT RONNIES 'WILD WEST' 50TH BIRTHDAY PARTY

RON AND JESS

RON AND BO DIDDLEY - GUNSLINGERS!

JO WOOD

KRISSIE WOOD

RON AND LONG TIME GUITAR TECH CHUCH

RON AND KIM GARDINER, PERDORMING AT ART WOOD'S 60TH BIRTHDAY PARTY

RON AND BIG BROTHER ART

HONEST RON...

RON AND HIS LATEST FLAME, BRAZILIAN POLO COACH ANA ARAUJO

OLD MATES RON AND ALI MCKENZIE - ART WOOD'S WAKE...

A few 'hellos' were exchanged, a few beers were downed and then Rod promptly departed for a hidden vantage point at the top of the stairs. From the safety of his hidey-hole, Rod could hear that the band lacked direction. He could also hear they needed a forceful lead singer.

He listened for a few numbers and left, but returned the following day and repeated the same process - brief 'hellos', a couple of beers and then his disappearing act.

This continued every day for well over a week, as Rod found that he actually liked what he heard, he loved the band's easy-going approach, and enjoyed their seemingly united spirit and humour. Their music appealed to him too, and it wasn't long before he was incessantly humming certain tunes that had wafted their way up the stairs and lodged permanently in his subconscious. "I don't know if I could ever lead a band," Rod was quoted in Record Mirror at the time. "But I need the security of a band before I can get back in front of an audience."

He was almost hooked! Still, Rod didn't want to appear obtrusive. "I was too embarrassed to ask Woody if I could join and he wasn't sure if the band would even want me as their lead singer. Ronnie wasn't being very helpful - he was being as vague as possible on the subject. So it was left to Kenney Jones to stick his neck out, as he did at the Spaniards pub in Highgate after one of their rehearsals".

It was a day Kenney remembers well "We'd tried out everyone as lead singer; Woody first and then Ronnie Lane - even Mac, but it still wasn't right. Although their singing was nice, it wasn't strong enough to front man a band like the Small Faces. We carried on every day and it got more and more painful, until I couldn't stand it any longer. Rod used to go to this pub near where he lived after he'd been to our rehearsals, and one day I asked if I could meet him there and went along without the others knowing.

"Then I simply asked him outright to join the band. I knew that he wanted to, but he wasn't sure the others were into it, except for Woody, who'd invited him in the first place. He said "Do you think the others will let me?" So I said "Yeah, I don't see why not", and I went back to tell them.

"I thought they'd love the idea; I was really excited because Rod had a fantastic voice and all we were doing was rehearsing our self stupid without a singer. I didn't expect the reaction I got, they hit the fucking roof! Ronnie Lane went mad shouting, "We don't want another fucking lead singer", and Mac, he was saying "Oh fuck no! We don't want another prima-donna". I thought, "fucking hell, you can't win with this lot"."

From Ronnie Lane's point of view at least his reservations were quite justified, he had a right to be sceptical and worried. After all, alongside Marriott he'd been one half of the era's most successful pop song-writing teams. Only to have Marriott's ego send it crashing down around his ears while belittling his musical ability in the press.

Now, with their self appointed leader gone, Ronnie Lane saw himself as heir apparent; the new front man and spokesperson. It was a position he wasn't about to relinquish easily.

"I understood why Ronnie was against Rod joining so soon after Steve had walked out" Kenney admits. "He was the songwriter now and he wanted it to be his band, he even wanted to call it Slim Chance. Mac was the same, he agreed with Ronnie and he kept saying "Yeah, fucking right, we don't want another bleedin' Steve Marriott!"

"So this went on all day, and in the end we all went round to Alvin Lee's house where Woody was living and sat up all night arguing about it. Woody agreed with me because he wanted Rod in, the same as me. Eventually they gave in and I got my own way."

It was morning by the time the three Small Faces finally settled their debate and Ronnie was exhausted. Not by anything as trivial as missed sleep, but by the level of heated conversation and hostility he'd witnessed.

He wished his new band mates a good morning and left them to discuss the ramifications of their decision while he went to the bedroom and slipped into bed beside Krissie.

Krissie vividly remembers Ronnie's dismay at what he had witnessed, particularly Ronnie Lane's reaction.

"He couldn't understand why he thought Rod could be a problem. Jeff Beck was an ego, not Rod. He was saying "Fucking hell! Rod's brilliant, he's not the sort to get carried away. When we were with Jeff, Rod used to stand behind the fucking amps to sing. That's how much of an ego Rod has!" All Ronnie knew was that he worked best when Rod was around. He used to say they were true soul mates, that they shared this special chemistry. That Rod had this crossover swagger that appealed to both men and women. For me, the charisma really shone when they got together both on and off stage. Theirs was a truly great partnership."

Maybe that partnership reminded Lane of what he'd lost when Marriott walked out. Maybe he felt threatened by it. He'd achieved far greater success than either Ronnie or Rod Stewart put together, and for far longer, but thanks to Arden, Oldham and even the Small Faces themselves, had nothing to show for it. He was riding a pushbike, and Rod Stewart had the sports car. Even Ronnie had successfully passed his driving test, and was whisking Krissie around town in a (second-hand) Mercedes.

Despite his diminutive stature and beneath his seemingly happy go lucky demeanour, Ronnie Lane was a formidable character. He could cut anyone down to size with his savage wit alone - he could be cold and calculating, and he also bore a grudge.

"He and Rod Stewart were never at ease with each other" Krissie reflects, "they were poles apart in their outlook, and as people, I sensed that there was an underlying standoffishness between the two right from the start.

"Ronnie noticed it too and did his usual best to mediate, but at times he'd say the atmosphere could become every bit as unbearable as it had been in The Jeff Beck Group - and this was before they'd even really got started."

Lane and McLagan weren't the only ones with misgivings about the band's new line up. Rod, too, had his anxieties.

"The Small Faces were seen as the poor man's Who" he explains. "They were somewhere between a teeny-bopper band and a progressive outfit. They were always one of England's finest bands, though. I've always dug the album "Ogden's Nut Gone Flake" - that was a masterpiece, but it was ahead of its time and Tommy got in there later and cleaned up, where Ogden's should have scored.

"There was always a link between the Small Faces and The Who, but actually there was a closer musical one with Free. The Small Faces played that tight sort of sound, but Free did it a lot better."

Nonetheless, once Ronnie Lane had resigned himself to the inevitable, he was astute enough to see that the addition of Rod Stewart's unique vocal talent and Ronnie Wood's versatile and inventive guitar playing did offer certain possibilities. "I could tell the sound would make a nice band. We all played together easily, because we all listened to the same records: Booker T, Gladys Knight, mostly Black American stuff. Our taste was stuck back in 1964 - a good year, that. On the other hand, 1969 was a fucking gloomy year!"

Curiously, nowadays McLagan remembers the birth of The Faces a little differently.

"When Woody came along we were a group again. Then along came Rod, which was even better. The Small Faces had gone stale, mainly because Steve was in total control. He would never ask me to do anything; he would always tell me exactly how to play or what to play. But when Ronnie and Rod arrived, we began really supporting and encouraging each other. That would never have happened with Steve."

So there you have it; Ronnie and his old pal had signed on with a group who couldn't agree on anything, were financially destitute, contractually beleaguered and facing a future that was nothing short of dubious. Moreover, Ronnie was the only band member without a contract. The three original members were still locked into a worthless deal with Immediate Records, whilst Stewart was now contracted to Mercury. Jones, McLagan and Lane were all bankrupt, Rod was living with his parents, while Ronnie was ekeing out what little money he hadn't blown since leaving Beck - but mostly, relying on Krissie's wages.

Record companies were firmly of the belief that the rejuvenated Faces were no more than the unwanted remnants of what had once been two very successful bands. The real stars had been Steve Marriott and Jeff Beck, and they were the ones the industry and the public wanted.

The band needed to do some serious work if they were going to change such a widespread preconception. It was decided a manager was the first step forward and Kenney Jones was appointed to find one.

He first approached the composer and arranger, Jimmy Horowitz, whom he'd met early on in his Small Faces career, and explained the band's dilemma.

Now, it is generally believed that any good manager needs two basic skills. First, a good business mind and second, the patience of a saint. ('Good' as in making the band rich, happy and content, that is, as opposed to ripping them off which is often seen as the hallmark of a successful manager.) The Small Faces also needed someone blessed with enough imagination and foresight to counter the industry's negativity and indifference. They also needed someone strong enough to take on five very disillusioned and by nature, very uncooperative and volatile individuals. Or as Kenney pointed out: "We didn't need a manager, we needed a fucking referee." Jimmy Horowitz knew just the man: Billy Gaff.

Gaff was a twenty-two year-old ex-economics student from Woolwich Polytechnic, who'd gone to work as an agent for RSO (Robert Stigwood Organisation). His first assignment had been Cream.

Gaff recalls: "When I was offered the job I told Robert I wouldn't know where to start, and he replied "Have you ever looked after children?" So I said "yes, my sister's got three" and Robert replied, "Good, just think of it like that and you'll be fine" so I did, and I was."

Horowitz arranged a meeting between Kenney and Gaff at the Speakeasy Night Club on Margaret Street in London.

"Gaff had this little leather hat perched on his head" Kenney recalls, "He looked like a little poof. I told him that we basically couldn't get out of our deal with Immediate and we couldn't work as the Small Faces because of it.

"He listened attentively to all this and then he says that he thinks he can sort everything out. Our old solicitor had frozen everything up for the last two years, so I didn't hold out much hope."

Gaff's intervention managed to get a mention in the 31st May edition of Disc and Music Echo under the heading: 'Hang Ups Over Contracts', where he let it be known he was looking for ways to release the Small Faces from their Immediate deal. But he made no mention of Ronnie or Rod Stewart.

Gaff called a meeting with the group's solicitor and accountant the following day and after much deliberation, miraculously secured the release of Messrs Jones, McLagan & Lane from all previous contractual arrangements. Much to the surprise of Milton Mark, the Small Faces' accountant: "I'd once gone to Immediate myself to try and get money for the Small Faces. I went to see Andrew Oldham and Tony Calder at the office they had in Gloucester Avenue. It was a listed Georgian hall of residence building, a beautiful place, but they had these builders in smashing the walls down with hammers and building these huge arched alcoves.

"I said to Andrew "that's a bit unusual isn't it? Are you sure you're allowed to do this?" and he replied "Yes; who'll know?" Then I asked what the alcoves were for, and he replied "oh that's where we're putting the thrones!" They were putting these huge great thrones on blocks set back in the alcoves for him and Tony Calder to sit on. I never got any money, it was too chaotic to deal with."

Gaff phoned Kenney with the news, and an offer to find the band a new recording contract, plus £500 to tide over the more impoverished members of the band. "That's when we asked Billy to manage us," says Kenny, "and he said that he'd always had that in the back of his mind anyway!"

The Small Faces' next step was to start playing again, but with no gigs booked - and with no agent to arrange any - they quickly discovered that club owners were as unwilling to give the group a chance as the labels were to sign them.

Meanwhile, Gaff was receiving more or less the same response from the record labels. Polydor had practically thrown him out of their Oxford Street offices, after informing him the band was nothing without Steve Marriott. Track and Apple's A&R department had simply asked if he was joking.

The record label problem was eventually solved by the persistent Gaff, on 1st November, 1969 when he successfully managed to sweet-talk a reluctant Warner Brothers into giving the Small Faces a £30,000 advance and a five-album deal.

It was a victory snatched from the jaws of defeat, as the British arm of the label, headed by Ian Ralfini, hadn't wanted to sign the band.

However, the visiting American chief, in the shape of Joe Smith, was eager to sign new British talent for the US Warner Reprise label. Smith saw potential in a Ronnie and Rod-led project for both were well known to American fans courtesy of their time with Jeff Beck.

The group breathed a collective sigh of relief and, as Kenney remembers, took great delight in letting the disbelievers know that a new band really had risen from the ashes.

"I remember we still had this horrible accountant, another relic from the early days and he said, "Oh, you've started a new band then have you?" Really sarcastic. Then he said, "So how are you going to fund it?" So I said, "we'll get an advance, go on the road and make records. To which he replied, "Oh yeah, what kind of money do you think you'll get?" So I came out with the first figure I thought of, which was £30,000! and he laughed, "Ha! Telephone numbers!" So when Billy asked me how much we thought we needed, I said it again. He wasn't sure he could get it, but he did. It was great telling that guy afterwards. Then we fired him."

Although the Faces weren't exactly well off, Krissie was determined that Ronnie would make good on his promise: he had his Revox tape machine, now she wanted a secure home. Ronnie would probably have rather had a recording studio, or at least a new guitar, for in his heart he already had a secure home: Number 8, Whitethorn Avenue, where the box-room was always ready.

Nonetheless, a promise was a promise, so he turned to Perry Press and his Little Pink Pig estate agents and asked for help. Press arranged for them to rent the Old Forge in Henley while he applied a little creative accountancy to the Wood finances.

This eventually helped Ronnie secure a mortgage on a spacious flat at the aptly named Ravenswood Court on Kingston Hill, Surrey, not far from where he lives now when he's back in the UK.

Not quite the stockbroker belt, which had been discovered by the Beatles a few years previously, but still a marked improvement on Shepherd's Bush and of course, Ronnie knew all the best pubs in the area. Old family friend, Jim Willis, who'd first taught the infant Ron how to play the guitar, moved in with his wife Irene to help pay the mortgage.

"Actually, I've no idea how Ronnie and Perry worked it," Krissie admits. "Ronnie never used to involve me in money matters. He just came home one day and said he'd managed to sort out a mortgage, which was unheard of at the time for a musician unless they were the Beatles or someone. He did it when he came home with the Bentley as well. That was such a lovely car."

The band finally found a new agent in the familiar shape of Robert Stigwood, possibly because he owed Ronnie a favour from standing by as The Birds had plummeted to earth. Gaff, of course, still worked for him, while Rod Stewart was tipped as a hot property. Hold the favour, this was a sensible business decision.

In fact, Ronnie wasn't the only ex-Bird to be occupying Stigwood's mind at the time. Kim Gardiner was firmly ensconced with Stiggie-poo's earlier project, Ashton (Tony, keyboards), Gardiner and Dyke (Roy, drums), but for some unaccountable reason had taken an instant dislike to the Bee-Gees, Stiggy's current fab five.

"They were never my cup of tea," Kim freely admitted, "and I played a terrible trick on them once. We were recording at IBC in London and Stiggy brought his new boys to see us. I knew who they were, because we'd stuck them with our old van - the one the Torture Boys had bought for us. Anyway, Stiggy doesn't know this so he says, "Kim I'd like you to meet

The Bee Gees", and they were all standing there in matching white suits; even then, they looked like a bunch of dicks, and I go, "Oh, very nice." Me, Tony and Roy were right in the middle of a track, a little bit stoned, and very laid-back.

"Some bloke called Ozzie, who I think was their father or uncle or something, said they wanted to use the toilet. So I showed them where it was, taking the lift upstairs, and they all went in the bathroom together, and I locked them in! I got really chewed out by Stiggy the next day, because I'd forgot about them and they were banging on the door all night until the cleaner let them out at seven in the morning!"

The first engagements that the new The Small Faces undertook occurred later in November when they played a week of low-key dates in Effretikon, near Zurich in Switzerland. Then, in December, the group entered the Olympic Studios in Barnes to begin recording their first album under the truncated name of The Faces.

"It was simply a way to separate the old configuration from the new" was Ronnie's reasoning, "plus Rod and me were a few inches taller than the others!"

Warner Brothers, however, wanted the band to retain their original name and capitalise on their only US success, "Itchycoo Park" a stateside hit back in 1967.

"We told them to fuck off!" Mac explained. "There was no way we were going to cover anything we'd done with Steve. I was heartbroken when he left, and there was still a lot of bad feeling around towards him, especially from Ronnie Lane."

Unfortunately, Warner brothers were equally adamant and were not budging. A long drawn out battle loomed, which threatened to bring the group to a grinding halt.

The two Ronnies gave the group's first round of interviews in December where Ronnie went to pains in order to hammer home the band's shortened title. "Now we're the Faces, I don't think we're heavy. That's a label, rather like being labelled teenybopper. There are a lot of influences from the old Small Faces in the group, of course, but labels don't mean a thing. Now we're the Faces, everyone goes on calling us the New Faces. We're called the Faces, not New Faces, that's a label, too."

While Ronnie Lane stated, "Steve Marriott had left us to get Humble Pie together, and we had to think seriously about what we were going to do. We had essentially, up until that time, been a group that was in the public eye all the time. Once people have decided what it is they want you to be, when you're in the charts then you're expected to keep fulfilling that image, which at times can be extremely demanding."

Eventually and sensibly, the group and label came up with a compromise everybody could live with whereby the band agreed to be known as The Small Faces in America, and simply The Faces in the UK - plus all of the old band's repertoire would be replaced by new group compositions.

So, with that settled The Faces (UK) finally entered Olympic Studios in Barnes and began recording their first album, unsure if they even still had an audience. First, they assembled a grab-bag of a dozen half finished ideas and near completed compositions.

Next, Ronnie played the demo tapes to Glyn Johns an engineer/producer who he'd worked with back in his Creation days, in the hope of persuading him to produce the album.

Johns agreed, asking for a two percent royalty per album. Given that Johns was one of the fastest rising young producers in the country, and the band was yet to play live at any serious venue in the UK, two percent was a good deal.

Of course, the band didn't see it like that and they turned him down flat, which resulted in them releasing a press statement that read, "The Faces don't need a producer, they are a dying breed."

The result of such actions meant the production seat and control room were deserted, save for lone engineer, Martin Birch. It also meant the band were without an encouraging or critical ear to guide them. The eventual production credit went to The Faces themselves.

Ronnie and the brilliant, lyrically-astute Lane commandeered the lion's share of the song writing credits, either penning or arranging seven of the ten finished tracks. Stewart lent a hand with three, leaving Mac to appear twice, and Jones just once.

It was a decent enough mix that combined the group's five individual styles and influences, from Lane's whimsical folksy ode to reincarnation, "Stone" and the soulful mournful ballads "Devotion" and "Nobody Knows", to Mac and Stewart's solid working class rock-based "Three Button Hand Me Down" a stellar tale of bar stool advice concerning sartorial matters and cultural baggage.

The public, however, thought it was about a Granddad's old suit. The first inkling of any future song writing partnership between Ronnie and Rod came with a reworking of the Beck period "Plynth (Water Down The Drain)". Originally credited to Beck-Stewart-Wood, it re-emerged as "Around The Plynth", with Beck's arrangement omitted, along with his name, and the credit firmly assigned to Stewart and Wood alone. They'd got over being mad, and now they were getting even.

The album kicked off with Dylan's "Wicked Messenger", followed by two instrumentals: Ronnie's salute to Booker T, called "The Pineapple & The Monkey" and "Looking Out The Window" essentially a filler work-out featuring Kenney and Mac.

All very diverse, and neatly summed up by the album's title, "First Step" released in March 1970. The cover shot showed the band sitting timidly in a row, with only Ron and Rod looking uneasily at the camera. Rod holds an imaginary glass, while Kenny, Mac and Ronnie Lane are engrossed by two different Mickey Mouse caricatures. Ronnie is holding a guitar-tutoring manual as if to comment on the public's perception that he was really only a bass player. The overall idea was to pre-empt any critical bitchiness by admitting they were indeed just starting out. They could only hope that they hadn't actually shot themselves in the foot.

Rod Stewart's solo album, "An Old Raincoat Won't Let You Down" had been out for a month in America and although it was selling a reasonable amount, there were still no plans for a UK release.

At first, Rod didn't seem bothered about the situation, preferring instead to get behind The Faces and promote "First Step" and a single taken from it called "Flying", backed by "Three Button Hand Me Down".

The band made their BBC TV debut performing the song on "Top Of The Pops" - a programme that at the time was attracting a staggering 17 million viewers. Unfortunately, none of them appeared to like the record and it failed to chart.

Ronnie Lane tried to rationalise the singles poor showing when he said: "We didn't really want to put out a single but our record company said that if we were good boys, there'd be some money in the bin for us. "Flying" is more a trailer for the album than anything else. We didn't really care if it was a hit, but it would have been nice if it was."

It would have been nice if the album had been a hit, let alone the single, but it was not to be. 17 million potential record-buyers had heard, seen and apparently disliked The Faces. For a while the band wondered whether "First Step" would turn out to be their own last hurrah.

Thankfully, live dates soon began to trickle in. The group had already played London's Lyceum Ballroom on New Year's Eve 1969, predictably billed as "The Faces' First London Performance" where they'd showcased some of the "First Step" album tracks. Now they began playing at various low profile or diverse locations, ranging from a US Army base in Cambridgeshire, to the University of Sheffield, and a Birmingham nightclub called "Mothers".

On 14th March, the group were once again booked by the BBC. This time to appear on the late-night BBC2 live music programme, "Disco 2". Things, it seemed, were beginning to look up.

Wrong! By now reviews for the "First Step" album had begun to appear in the music press and they weren't great. The NME reported: "The Faces come up with some weirdo sounds on the ten tracks. They are striving for a heavier sound and getting it, but whether the former fans of the Small Faces will like it, remains to be seen."

"The Faces have retained much of their original appeal, with a much heavier feel,' sniffed Melody Maker, 'but the album is rather patchy."

Only American Billboard showed any encouragement: "The most together of any first album I've heard in a long time!" If Ronnie was in anyway worried about the album's lukewarm reception, he certainly never showed it. If anything, he was more upbeat than he'd been in a long while and eager to get started on the band's first major tour, a 28-date trek across America:

"Rod and me had already made a bit of a name for ourselves in the States thanks to The Jeff Beck band, so I wasn't worried about getting a good reception, but it was all new for the others. Ron, Mac and Kenney had never played there… in fact, I don't think they'd ever set foot there!"

Which wasn't totally accurate, for the Small Faces, with Steve Marriott, had actually spent one night in America during February of 1968 following their deportation from Australia. They'd missed their connecting flight in Los Angeles and were put up at the airport's Holiday Inn Hotel.

Kenney Jones' memories of the Small Faces' first taste of America revolve around television. Actually, a swivelling television attached to the hotel room wall. Neither he nor the rest of the band had ever seen a wall-mounted TV before, and marvelled at the hotels' forethought.

A screwed-down TV set was so much harder to throw out the window and they'd even put it out of reach of the diminutive band. That initial thought was overshadowed by their first taste of American programming.

"There was a news-reel about Vietnam," Jones remembers. "I turned the TV on and the first image I saw when the screen came into view was that famous clip of a Vietcong prisoner being shot in the head. It was like a split-second, bang! I thought, fuck me, welcome to America! We'd never seen televisions or TV news like it. We were used to seeing the news end up with a happy animal story, like a dolphin or a giant panda giving birth in a zoo somewhere, not people being shot in the head. The funniest thing I remember about that hotel was later on we were all in the hotel lobby and this basketball team walked past us. The contrast was hilarious - we'd never seen people that tall."

Rod had helped smooth the band's imminent arrival Stateside some months earlier with a week long promotional tour organised by Mercury Records to plug his first solo album. He also used the opportunity to enthuse about how happy he was to be working with Woody again and thanked the record company for allowing him to play with The Small Faces.

He also expressed the desire that by promoting his solo work abroad it would, in turn, raise the band's profile. A reasonable assumption, but one that was wasted on some newspapers and DJs who turned up in some cities to ask, "Was Rod Stewart the guitar player in the Jeff Beck Group?"

Still, the band was geared up and ready to go, leading Rod and Ronnie to say: "Half the battle is already won. The Faces will go down fantastically well because everyone in the band has improved musically so much. It's Ronnie, Mac and Kenney's first trip to America and they're all going to get very homesick. God, they went to Australia for a week and got homesick! This is going to be a great two months. I really think that Marriott was holding their playing back. Since he left, they really seem to have come into their own."

Ronnie Lane hadn't wanted a leader for the new band. Now, it seems, he had two.

"The whole set up in the band was a bit stacked against us right from the very start," Kenney stated. "Rod and Ron were all cocky about going to America because they had been there before. They had their following, knew their way around, and became all flash by saying things like "Oh we know this great place in New York that does boiled eggs" and all that. We were seen as Rod's and, to a lesser extent, Ronnie's band, which I could see was going to be a problem, but it was a case of waiting and seeing."

1970 was a good year for English groups in America. Rolling Stone magazine was predicting a decade of 'Renaissance Rock' in the wake of the frantic chopping and changing that been prevalent amongst several top bands at the end of the 1960s. Then it had been dubbed the era of the 'super group', with Cream at the helm leading the way, followed by groups like Humble Pie and Jon Hiseman's Colosseum. It was a musical climate that by all accounts awarded the (new) Small Faces a curious, but sizeable, ready-made audience.

The tour kicked off on 25th March 1970 at the Varsity Arena in Toronto, Canada with the band playing third on the bill to home-grown crowd pleasers such as Canned Heat, and Detroit's demi-gods, The MC5.

It was here that the group got their first taste of things to come. The posters advertised the band as "Rod Stewart & The Small Faces".

"They gave me hell!" Gaff remembers. "I knew perfectly well that behind the scenes the promoters were advertising the band as "Rod Stewart & The Small Faces" I just hoped for the best. Promoters would try and change the signs on the front of the theatres at the last minute, but not always in time. Anyway, they had a meeting and sent Ronnie to tell me that the American promoters were never, ever, to give Rod star billing. I didn't know him (Ronnie) that well, but he'd always seemed like a pussy-cat.

"I figured that it was mainly Lane and McLagan. It was all pointless nonsense anyway because Rod Stewart was going to be a star no matter what they did. It was obvious to everyone that Rod would become one of the biggest rock stars the world ever saw, and there was nothing the band could do about it - the resentment was there right from the start."

Krissie Wood also believes that Ronnie was used as a front man for the other three: "He loved Rod and the others. I don't think he was aware that there were potential problems ahead. I don't think he foresaw any conflicts. He went along with what the others wanted because he knew Rod better than anyone, so he was always the one to have to talk about Rod to Billy."

If there was trouble brewing amongst the group then it wasn't obvious to the crowds that stated flocking to the band's sold out shows. From the very first note that The Small Faces struck during their opening American concerts, they had the audience crowd awe struck. Their magic was so instantaneous and their apparent camaraderie so infectious, it seemed the most natural thing in the world for them to create an atmosphere of snug-bar intimacy in auditoriums as big as Aircraft hangers.

Right from the very start their stage presence was both inspiring and awesome.

Fuelled by enough booze to knock out a horse, the group exemplified good time rock 'n' roll, every night was party night and everyone felt invited. Rod mastered a unique acrobatic baton-twirling routine with the metal mike stand, while Ronnie Lane stomped around him in ever widening circles, like a little drunken gnome. His chugging locomotive bass lines accentuating Kenney's thunderous drumming as Mac's swirling Hammond organ meshed with Ronnie's driving riffs.

Ronnie perfected his caricature image of constant cigarette puffing cool as he swooped around the stage like a cartoon rooster, his guitar screeching in torment from a bottle-neck pummelling that would reach such a crescendo that the band ended the show every night collapsed in a drunken and exhausted heap on the stage - and not always at the end of a number.

They soon gained the reputation as an impossible act to follow, and their live shows a yardstick to measure feel-good boogie bar room bawdiness by. It was a completely different story off-stage off course.

Midway through the tour they were regularly blowing away the 'bill-toppers' and anyone else that dared flex a musical muscle in the same city. Revered bands such as Savoy Brown and a Joe Cocker-free Grease Band learned the hard way. Even Motor City crown holders, The MC5, saw their Detroit stranglehold lose its grip to The Small Faces.

"We thought no one else would take us seriously," was how Ronnie described these early dates, "so we'd get totally plastered beforehand - Dutch courage. We were basically lacking in confidence, especially Ron, Mac, and Kenny we'd get so pissed we'd lose any inhabitations and have a good time and it worked."

News filtered back to England that The Faces were taking America by storm, albeit a drunken one, but an indifferent English press were not impressed and column inches remained Faces-free. Who cared how big anyone was across the pond if they couldn't cause a mini-riot on Top Of The Pops or make the gossip columns by hanging out at the Speakeasy club? Also, if their management wasn't schmoozing journalists by the gross, well hey, they just didn't exist. Then there was also the question of the Faces' uncool heavy drinking image.

"We didn't set out to be different or get a reputation going with the press with a gimmick," Rod states, "it wasn't a conscious thing. We just all enjoyed a drink. All the boys enjoyed a drink - we wanted to be drunks. There was a general smile whenever anyone played a dodgy note."

"My whole family is good at emptying bottles," Ronnie grins.
"Booze; terrible stuff. The ruin of me mother. It's nice really, quite okay. Why? Do we have a reputation of being a bunch of juice-heads?" Lane innocently enquired at a press conference.

Which was a problem because while drugs were hip and cool, booze was strictly down-market thuggish, even rock music had begun to be heavily influenced by class and former working class music journalists - never very many - were desperate to establish their middle class credentials and the power of their intellect.

As it was, when the band returned to the UK in June, the first concert they played was at the unlikely venue Dudley Zoo in Epping. It was a reality shock to say the least. According to Ronnie, a very unwelcome one: "We were on a roll and yet we came back to England after a very successful two months to virtually nothing.

We expected a flood of gig offers and some decent publicity, but nothing happened, nobody had thought to capitalise on our US success and no one had fixed up a single thing for us. We were right back to square one in the UK and we had quite a job to do, it just hadn't taken off at all.

"I remember saying I'd rather go straight back to the States than bash people's heads against a brick wall in England. Over in the States, they hadn't had anything to go by, or judge us by, except a couple of chart entries by the old Small Faces.

"They hadn't seen that band live, they'd only ever seen Rod and me, so there wasn't the problem that we had in England, where people linked the old with the new. In America we'd started fresh and new because they didn't have our history down pat; they didn't have anything to match us to. So we didn't have anything to live down - we didn't have to prove anything to anyone.

"Although, come to think, of it someone did call out for "Itchycoo Park" one night, which pissed Rod off! Ronnie, too, if I remember rightly.

"Don't get me wrong, I really wanted the band to make it in England, but by the back door, by hard work, not by hype, but people, especially the press, were very critical of The Faces at the start; either that or they just ignored us - there was no middle ground.

"We weren't given a chance in England. Music journalists in the UK think bands should simply play to please them. "Come on you bastards entertain me!" they have a preconceived idea of what they expect and if you don't pander to them, they slag the band off and then everybody gets on the bandwagon.

"It happened at Dudley Zoo. We supported T Rex and were introduced by jazz-snob Edgar Broughton as: "A bunch of drunken East End yobbos!" Journalists heard that and that was the headline. Nice one, Edgar!"

He has a point; but then again, Ronnie's frustration might just as easily be explained by the fact that he was probably concerned his career was once again going round in ever decreasing circles. Certainly it seemed he was experiencing a repeating cycle of events. The same thing had happened with The Creation - huge in Germany and Holland, minuscule in the country of his birth.

Jeff Beck too was always more popular overseas than in the UK - why, even The Birds had been big in Cheshire.

Sadly for the UK it's still pretty much the same today whereby highly-regarded bands and musicians like Ten Years After and John Mayall can still command a large and respectful following abroad, but not in their own country, and certainly not in the mainstream music press. Not because the foreign media and music industries are less knowledgeable or hip, but because they are less age-obsessed, more appreciative and far broader minded.

Ever noticed how only Black blues musicians are allowed to grow old in England? In America, the Rolling Stones can appear on the same stage as Muddy Walters or BB King, and will be simply judged by the quality of their music. Which in these three examples, are still amongst the best in the world.

In England, however, the same gig will be greeted with a headline sneering: "Lock Up Your Grandmothers - Strolling Bones Play With Blues Greats." Which is nothing but lazy journalism coupled with spineless political correctness.

Part of the problem is that the British music press loves to elevate one person or a group to near-Godhead status, in the hope they achieve mass-market appeal, which in turn eventually results in a panicky overkill, followed by the inevitable ritual sacrifice.

It's true that a record company's back-catalogue makes money - if it's properly handled - but in real terms, there's nowhere in England for yesterday's men, band, or star to go after their fifteen minutes of fame; its sad but true.

So, they become a nostalgia act, then break up or disappear which eventually leads to the inevitable reunion or individual re-appearance on morning television. And oh, how the industry loves a reunion or a come back, as does the media, since it makes for 'hilarious' knocking copy and bad pun headlines, it's as easy as shooting fish in a barrel.

And bizarrely everyone rolls over and plays the game, no matter how sad or gross or obvious, because that's the way it's always been done on these small, wet, grey islands. The UK slavishly copies marketing trends and techniques developed in a country (America) where a minority audience can still be the size of Holland.

At the same time, the industry also suffers from making the British public believe that if you're big in the UK you're big everywhere. Which is nonsense, but it still goes on. People laugh and sneer at bands that are big in Germany, France or Spain - in the eighties, a band even called themselves Big In Japan to make the point. You might have thought it preferable to be big anywhere, rather than small in Britain, but you'd be wrong.

Ronnie had realised all this when he'd toured with The Creation and Beck. All he wanted to do was to make a living as a musician, and where he did it wasn't important. Sure, it would be nice to make it in your own country, but if America and Europe were more open-minded, then that's where The Faces and his future lay.

It's a view he admits too even now: "We had strict ideas about the States. We had a direct approach. We knew how to go in and we pretty much organised it so that the places we played were the most important.

"The gigs we had previously done had got us the enthusiasm to slog it out. We could have gone back and done the Fillmore East, but if we'd played a dud there, that would have had a bad effect on us, smashing what little confidence we'd built, so we didn't do it.

"We never played it until we were ready. Bill Graham wasn't the first businessman I'd ever met. I think we were the first band to turn him down. A lot of bands turned him down after that. He expected groups to kiss his boots. He was a slave driver! He was one of the people you could do without. He got people at the lowest possible prices.

"At first you needed to play the Fillmore but as America opened up, you didn't. You could get by without it. We were learning the business side of things because we had all these raw deals and big debts we'd inherited from the old Small Faces days.

"We started off the new group full of new hope and old problems. It was enough to make us give up, but we got our heads down and ploughed through it all and America helped that. American audiences can discover a band, they can break a group would wide whereas in England they're used to having it all on a plate, reading about it, letting the stories get back to them so if they read about a band that has conquered the States, they're ready for them.

"But in England they'd already made up their minds about us, they simply saw The Faces as a washed up affair that were trying to make a second life for themselves abroad, using a name that had been and gone. Naturally, we stood little chance with that attitude, so America became all important because it gave us all another chance."

America also gave the band something else as Ian McLagan's then wife Sandy Sarjeant remembers: "They all came back from that first trip to the States with the clap - Woody, Rod and Mac. I think probably Kenney got away with it, maybe Ron, but not the other three.

"I remember thinking, "oh, I can see this is a sign of things to come." I could tell what our lives were going to be like. They all came back really excited, raving about all sorts of crap like Thousand Island dressing, which they'd never seen before. It was as if having the clap didn't matter, they'd discovered salad dressing.

"So the rot started straight away with all the wives and girlfriends; never mind the troubles they were facing within the group, their biggest trouble was with the girls. They spent more time trying to sort out their various domestic situations than they did being a band. It became their biggest distraction.

"Eventually, it caused so much trouble in their personal lives that the record company started flying the girls over to be with them. Ronnie Lane's wife, Sue; Kennye's wife, Jan; Krissie Wood; and myself. That was a real shock to all the girls, because we saw for the first time what was out there regarding other women. They had hundreds of them literally throwing themselves at them everywhere they went. They didn't care if you were the wife, that didn't put them off at all. Some of them were terrifying; they'd kill you if they had to. I remember going to one reception where the group were all seated in this sunken booth and there was a balcony with seats positioned right about head height and all these girls were sitting along it with their legs open and not one of them had any knickers on. There was a whole row of them just winking at them. That was it after that - the wives would try and go on every tour possible.

"Rod had a girlfriend called Sarah Troops at the time, who was fabulous, I loved her, she was a sweetheart who came from a really nice family, but Rod would never let her join them on tour because he didn't want to be seen with any girlfriends. That would have cramped his style and she wasn't as strong-willed as the other wives and girlfriends, so she'd always be left behind. Not that we all got on with each other, oh my god no; we would have the most ferocious rows between ourselves. There were times when there were like two forces at war - the band and the wives. There was always 'happenings' on the road, like some silly little remark would trigger someone off and one of us would find we were out of favour with the other three, and all the guys would get dragged into it, sticking up for their respective other half.

"We were so adolescent it wasn't true! I remember when Dee Harrington came on the scene with Rod and she was very aloof, and no-one would have anything to do with her because we all decided we liked Sarah better."

The Faces' second US trip, which included four sold-out dates at the Atlantic City Music Hall in New Jersey on the 7th, 8th, 9th & 10th August 1970, broke Joe Cocker's in-house record and netted the band a handsome $30,000 profit! The group then flew directly onto Scandinavia for a further three days of concerts before flying home in order for Ronnie to join Rod at the Morgan Studios in Willesden to cut his second solo album.

"Gasoline Alley", the album's title and lead track, was the first definitive evidence of Ron and Rod's maturing song writing, and musical, partnership. The song, an entirely acoustic composition, deals with the stark realisation that the grass is not, by any means, greener in pastures new.

The lyrics originated from a meeting with a girl whom Ronnie and Rod had met at an after-show party thrown for The Face's following their (eventually) sold-out concert at the Fillmore East. That was the gig that saw the band take to the stage following Bill Graham's introduction of "Ladies and Gentlemen, the Mateus Wine Company presents... The Faces!"

The girl had casually mentioned to Rod that she should be getting home before her mother could accuse her of being down gasoline alley again. The phrase struck a chord with both Ronnie and Rod, who were feeling a little homesick and lonely after so many nights on the road. The result; a beautifully crafted lament, that had the listener yearning or appreciating the old homestead, or local pub.

When Ronnie and Rod were asked about the song's 'no place like home' inspiration and where, in particular, they actually felt at home, Rod replied, "Highgate, where I was born and bred." However, Ronnie seemingly misunderstood the song's moving and well crafted message and replied: "It's just about some prostitute we met at a party!"

The players on the album naturally included all of The Faces, with the exception of a 'holidaying' McLagan, who blamed a 'bus strike' for his absences.

On the surface, it looked as if Ronnie Lane, and Kenney Jones had accepted and welcomed Rod to their collective bosom, but McLagan was remaining aggressively neutral.

Other musicians included Micky Waller, acoustic guitar player Martin Quittenton, and Pete Sears from the pub-rock band Stoned Ground on piano. Plus several session players whose names escaped Stewart, with the result that the credits went instead to his football heroes like Stanley Mathews and Dennis Law. A little bit of British humour that understandably escaped the American reviews which lavished praise on the musical skills displayed by some of Britain's greatest footballers. All things considered, it would have been churlish and ungrateful to explain the mistake, so no-one ever did.

`The Faces played as a unit on two tracks, "You're My Girl (I don't want to discuss it)" and a reworking of the old Small Faces classic, "My Way Of Giving", obviously included as a tribute to the group's fondness for the Chris Farlowe's version as opposed to, according to Stewart, "The monstrous version cut by the original Smalls in 1967 on their first Immediate album."

Just as Ronnie's suggestion to cover the Bobby and Shirley Womack chestnut "It's All Over Now" owed more to his admiration for The Rolling Stones' interpretation than the earlier, and superior, original. Still the group managed to inject their own unique brand of football-terrace sing-a-long, complete with Billy Gaff's final whistle blowing towards its crashing climax.

It became an instant live Faces favourite, but strangely only a Rod Stewart solo single when it was released that September.

Ronnie doubled on bass and guitar on most of the remaining numbers, including "Cut Across Shorty" where his fluffing of a chord change caused Stewart to miss out a line completely.

"That was Woody's fault! He forgot it when we were laying the track down, but I think it's great. It doesn't sound wrong, it's a lovely sort of mistake really," was Stewart's unusual response to a recording error that he wouldn't have tolerated from any musician other than Ronnie. "He's brilliant. I can't think of any anybody else I could use to play bass and guitar, and there are loads of good players about. I could have used musicians like Paul Kossoff, but as far as bass players go, you know I wouldn't look anywhere other than Woody. He'll be the only one out of The Faces that I'll use on a new album. I used to tell him he would never make as good a guitarist as he was a bassist, but he proved me wrong!" One can only imagine how well that comment went down with Ronnie Lane and the rest of the Faces.

Rod also excitingly explained the loose working liaison that the pair were building. "Woody comes up with a chord sequence or a tune and records it on tape. Then I take it home and work out words for it. For instance, Ron's got this one called "Had Me A Real Good Time" which seems to suggest a party, so that's what I wrote about - we've already recorded a version of it."

Ronnie summed up his own contributions to "Gasoline Alley" in the album's liner notes, which read:
"Well, it's like this. Now I am definitely not one to complain, no way can I be accused of that. I turned up promptly at each session with my guitars, a shoelace and a small wireless. I couldn't be fairer than that. Everyone had a good time. Nobody came without being invited and no one arrived who didn't come. All in all a finer gathering of vocalists and musicians I've yet to see. I mean, we all share a good deal of satisfaction and respect for Rod and the lads on this album and also…"

The album was released on 11th September and charted no higher than 62 in the UK. Yet once again, the sheer disparity between Stewart's career on either side of the Atlantic was emphasised when "Gasoline Alley" entered the Billboard chart at number 27.

The Faces prepared for yet another North American marathon to follow the album's release, starting in Vermont at Goddard College in Plainfield on 1st October. The band intended to use the tour to work up new numbers for inclusion on a second Faces album, a not altogether unfamiliar practice, but one The Faces decided to take a step further and excluded the songs that the crowd knew and expected, in favour of all new material mainly worked up on stage.

As unbelievable as it seemed, The Faces were about to fall into the age-old trap that has befallen many a band, whereby they think they're so important and vital an audience will pay out good money and blindly accept an hour and a half's live set of completely unknown material.

It's unclear who came up with such an arrogant and naïve idea so early in the band's live career, but given that the band could rarely agree on anything, it's safe to assume all five members agreed to it.

The first time the plan was put forward as a fait accompli to Billy Gaff, the manager was suitably aghast and was overheard to describe his charges as "a bunch of cocky little bastards with an over-inflated opinion of their own importance."

"I told them it was too early to even think about it, that to leave out what little numbers the crowd knew would be disastrous. Of course, they ignored me because they'd forgotten their job was to entertain. The show was a complete fiasco; the worst kind of flop and the audience let them know it. You should always try to at least meet the audience halfway. Anyway, never let it be said that The Faces weren't fast learners, the next night they sang all the crowd-pleasers.

"It was a lesson learnt the hard way, and they never tried it again. I never asked them who had suggested such a thing, but I had my suspicions. They had such diverse personalities that you instinctively knew who had come up with such and such. Ronnie Wood is a lovely bloke, one of the nicest people in the business. Kenney Jones is very straightforward and genuine. Ian McLagan, and Ronnie Lane have their dark sides and can be quite vicious at times; they were both really jealous of Rod Stewart, who's one of the most professional people you could ever hope to work with."

Gaff was obviously less than enamoured with two of the Faces, but that wouldn't prevent him producing hand written individual "This Is Your Life" type books to each of them, listing those qualities that Gaff thought made them special, complete with photographs and even a poem.

The back-in-their-stride Faces were supported on the rest of the tour by the Joe Cocker-less Grease Band, and Savoy Brown, who'd come to the end of their limited success on Decca Records and had wisely bought and paid for their own warm-up act in the shape of the singer-guitarist Gerry Lockron. No sensible band on the slide wants to be seen as the warm up.

On 5th October, four days into the tour, The Faces breezed into Boston for a show at the Tea Party only to find that the local promoter and publicity hounds had been up to their old tricks again. "Rod Stewart and The Small Faces" read the posters and Ronnie Lane began sharpening his wit. Ian McLagan looked for someone to blame and Billy Gaff wisely kept out of the way.

Rod Stewart managed to defuse the situation by spending most of the evening's performance hiding from the audience, except when he was singing, leaving the rest of the band to take as much spotlight as possible. They sought him here, they sought him there, all to no avail as he was either behind Kenney Jones's drum riser, or McLagan's Hammond and Vox Continental combination.

It worked to some degree and eventually the usual Faces humour returned. As when, for example, Stewart lifted the vertically-challenged Lane bodily up to the height of his (Rod's) microphone for the chorus of "Three Button Hand Me Down".

There was the usual booze-aided pub chorus sing-along to close "Gasoline Alley" and the obligatory collapsing-in-a-heap finale, but the show was over quicker than usual and the band strolled separately off-stage.

The following night, the band played the first of a two-show engagement at the "The Club" in Rochester, New York State. The gig was correctly billed as The Small Faces and did much to re-unite the group. Unfortunately, Rochester was a mistake booking for the band, since in the early seventies the town wasn't known for live music in any shape or form.

Ron and Rod knew this from earlier experience and ruefully informed the rest of The Faces that they'd be lucky if they filled half a house at each performance.

They were right, too. Most, if not all, of the tickets sales had gone for the second gig only, so the first night became nothing more than an impromptu rehearsal for the main event, which turned out to be a marathon all day drinking session with the crew at the local Holiday Inn.

As show time approached, it took all of Billy Gaff's well-earned management skills to shepherd the band into the waiting cars and back to the venue. He began by fretting, which they ignored. Then threats, but that just made them laugh. It was only when he tried pleading that they relented.

All five band members and most of the crew were either completely drunk or well on their way, one or two had difficulty focusing, and all had trouble walking in a straight line. Fortunately for Gaff, their collective mood was, unsurprisingly, up and everyone was determined to deliver a good performance.

Unfortunately, their happy dispositions were soon dampened by the news that thanks to "Savoy Brown's late arrival at the venue", the show was running an hour over and rising and that The Grease Band were now refusing to vacate the stage.

This knock-on effect now meant that according to the programme schedule, The Faces would have under 30 minutes to play their set. As the Grease Band played on, Billy Gaff managed to negotiate with the local authority an extra half hour for The Faces, which still left a ludicrously brief amount of time to pull it off, and anyway, quite irrelevant.

It was now 12.30am and the Grease Band were still ploughing defiantly on with their sober roadies forming a protective ring around them. They hit their final, cracked note at 1.00am, allowing The Faces to clamber on stage in double quick time and surge into an ironic rendering of "It's All Over Now".

The set was naturally over far too quickly and the audience, feeling short changed, cried out for more. The Faces, only too ready to oblige, tried to return to the stage only to be barred by at least a dozen heavily-unionised stewards and stagehands backed up by a further dozen or so Rent-A-Cops armed with two-foot nightsticks.

The Faces' booze-fuelled roadies waded in regardless and created a distraction long enough for Kenney Jones to slip past, followed by the rest of the band.

There was a roar of appreciation from the crowd as the group bounded back on stage and then nothing. The power had been switched off and all the audience could hear was Kenney Jones drumming in the half darkness. Stewart slung his mike stand hard into the backcloth and all five Faces stormed off-stage to join the fracas.

Meanwhile, the crowd had started a fist-saluting chant, of "Faces, Faces, Faces" which lasted well over a quarter of an hour until the house lights were brought up in a vain attempt to empty the auditorium. That was met by a shower of small change hurled at the stage and the band's equipment, ricocheting tunefully off Kenney Jones' cymbals.

Enter the real cops, with the message that unless everyone went home peacefully,' the guy with the funny hair-do' who threw the mike stand would be charged with incitement to riot.

Meanwhile, the guy with the funny hair-do was hurriedly swapping jackets with Billy Gaff in a ridiculous attempt to disguise himself, while the rest of the Faces grabbed as many bottles of after-show booze as they could humanly carry. They then made a dash for the exit and the safety of the waiting limos while a satin-jacketed Gaff stayed behind to try and sort out the mess.

As the crowd set about ripping the place apart both inside and out, Ronnie emerged first. He was met by a torrent of thrown bottles, beer cans and rubbish aimed at the music hall windows by an angry mob of fans who had congregated outside the venue, screaming "Kill the pigs!" The entire band piled into the first car and sped off, whooping and laughing towards the Holiday Inn, leaving the crew to, hopefully, rescue their equipment, clear the stage and, maybe, pick up some small change for their trouble.

Rock 'n' roll had come to Rochester.

The tour progressed down the East Coast to New York and then across country to Detroit, and premièred several new, live numbers like "Had Me A Real Good Time", "I Feel So Good" and the Paul McCartney classic, "Maybe I'm Amazed" - all of which were recorded live at their show at the Fillmore East using the Electric Lady Mobile Recording Unit.

This new material was wisely interspersed throughout the group's nightly live favourites and was well received; well enough for them to be earmarked for inclusion on what would subsequently be The Faces' second album.

Ever since The Faces had so convincingly demolished The MC5 a mere six months earlier, Detroit had adopted the band as Motor City's very own. A giant "Detroit Welcomes The Faces" banner greeted the bewildered fivesome at the East Town Theatre, which had to post house-full notices for the next two nights. It would be the same story at every show from now on.

On 18th October, when the band was playing at The Scene in Milwaukee, news broke that the remaining sixteen dates of the tour were complete sell-outs.

Naturally, the group celebrated by invading Billy Gaff's hotel room in the middle of the night in order to overturn his bed, steal his pyjamas, flood his bathroom and exit with the light bulbs. This left the bewildered and dazed Gaff naked under an up-turned mattress in an inch of water, while his assailants whooped and screamed off down the corridor.

This was the beginning of regular hotel rampages and wrecking sprees that came to be recognised throughout the 1970s as a particularly English trait amongst its visiting rock bands to the US. As Ronnie admits: "Keith Moon turned it into an art form, but The Faces definitely pioneered the craft of hotel demolition. We didn't always get the blame for it, but we were responsible for some of the worst examples of hotel destruction. We got away with a lot of it because most of the times we'd book ourselves in as Fleetwood Mac.

"Those hotels couldn't tell one English group from the next; they'd just hear the accent and roll their eyes. It caused Fleetwood Mac no end of problems, but it also got them a lot of press, if not a few lawsuits!

"A particular favourite on that tour was removing every stick of furniture and setting it all up either in the lobby or in the corridor and we'd sit there drinking as if it was our room then we'd party in the empty rooms and see how many people we could cram in it. We'd round up everyone we could, all these strangers and people walking by and cram them into one room and get completely pissed, waiting for the first person to fall over, which would start the domino effect. We would completely dismantle entire suites right down to the plumbing.

"The worst thing we did was blow up a train. There was a hotel - I think it was in Miami - that had its own train, a real steam train that went round the grounds. One night we started it up and all got in and the fucking thing flew, we couldn't control it so we all jumped off and it fucking derailed and blew up. There was this massive explosion and huge flames. I think we gave that one to Fleetwood Mac too."

Why did the British rock fraternity trash so many American hotel rooms? Aside from the obvious reasons of drugs and booze, was it revenge for the war of independence? Clearly, defenestrating television sets goes beyond youthful high jinks. No, the simple truth is that they could get away with it, so why the hell not? Think of little kids breaking windows in an empty house. Evelyn Waugh got it wrong: it wasn't only the English aristocracy who bayed for the sound of breaking glass. The Faces, The Who and their ilk were the first British working-class generation who hadn't had to learn discipline the hard way either in the armed forces, or on the factory floor; they were the generation who'd never had it so good. They were also writing the rock 'n' roll rulebook as they went along, doing it first and creating history while they were at it.

It's like Ronnie says, "People thought that's what rock bands did, and on the whole they indulged them, and so they indulged themselves. It's taken for granted now, but back then it was new, there wouldn't be films like "Spinal Tap" if it wasn't for those bands - you're welcome."

The tour continued to snake its way around North America, crossing to San Francisco and the Fillmore West on 28th October, Santa Monica on 30th, then up to Canada before arcing back to the East Coast to begin the second leg in Wisconsin on 3rd November. A further date in Detroit saw The Faces upgraded from the East Town Theatre to an open air appearance at the Olympic Stadium on 7th November, a gig which caused Gaff to suffer another of his familiar and almighty headaches.

As the band drove closer to the Stadium, the front of house billing began to loom up at them. They drew to a halt feet from the gate and sat in their limo staring up at a billboard that announced in letters several feet high "The Small Faces Featuring Rod Stewart".

The band plus Gaff sat there in silence. Gaff was horror struck for he realized he'd been had, he'd been adamant in his demand with the promoters that they never advertised the group as "Rod Stewart And The Small Faces" and sure enough they'd stuck to their word.

This was different; this was "The Small Faces Featuring Rod Stewart".

After what seemed like an eternity, McLagan broke the silence by hitting Gaff on the head with a beer bottle and shouted at the driver to move on.

Luckily for Gaff, he successfully shifted the blame to the tour's publicist, Peter Burton, who remembers, "I thought the game was up that early, they so deeply resented those marquee signs advertising Rod separately to The Faces.

"They quite rightly, I suppose, refused to be relegated to the backing band. Ronnie Wood was a charismatic performer in the States in his own right; he's an awfully nice man, who had his own space and somewhere to go. But the other three felt marginalized; Ronnie Lane in particular felt it as a songwriter as much as anything else. There was a lot of power play and whispering jealousy going on, which added to what I felt was a constant tension in the air, and then the girlfriends would arrive and start adding to it. It was always much worse when they were flown in."

All things considered, it's a wonder that The Faces lasted as long as they did. Although Rod Stewart did feel uneasy enough about the duo billing that he began arriving at the venues early, in order to check that promoters had removed his name from the hoardings. It was either that or risk a cold shoulder or a mouthful of abuse from the rest of the band.

The Faces played their final date of the tour at the Commodore Ballroom in Lowell, Massachusetts on 15th November and flew back to England to play London's Marquee Club.

In their absence, Warners had put out a single, the Ronnie and Rod composition "Had Me A Real Good Time". It had been released on 13th November to coincide with their return to England. It also served as a taster for the forthcoming album, the follow-up to "First Step" which was titled "Long Player".

The single's B-side, "Rear Wheel Skid", was long thought to be a derisory dig at Jeff Beck's custom car obsession and a jibe at a more recent road accident involving the petulant guitarist. But according to Ronnie, "It was more of a derogatory reference to the Cockney slang for Jews - real wheel skid = Yid" which was forming the basis of the group's preoccupation with all things 'un PC' and 'Laddish' and, in particular, Cockney rhyming slang and sayings.

Once again, the album was produced by the band themselves, continuing their determination to keep a tight grip on the artistic control and an even tighter grip on their finances. In England this was seen as an even greater example of the band's arrogance, prompting the "Record Mirror" headline: "Faces Ditch Producers" and an admission from Lane that: "Some of the band's past efforts had proved to be disappointing."

Nevertheless, the group was publicly adamant that the band still viewed a producer as an unnecessary ingredient.

Ronnie was quietly not so convinced: "I think it's a valid point that a producer can act as a referee if there's indecision, but a producer is only of value if he works the buttons himself. And back then, Glyn Johns was one of the few who did."

But as Ian McLagan added: "Producing is a musical thing and most producers didn't know or wouldn't know one note from another. We didn't really know the notes but we could play them."

The producing problem made Ronnie think about the possibility of building his own studio, but not having a house big enough to accommodate one meant this had to remain a project for the future.

"One thing that bothered me was that in most studios the sound that came through the cans was never the same as the sound you got when you were playing. That's when I began looking for somewhere in Richmond, a big house, plus I fancied walking over the bridge in the morning to get the milk in!"

The Faces had been given an initial six months in which to produce "Long Player". A reasonable time limit for a band as well rehearsed as The Faces, but left to their own devices, the group was revealed as sadly lacking in any form of self-discipline, as Kenney Jones admitted: "Rod and I were very frustrated when it came to recording with The Faces. If you can believe this, Rod and me were never on anything when we were in the studios. We had a bit of a drink and that's all. The others were already getting a bit out of hand on other things.

"Everybody else in the band took a lot of other things, we were night owls, we lived through the fucking night! Rod and I would have preferred to have gone in the studio at eleven or twelve in the morning, worked through the day, finished at eight and then gone out and partied.

"That's sensible and that's how you do things but in those days, the earliest we could persuade the others to come in was about seven at night! Rod and I would get there at six just to loosen up and play a while and we would inevitably be waiting there until gone ten o'clock and in most cases midnight. In the end we'd think 'Fuck this, I'm going home; we couldn't handle just hanging around. It was that sort of in-house behaviour that eventually let the group down recording wise."

To say the band approached the recording of "Long Player" with a less than professional approach is an understatement. The Faces may have insisted that their attitude towards the record-making process was, in fact, saving rock 'n' roll from taking itself too seriously, but when "Long Player" was finally finished, this proved just an excuse.

Only two weeks out of the band's allotted six months were ultimately used for recording the album's eventual nine tracks, with the ninth being a two minute, solo slide guitar rendition of the hymn "Jerusalem" played by Ronnie, a track for which he incredibly claimed the publishing rights!

The album also included two live versions of "I Feel So Good" and "Maybe I'm Amazed" recorded at the band's Fillmore East show, together with the two Ronnies' "On The Beach", which was recorded acoustically on a porta-studio at Lane's new flat in Richmond. This left only four fully-fledged studio recorded numbers and one of those, "Bad 'n Ruin" was recorded one boozy night using the Rolling Stones' mobile, while it was parked outside Mick Jagger's stately home in Hampshire.

This shoddy and haphazard approach to recording an all important second album wasn't something that escaped the band's critics either. As American Creem magazine's Ed Ward was quick to point out in his review:

"Well, The Faces took their first step and like any other first step it was greeted with reserve. After all, the baby might fall flat on its face with the second step. Here then is The Faces' second step and I think we'll have to wait a while before we can categorically state that the baby's learnt to walk yet. After playing it numerous times, I find that I can still look at the label and not recognise some of the titles; nor I find, can I remember what most of the songs sound like, but why deal with the album's shortcomings and why bother with these babies at all?"

Ouch.

CHAPTER ELEVEN
"IF YOU DO TO ME WHAT HE DID TO HER."

"Long Player" was universally seen (critically) as a step backwards for The Faces. Yet was this really fair? Given that the first album had (eventually), thanks to the group's high profile touring persistence, managed to limp back into the lower reaches of the US chart. "Rolling Stone" magazine had even decided to re-appraise it and were currently hailing the band as their third favourite group of the seventies. They'd also won over the normally unshakeable and heavy critic, John Mendelsohn, in the process.

American hearts it seemed had warmed to the band's particular brand of humour and charisma, and applauded their readiness to flaunt their unmistakable Englishness in the wake of such unashamed Americanised Brit rockers as Free, Led Zeppelin and probably the most guilty, Humble Pie.

Sure, the band hadn't bothered too much about the overall quality of the new album and certainly value for money didn't seem to be high on their agenda either. But at least the band knew it.

They would argue that one reason "Long Player" sounded so patchy was due to their extensive touring schedule; but they secretly knew that wouldn't wash with most reviewers. Ronnie knew they were in for some flak from the music press, it was inevitable, and he was prepared for it. However, what he wasn't prepared for (and what surprised him the most), was the fact he was singled out for criticism.

Ronnie's guitar had dominated the album and although it was some of his most innovative playing to date, it did sound laboured and hesitant; something "Rolling Stone" - a tad unnecessarily - highlighted when it said: "The Faces seem to lack any clearly defined sense of direction. They are obliged (or disposed) to look aside from infrequent contributions in the grand old style by bassist Ronnie Lane, to late addition Ron Wood for direction. Wood most frequently fancying pleasant if dispensable bottle-neck laden variations on De Booze is not the Face to provide that direction."

Meaning they didn't like him.

Rod Stewart didn't escape unscathed either, his contributions were later described as: "....And Wood's friend with the haystack haircut doesn't seem nearly so intent on providing as differing to the other chaps tastes for purposes of saving the group from becoming Rod Stewart (with The Faces). But so intimidating is Stewart's presence apparently in what should, of course, but hasn't thus far been a mutually beneficial way, that the other chaps are all too eager to defer to Stewart's tastes. The present result being that instead of getting both Faces albums and Stewart albums, "Long Player" ends up being nothing more than a grab bag of tit-bits good enough to tide us over until Stewart's third solo album."

Other reviews were equally damming and most singled Ronnie out as their target.

"Ron Wood is probably one of the best guitarists for a beginner to copy" sneered Disc & Music Echo.

"First off you need to have played bass to have a good excuse for not playing fiddly!" Was Ronnie's reply, referring to all the intricate guitar work that was then in vogue, courtesy of the likes of Beck and Plant.

"When I started out I was copying riffs. I used to listen to early Motown records and try to find out what the hell the chords were, but that was hopeless and my playing was grinding to a halt. I came off a two-year stint playing bass and leaped into slide guitar which I'd not tried before. I heard Duane Allman and it was 'wow!' I felt a natural pull towards that. It was a whole new style of bottleneck because we started playing slide guitar using regular tuning and I tried to copy that. I never realised it was the most difficult way to start. I was aware of Steve Cropper, Buddy Guy,

Kenny Burrel and Wes Montgomery, but Duane's playing on Aretha Franklin's version of "The Weight" was my main inspiration. That was what I was trying to do."

So there.

Ronnie's intentions may have been honourable and it was obvious he knew just what he wanted to achieve in his head, but on "Long Player" he never managed to put it across. He was basically accused of gross self- indulgence by experimenting in public and using The Faces as a vehicle with which to pursue his own personal agenda, despite the obvious shortcomings and over-compensating clumsiness.

This popular train of thought wasn't helped when Ronnie Lane, (whose own compositions had been slightly less rubbished, ie "Horrendous production!" and "Insufficiently developed arrangement!") did little to help Ronnie's reputation as either a recording artist or a live performer when he stated, "Ronnie's got this thing about jamming, but it usually means fuck all! Jamming is alright for a bit of fun on your own, but in front of paying audiences... I ask you, is that fair?"

Ronnie defended his work on "Long Player" by (as expected) blaming the impossible demands of constant touring, and the lack of any serious time with which to work up any new material or ideas. But he was honest enough to acknowledge that his attitude had become sloppy and accepted that maybe the drinking was, in fact, getting just a little out of control. "I don't rehearse enough and I didn't practise. The only time I'd practise was when I put new strings on before a show, and then we'd usually be pissed anyway!"

Ronnie's playing throughout "Long Player" may have received a trouncing, but his lyrical contributions to the tracks, "Had Me A Real Good Time", "Sweet Lady Mary" and even Lane's "On The Beach" were met with grudging approval. In fact, Ronnie's "Sweet Lady Mary" was regarded by most reviewers as the album's standalone track and highlight.

Funny people, those 70s rock critics.

It's a story about separation, incompatibility and the doomed love of a travelling man that may well have owed its origins to "Gasoline Alley" but Ronnie's' harder edged realism had maybe pointed The Faces (for the first time) in the direction of hit-making potential.

"Her Spanish habits are so hard to forget,
The lady lied with every breath I accept,
It was a matter of time before my face did not fit."

Ronnie was more susceptible to any form of criticism in the run up to The Faces playing to British crowds. They had a handful of UK shows lined-up across the country and he grabbed the opportunity of an interview with "Melody Maker" prior to the first show at the Orchid Ballroom in Purley Surrey on 11th April.

In it he explains how he saw The Faces progressing in the UK. He also defended "Long Player" and the intended new single, "Maybe I'm Amazed". The latter was eventually produced as a limited edition pressing of 500 copies, given away free to the fans entering London's Chalk Farm Roundhouse on 29th April: "The first album was simply to show the direction the band was taking and this one was us levelling out. But the next one will be "Wow! That's how it should be". I don't think the band realise that we've got something to live up to. The next album will supersede "Long Player" - we've got to keep up a high standard of work and even the Stones have re-recorded "Honky-Tonk Woman" that's why we've re-recorded numbers today that would have been considered great about six months ago. I really think we get a very high standard of performance on stage. If there's more than a minute between numbers now, Rod goes potty and the rest of us get very edgy. I mean I've watched The Grateful Dead constantly tuning up and it makes my nerves bad. Now when we go out on stage, there's no time to be messing about tuning up, so if the things are not in tune when you go out there... beware!"

The Faces had also come up with a highly unconventional, but nonetheless novel, way of ensuring a convivial response from their audience. They had decided to dispose with the usual approach of using a support band at most of the shows in favour of distributing free crates of wine and beer from the stage.

"We'd get the roadies to dish out fucking great crates of the stuff," Ronnie laughs. "Crates of wine and then wait for about an hour and a half while the audience were soaking it all up and come on when they were completely pissed!"

The group had already performed shows in the US with the aid of a fully stocked, and functioning, bar set-up on the stage from which waiters dressed in white shirts, bow ties and waistcoats would serve the band with drinks throughout their set. This would later expand to two, the standard size bar run by cocktail waitresses, and a little mobile one pushed from player to player by a dwarf in white tie and tails.

Meanwhile, the roadies would cut and leave neat lines of cocaine on the top of flight cases and amplifiers positioned just to the side of the stage out of view of the audience.

It was a 'devil may care' approach to performing, born from sheer insanity. Not surprising, Ronnie remembers little of these shows: "None of The Faces remember much about those shows, but that was just the beginning. Things got much worse on the later tours."

Their attitude to playing in the UK was still very much chore like, and the idea of getting the crowd as drunk as themselves was probably as calculated and self-indulgent as The Faces would get, but hey, it worked!

The images of Rod & Ron singing head-to-head around the one mike may have been reminiscent of Lennon & McCartney, but their cartoon-like features forged an identity very much their own, and it's an image that has stayed indelibly fixed in the memories of Faces fans ever since. The whole band had almost subconsciously honed their stage presence whilst on those long hauls across the States. It still retained their trade-mark of slipshod, good natured, men-of-the-people, but now they added a dash of panache which gave them that true, pop-star quality.

"I wouldn't say American audiences made us into a great band overnight. But they certainly made us into a big one," remembers Rod Stewart.

And Ronnie was a major reason. There was little doubt that he'd learnt to project the very charisma and self assurance needed to elevate himself from the shadow of Rod Stewart in very much the same way as Pete Townshend had done vis-à-vis Roger Daltrey, or Jimmy Page with Robert Plant.

Ronnie was also a lot less menacing, and a sight more entertaining than Jeff Beck had ever been in the same situation. The magic didn't only work with Rod Stewart, either. When he got it together with Lane, the picture was perfect: the duo's plumes of thick cigarette smoke wreathing their faces as one by one they'd chug over to the bar in order to take more booze on board, like steam trains going to the water tank.

McLagan and Jones completed the scene. Mac sat bolt upright at his white grand piano complete with candelabra and crystal wine glass, ever resplendent in one of his seemingly-inexhaustible supply of brightly coloured waistcoats.

He always gave the impression that he felt a little resentful about the obvious restrictive nature of his chosen instrument, trapped and confined to the right of the stage. Especially when Rod and Ronnie would drag on a net full of footballs and together with Lane boot them into the crowd. He'd be forever craning his neck over his shoulder watching the antics of the band's centre forward and his pair of knock-about team mates.

All the while, Kenney would thunder on relentlessly behind them, tight-lipped and staring madly heavenward, barely visible behind his custom built Liquorish Allsorts-coloured kit.

British audiences were finally waking up to something that America had known for more than a year: that here was a band whose natural vitality, humour and undeniable hospitality set them worlds apart from anything else currently on offer, either side of the Atlantic.

Britain was finally ready to welcome them into their own, often inebriated, heart.

It's fair to say that at this point, had The Faces' rapport fallen flat with a larger, home-grown audience then Rod Stewart would certainly have taken to the road with Ronnie and the rest of his studio band.

It's also true that they could have sustained a small part of the magic.

However, that particular group of musicians could never have linked together so perfectly Britain's three major passions outside of sex - music, football and booze.

You can rearrange the order to suit, but the fact remains The Faces were the very embodiment of the real working-class dream. Two hours spent watching them strut around the stage bolstered the belief that if this bunch of befuddled piss-heads could take on the world and succeed, then there was a very real chance that the audience could too.

The success of these live shows even had a rejuvenating effect on the UK sales of "Long Player" pushing it as far as number thirty one in the charts, only two places lower than the US showing. Billy Gaff added extra dates, hoping to keep up the British momentum, and extended the live itinerary through April, May and into July - at which point another American excursion would kick in, their fourth in under two years.

The band also managed a TV appearance on 22nd April, when they were the stars of BBC Two's music show, Disco Two, where they performed three numbers from the album: Ronnie's "Sweet Lady Mary", Lane's "Tell Everyone" and "Bad 'n Ruin".

Ronnie and Rod Stewart added to their workload, whenever possible, by meeting up between dates at Morgan Studios to record tracks for Rod's third solo album which Mercury had scheduled for release on 9th July - the date of the group's next live date in the US.

The ridiculousness of such a gruelling schedule meant Stewart sticking pretty much to the same established formula and components that had worked so well on his first two albums. Ronnie and Rod were the nucleus, aided by Micky Waller, Martin Quittenton, and assorted Faces where needed. They recorded the usual Dylan song, some old soul covers, a Tim Hardin number and two Stewart originals. There was also a Rod and Ronnie newie, the opening and title track: "Every Picture Tells A Story".

"Every Picture Tells A Story" was as close to a conceptual, autobiographical Rod Stewart album as it's possible to get, without meaning to be. The title track itself revives the familiar tale of the wanderer, which harked back to Stewart's days as a busker in Europe; albeit with large portions of poetic license. You know the kind of thing: trouble-prone traveller and his meandering memories of unfulfilled relationships, and lustful encounters in far-off lands.

Which slightly begged the question as to why Stewart gave it all up to become a gravedigger.

Nonetheless, it's a mini masterpiece of a song, and one that managed to encapsulate the entire feel of the album in under six minutes. More importantly, it highlighted the definite coming-of-age of Ron and Rod's musical partnership. It might even have stood out as Rod Stewart's finest moment to date, had it not been for a certain other track entitled "Maggie May". Yet another fabled slice of the Stewart sexual legend, which deals with the loss of virginity to an older women, heartbreak, pool playing - and even joining The Faces: "Find myself a rock and roll band that needs a helping hand".

All of which make both songs a virtual Rod reference fest.

The album also displayed Rod's uncanny knack at picking the right songs to cover. Numbers that suited and complemented his very distinct vocal style, yet at the same time sat comfortably alongside the admittedly brilliant, but few, originals.

Despite the album's heavy covers quota, the finished result sounded complete, slick and passionate; three qualities that had been arguably missing from both Ron and Rod's work with the Faces so far.

Ironically, both Stewart and Mercury Records were slow to recognise "Maggie May's" massive hit potential and relegated it to the B-side of Rod's next single, "Reason To Believe". However, some keen-eared DJs on both sides of the Atlantic knew a hit when they heard one, and took it upon themselves to flip the disc over in favour of Maggie.

It was played non-stop until it bounced simultaneously to the Number One spot in both the UK and America.

Needless to say, Rod's massive single success had a positive knock-on effect regarding The Faces' popularity in the UK. An example of which was witnessed on 29th August 1971 when the band played a support slot for T Rex at the Weeley Rock Festival, just outside Clacton-on-Sea in Essex.

"WEELEY - A ONE GROUP FESTIVAL!" screamed the "New Musical Express" front page the following week. Inside ran a story of how Britain's then premier attraction, T Rex, had been totally humiliated by a crowd shouting and banging beer cans together as they demanded more of The Faces for a full fifteen minutes into T Rex's set.

The report also said that the Faces' rendition of "Maggie May" brought the best response of the entire festival, with the hundred thousand plus crowd standing singing along with the words. The reviewer's sympathies were with T Rex, of whom he said, "couldn't hope to match the sheer brilliance of The Faces".

Flash back three months and The Faces were playing pubs like "The Nags' Head" in Northampton and "The Croydon Greyhound" with a maximum of two hundred and fifty drunken punters at each gig. All of whom invariably shouted out for the old Small Faces hits, "All Or Nothing" and "Lazy Sunday". Now, they were knocking the sequins and feather boas off Marc Bolan and T Rex.

Ah, but wait, there was a price to pay for that sort of unexpected wind fall, especially in a band where the levels of paranoia were rising as fast as their popularity. The attention scales were tipped even more in Rod Stewart's favour, and the rest of the band's mental scoreboard flashed up Rod Stewart One, The Faces (plus Rod Stewart) Nil.

What's more, it was about to get worse. Within weeks the phenomenal success of "Maggie May" saw the album also propelled to the number one position, an amazing feat which meant that for the first time in recording history, the same artist held the top spots simultaneously on both the American and UK singles and album charts.

Oh yes, he also had album and single Number Ones in Canada, New Zealand and Australia.

Rod Stewart Seven, The Faces (plus Rod Stewart) still Nil.

The rest of the group's fate as Rod Stewart's backing band now looked cast in stone. For a while they clung to the hope that Rod's recording success might somehow rub off on his team-mates, so they made do with shamelessly plugging "Maggie May" with all the intent and purpose of making it look like a group effort. They ignored the fact that only Ronnie was a member of Stewart's studio band of writers and regulars.

Micky Waller, for one, was understandably shocked to see Kenney Jones uncomfortably miming to his drum fills when he tuned in to see The Faces performing the song on Top Of The Pops.

"To this day people don't believe it's me playing on Maggie May, because they wanted people to think it was Kenney. They wanted to make The Faces look better than they really were. But anyone who saw them knew they weren't capable of recording anything as remotely good as that. The Faces couldn't make a fucking half-decent record, they were useless, you've got to ask yourself if they were that good, why didn't Rod use them all the time?"

Kenney to his credit has never claimed to have played drums on "Maggie May" and defends the group's performance in his customary matter of fact manner. "We were so obviously fucking miming its not true. We kicked a bleedin football about on the set to show it wasn't really us playing. What Micky forgets is that before you did "Top Of The Pops", certainly back in those days, every band would have to re-record the backing track you mimed to."

Fair enough, but in reality, the band did want to have their cake and eat it, too. The fans in the know, knew the clowning-around demonstrated that The Faces weren't trying to take credit for "Maggie May", but they were also banking on the fact that the vast majority of the record-buying public didn't have a clue.

Micky Waller aside, certain British rock journalists were also sceptical about the band's real musical abilities, some even sniped that The Faces had only triumphed at the Weeley Festival because they were only up against a field-full of has beens and teeny bopper favourites like T-Rex. Quite what The Grease Band (who were given yet another hiding); Mungo Jerry; the Groundhogs; Heads Hands and Feet; Juicy Lucy; and the newly be-denimed Status Quo thought of this is any one's guess.

The Faces' next show was at the more sedate, but prestigious, Queen Elizabeth Hall on London's South bank. There it was announced that Rod Stewart had been voted best male Vocalist by the readers of Melody Maker, Maggie Bell, Stewart's chosen backing singer was voted Best Female Vocalist, and the single "Maggie May" made third place in the International single's listing. Lane, McLagan and Jones all fared reasonably well in their chosen instrumental categories, but there was no mention of Ronnie, anywhere.

Next up The Faces were second on the bill at the Oval Cricket Ground, where they gave the mighty Who a run for their money in front of thirty-five thousand fans.

"For a live show," wrote Chris Charlesworth in his "Melody Maker" review, "it has long been my opinion that The Who couldn't be topped - but watch out, Who, The Faces are breathing down your necks." The Faces seemed to be silencing their critics at last.

"I had a few doubts about The Faces to begin with." Rod admitted in the same edition "Me and Woody used to think, "Christ' we'd better ring Jeff (Beck), this isn't going to work." Ron and me had come from the so-called underground, The Faces were more pop and it was hard to match the two of them up at first. But it's working out fairly well."

Well, it certainly was for Ronnie and Rod, both of whom were obviously benefiting from Rod's solo career. The royalties were mounting up from their joint compositions and it was time to go house hunting.

Stewart bought his first, obligatory rock-star mansion, Cranbourne Court, from Lord Bethell. A thirty-two roomed monster pile near Windsor in Berkshire surrounded by fourteen acres, with a lodge, a stable block and swimming pool for which he paid £89,000 cash (over £1.5 million today). Girlfriend Sarah Troops got lost in the move and new flame, Dee Harrington, became the lady of the house.

Ronnie, too, was looking to move up the property ladder, encouraged by Krissie's conviction that they needed something a little more distinctive than the Old Forge in Henley.

Perry Press was once again set to work to find them something appropriate in the Richmond area. Now, it's a little difficult to hide wealth from close, working colleagues and the rest of the band duly noted that the two newcomers were doing vastly better than they were.

Ronnie was now driving a new Bentley and Stewart a bright red Lamborghini. The rest of The Faces were doing okay, but it was obvious they were nowhere near as well off as Ron and Rod. It seemed to them that the pair were moving into different musical and social orbits, or to put it plainly they were leaving the boys behind. Whether the feelings of distance and resentment were warranted is beside the point. They were inevitable.

"We never saw the Rod thing being quite so big," Ronnie said at the time, trying to paper over the cracks. "We were extraordinarily close and we'd all reached a stage when we co-operated with each other. With the Rod thing it was all of a sudden Bang! and he was huge. He was getting lots of offers, people dangling carrots under his nose, but Rod was incredibly good about the whole thing, and despite all the temptations of going solo, he swore The Faces were still his cup of tea. However, I don't think the others saw it like that, and they looked for someone to blame."

Over thirty years later, Ronnie looks back and sees the situation a little differently. "The wives started the break-up. They were always setting their husbands up against one another arguing and rowing with each other, and just making life unbearable. It made you want to get away from it, because they acted as if they were the band instead of us. That's one reason we toured so much - and then they started coming on tour with us, and that was the beginning of the end."

The three original Faces had all married young, in their very early twenties, and all would divorce young. Ian McLagan married Ready Steady Go dancer Sandy Sarjeant, Ronnie Lane to the singer Genevieve, real name Sue, and Kenney Jones to Jan Osborne, daughter of the composer Tony Osborne. Rod Stewart's relationships are a book in itself.

None of the marriages survived The Faces. None of the girls remarried and only Sandy, a particularly feisty character, reverted to her maiden name.

Years later, Krissie Wood summed up the first (rock) wives club dilemma when she was asked why she'd never re-married? She replied, "Well in a way I wanted to… but that meant changing my name and I wouldn't be a Wood anymore."

Then again, the wives all say they had to put up with a hell of a lot from their men.

At one party all the couples attended, Ronnie Lane went missing, as did Sue's best friend and neighbour, Kate McInnerney, wife of designer Mike (Tommy album cover).

They were discovered having sex by the extremely put-out Sue.

It then transpires Ronnie and Sue had an open marriage and often swapped partners with like-minded friends and groupies. However, there were rules to this practice and apparently they didn't stretch to best friends and neighbours.

Besides, they were at it in Sue and Ronnie's bed.

Ronnie topped it off by announcing to the embarrassed guests afterwards that in fact he preferred Kate now anyway. So that was all right then. Two marriages broke up that night.

This little act of indiscretion sent shock waves of insecurity through the other wives and girlfriends as they realised how easily and callously they could be replaced. After all, none of their relationships were what could be called conventional, and God only knows how much temptation their men-folk faced everyday. It was a worry and fear that gnawed away at Krissie in particular.

"That business with Ronnie and Sue Lane had obviously played on her mind," Sandy Sarjeant recalls. "One time we were all in America together, and the boys were on stage. Krissie was all done up in her usual manner - feather boa, big floppy hat and silk dress. She was also totally pissed, and one of her tits had popped out of her dress.

"She had really great tits, I would have loved to have tits like Krissie's. Anyway, she was standing by the side of the stage, obviously mulling over something in her head.

All of a sudden she walks straight out on stage, glass of champagne in one hand, and her tit still hanging out. This is in front of thousands of people; she walks up to Woody, who hasn't seen her yet, and she tapped him on the shoulder. Ronnie turned round and he couldn't believe his eyes,

Krissie started wagging her finger in his face and shouting: "If you ever do to me, what he (pointing a finger at an equally-shocked Lane) did to her (Sue), I'm fucking leaving you!"."

Kenney Jones remembers that night very well, and was the first one to notice Krissie's arrival on stage; "I saw her come out and thought, where the fuck is she going? None of the others had seen her because they all had their backs to her and me. Ronnie was dumbstruck. Rod broke it up; he was fuming and gobbed on her back, she was hustled off the stage and we tried to finish the song. It was fucking unbelievable."

The next night Kenney turned up on stage wearing a T-shirt that read: 'If you do to me, what he did to her...

Sandy admits: "I've never been able to work Krissie out. Even to this day. She was absolutely beautiful, she was everything I wanted to be; gorgeous figure, blonde, blue-eyed, hair down her back, but she was like she was on another planet. She'd either be as thick as shit, or she'd have flashes of brilliance. I never knew whether she was playing the dumb blonde or if it was for real, and I still don't know."

In October 1971 the band left for America, for a two-week tour that included a sellout show at Madison Square Garden, where they previewed the song that would become the band's first and finest hit single, "Stay With Me."

"That one song and in particular the intro, turned my career around." Ronnie says. "It came at the time when everyone was kissing the arses of Led Zeppelin. That song and the album "A Nod's As Good As A Wink To A Blind Horse" made people really sit up and take notice, that was when the band finally came together."

Not just the intro, Ronnie's playing throughout firmly established him as a class lead guitar player, and also led to one of the most embarrassing moments of his career.

"It was that Madison Square Garden show. We had this idea of walking through the crowd like boxers to get to the stage. I had my guitar strapped on and I must have knocked it out of tune getting through. There was a big introduction when we got on stage: 'Ladies and Gentlemen… The Faces' and we were supposed to kick off with "Stay With Me" my cue to start the gig with those big opening chords. Except I played the most out of tune shit, I'd ever heard in my life. Then there was dead silence and the whole band are looking at me wondering what I'd played. I had to walk up to the mike and tell twenty thousand people to talk amongst themselves while I stood there and tuned my guitar. Rod was pacing around, and it put me off for the rest of the gig. I should have been my biggest moment, but it turned out a nightmare.

"I was still pleased with the attention I started to receive as a guitarist. Because I was getting a bit worried that I was always going to be left in the background. It's nice when the little things you come up with get picked out, and you realize you've got something across to people. At one point I felt that being stuck away was going to be my position for life. I'd started out experimenting with slide guitar on "Gasoline Alley" and then I was using a twelve string and a six string and over dubbing the slide. Then I found I could get the same sound live by using open tuning and fiddling around.

"I found I could easily mould the guitar around the organ and bass. I think that guitarists had gone out of style for a while back then. It was the dawn of the piano players like Leon Russell, Billy Preston and of course, Elton John. Hendrix had gone and Beck and Eric Clapton had faded away into the background. It's like every style, it comes and goes - t's basically the public's whim."

There's probably one other important factor in the success of the band's new found confidence, they'd finally hired Glyn Johns as their producer. Although Johns now seems less enamoured about his involvement or his experience. "It was obvious to me as soon as I got involved with them that it was a case of Rod Stewart and his backing band. That wasn't necessarily anyone's fault. Rod was a success and the band wasn't. I doubt if I'd work with them again though, too much hoo-hah went down in the end and I made myself unpopular. Rod's vocal abilities are wider than he gives himself credit for. He was the one person I never produced. You don't produce him, he has a particular way of recording and it works for him."

The album reached number two in England and number six in the US. The single made it to number six in England and number seventeen in America. Both single and album would have undoubtedly reached the top spot on both sides of the Atlantic if it hadn't been for a last minute re-call by Warner Brothers.

The record label in America had apparently been inundated with complaints concerning the contents of a huge fold-out poster that came with the album. It was made up of hundreds of little snap shots taken by the band and crew on tour in the US and some of them featured (presumably) groupies in various states of undress.

Nevertheless, the year had ended on a high note for the band and an even higher one for Rod Stewart. A list compiled by the British Market Research Bureau named him as the top-selling album artist of the year, and the third biggest singles. As Glyn Johns said, Rod and his backing band, or as was becoming increasingly apparent, Rod Stewart And The Faces, also featuring Ronnie Wood.

CHAPTER TWELVE
"MY WHOLE FAMILY'S GOOD AT EMPTYING BOTTLES."

The Wick in Richmond, now owned by Pete Townshend, is one of the loveliest houses in the London area. It's a classic Georgian, twenty-roomed house standing just below the brow of Richmond Hill, overlooking that lovely curve of the Thames, which gave its name to a similar view in Richmond, Virginia. The garden slopes down to the towpath, and includes a three-bedroom cottage - very important, The Wick cottage, because without it Ronnie could never have afforded the house's asking price of £100,000.

He was doing well, but not that well. Not yet.

The problem was solved by Ronnie Lane, now homeless and separated following his affair with a girl named Kate McInnerney. Ronnie bought The Wick and Lane bought the cottage, partly because he could also park his mobile recording studio (housed in a classic American silver Air-Stream caravan), in the garden. On the face of it, a good deal for everyone, and at first Lane was delighted with the deal.

But not for long, for every time he walked out of his own little home he'd be confronted by the evidence of how much more successful his band-mate had become. Ronnie owned the mansion on the hill, while he had what were effectively the servants' quarters. Lane had always seen himself, along with Marriott, as the moving force behind The Small Faces. Now he'd been sidelined by two outsiders. The Faces weren't even relying on his song writing talents as much as before, now it was all Ronnie and Rod, and there was that bloody great house to prove it.

Now firmly under the influence of Kate McInnerney, a great one for the myth of the raggle-taggle gypsy, o! - Lane himself began to adopt a gypsy-like approach to life. Possessions no longer meant anything, he would preach: "I know big houses and big cars won't make me particularly happy. It's work, friends, the company I keep, and the old lady."

Subsequently, Lane adapted his wardrobe to suit. He began wearing earrings and allowed his hair to become romantically straggly. The only exceptions to the no-possession rule for Lane were guitars and caravans, a lot of caravans.

"I had so much trouble adapting that fucking Air-Stream caravan for British electrics." Lane joked in 1990. "Nothing fitted, the plugs were all wrong, the voltage, the sockets everything, and when I'd finally finished it, I realised the only reason I'd bought it was because I liked the look of it.

"Funny thing was, years later, after I'd split up with Kate, it got vandalized when I left it parked on a council estate in Hackney - and I discovered that the only thing insured was the fucking wiring."

The irony of course was that here was a man trying to become a gypsy, while a real, full-blooded Romany lived in the big house on the hill.

Meanwhile, the caravan collection continued to grow and grow and came to include a traditional, brightly painted, horse-drawn example that remained slowly mouldering in the garden long after Lane had gone.

His appearance continued changing, too. The more glamorous the other Faces became, the more down market Lane became. He'd turn up in dirty old jeans, a long costermonger scarf, high lace-up boots and a four-day stubble. In The Small Faces, Lane's persona as a down to earth East End mod from Plaistow seemed so right when surrounded by his three little mates from Mile End and Stepney; all cheeky, cheerful barrow-boys with an eye for mischief and a wicked sense of fun. Even in the early days of the New Faces, his dapper, teddy-boy drape suits hadn't looked out of place.

However, from 1972 onwards his look of ragged introspection was totally at odds with the others' naturally flamboyant style.

His point about possessions didn't last either. After he left The Faces, he finally got over his hatred of large houses and bought a working sheep farm in Wales.

Tragically diagnosed as suffering from multiple sclerosis, he later discovered that his condition had been made worse by the chemicals used in sheep-dip.

Ronnie had bought The Wick from Sir John Mills and his wife, the writer Mary Hayley Bell, who'd decided to move out of London, although they regretted their decision almost as soon as the papers had been signed, and asked Ronnie to sell it back for more than he'd paid.

Ronnie declined the offer. In his mind he'd already spent £25,000 to equip the recording studio he planned for the basement.

Besides "I fell in love with The Wick as soon as I saw it. I'd always wanted a nice, big house and Krissie and me were fed up living in chaos, always moving. Even when I'd lived at home with my mum and dad, it was chaos because there'd be parties every week - my family has always been good at emptying bottles. When we moved into The Wick, I got Art's then wife, Doreen, to come in every day as my secretary and mum used to come and cook breakfast every morning and do anything to help out. Art and Ted were always there, offering to fix things, which they were no good at, but it was lovely, just like being at home - there was always people coming and going, but mum was used to it, she'd known chaos ever since she'd had children. And my dad was so proud, too!"

Krissie had fallen in love with the place too, "Ronnie just said to me one day, "Kriss I've found the house for us". I didn't know he'd even been looking. Then when I saw The Wick I couldn't believe how beautiful it was, I kept on saying, "Is it really going to be ours?" Sir John Mills left us a note on the mirror, saying "I hope you will be as happy as we were at The Wick." He was such a lovely man - the fact that he and his wife lived there for so long and they'd brought up their children, Hayley, Juliet and Jonathan, there, made the house even more special."

Even so, not everything in the garden was rosy. While there had been no serious affair to disrupt Ronnie and Krissie's relationship so far, their idyll had begun to tarnish a little. They'd been together for nearly eight years. Ronnie had grown in stature as a musician, and Krissie had grown in stature as a musician's woman. It was no longer the two of them against the world, nor was there a case for Krissie to have to work to keep them.

As the band became more and more successful, they toured relentlessly, back-to-back treks across Britain, Europe and their second home, America, where they were regularly spotted fraternizing with the likes of Crosby, Stills and Nash, the Allman Brothers, the occasional wayward Beatle and the Stones.

All the while, the wives seethed and bickered about not being able to join their men 24 hours a day.

Ronnie and the band's schedule for 1972 went something like this: Germany in March; the UK and the US in April; back to Germany and the UK in May; another US tour in August (their seventh), all interspersed with recording sessions for the next album. Then there was Ronnie and Ronnie Lane's side project, a film score for the movie "Mahoney's Last Stand", sessions for Rod's fourth album, a single and yet another trek across the States. All of which kept Ronnie and Krissie apart for some considerable lengths of time and delayed the day The Wick would begin to feel like their new home. So basically it was hardly surprising that Krissie began to suspect that Ronnie must be sleeping around.

Ronnie had known George and Patti Harrison for a couple of years, and Ron had introduced Krissie to the ex-Beatle in Los Angeles that same hectic year. It was common knowledge at the time that the Harrison's marriage was heading for the rocks and that George had (briefly) ditched his daily meditation marathons in favour of some slightly more earthy pursuits.

Krissie believes that Ronnie began an affair with Patti around this time, but this has been hotly denied by both Ronnie and Patti even to this day. So, it's possible Ronnie was simply a shoulder for Patti to cry on at a particularly difficult time.

Even by Krissie's admission, Ronnie could be very sympathetic when needed. "Brian Robertson (Thin Lizzy guitar player) once said to me that Ronnie had the ability to make you feel that you are the most important person in the room all the time he's with you, but it's a mistake to hold on to that moment. I thought wow! That's it, that's what was wrong, he can do that… and once you've moved on, it'll be someone else and you're a fool to think otherwise. He never calls you back, he's got that wonderful thing that allows him to live in the now, he doesn't live for tomorrow or yesterday.

"People mistake it for innocence, but it's not, it's actually very calculated and intelligent. I was speaking to Pete Townshend just the other day and he agrees. There's also a cutting side to Ronnie; he can really cut you down very quickly with a smile on his face. I think it was something he developed while being on the road all the time. He didn't live a life like an ordinary person who sometimes woke up with a hangover and went down the pub to get over it. He woke up like that all the time, but he'd have to perform for people both on and off stage. So he learned to develop this way of dealing with people who are naturally drawn to him."

In other words, people gravitate to Ronnie and receive what they think is his total support and interest which it is at the time. He's also incredibly discrete and jealously guards his private life, which was one of the reasons why his friendship with George lasted like it did; his privacy made him an ideal confidant, for him a secret shared is a secret never repeated.

Whatever the truth of Ronnie's close friendship with Patti, Krissie remains convinced of the worst. At the time she felt more and more that the growing distance between them wasn't only a matter of mile, but more a case of them moving emotionally apart. Such is the downside of being a rock wife in a situation made all the worse by the suspected rival being married to a Beatle, for in rock wifedom's natural pecking order, there's no wife more important than a Beatle wife.

It wouldn't even have been necessary for Ronnie to have slept with Patti for what came next to have happened. Simply being close to her was enough.

Krissie vividly remembers her first meeting with George Harrison, in Los Angeles at a party for The Faces. "George started chatting me up. He had no idea I was with Ronnie. He was so calm, but very charismatic with that great crooked grin. He seemed to be a million miles removed from all the rock-star bullshit going on around us. He just sort of glided in and suddenly there he was, talking to me. I never dreamed anything would happen between us, I just remember feeling really flattered."

The next time they met was in October 1972 at a party at The Wick. Ronnie had only recently settled in at the house and a string of house-warming parties were a regular happening. George stayed over that night and the next morning, Krissie breezed into his room to offer him a cup of tea. Her third meeting is probably her most vivid and she still giggles at the memory of it. "The first thing I saw was George's naked bottom bouncing up and down in this big brass bed. I didn't recognize the girl because I couldn't see her face, if you know what I mean. I slipped out pretty quickly and thought maybe the tea can wait."

George had undoubtedly made a lasting impression on Krissie - one that would ultimately lead to her first serious affair.

Mansions, luxury cars, a seemingly inexhaustible supply of money and drugs, especially whilst touring America, famous friends, adulation, jealousy, and a entourage of twenty four hour ego masseurs. That was now the life of Krissie and Ronnie; the average age of the rock star fraternity was around twenty five years old and they felt like gods. It seemed nothing was beyond their reach, and they were almost expected to behave with a wild disregard for society's values.

Someone needed to keep such lifestyles in check, or at least the worst parts out of the newspapers. Enter Shirley Arnold, who as a former secretary to the Rolling Stones (Brian Jones in particular) understood a bit about drugs, chaos and scandal. Most importantly, she knew how to deal with such matters. She'd started work with the Stones as a naïve sixteen-year old. Nine years later she'd be forgiven for thinking she'd seen it all.

"I was working at their New Oxford Street office, when Ronnie Wood and Ronnie Lane came up to see Ian Stewart (Stones roadie and session piano player) about the film soundtrack they were working on. Ronnie Lane's car got towed away while they were there and they didn't know what to do. They were so vague, it wasn't true, "Oh, blimey, the car's gone!

What do we do?" They really didn't have a clue. Luckily the Stones organisation was very professional and we could sort almost anything out. So I got on to the car pound and within an hour I'd got the thing back. It was as if I'd pulled off the most amazing thing in the world, they were so impressed. I thought "My God! They need someone to look after them." I'd been thinking about a change for a while, but I wasn't sure I wanted to jump from one band to another. But I remember watching them both and thinking, compared to the Stones they were like two little kids. They were saying "Oh we need someone like you, we need a secretary. Shirl, could you do some things for us?"

"They kept on and on until I said, "I might be able to Ron, I'll give it a try." There was a lot of nonsense starting to happen concerning Billy Gaff; some of the band didn't think they were being well managed, and I think they thought I was more high-powered than I actually was.

"They thought I could take them away from Billy, they all did; all but Ronnie, who didn't seem to care either way. Anyway, to cut a long story short, I eventually went to work for them and after about two weeks, I realised what a God-awful mistake I'd made. There was nothing you could do for them; they were so unreliable and un-united on every little thing. There was so much bitching going on amongst themselves and amongst the wives.

"Ronnie Lane was constantly bitching on about Billy, Kenney was bitching about Woody and Mac being forever late at the studio and both Mac and Kenney bitched about money. The only thing all three bitched about together was Rod. They were still on about the separate billing they'd got in America, some banner they'd seen, it was terrible. My God, they were not the happy go lucky band people thought they were, not in the slightest.

"They all got incredibly moody over the pettiest of things, trivial silly things that would then get blown up out of all proportion. This was around the time Kenny started insisting his name was spelt with an extra 'E' - as in Kenney, it would get so bad at times I'd be relieved when they finally went on stage, that was the only time they'd stop moaning.

"I started leaving the venues while they were on so I could have a cigarette in peace, that's when I'd wonder to myself, "what had I done" and remember I'd worked for Brian Jones. On top of all that, I was constantly having to quash the rumours flying around that Woody was secretly seeing Patti Harrison."

The Stones had thrown a leaving party for Shirley, the week she left. "Mick was lovely - he'd organized it all, ordered a huge cake and champagne and flowers. He kept saying he didn't want me to leave, I should have listened to him. What was funny was The Faces were all downstairs, frightened to come up in case my leaving had upset the Stones. It was hilarious, Woody was the only one up there helping himself and slowly, all the others drifted in one at a time.

Shirley joined the Gaff Organization as a secretary, not a personal assistant or managerial figure. However, none of the band bar Rod (he already had one) seemed to realize this. They all wanted to be looked after, which is what personal assistants do, so Shirley found herself just that, and doing it extremely well.

"I soon worked out that Krissie wasn't very good at the domestic side of things. So I offered to cook for them one day. Ronnie asked if I could make a shepherd's pie, and I remember doing it in their kitchen and every one coming back for seconds. I don't think that kitchen had been used for cooking since they'd moved in. I once saw Krissie trying to make toast and I'll tell you one thing, it was just as well Ronnie didn't eat much. I eventually realised that he wanted some normality in his life, because nothing in his life was normal any more; he was totally surrounded by so many abnormal things."

Shirley had done a great job of dampening down the media rumblings concerning Ronnie and a Beatle wife... little realising that Krissie was about to give the papers a story that was really worth writing about.

Shortly before The Faces started their run of Christmas gigs, Ronnie and Krissie were invited by Mick and Bianca Jagger to stay at the Guinness family's castle in Ireland. The invitation hadn't come out of the blue, for Ronnie and Mick had become firm friends over the last couple of years. For while it was Keith Richards who would ultimately become Ronnie's soul mate, it was Mick who initially took him under his wing.

"He's a shrewd boy, Mick." Ronnie says. "He'd always kept an eye on what I was doing, right back from when he'd rung my house that time. I started hanging out with him a lot at that time. So it wasn't unusual for us to go on a break together. When we were in Ireland he wrote "Daddy You're A Fool To Cry" and he played it to me on an acoustic guitar, I was blown away by that - it's an incredible song."

While Ronnie and Mick immersed themselves in song, Krissie spent most of her time alone. She'd found it difficult to connect with either Bianca or the Guinness family. "They were nice but very aloof; I felt very out of place and uncomfortable."

Eventually these feelings proved too much and fuelled by what she now admits to a little too much hash, she made her excuses and metaphorically and physically flew home alone. Only she didn't return to The Wick. Instead, she went directly to the gothic pile which is Friar Park and its owner, George Harrison.

"What people don't realise or for that matter, appreciate" Krissie explains, "was how young we all were. I mean really young. None of us had grown up in a normal environment; we weren't living in the real world. We were all very childish and selfish in so many ways and suddenly we had all this money and privileges, and no one to tell us how to behave, so we didn't stop to think."

In Krissie's mind her brief affair with George Harrison should also be seen as payback to Ronnie's hotly denied, yet more than likely, fling with Patti. It would certainly explain how the whole episode was so quickly forgotten.

Ronnie and Krissie would stay together for a few more years but the damage had been done and in effect, it signalled the beginning of the end of their relationship.

Still, she'd proved a couple of things to herself. First, was that one of the most famous and eligible men in the world had found her most desirable, and second, Ronnie was no longer the centre of her world. How could he be, he was now so rarely in it.

They'd met as kids, and in many ways their relationship had never grown up. Krissie had never had a career, or had any thoughts of starting one. She did harbour the idea of becoming a model once, after all she had the looks, but then again didn't most rock stars' wives nurture similar dreams? Anyway, being Mrs Wood and part of the trendy London crowd was career enough. So, why had she begun to feel the first glimmerings of discontent, coupled with the vague suspicion that just possibly she was living in a fool's paradise.

Krissie and George's affair never made the same media splash that the later Patti Harrison, Eric Clapton one did. This was due in part to the quiet Beatle's obsessively secretive nature, and a testament to Shirley Arnold's professionalism.

Rod Stewart's fourth solo album, "Never A Dull Moment" had been released in July 1972 and it had notched him up yet another number one. The Faces started performing various tracks from it including "You Wear It Well", which also hit the top spot and saw the band once again hamming it up on "Top Of The Pops". They performed it once in August and then again on Christmas Day and both times, Kenney found himself in the awkward situation of once again miming to Micky Waller's drum track.

"I sometimes wonder what I did to upset them," Waller says, "I've never been able to forgive Rod and Billy Gaff, I don't think they cared who they upset. The saddest thing about all that was, my father had just died and I remember my mum getting into an argument with a neighbour, after she'd told her I was Rod Stewart's drummer. Of course, the neighbour saw "Top Of The Pops" and there was Kenney pretending to drum. The neighbour called my mum a liar, which made her cry and I've never forgotten that."

The Band never looked totally comfortable playing Rod's solo hits on those Christmas dates. Preferring to play instead his cover versions and in particular, his rendition (and second single from the album) of the Jimi Hendrix classic, "Angel".

"Angel" saw the band back on "Top Of The Pops" - once again without Waller and this time without Ronnie Lane, who sent along a life-size cut out of himself indicating that he was no longer prepared to take part in the farce.

For Ronnie there was no such misgivings; he'd played lead guitar on all Rod's recordings and therefore had every right to mime to his own work.

One might think that the rest of the group would have been just as sceptical and critical about Ronnie at this particular time, and one would be wrong. For even though he was an integral part of Rod's solo set-up, his charm and disarming air of not being totally a part of anything very much, deflected any anger or suspicions.

As Shirley says, "Ronnie let everything go over his head, He wouldn't be drawn into any silly squabbles. He wouldn't have anything to do with petty jealousy, either."

Which is commendable, considering a fair bit of jealousy was being directed at him, albeit in a sort of offhand, friendly kind of way. It was something Sandy Sarjeant noticed: "There was a bit of that going on, silly jealousy, over silly things. Like Ronnie's hair for example. Ronnie had this amazing shock of jet-black hair, you could take a pair of garden shears to it and it would still end up looking fantastic.

"Mac tried to copy it, but his hair was fine, he was always at the hair spray, setting lotion and gel. He managed it, but with a lot of hard work. Oh, and they all loved Ronnie's clothes, oh, God it was a disgusting era, just look at those old films and cuttings!"

Or, as Ronnie's dad would say, "If you go out looking like that son, it's up to you."

As 1973 began, any impression that the band had gained some ground on their lead singer's meteoric rise to superstardom was purely illusory. Rod and Ronnie had written most of the songs on the new Faces album, "A Nod's As Good As A Wink To A Blind Horse". Rod was back in the charts with a song he'd recorded as a session singer, credited to Python Lee Jackson (Number Three) and all of his previous albums remained in the chart. It was beginning to look as if all Rod had to do was read the phone directory and it would shoot to the top.

It was obvious by now that two very distinct but interlocking musical styles had successfully emerged, based on two very different aspects of Ron and Rod's collaborations. There was the folky, introspective, story-telling ballads reserved for Rod's solo outings. And then there was the boozy, bar room rockers that they shared with The Faces.

Ok, "A Nod's As Good As A Wink" was the first Faces effort to do anywhere near as good as a Rod solo and the band did go on to have two big hit singles with "Stay With Me" and "Cindy Incidentally", but it was still Rod who was capturing the world's attention and leaving the others standing at the bar.

In truth, Rod had a shed load of what none of the others (Ronnie excluded) had; and that's star presence. They may all have shared a similar sense of humour, Ron and the others more so, but none of them was seen as charismatic enough to warrant a front cover of a publication like Rolling Stone or even Melody Maker. It was all too easy to ignore the superb writing contributions made by Ronnie Lane, and ignored it was.

His material was always of a more gentle nature, wistful and insightful - actually a lot closer to the more nostalgic material Rod reserved for his own albums.

It wasn't only Lane's appearance that was out of step with Rod and the other Faces. His voice no longer suited the set-up. His singing was frail but blessed with sincere emotion, whereas Rod's sounded soaked in booze and dried out with cigarettes. Rod's singing had a cocksure powerful rawness, whilst Ronnie Lane's expressed a resigned nature.

The songs that Lane had first contributed to the group had once served to diversify their ramshackle repertoire, but now seemed far too parochial, and harked back to the old time music halls of the war years. Basically they now sat uneasily in The Faces' auditorium rock crowd-pleasing set list.

Ronnie's gift was his ability to flit effortlessly between the two camps, and why not since he was integral to both. Yet he was beginning to make no secret of his unhappiness at the band's inability at nailing down that all important cohesion; "Some tracks on The Faces albums didn't even sound like us."

Rod, as usual, was a little harsher; "people must hear something I can't hear. The Faces sound so out of tune to me, out of tune and out of time. We never had the musicianship. Individually, we were good, but we never came together as a band. Don't get me wrong, it's still a great band to be in."

Lane believed Rod had a coldly calculated agenda that involved cherry-picking his best work and holding it back for use in his own personal career. Not only did he believe this, he told him so, repeatedly and very loudly at the increasingly few occasions the band got together.

"Little Ronnie Lane was such a lovely man" says Shirley Arnold, "but he was extremely unhappy with the band's situation. He saw Rod's solo success as being promoted by Billy at the expense of the group, and that really hurt him."

Lane started travelling separately from the others, commuting between gigs wherever possible in his Range Rover. "When he wasn't moaning about Rod with Mac and Kenney he'd be on at Billy" Shirley says, "all three felt there was a divide. I thought Billy was a nice guy, he was a good manager, and they treated him so badly. I remember one day Billy had a car crash and he ended up in hospital. All three were ringing the hospital asking for him, because none of them believed he was really in there. He was in a lot of pain and in traction and all they wanted to know was when he was going to get back to work. Can you believe how gutted he felt. They kept asking him "When are you going to do this and that? When are you coming back in? When are you going to get us some publicity?" Then Kenney threw an almighty strop, it was just before they were due to go back to America. He rung up and said he wasn't going. I have no idea why; he just decided he wasn't going. I didn't know what to say to him because I'd never had that with the Stones, they lived to tour, but Kenney was adamant he wasn't going.

"Billy and me was so fed up and exhausted by them that I rung Rod and said "do you know what I'm going to do? I'm going to ring Woody because he's a good mediator and tell him that you've asked me to get in touch with Micky Waller." So I did just that and five minutes after I put the phone down on Woody, Kenney rang me and said 'oh hello Shirl, I'll go on the tour now."

"Sandy Sarjeant saw it all a little differently. This was around the time all the girls went to New York and we were all supposed to be staying at the same hotel together.

"It was the first time we all got the feeling that the split was coming. We'd all been out to some club after the first show and everyone was hyped up; it was a great night, boy we really went for it! The drugs, the drinking, you name it - it was ridiculous. I remember trying to find an all night chemist for Mac because he was in a real mess. The next day all the girls were meant to fly home while the boys flew on to LA.

"When I came down in the morning, Ronnie Lane, Kenney and Mac were all sitting around the foyer looking like shit, they were really down and deflated because they'd just been told at reception that Woody and Rod had already flown on ahead without them.

"It was only a matter of time before it all blew up, and when it did, everybody blamed everybody else."

CHAPTER THIRTEEN
"FAR TOO MANY BRUSHES WITH ROD."

Amazingly enough, despite all the bickering and backbiting The Faces somehow managed to produce a fourth album. Admittedly, it had taken the best part of the year, but media speculation was rife that at last the band was about to offer up the crucial record they needed: their very own "Sergeant Pepper", or "Pet Sounds".

It was a fair enough assumption because with each consecutive release, the group had shown a gradual improvement and silenced their critics on both sides of the Atlantic. It had been a hard up-hill struggle to "A Nod's As Good As A Wink", so surely the next one (with so much collective experience behind them) would be the one to establish the band as one of the top acts of the day.

Yes, surely "Ooh La La" was that album, wasn't it?

Eh, well... No.

"It's a bloody disgrace," Rod said to Melody Maker's Roy Hollingsworth, in a controversial interview a few days after its release in April 1973. "It's a bloody mess" he went on, "But I shouldn't say that should I? The public aren't going to like me saying it's a bloody mess. Maybe I'm too critical. One of the best tracks is one I don't even sing on and that's "Ooh La La". But all that fucking about to do an album like this doesn't prove anything. But I'm not going to say anything more about it, that's it.

When Hollingsworth asked if Stewart was thinking of leaving the band, Rod replied: "Er... No. We're together for life. I don't think there's really anything else I could do. I just want to make good albums."

If this was an exercise in fence-mending, then it was defiantly a case of too little too late. Nor was "Ooh La La" as bad as he painted it, reaching number one in the UK, and twenty-one in the States. However, it wasn't the magnum opus the band wanted or the critics hoped for.

Ronnie diplomatically defended the album without direct reference to Rod's barbed comments, when he said, "I think the work's been spread more evenly throughout the band this time. Five of us getting involved equally does help. It takes a lot off of Rod's back for a start. It's certainly the closest we've got to our stage work. Every track stands up. I feel that with this album, more than the others, there are no throw-aways. But I also think some of the tracks aren't very identifiable as us."

Ronnie was obviously treading carefully and made no mention of the fact that the one song earmarked by Rod for any sort of praise was the album's title song, "Ooh La La" a track that marked his singing debut.

Today though, Ronnie's scornful about Stewart's oft-quoted comment that it was the band's lack of studio discipline that led to them recording substandard material. He's also keen to put the record straight regarding his quote that only he and Kenney Jones took the recording sessions seriously. Stewart would apparently complain to journalists that only the two of them would be waiting to begin work while the others were still pissing it up in the pub (thus giving the impression that they were the only professionals amidst a bunch of irresponsible drunkards).

"Rod's been telling that story for years," Ronnie says wearily, "and it's a fucking useless story. All Rod and Kenney would do was turn up and jangle their car keys at a Faces recording. They couldn't wait to get out of there. They never put their hearts into it - or maybe for one song they did. I would have to bribe them to stay there most of the time. Rod was in the pub as much as we were - 'old short arms and long pockets' Ronnie Lane used to call him. He'd always make an excuse and be off to the toilet when it was his turn to buy a round. We had the greatest time drinking with that Liverpool supporter, John Peel. He was great to go round the pub with. We'd get totally pissed, then go back to the BBC studios and go out live on air. We never had any idea about what songs we were going to do, or who was doing what. We'd give each other piggy-back rides on the stage, Ronnie Lane was always on mine or Rod's back. It's a shame none of that was filmed.

"Rod can say what he likes now, but he was there and very much a part of it. As a matter of fact, that's how Rod, Mac and me came to write "Cindy Incidentally". It came out of a pub session where every sentence you said had to have the word incidentally in it. Like for instance you'd say "I'll have a pint of Guinness incidentally.""

Perhaps another interview Stewart gave back in the early seventies pinpointed what his real problem with Faces recording sessions was. In it Rod stated, "If I have to be frank, I must admit I tend to enjoy my own recording sessions best. It's just that I'm producing them and everything is arranged around my voice." The inescapable truth appears to be Stewart really only ever saw the Faces as an occasional light relief side-line to his own career, as did Billy Gaff.

Justified perhaps given the grounds that Stewart was fast becoming one of music's greatest performers. Small comfort for Kenney, Mac and Ronnie Lane of course, all of whom hoped for something similar. Whether or not that was ever possible is besides the point, because with Rod Stewart as their lead vocalist they were never going to be given the chance. The music world's critics had long since written them off as Rod Stewart's backing band.

Rough justice considering the Small Faces album, "Ogden's Nut Gone Flake" was and still is recognized as one of the all time classics.

Ronnie was also carving out a career that was threatening to eclipse the other three. In January 1973 he'd started rehearsals at The Wick for two concerts to be held at the Rainbow Theatre in London's Finsbury Park to mark Eric Clapton's return to live work following heroin.

Besides Ronnie and Clapton, the concert's line up included Pete Townshend, Steve Windwood, Rick Grech, Jim Capaldi and Jimmy Karstein. Both gigs and the resulting live album were a resounding success, and put Ronnie on an equal footing with England rock royalty… a position that further underlined the widening gulf between Rod and himself on the one hand and the rest of the band on the other.

By the time "Ooh La La" was released, it's safe to say the entire band was becoming unhappy about their performance, either on stage or in the studio. Two months earlier they had even walked out of a BBC recording session for Radio One's In Concert programme. A somewhat shocked BBC memo states, "Halfway through the recording, the band walked off stage and returned to their dressing rooms. They were unhappy about repeating all their old material and in fact, some members of the group had not wanted to accept the booking until their new material was ready for a stage performance.

"They had been talked round by the other group members and their agency (Gaff). After about twenty minutes they were persuaded to finish the recording, but the result was a bit of a shambles and no one was really happy with it. Unfortunately the producer, Jeff Griffin was in the States so the final decision had to wait for his return. He has now listened to the tapes and decided against broadcasting it as "It was not as good as we would all have wished"."

The memo went on to say that the BBC would not pay the group, but they would pay £20 to cover the band's expenses. It also stated that Jeff Griffin wanted to re-book the band when their new material was ready, but the BBC's management should be put in the picture' and the event should be duly noted in case anything similar ever occurred again.

In the meantime, Stewart's comments regarding "Ooh La La" did nothing to soothe the dissatisfaction felt by the rest of the band, and for once it was Kenney Jones who let his thoughts be known. "I didn't fucking understand Rod saying that, how could it have been a fucking bad album if it got to number one?"

So, what exactly is his gripe? He's not even on half of it. Two tracks on the album were sung by Ronnie Lane and another by Woody and Ronnie. Tracks that were originally earmarked for Rod, but he'd flatly refused to sing them.

"The album came out with a bang and then lapsed into obscurity." Lane complained, "Rod wasn't into it from the start. We'd do a song and then a month later he'd hate it. That's why me and Woody ended up singing so much of it. Those songs are all in the wrong key because they were written for Rod."

One track never even made it onto the finished album. A composition entitled "Its Only Rock And Roll (But I Like It)" a song conceived by Ronnie and based on one of his favourite sayings. Ronnie recorded the track at home using Kenney and Mac plus Mick Jagger, Willie Weeks and David Bowie. Jagger so loved the song he asked Ronnie if he could have it for the Stones, and offered Ronnie the vastly inferior "Black Limousine" in exchange. It was a somewhat bizarre swap, but Ronnie accepted only to see the track released complete with a Jagger/Richards song writing credit.

"The track stayed almost exactly the same as when we recorded it" Ronnie explains, "they even kept Kenney's drums on it. Charlie apparently heard it and said he wouldn't have played it any different, so they kept it as it was, which was the first and only time Charlie isn't on a Stones track. They put it out as a single and it was the name of their next album, which meant I was playing on a Stones record long before I joined. Talk about what will be will be."

Considering how harmful Stewart's comments could have been to the sales of "Ooh LaLa" it's strange that Billy Gaff remained so neutral. Weird for a manager of a band whose latest material had been so utterly rubbished by their lead singer.

Surely Gaff's failure to even mildly reprimand Rod gave the rest of the band the impression that he somehow agreed with him. Did Gaff see Rod's involvement with the The Faces as an irritable distraction to his escalating rise to superstardom.

His only comment at the time certainly lends some evidence to this theory: "To me, Rod Stewart will always be a great performer," he told The New Musical Express, "I'm one hundred percent sure he'll be singing in twenty years time, simply because he can manage any sort of material." Anything but the latest Faces material, we assume.

Ronnie for one could see what was coming. All the bands he'd ever been in had broken up well before reaching their full potential and The Faces looked like following suit. He knew the signs better than most; he still clung on to his dream of one day becoming a Rolling Stone, but Mick Taylor was holding that job down (just). In the past, Ronnie had always been able to move from one musical home to another with ease. But he was astute enough to realize that as time moved on, it was becoming a little bit harder to make such transitions.

To begin with, there weren't any decent bands on the lookout for another guitar player. The super group phase had been and gone and Ronnie was high profile enough to be choosy as to where he laid his Strat.

By 1973, the same fate had befallen Jeff Beck and Eric Clapton, now both going it alone. Naturally Ronnie considered the same option, but he wasn't about to jump head first in that direction just yet; after all, he was happiest being a team player not a solo artist.

The Faces still provided him with a musical base (for the time being at least) and a pretty good income too, so the smart thing to do was dip only a toe in the solo pool and announce that with a little help from his friends, "I've Got My Own Album To Do". It's a common enough practice for guitar players in Ronnie's position, but alas not one that's ever taken too seriously by a cynical music industry.

Ronnie Lane wasn't nearly as calculating. His situation within the group had driven him to breaking point, and his big finale was just about due. It came on 3rd May at a gig in Providence Rode Island as part of The Faces' eighth American tour, (their eighth in under three years).

The band had just come off stage when Rod Stewart, dressed in pink satin trousers, a feather boa and running mascara, turned to Lane (who was wearing his rag and bone man's Sunday best) and sneered "What are you, a fucking Spiv or a fucking Teddy Boy?"

Lane, as quick as lightening, snapped back, "I'd rather be a fucking Teddy Boy than look like a fucking prostitute who's going through the change of life."

With that Lane swung a punch at Stewart and the pair grappled to the floor. Shirley Arnold watched in horror, "It was very sad. It developed into a full-scale punch-up in the dressing room. There was a lot of swearing and shouting and tables and chairs going over. Pete Buckland, one of the roadies, had to pull Ronnie Lane off Rod. Woody was there, but I can't remember what he was doing (If past history was anything to go by, he sensibly left them to it). The room was wrecked; broken glass and food on the floor - it was horrible. There was just the worst atmosphere after that.

"The next day we had to take a small plane to the next gig and Ronnie Lane said he wasn't coming, so I remember we all took off without him. I rang him later and he told me he was leaving the group, and asked me to go and work for him. But I said I couldn't leave the others and somehow managed to persuade him to rejoin the tour, which thankfully he did, hiring a car and driving himself. Then he told Billy he'd finish the tour and the forthcoming London shows out of loyalty to the others. But that was it, after that he was definitely leaving."

Sandy Sarjeant blames the final bust up on competing egos: "Those were terrible times. There was no camaraderie left anymore. They were all acting like superstars. I suppose in hindsight, you can see why it got out of hand and you can see how difficult it was for them once the egos took over. It was a very egotistical band. I remember thinking that they still looked like the people we knew; Ian still looked like my husband, but he started acting like God. One morning at home he demanded to know why I hadn't cut his bread up into soldiers (thin strips) so he could dip it in his boiled egg. That was the last straw, I packed my bags and left."

Lane was good to his word and made his last appearance with the band at the Sundown in Edmonton, North London, where he was greeted by hundreds of banners and placards saying, 'Good bye Ronnie' and 'We love you'. When the band finished that night, Rod - with his arm around Lane's shoulder - shouted to the crowd; "Good night, we're off down the pub" to which Lane quipped, "Too late, they're shut."

Which pretty much summed up their relationship.

It would be ten years before the two men could bring themselves to speak to each other again. Ironically, the end of his Faces career helped Lane renew a short-lived friendship with his old band mate and writing partner, Steve Marriott. "I went over to see Steve soon after I left." Lane said. "I'd started to miss him, because we'd been so close once. I realised I hadn't been able to give him any help when he'd left the Small Faces because I'd never left a band before. Once I left The Faces I understood at last how he must have been feeling and why if he wasn't happy, he wanted to go. I suppose I'd have been better off talking to Woody because he'd been in more bands than any of us."

"I knew that once Ronnie Lane went that was the beginning of the end," Ronnie reflects. "You couldn't replace Ronnie Lane; he was the heart and the soul of that group. But he'd had far too many brushes with Rod for me not to understand why he wanted to leave. It was very sad and sobering to us rowdy rock and rollers to watch what happened to him." (Lane died from multiple sclerosis in 1997).

Another ironic twist came one year later when Rod Stewart recorded a version of "Ooh La La" one of The Faces tracks he'd initially refused to sing. He gave the money to Lane's family.

With Lane gone, the first order of business was to find a replacement and one that would sense he was joining an already sinking ship. They found one playing in a group who'd disintegrated even faster than The Faces - Free.

Tetsuo Yamauchi was the first Japanese-born musician to make any sort of a mark on the English music scene. He'd joined Free as a replacement for Andy Fraser and endeared himself to their fans less for his musicianship (which was questionable at best), but for his unquestionable ability to be able to drink most people under the table. In short, a true rock and roller in spirit, if not ability.

Consequently, joining The Faces was a dream come true, unfortunately within a matter of weeks Yamauchi was having to be tied to his bass stack with rope to stop him falling over on stage. To this day, Ronnie has no idea how he was hired in the first place. "Perhaps it was due to having a string of dates booked in the Far-East? I don't know. He certainly wasn't mine or Rod's choice, we wanted Phil Chen, but he was busy. Then once we got Tetsu the Musicians' Union kicked up such a fuss, so we ended up keeping him.

"One thing I do know is, he must have lied about his age because years later we were trying to locate him for some function or another and Kenney tracked him down. He said he looked like David Carradine's kung fu instructor off the telly. Kenney said he looked about a hundred years old."

Tetsu joined the band at the beginning of August. By the eighteenth, he was banned by the Musicians' Union (backed by the Government) on the grounds that he was depriving a British musician of a job.

The group started a lengthy battle to settle the dispute and left the UK in January 1974 for their Far-East engagements. Ronnie was pleasantly surprised to find that whatever musical reservations he had about the new recruit, these were more than compensated for by the welcome they received in his homeland.

Although Stewart apparently never saw it that way, as Shirley Arnold witnessed. "Rod had a complete strop when we flew into Tokyo airport. There were hundreds of fans all screaming for Tetsu. I think Rod wanted to split the band up right there. He just didn't want to be the one to do it. He felt he'd proved he was the big star in the group, and yet here was all these girls mobbing the new boy and ignoring him. He was so pissed off that when we got to the hotel, Rod locked himself in his room and sent a message down saying he wasn't going to play the first night's show. He made out he had laryngitis, but everybody knew it was because of Tetsu.

"There was a full-scale riot at the stadium when it was announced and it was on the news. Then we got another call from Rod saying he felt better now and could we get a meal. Billy was mad and said "No, stay in your room. They're tearing the stadium to pieces." He calmed down and even saw the potential in the great publicity we were getting, but the rest of the band was not at all happy."

In addition to the Japanese dates, the group also played their first Australasian shows, which was a strange experience for Kenney and Mac. The last time they'd been in Sydney was as two members of the Small Faces in 1968. Then they'd found themselves deported from the country, along with Steve Marriott and Ronnie Lane, for allegedly assaulting an air stewardess and inciting a riot. Incredibly, no one in authority or immigration connected the two groups, or their personnel.

To coincide with the Australian trip, a live album, "Coast To Coast Overture For Beginners", recorded on their recent US trip was released, strangely enough by Mercury Records. This became the subject of a curious deal orchestrated by Gaff and Stewart whereby Warner Brothers ended up releasing the same album simultaneously, but on cassette only.

Naturally enough, when it first came to light Warner's issued an injunction against Mercury, prohibiting Stewart from delivering any new material to his own label. The lawyers had a lucrative few months, and eventually a compromise was reached and a deal was struck. The situation reverted to normal, or what passed as normal where The Faces were concerned.

With no new studio material available, the band issued an EP of old favourites in June. It featured "Cindy Incidentally", "Stay With Me" and "Pool Hall Richard" which had been released as a single the previous December and reached number eight.

It was a blatant cash in and as far as the great record-buying public were concerned, one filler too far. They understandably stayed away from the tills in droves and the record failed to even chart.

CHAPTER FOURTEEN

"I DREW THE SHORT STRAW ON THAT ONE."

Krissie Wood had first met Jimmy Page back in his Yardbirds days. Which was way back in rock history, now she was married to The Faces lead guitar player and Jimmy was playing lead for arguably the biggest-grossing rock band on the planet, Led Zeppelin. The band Ronnie could have been playing bass for if he hadn't opted to tour America with Jeff Beck that one last time.

Ronnie and Krissie met up again with Jimmy at a party in Los Angeles during The Faces' ninth American tour. Observers noted an instant attraction between Krissie and the latest rock God - an attraction Krissie now attributes to the fact that she found Jimmy to be one of the most interesting men she'd ever met. It so happened that both bands were booked on the same flight back to England.

"I can't remember whether Jimmy came to sit with us or we went over to him" Krissie says now, "but I do remember that Ronnie must have felt threatened because he sat in between Jimmy and me. That sticks in my mind because we were talking all the time about stuff that really didn't interest Ronnie. I started to get embarrassed because Ronnie was making an issue out of nothing. I didn't fancy Jimmy and I didn't think Jimmy fancied me. Ronnie obviously picked up on something though. He was very threatened by our energy and the fact that Jimmy and I communicated. Which we did, we really hit it off because we could talk about a wide range of subjects and not just rock and roll.

"Ronnie wasn't the only one who noticed. Kenney said to me much later he had sensed something was up. So did the other wives, because they were all giggling or being really sarcastic; they were jealous because Jimmy had this big sexual reputation, he was known for being, well, a bit dangerous."

Krissie could have put it all down to being Aleister Crowley's fault. Or to be more precise, Jimmy Page's openly admitted fascination with the man once known as 'The Great Beast'. Crowley was a one time a member of the occult society known as "The Golden Dawn" a group that included the poet W.B. Yeats amongst its flock back at the turn of the last century. Crowley was a founder of the Abbey of Thelema in Sicily, from where he was deported following a case of unexplained death and several cases of insanity and orgies.

He was also a noted mountaineer, a scholar and a writer of embarrassingly bad pornography. Crowley had been given the title "The Wickedest Man In The World" by a Daily Express journalist back in the 1930s and had been used by Somerset Maugham as a model for the central character in his novel, "The Magician".

Whether or not Crowley was a Satanist is debatable, but he clearly saw himself as a master magician and an heir to an esoteric tradition that pre-dated Christianity. Magic was rediscovered by the rock and hippy fraternities in the 1960s and Crowley in particular was back in vogue. They particularly liked Crowley's well-known sayings like "Do what thou wilt shall be the whole of the law" and other such gobbledegook, while getting bogged down in his so called 'Magickal Writings' which need a pretty broad knowledge of Latin, Hebrew and Greek, as well as several comparative religions.

Page's interest in the subject would lead to a collaboration with Kenneth Anger, the ageing Hollywood bad boy (and another rumoured Satanist), on a film called "Lucifer Rising". This all ended badly when Anger pulled out of the project, citing Page's music as too sombre and depressing.

Anyway, back to Jimmy Page's reputation as a sexual deviant, which at this point in time was almost as famous as his music, with much talk of whips, chains and a fair bit of S and M. all of which made him a bit of an adventurous and complex character. Whether any of it was true is of course irrelevant, what is true is that Jimmy Page was and still is a highly intelligent, cultivated man with a wide range of interests.

That then was the man Krissie found so deeply fascinating on that return flight, much to Ronnie's very real concern, especially as Page had let it be known he'd recently split from his long-term girlfriend, Charlotte.

Which doesn't quite explain why the three of them went back to The Wick straight from the airport? Once there, Krissie and Page continued talking until the early hours. Eventually, a jet-lagged Krissie retied for the night and left Ronnie and Page to talk - presumably about rock 'n' roll. The next day Page left, having invited Ronnie and Krissie to visit him at his home at any time.

Some months later they did just that, dropping in on the guitarist at his sprawling country home, Plumpton Place, deep in the Sussex countryside.

"Actually we were looking for some coke," Krissie now admits. "We knew Jimmy would have some, so that's where we went. His home was so beautiful, a real moated castle, with a drawbridge surrounded by an orchard.

"I'd never seen such a beautiful place. It was getting dark and I remember the drawbridge was down, so we walked over it and we were laughing about it, because how many people do you drop in on who have a drawbridge. That's when the strangest thing that's every happened to me started to occur. I'd never been there before, I'd never even seen a picture of the place, but I instinctively knew where to go. I was calling back to Ronnie saying 'come on, I know the way' and he was following me. I just somehow knew how to find the right door once we'd crossed the bridge, and what was even stranger than that, I knew how to open it. It was a really old oak door that had a set of wooden handles that you had to pull in a certain order, and I knew how to do that too. I pulled the levers and pushed the door and sure enough it opened, and there in front of us was Basil, Jimmy's black cat, which would have normally hissed at anyone and run away. But he didn't, he stared at us as if he knew us and rubbed around my legs. It freaked Ronnie right out, and he was saying 'fuck this Kriss let's go!' But I had to go on, it was pitch dark inside but I still instinctively knew where I was going, I knew where to reach for a torch and find the stairs. I even found Jimmy's bedroom, which was the last straw for Ronnie, he was totally spooked out and saying 'I'm going fucking home'. I turned a lamp on and Jimmy was asleep in bed with Charlotte. Which I was really happy about, and I said to Ronnie 'Ah look, he's back with Charlotte, isn't that nice? But Ronnie couldn't have cared less, he was trying to drag me out, and that's when we saw Jimmy had a gun on the bedside table. Ronnie was going quietly hysterical now and half whispering "you fucking idiot, he could have shot us"."

To this day, Krissie professes wide-eyed amazement at just how she was able to find her way to Jimmy's bedroom in a strange house in the dark. Yet one assumes nowhere as amazed as Ronnie, who despite being fairly superstitious and open minded, must have initially wondered whether Krissie had in fact been there before.

"I don't like weird things, one of the reasons I loved The Wick so much was because no one had fucking died in it. Well not that I knew of."

Still, Krissie swears that she'd never set foot in that house before and I suppose she deserves the benefit of the doubt. So maybe Page was as accomplished a magician as he was a musician.

If Jimmy Page was at all annoyed to be woken up by a beaming Krissie and a puzzled Ronnie Wood standing at the foot of his bed, he graciously never showed it. Well, he never shot them. Pretty soon a mini party was in progress downstairs, where the foursome were joined by Jimmy's house guest, Gerry Beckley from the American band, er… America.

"You know how some parties are" Krissie asks, "I don't remember but I must have eventually conked out, and the next thing I knew it was morning and I felt someone covering me up with a fur coat. I thought it was Ronnie and half asleep turned my face round and kissed him, and when I opened my eyes I saw it was Jimmy. Right at that moment Charlotte walked in, no one knew what to do. It was very awkward. I'd innocently thought it was Ronnie, but Jimmy knew very well he wasn't covering up Charlotte. Anyway, I stood up and feeling silly looked out of the window while Jimmy went in to another room with her. I remember I had dungarees on, hardly dressed to kill or anything, and it was a really hot sunny day so I suggested we all went for a walk. Of course, Charlotte said "No thank you, I don't want to go for any walk." She was really pissed off with us. And then Jimmy said, "Well I do." Ronnie was still partying with Gerry, so off we went.

"The castle was surrounded on three sides by lakes, and we walked for hours across the meadows and streams until we came up to an old water mill, it was so hot and we were so tired that we feel asleep. When I woke up it was night again, and pouring with rain and I was in Jimmy's arms. He was keeping me warm; nothing had happened, but it looked pretty bad. So said to him "listen, we are in big trouble. We've been on the missing list for hours, this is very serious."

"We could see the lights of Jimmy's house miles away off in the distance and Jimmy said "don't worry, I'll get us back." He knew his way in the dark; he even knew how to take a short cut across one of the lakes because it had these flat stones placed just below the surface, which made a path. It gave the impression you were walking on water. George had the same thing in his garden, they were dated back to the middle ages.

"It was raining really hard now and we were soaked though so we stopped at the ground-keeper's cottage. We tried to warm up and I put my feet in a bowl of hot water and that's when I heard a car drive past and it was Ronnie with Charlotte and Gerry.

They'd all got fed up waiting and decided to head back to London. Nothing had happened between Jimmy and me, but there was no getting away from how bad it looked and it looked really bad and now I didn't even have a chance to explain.

"So I just stayed with Jimmy. I never left; all I had was the clothes I stood up in, I had absolutely nothing and Charlotte went back to The Wick with Ronnie."

Outwardly, at least, everyone concerned with the bizarre outcome pretended they were happy with the new arrangement. However, Ronnie's relationship with Charlotte proved to be short lived. It was, after all, a relationship Ronnie had neither wanted or needed - a fact he was eager to point out to Led Zeppelin road manager, Richard Cole: "I drew the short straw on that one. I got the worst end of the deal."

Before Krissie had started her relationship with Jimmy Page she did one thing for Ronnie that would ultimately change his life.

"It was whilst I was recording my first solo album in the basement at The Wick" Ronnie explains, "Krissie had gone off to the Speakeasy one night and she'd noticed Keith Richards was lumbered with a crowd of people he obviously didn't want to be with. So interrupted them and she asked him if he wanted to come back and hear what I was doing in the studio. Keith saw what she was doing and was grateful for the excuse to get away.

"He came back with Kriss and stayed for five fucking months. He moved into the cottage that I'd just bought back from Ronnie Lane, so he could buy that farm down in Wales. Keith and me have been mates ever since, give or take the odd punch up that is. So I have Krissie to thank for that."

The first time Art Wood saw his little brother and Keith side by side, he was taken aback by the pair. "I thought, fucking hell they look like a couple of book ends."

Aside from hooking up with Keith Richards, this particular period in Ronnie's life is not a time he likes to talk about much, other than to say "It was a fucking horrible time." Krissie's brief fling with George Harrison had been one thing, but her desertion to Jimmy Page was quite another. The trouble with rock stars is they're expected to behave with a certain insouciance as regards conventional morality. So when someones who's (spent the best part of his life trashing hotels, graduating from speed to coke and beyond, and taking advantage of as many groupies as humanly possible) wife takes it upon herself to go off and do her thing, then he can't really be surprised can he?

Well, maybe Ronnie can. That's how Shirley Arnold sees it, "Ronnie doesn't have a malicious bone in his body, not even a slightly cross one. That's why it was hard to see what had happened with him and Krissie. So, unlike the average person in that situation Ronnie didn't even bitch and moan about it, but he must have been upset inside. The other thing was, they were all so wrapped up in their own little worlds there wasn't any one in that band who probably would have listened."

Besides, rock stars are often well shielded from the reality of their own emotions: groupies and hangers-on provide a twenty-four hour ego massage: booze, acid and cocaine dull the pain: and when all else fails, you can go shopping. The net result is maybe twenty minutes of naked reality every forty-eight hours - which sobering angst Ronnie could always blot out with his music. Even so, there are those few seconds on waking when you realise that the body you've been used to cuddling is no longer there and if there is a replacement, she doesn't react in quite the same way. Ronnie's solution was to start staying up for days on end, enthusiastically tutored by Keith, who still holds the all time record - and was hardly likely to have been teaching Ronnie yoga.

"I can't do the nine-day-and-night stints any more," Keith recently admitted. "About three days is all I can manage now." Later he capped that idiosyncratic remark with the classic line, "Now days I think the older you get, the older you want to get."

For her part, Krissie has no doubt why she spent a year with Jimmy Page, "It was just something I needed to do," she says today, and for a moment you're looking at the sixteen-year-old who first attracted Ronnie's attention. "I'd been terribly lonely with all the touring Ronnie had done and Jimmy could teach me about all sorts of things that Ronnie had no interest in, especially to do with the countryside. But, never anything to do with the occult - I mean, I admit he did own Aleister Crowley's cloak and his stick, but I never saw anything like that going on. If it was, he kept it from me. I just needed some time to grow, and someone to help me do it, and Jimmy was perfect.

"Once I got away, I realised I couldn't live Ronnie's lifestyle any more. So I put my true feelings on hold for a while. Jimmy always said I was just infatuated with him (Page) and in hindsight, he was probably right. George and Jimmy were both incredibly calming and sensitive men - they could both be crazy, but not like Ronnie. George had always known Ronnie was the only one for me - but George was a great one for letting people find their own way."

Meanwhile, Ronnie still had his own album to do, and he threw himself heart and soul into it. Especially as he had a new best friend on hand to help him. During the rest of 1974, Keith helped him pursue his solo project, appearing with him on 13th and 14th July at the Kilburn Empire in North London, with a line-up that included Willie Weeks on bass, Ian McLagan on keyboards and Andy Newmark on drums.

A fantastic line up and a brilliant show, but unfortunately it was clear from the opening number, that Ronnie was not destined for solo stardom.

Mainly due to his voice. The problem being is Ronnie's vocal style has the same draw back as Ronnie Lane's and George Harrison's, or for that matter Keith Richards - it's slightly fragile. Expressive yes and quintessentially English, but these are qualities that lend themselves more to folksy bluesy material, rather than out and out rock.

More importantly, he is a man whose talent is most evident when someone else is fronting a band. He's far too easy going to be a successful leader - all that Ronnie's ever really wanted is the security of a group in which his abilities can properly flourish.

And talking of groups, the Faces were still gamely carrying on, rather like a wounded animal desperately looking for someone to put it out of its misery - only to find itself surrounded by Animal Rights campaigners, none of whom can bring themselves to do the merciful thing. They'd topped the bill at the Buxton Festival on 6th July, when one of the supporting bands had been Steve Marriott's Humble Pie.

By now the Faces' record output had equalled Rod Stewart's: four albums apiece, not counting Stewart's greatest hits compilation, Sing It Again, Rod, another number one when released in August 1973, or the Faces' live outing "Coast To Coast Overture And Beginners". Stewart had already recorded most of the tracks for his fifth LP, using his usual studio band; but the legal problems between Warner Brothers and Mercury Records flared up again, with both claiming to hold the only binding contract with him. This fight over the singer's lissom body would delay the LP for a further five months.

Meanwhile, the Faces had no real plans to follow up Ooh La La; 1974 looked like being a barren year for new product from either Stewart or The Faces. Nevertheless, Stewart continued to record and Ronnie went on working on his own album. Naturally enough, the news that two solo projects were underway only served to fuel rumours that The Faces were about to split. But all of this passed Ronnie by, shut away as he was in his basement at The Wick, with Keith and assorted musical cronies.

"Keith just sort of stayed and stayed (at the bottom of the garden), Willie Weeks and Andy Newmark were supposed to be in a hotel, but ended up staying at The Wick as well. George Harrison came by and we did "Far East Man". At times, the house was like a fucking hotel," Ronnie laughs. "The album cost around £40,000 and that was just the booze. I was going to set up a bar and charge for drinks for all the people that just dropped in. Everyone had roadies and friends with them. Then the neighbours got a bit annoyed at the constant rehearsals. So I don't think you can say it was well organized. Fun yes but, definitely lacking on the organization front."

Micky Waller remembers one instance that seems to have been fairly typical: "Ronnie and Keith wanted a drummer for one track they were doing, and they just came and got me from a studio I was working in. We went to a pub, where Ronnie tried to explain the song, which took several hours, then got back to The Wick at around midnight to do it. Ronnie and Keith were so stoned that they played the same riff for the next six hours!

"I finally put down my sticks because I was so tired, and said, "This is bloody ridiculous! I'm going home!" And Keith looked up and said, "That's the trouble with you Micky, no stamina." I just got up and left, just as Ronnie was saying happily, "Yeah, Keith, this is a different class, isn't it?"."

Ronnie now thinks that doing his own album had far more of an effect on the break up (or certainly the rumours of it) than anything Rod had done. If only because Stewart had already established his solo career. "It was all nonsense in the long run anyway, Rod sang on my album," Ronnie points out. "So I think any one of us could have made a solo record at that point. Kenney eventually made a solo single and he never used any of the band."

That particular record was "Ready or Not", unfortunately the public wasn't and it sunk without trace.

"I just couldn't resist doing my own album," Ronnie continues, "but I was worried that people would think - what's so special about him? Is he on an ego trip, a name dropping ego trip?"

As the year wore on, Ronnie toyed with the idea of playing more gigs with his studio band (now firmly including Keith), while denying any prospect of the Faces splitting: "We're rather like the Who insomuch as we don't see much of each other when we're not working. I think that's what keeps us together; it's the secret to staying successful." He somewhat unconvincingly said to the New Musical Express.

In fact, the secret to staying successful as a world-class band, in addition to being a great live act - which they were - is an agreed musical direction, a leader and at least one seminal record. One out of four wasn't enough, and Ronnie must have known it. Which is probably why his insistence on The Faces' solidarity sounded so weak.

"I've Got My Own Album To Do" was released in September 1974 by Warner Brothers, who organized the obligatory party at which Ronnie saw someone else he'd rather lost touch with over the past few months. Krissie showed up on Jimmy Page's arm, but they both left rather quietly and quickly. No fights, no fuss, no tantrums but as Krissie explains: "Jimmy was so worried about what Ronnie thought. He didn't want to upset Ronnie, he really loved him."

So why show up in the first place? Perhaps the answer lies in the rest of Krissie's explanation: "The situation had gone on for so long, I was going to marry Jimmy and we had the divorce papers drawn up and everything."

It was that kind of era, and those sort of people. Just so long as you were sincere and meant well, you could do and say almost anything and if anyone criticized you, they were a bad person. Worse, they were uncool. In time, that sincerity would become political correctness.

Despite Ronnie's stellar line-up, "I've Got My Own Album To Do" sunk without trace by the time Stewart's new album, "Smiler" hit the racks in October 1974. Like clockwork, it shot to number one in the UK, totally overshadowing Ronnie's efforts, although in the US it made a less-impressive number sixteen. There was clearly only one star in The Faces good enough to achieve solo success. Which was why Mac quite wisely decided that any solo effort by him could, and would, wait.

A hugely successful UK tour managed to put all problems on hold for a while and even renewed the group's confidence enough for them to begin developing new material.

This would include (what in a lot of people's minds is perhaps the band's finest single, co-written by Ron and Rod): "You Can Make Me Dance, Sing Or Anything". "It was a great single," Ronnie declares happily. "It was a good step towards how we were feeling momentarily. It started off with about four different riffs and we sewed them all together with the lyrics we'd rehearsed at The Wick. But the guitar part didn't come together until the last minute - I pretended I was Barry White's guitar player."

But once again, Stewart poured scorn on what was an unquestionable Faces benchmark saying: "I don't think it's our best release, I don't think it's our best single. I think "Pool Hall Richard" was." Interestingly, the new song was credited to all of The Faces, in an attempt to promote a feeling of solidarity within the band. Presumably, solidarity as in 'we're all equal' was the very last thing Rod Stewart wanted.

The British tour had been the largest-grossing one by any band in 1974, netting The Faces over £100,000 in only twenty-four days; taking into account inflation and money skimmed off the top, the equivalent of over £1.5 million today. This encouraged the band to forgo the pleasures of an English winter and head off for another tour of Australia, New Zealand and Japan… just as the rumours about Ronnie joining the Stones began to surface.

Mick Taylor - a genuinely gentle and unassuming man had been with the Stones for a little under four years. He was a gifted guitarist, but he'd never managed to connect personally with the rest of the group. Nor could he cope very well with the pressures of touring material he wasn't that interested in. Plus, all the while, Stones fans the world over were becoming divided into two main camps: Stones plus Brian Jones era, or Stones plus Mick Taylor.

Taylor made no bones about wanting to return to playing more classical blues - an excuse similar to Jeff Beck's when he'd left The Yardbirds.

Privately, he was cracking up and there was nothing anyone could do to help. It takes a very strong type of character to remain even relatively sane as a Rolling Stone. Taylor didn't have it. He wasn't even a real Rolling Stone either, inasmuch as he was still on a wage.

Ronnie was the obvious replacement for Taylor, if only because Keith was living at the bottom of his garden and, as Ronnie claimed at the time, the two men had become inseparable, Even so, he made a point of adding: "Despite all the rumours, I will not be joining The Rolling Stones - we've never even talked about it. I suppose in another time or era I would join the Stones. Aesthetically, I'd join because my roots and influences are there. But it's like I said - another time, another era. It just couldn't happen while I'm with The Faces, the Stones know that and that's why they wouldn't ask me."

Actually, they had already.

"Mick sort of sidled up to me at this party." Ronnie now admits, "and said, "What if Mick Taylor left, do you think you'd be interested in, you know, helping out?" But I said no, I couldn't do anything to upset the Faces, or to make them break up. And Mick's going, "No, no, no. no, I wouldn't want to break up the Faces." And I'm thinking, "Fucking right I'd join!"."

In February 1975, the Faces were back in the States, and this time the debauchery would reach all-time records, even by the band's demanding standards. Strangely - or not, given Tom Wolfe's acid comments about radical chic - they still managed to attract America's most socially prominent, and the ladies-who-lunch. But it was only Stewart who took the celebrity circus at all seriously. He'd discovered that George Harrison's last visit had received a First Family audience on his US tour, so it seemed only natural to invite the Ford daughters to the Washington DC gig.

The best-laid schemes of mice and social climbers. Only Susan Ford showed up with a few friends - no President, no First Lady, and Harrison's tour hadn't even been all that successful. Still, Billy Gaff and The Faces press officer, Tony

Toon, made the most of it and ensured that the press got their shots of Susan chatting to the band backstage. Immediately afterwards, a put-out Stewart flew off to New York for a party being thrown by Led Zeppelin.

Ronnie and the rest of the band stayed behind, Ronnie because he knew that Krissie was accompanying Jimmy Page. And oh! How they laughed when they discovered that Stewart had just been sent an invitation, at his Washington hotel, to join Gerald Ford and his family for dinner at the White House, as a thank you for being so kind to Susan. For by now Stewart was in New York, and the fog was rolling in.

All flights were grounded. To make it even better, or worse, depending on who you were, a rumour planted by Tony Toon surfaced in the British press that Stewart was now dating Susan Ford, causing Stewart to send a bouquet of red roses to the White House by way of apology.

The band reunited in New York for another sold-out show at Madison Square Garden. A gig that Kenney Jones remembers particularly well: "Ronnie called me into his room backstage before we went on, and there was blood everywhere. It looked like someone had been murdered. I looked at Woody and his fucking nose had come away at the top. All the coke he'd been snorting had eroded the bridge of his nose away.

"I'll never forget he made this looking-down-nose face, cross eyed and said, "Fuck me, Kenney, I can see the sink from here!" Anyway, we cleaned him up and stuck his nose back on with gaffer tape, then put on this huge pair of dark glasses to hide the join. But he wasn't worried, he was laughing and said, "I'll get one of those plastic things that Stephen Stills has got, he's had a couple.".".

So Ronnie became the latest in a long line of rock stars to have a plastic septum inserted in his nose.

Stewart later admitted that this little incident led to some members of the band using cold capsules to administer coke. "They'd empty out what was already in there, usually a cold cure, and replace it with cocaine. They believed it would do less physical damage that way."

At the end of the tour the promoters, Pacific Productions, threw a lavish party for the Faces at a Hollywood eaterie called the Greenhouse, where the band rubbed shoulders with the music and film-world's A list elite, which included a visiting Paul and Linda McCartney, Cher and Greg Allman, Joni Mitchell, Jon Lord, Ryan O'Neal, Tina Sinatra, Bob Dylan, the odd Beach Boy and even Kim Gardiner, who had taken up US residency after the failure of Badger, his last musical venture. Oh yes and Rod Stewart unveiled his latest blonde babe, Britt Ekland.

Billy Gaff announced that the tour had gone so well that it would stretch on throughout the rest of the year, but would allow the band a break from June to July, before once again visiting Australia and Japan. That break would allow Stewart to record another album and the band to spend time at home. There would also be the possibility of a short UK tour, including five dates at Wembley's Empire Pool, and even a new Faces album. The old camaraderie seemed to be back in full force. It all sounded too good to be true. It was.

No sooner had the band (plus Britt Ekland) returned to the UK, Stewart flew back to the Americas West Coast, for what he described as a working holiday, otherwise known as his next solo album, "Atlantic Crossing".

It was the first time Ronnie wasn't going to feature, either as co-songwriter or session musician. Not because he didn't want to, but because he simply hadn't been asked. Nor had any of the others - their places had been taken by Booker T and the MGs plus guitarist Jesse Ed Davis and the Memphis Horns. Aretha Franklin's producer, Tom Dowd would also replace Glyn Johns.

Not that Ronnie was worried, for he had his eye on a temporary job abroad, and one that paid far better. On 15 April 1975 it was announced that Ronnie Wood would be joining The Rolling Stones in June as a replacement for Mick Taylor for the band's up and coming American tour. It had all happened very quickly.

"I was at a party for Eric Clapton at Robert Stigwoods's house," Ronnie explains, "when Mick Taylor told Mick Jagger that he was leaving. He told him right in the middle of his salad, and Mick was shocked, he wasn't happy at all. So he came up to me and said, "Fucking hell! Mick Taylor's just told me he's leaving the fucking band and there's a whole tour lined up."

"It was obvious he wanted me to say, "oh really, well I'll help you out," but I still said, "Well, I don't want to break up The Faces, but give me a call if you get stuck, keep in touch." The word had been out for some time that Mick Taylor wanted to go and there was everyone waiting in the wings wanting to join. For instance, Steve Marriott said he'd been asked by Keith but Mick had said no; every guitar player alive was supposedly in with a chance, even Wayne fucking Perkins was rumoured.

"Clapton actually auditioned, but he didn't work out, although he still says to this day, "I could've had your job," but I always say to him, "No you couldn't, you need a personality." The Rolling Stones were holding auditions for the job in Germany and I got a call from Mick saying come out. So I went, they'd rented a lot of rooms for every one at the Munich Hilton, and Jeff Beck was in a room next to me. How fucking hilarious was that."

The announcement that Ronnie was joining The Rolling Stones was read with great interest by the Metropolitan Police's Drugs Squad because the accompanying press articles mentioned that Keith Richards was a permanent house guest at Ronnie's home.

It just so happened that the Drugs Squad had been wondering where Keith had vanished to. He had never returned to his regular Cheyne Walk address since returning home from a year's tax exile in France, with Anita Pallenberg.

The couple hadn't really been seen in England since their drug bust in June 1973, when they were arrested for possession of cannabis, heroin and Mandrax. Bail had been set at £500 and a court date set for 31st July.

Then Keith had sought sanctuary at his rural Sussex retreat, Redlands, which inconveniently caught fire, which delayed the trial until December when Keith was found guilty and fined £200. All of which had made Keith understandably nervous about remaining in any one place for too great a length of time.

The Wick Cottage offered a convenient bolt-hole. Besides, when he was working - as he had been on Ronnie's first solo album - he liked to shut himself away from the outside world.

The Drugs Squad, still smarting over what they'd considered the ludicrously light fine imposed on Richards, had been seeking him here and seeking him there. He'd been showing up infrequently at Cheyne Walk, but not long enough for them to pay him a visit. Now thanks to the News Of The World, they had another more permanent address for him. Moreover, it was the home of another probable drug user called Ronnie Wood. Why, he even looked like Keith Richards and he'd just joined that well-known gang of outlaws The Rolling Stones. A bust at The Wick was surely long overdue, especially as the local police confirmed that the neighbours had been complaining for weeks about people breaking and entering.

Re-enter Krissie. "I'd gone to dinner with some friends in Earls Court," she explains, "and it was too late to get back to Jimmy's place. I don't know why, but I just felt the need to go home, and The Wick was still my home, far more than Plumpton Place. I knew Ronnie and Keith were away in Amsterdam, and I asked a girlfriend of mine called Audrey Burgon, to come back with me because I didn't want to go there on my own."

As far as the descriptions were concerned, two women, one of them a tall blonde, had broke in at The Wick. Anita Pallenberg was tall and blonde, that was enough. Although, officially, the police were acting on 'information received'. When they barged in, they discovered not Keith and Anita, but Krissie and Audrey. Naturally, the police jumped to the obvious conclusion.

"It was a huge bed, bigger than a double bed, and the only reason I'd asked Audrey to share it with me was because it made more sense than making up a new one. Also, I was frightened of sleeping alone. I remember waking up at around six-thirty in the morning, and there were about twenty men in the room - I thought I was going to be kidnapped, I had no idea they were police. They'd even kicked in a two-hundred-year-old door. There were no policewomen there, and all Audrey had on was a pair of panties and I had a night dress. So obviously we had to be lesbians!"

The raid netted a pestle and mortar containing the faintest residue of cocaine and an antique rifle (the latter left behind by Sir John Mills). While the police waited for a female officer to arrive, to search what little clothing the girls were wearing, they played Ronnie's jukebox, banged his drums and strummed his guitars. Both girls denied the subsequent charges of possessing a controlled substance.

When the case finally came to trial, Krissie painted a harrowing picture of the pressures that came with being married to such a high-profile musician. She told of the hangers-on and the parasites that surrounded their lives, any one of whom could have been responsible for the minute amounts of cocaine found in the mortar.

The jury understandably believed her and both women were acquitted. The trial received extensive coverage, but nowhere was it mentioned that Krissie had actually been living with another man at the time of her arrest.

The legal proceedings would last well over a year, and by the time they were over, Krissie would be back with Ronnie - pregnant and married to a Rolling Stone.

CHAPTER FIFTEEN

"NOT A BAD BIRTHDAY PRESENT."

Ronnie's long-term friend, Rick Cunningham, remembers guitar player Nils Lofgren desperately wanted to join the Stones: "He actually phoned Woody up and asked him to put a good word in for him. Ronnie was laughing because it was a foregone conclusion he'd got the job, but he still said to Nils, "Of course I will mate, I'll talk to Keith about you" and then he turned to me and said "how fucking out of touch is Nils Lofgren?"

Ronnie's own press statement said that "at first I couldn't accept the Stones job because it would have meant leaving The Faces and I am too close to the idea of that band to turn my back on them." He went on to say "Mick Jagger understood this as well as anyone, and I only agreed to the offer after a deal was worked out and a satisfactory compromise reached. I will therefore become a part-time Rolling Stone and remain a full time member of The Faces. I will also be free to carry on with outside interests and solo work."

Who was kidding who here? Rod was thousands of miles away doing his own thing, and the abandoned-feeling Kenney and Mac were already talking about rejoining Steve Marriott and Ronnie Lane in a reformed Small Faces.

Ronnie had waited his whole musical life for a chance to join his boyhood idols and he wasn't about to blow it now. Even if he (like the departing Mick Taylor) would be a salary employee only.

"I was very worried for Woody" Shirley Arnold admits. "So much so that I pulled Mick aside one day and said to him: "Now listen, Mick, you can't go and treat Ronnie in the same way you all treated Mick Taylor and just pay him a wage. You've got to give him a fair deal and a cut of everything. Of course they didn't do anything of the sort. But Woody would have been happy with whatever they gave him. You could tell it was the happiest he'd been in his entire life."

So Ronnie accepted his hired hand wage, and it was a bloody good one; a reported £50,000 for the one tour. Even so, he still managed to return home almost broke. According to Rick Cunningham, "He'd basically spent all his salary without realising it. It turned out he had signed for everything. Imagine, if you will, there'd be eight or nine of them out in a club for hours on end, and at the end of the night the waiter comes up and says someone will have to sign off for whatever they'd had all night. It would have to be someone from the band that signed for it, so Ronnie would be the first one to say "Oh, I'll do it." He didn't realise that it was all coming out of his wages; he assumed he was signing on behalf of the whole band and he did it every night. It was also easier for the waiter or whoever needed the signature to approach Ronnie than it was to go up to Mick or Keith and ask. Ronnie was the green new boy who'd go, 'Oh yeah sure, how you doing, give it here and I'll sign it."

"At the hotels he thought everything was being charged to the Stones, so he'd be opening bottle after bottle of champagne, and having people up partying in his room and he was paying though the nose for it. He told me after that once all the deductions had come off his wage, he walked away with a cheque for £2,500."

Ronnie joining The Rolling Stones on whatever level became the top tabloid topic of 1975; the other burning question was who was hastening the eventual break up of The Faces? Ronnie, Rod or Kenney and Mac? Was it even her Majesty's Inspector of Taxes, who had been taking a keen interest in the band's financial affairs for some time? The top rate of tax that year stood at a crippling eighty three pence in the pound, and while many businessmen at the time managed to avoid paying quite so much (the Vestey family, for example, with their fortune from meat packaging plants and butchers' shops), entertainers always seemed to be a soft target.

Not for them (well, not yet anyway) the sensible luxury of trusts based in Lichtenstein, and a web of companies all apparently running at a loss. No, instead, rock and rollers opted for a lifestyle conspicuous by its consumption and flamboyance, financed by an income that even the most junior tax officer could easily estimate.

Add to that the fact that almost all the bands from that era were being badly advised and you had a recipe for financial disaster. In short, a lot of bands became the fall guys to an industry never noted for its accounting integrity.

Talk of tax was top of the agenda for the band that year, and none more so than when Rod Stewart failed to return from a trip to LA and announced he had become a tax exile. He was applying for American citizenship and had instructed Billy Gaff to sell everything he owned in England.

A month later he contradicted himself, saying the story was only a rumour and entirely false. He was merely working abroad for the next few months and that his mum would never forgive him if he quit home for good. On 23rd July, the British press reported that Rod had refused to leave the international lounge during a stopover at Heathrow, so he could avoid being served with a writ for £750,000 in unpaid taxes. Rod subsequently initiated legal proceedings against the newspaper and journalist who'd reported the story.

Curiously, he'd been on his way to another safe tax haven, Dublin, in order to attend a press conference he'd called to promote his up and coming album ominously titled "Atlantic Crossing".

Once safely in Ireland, Rod continued to fan the flames of a Faces break up by telling the New Musical Express's Steve Clark; "I believe this latest album is the best I've ever done. I definitely needed new blood around me; suddenly I've seen the light of day. This is what I should have been doing two years ago."

He then outlined his plans to tour with a full orchestra, a reference to his already booked solo concert at the Royal Festival Hall. He also revealed his backing band for the occasion was Booker T and the MGs (the concert was eventually cancelled in October when the MGs' drummer, Al Jackson, was shot dead by an intruder at his home in Memphis).

The initial announcement of the Festival Hall show started another rumour that Rod planned to replace Ronnie with MGs' guitar player, Steve Cropper. When a reporter pressed Rod on the subject he replied; "I don't even know if our guitarist is still alive or dead. I've spoken to him three times; twice he sounded really on top of the world, and the last time he sounded really down." His only passing reference to The Faces as a band came when he added "we'll all be down in Miami in three weeks time to start rehearsing and obviously there's going to be a lot of egos floating around. I wanted desperately to re-create what I've done on this album on stage. I'd do anything to do that, literally anything. We've already got a fifteen-piece orchestra that's ready to tour with us, which Mac doesn't like. But he's going to have to lump it."

When journalists repeatedly asked about a break up, Rod wearily replied; "If we don't break up soon we never will. We're now as close to breaking up as we've ever been."

Note that Stewart was actually saying the next tour was essentially going to be a promotional exercise intended to push "Atlantic Crossing". Which basically had nothing to do with any of The Faces, hence his concern that the band undertook some serious rehearsals. This was the first time he'd plugged a solo album in such a manner and he couldn't have done so without the backing and encouragement of Billy Gaff.

On a cold day in May, whilst Rod was or wasn't becoming a tax exile, Ronnie Wood was very much alive and riding down Fifth Avenue on the back of a flat-bed truck playing lead guitar with The Rolling Stones. The world's press had been packed into the dining room of The Plaza Hotel, expecting the band to turn up there in the usual limos, never realising that they were about to witness the world's greatest rock 'n' roll band appear in the street accompanied by the live sound of "Brown Sugar".

The Stones were turning up in their own inimitable style to announce that their 1975 tour of America would soon be upon them.

"All these New York cops came up to the truck as we were playing." Ronnie recalls, "They all shouted out for me, 'Hey Ronnie can you get us tickets for the show? We couldn't get any for The Faces. New York's finest never miss a trick."

Ronnie played his first real show with the Stones on his twenty eighth birthday, on 1st June 1975, at the Baton Rouge, Louisiana. "I was thinking, Not a bad birthday present for a kid who'd always dreamed of being a Rolling Stone." People who were there said he never stopped grinning.

Meanwhile, back in the remaining Faces camp there was understandably a fair amount of consternation going on.

"I feel pretty browned off," Kenney said in an interview in July. "Ever since Rod moved to the States everything's got a lot more disorganized. The Faces haven't worked in four months and I've lost £80,000 because we're not playing Wembley any longer."

There was also the little matter of a new album, which Billy Gaff had announced a few weeks' earlier. Jones, Mac and Yamauchi desperately wanted to start recording, but without a guitar player or singer, that was out of the question - as was the band's next US tour. A fact bore out once Jagger announced that The Stones' own American trek was being extended throughout the year.

Strangely enough, it was Rod who appeared to be the most put out; "We've had to cancel three concerts in Miami at a loss of $200,000 a night because there won't be enough time to rehearse new numbers with Ronnie. I'm particularly fed up because I feel the Stones should have let me know about their tour extension earlier."

Amazingly, Ronnie did manage to juggle his commitments and rejoin The Faces in Miami just in time. It was the first time the group had seen their guitar player for two and a half months.

"I'd been playing with a lot of different people during the lay off," Kenney told reporters "People like Paul and Linda McCartney (who he charitably referred to as 'actually a pretty good player'). What with Rod playing with Steve Crooper and Donald Duck Dunn (MGs' guitarist and bass player) and Ronnie playing in the Stones, I would have thought all that added experience would have made The Faces sound better. I knew Rod wanted the band to sound like his studio records and we could have done that. Unfortunately, it wasn't put to us like that and everyone was still getting as pissed as ever. Plus let's not forget Ronnie went away as a Face and came back as a Rolling Stone."

Rod might have planned for The Faces to reproduce "Atlantic Crossing" live, but once he was confronted by the sheer bloody-minded attitude of Mac, a drunk Japanese bass player (who he never wanted in the first place) and a lead guitar player whose mind and loyalties were so obviously elsewhere, Stewart had clearly thought again. Only Kenney seemed to understand or even care about what his singer was trying to do. "Going back to join The Faces that last time made me realise how unprofessional we'd always been" Ronnie admits today. "I saw how much more organized the Stones were. We'd all treated the Faces as a laugh, too much of a laugh. The Stones had everything worked out beforehand, they had set lists worked out and they knew exactly where and what they were going to do. They all pulled together as a team, and were the ultimate in professionalism. Spontaneity is all right, but for years The Faces never even had a set list, so you wouldn't know what number was next. One song after another was a guess and everyone would be shouting at each other "what are we doing next?" Sometimes you wouldn't even know what song you were playing at the time."

Unable to stamp his authority on the group and so re-create his new album live, Rod changed tack. The orchestra was trimmed down to twelve players and individual string quartets, whilst pick up musicians were hired in each city the band played.

Mac was still against any change of format: "that's fucking Liberace, that's Elton John show business nonsense." He hated it so much he only suffered it for a few opening dates, before finally refusing to pay his share of the quite considerable costs.

This left Ron, Rod, Kenney and Tetsu to pick up the extra tab.

The intended set also changed. Only two songs from "Atlantic Crossing" were included "Three Times Loser" and "I Don't Want To Talk about It", while the rest was made up of tracks almost entirely cherry-picked from Rod's other solo albums. This left only two bona fide Faces tracks remaining "Miss Judy's Farm" and "Stay With Me".

Effectively, it was a Rod Stewart Greatest Hits package, performed by a six-piece Faces (Rod had insisted guitarist Jesse Ed Davis also join the tour) and a stream of session men.

Ironically, that tour proved to be the most lucrative one the band had ever undertaken. It was also one of the longest. It eventually stretched into November and gave Kenney, Mac and Tetsu the forlorn hope that the band really did have a future.

Well, until only three-fifths of the band arrived back at Heathrow.

Rod had stayed on in LA holed up in a rented house in Beverly Hills, while Ronnie had jetted off to join Keith on holiday in Jamaica, before flying to Switzerland and starting rehearsals for his first album as a Rolling Stone.

Billy Gaff had also stayed on in the States and was renting a house not far from Rod's. He was now answering calls as Rod Stewart's personal manager and had left instructions with Shirley to deal with any Faces business outstanding.

All of which prompted the three UK based Faces to call a series of press interviews in which they sounded both embarrassed and desperate.

It was a last ditch attempt at trying to convince a music industry that The Faces were still a going concern, despite the widespread knowledge that the group were already finished.

All that needed to be done was for someone to administer the final coup de grace.

That task fell to Rod Stewart's personal publicist, Tony Toon, who issued a press statement that said "Rod feels he can no longer work in a situation where the group's lead guitarist, Ron Wood, seems to be on permanent loan to The Rolling Stones."

Billy Gaff also added his tuppence worth and said: "Rod thinks the world of Ron Wood. I have repeatedly tried to telephone Ron, who is touring with The Rolling Stones (in fact recording). I've left messages for him to call me, but so far I've heard nothing. Therefore The Faces' proposed tour of Britain and the Far East (always tentative at best) has now been called off."

Incredibly, McLagan commented, "I won't believe he (Stewart) is leaving The Faces until I hear it from his own lips." Whereas the more realistic Jones said, "If this means the end of The Faces, then I'm not bothered. I expect I'll survive."

No one bothered to ask Tetsuo Yamauchi what he thought about it.

"Billy had told me he wanted nothing more to do with Mac and Kenny," Shirley explains. "When they finally learned the truth, they came in and smashed the office up. They then sent the roadies in to take everything away, even the furniture, because they felt they'd paid for it. Even their roadies were fighting each other now; Pete Buckland went for Chuch and there was another punch up there. It was so horrible and upsetting the way it finished, the place was wrecked.

"When they'd all gone I looked around the office and thought back to my first days with the boys, the early days when I'd realised how different the public's perception of the group differed from the reality. I put my coat on and called Doreen up (Art Wood's first wife and Ronnie's first secretary) and I said, "Do you want to meet me at lunchtime, I'm leaving." So we went to the pub for a drink and I never went back."

Ronnie in the meantime was doing his Macavity the Cat impression again, staying well away from all the arguments. As well he might, because on 19th December 1975, Ronnie Wood's face grinned out from front pages throughout the world when it was announced that he had become a permanent member of The Rolling Stones.

What's more, some newspapers printed pictures of Ronnie posing in an LA swimming pool with non other than Krissie, once again by his side.

"I hadn't spoken to Ronnie in a year," she explains. "He understandably wouldn't even talk to me on the phone. Jimmy had been very proper and asked my Dad if he could marry me, and I'd sent Ronnie the divorce papers to sign. But he still wouldn't acknowledge me, he still wouldn't speak to me; he never even said if he'd received them.

"He just ignored the whole thing. He was in Jamaica with Keith and I said to Jimmy, Ronnie won't talk to me on the phone, so I'll just have to go and see him in person.

"Which upset Jimmy - it was so hard, but he understood that I had to go. Jimmy also cared about how Ronnie was feeling... because none of this had been planned and he knew we had to get something sorted out. Because there had never been a big scene about it, nothing had been brought out into the open; there'd never been guns out blazing."

It had to be obvious to someone as intuitive as Page that some bonds between Krissie and Ronnie were still firmly in place. She'd repeatedly told friends how uncomfortable she felt sharing the guitar player's wealth and success:

"I wish I'd helped him achieve some of it." She explained: "I would walk wistfully around Plumpton Place and think "I'd be comfortable with it, if I'd been there to help you get it." It didn't feel right to suddenly be a part of it. It had felt the same with George (Harrison). I hadn't contributed anything to George, or to beautiful Friar Park! But I had with Ronnie and The Wick - we had grown together and built a foundation together, we were like soul-mates."

Page had once told her that he felt she was only infatuated with him. He must have felt that the infatuation was wearing off.

"I flew to Jamaica and met up with Ronnie," Krissie continues, "and he said no to the divorce. Just seeing him again made me realise I was still in love with him, and I never went back to Jimmy."

That Ronnie's future lay with the Stones was obvious to almost everyone who knew him. Yet he still had some niggling concerns and in an uncommon moment of hesitation, he called up elder brother Art and asked for his advice.

He rang me up and said, "Art do you think I should do it?" To which I replied "Ron, you're not joining just another band this time, The Rolling Stones is a way of life." He'd never spoken a truer word.

Yet by 1975 the critics were all but writing off the world's greatest rock and roll band, and slating their new album "Black And Blue" as patchy and poor.

In fact, it seemed the entire world's music press were united in dismissing the album, whilst unanimously agreeing that their album "Exile On Main Street" had been the group's last great record and a final hurrah.

It was of course only partly true, but nonetheless there was a definite cause for concern regarding the quality of The Rolling Stones' recent work. "Goat's Head Soup" (1973) and "Black And Blue" (1975) were at best a ramshackle collection of songs drawn from a period when the Stones could scarcely call themselves a fully functioning band. And although "It's Only Rock And Roll" (1974) had gone to number one in America, it featured a fractured Stones line up, bolstered by a whole host of guest players.

Not only that, Keith at the time seemed determined to travel his own personal path to destruction, while Mick (who'd written the title track with Ronnie, a track that featured more Faces than Stones) seemed to have forsaken most of his rock and roll links in favour of becoming a Sunday paper socialite.

Bill Wyman was seriously considering leaving the band and teaming up with Crosby, Stills and Nash, while Charlie Watts looked even more bored and disinterested than usual. No wonder Mick Taylor thought he could hear the fat lady singing. Although to be fair, Taylor's decision to quit had as much to do with his own drug use as it did to feeling the band was fading away.

In retrospect, Ronnie joining the Stones in 1975 wasn't the sure-fire career move it might have looked. True, The Faces were definitely finished, but Rod Stewart would always have found a place in his band for his pal, just as he had for Kenney Jones.

Only Kenney ultimately hadn't taken it, and he'd hauled his drums off the private plane leaving Heathrow for Los Angeles at the last moment: "I did it out of loyalty to Mac," Kenney later explained, for Ian McLagan hadn't been included in Rod Stewart's new plans or line-up.

Ronnie had enough credibility to form his own group, but possibly not the will. As Art says about his kid brother: "He's got his own thing. I don't mean his solo albums, I mean Ronnie's thing is and it's been said a thousand times, he's a team player. Even when he did his little solo thing, he always wanted to share the spotlight. He never had the genuine aspiration to be a solo star. Even if his albums had sold millions, I'm sure that he'd still be the same. Rod wasn't like that, and Keith wasn't for quite a while, but all Ronnie's ever wanted is to be part of a band. He was in the middle of three brothers and I think that has a lot to do with it."

Nevertheless, Ronnie was right to have had those last minute jitters. The Faces had always managed to weather their not inconsiderable bad press, but bad reviews and press was something new to The Rolling Stones.

"There are two things to be said about the new Stones album, "Black And Blue" before closing time," bewailed Creem magazine. "One is that they are still perfectly in tune with the times and the other is that the heat's off, because it's all over. They really don't matter any more or stand for anything. Which is certainly lucky for both them and us. I mean, it was a heavy weight to carry for all concerned. This is the first meaningless Stones album, and thank God."

Leaving aside the question of fairness - everyone's entitled to at least one bum album - nearly all the critics had, of course, totally missed the plot. The band was in crisis, but it was one of transition, not boredom. They'd been around too long to be rebels, but weren't quite old enough to settle into that hard-driving middle age that would become their hallmark for the next two decades. There was also the slight problem of an internal power struggle between Mick and Keith for control over the group.

Generally speaking, each rock band has a single leader. Very rarely have there been two - Lennon and McCartney of course and maybe Page and Plant in Led Zeppelin - but it's not common.

People naturally saw Ray Davies as leader of the Kinks, Pete Townshend for The Who, and Steve Marriott for The Small Faces, The problems arise when another member of the band thinks he should be leader, or at least co-leader... or when a Steve Marriott leaves, and the band flounders. Normally, the leader will be the lead singer, guitarist or both. He's usually also the chief songwriter. The rhythm section, by the way, rarely gets involved.

The Rolling Stones had changed the equation. The original leader, Brian Jones, had been quickly sidelined by their original manager, Andrew Loog Oldham. Aside from his photogenic good looks, Jones simply hadn't been dynamic enough on stage, nor could he write songs (his biggest weakness). He also appears to have had what the Americans nowadays call a 'bi-polar' disorder. A less understanding society would merely mark him down as being paranoid, manipulative and self-destructive.

Be that as it may, his departure had allowed the Jagger/Richard partnership to flourish and given the band one front man, but two leaders. Mick and Keith had been close since childhood, but times change and with Keith's descent into heroin addiction, the old partnership was no longer working. Mick had the ability to stand back and take an overall view. Keith's life had become bounded by his relationship with Anita Pallenberg and the next fix.

Long before Mick Taylor had left, Jagger wanted total control over the band - if only because Richards could no longer be trusted to take an interest. In fact, there was some doubt if Richards would be at liberty for much longer, or for that matter even alive (but people are still saying that). If Keith had gone to prison for drugs, he wouldn't subsequently have been able to tour America. So as well as wanting control - primarily for business reasons - Jagger, always a far-sighted and practical man, felt he had no choice but to be on the lookout for a possible replacement for the other half of the Glimmer Twins.

But spaced out or not, Keith was not about to surrender any iota of control over the band. Like all addicts, he knew he could still function perfectly. It was just a question of managing to keep awake and remembering which country he was supposed to be in.

Mick Taylor was never strong enough to be a kingmaker. Brilliant musician that he was, he lacked the drive and the will to support either Jagger or Richards against the other, no matter how much they individually canvassed his support. It was a lousy situation to be in, one that had undoubtedly contributed to his own heroin addiction and ultimately helped him make up his mind to leave. Besides, he'd grown tired of only being on a wage and never really considered a full band member.

No wonder he never looked as if he truly belonged: Mick Taylor was simply too nice. But with him gone, the way was clear for Mick or Keith to bring in their own lead guitarist, someone who would side with Mick (who incidentally was now playing guitar) against Keith, or vice versa. Someone, in Mick's terms, who could - at a pinch - replace Keith if and when he went to that great High in the Sky... or found himself doing a ten stretch in Wormwood Scrubs.

In Keith's terms, someone who would watch his back, someone who could take sides without seeming to, and someone who could basically be all things to all men.

The point to remember is that while Jagger and Richards might have been at each other's throats, they went back a long, long way. Anyone openly favouring the one over the other would undoubtedly have been smacked down, and hard. The argument between them was family... and above all, there was the Stones organisation itself.

Even in 1975 the Rolling Stones were worth, in terms of back catalogue alone, a conservative £50 million - and that was with their old manager, Alan Klein, taking his tidy profit. It wasn't a band so much as a multi-national corporation, and no one - but no one - causes problems for a multi-national, unless they're a shareholder. It was a point not wasted on many a guitarist who might have been thought the obvious choice to replace Mick Taylor.

Chris Spedding had known Mick Jagger for years. His band, The Battered Ornaments had supported the Stones at the Brian Jones memorial gig in Hyde Park. Even so, he was a little surprised to be called by Mick Jagger one day in early 1975 and asked: "What are your plans and are you free?"

Spedding knew that the Stones were looking for Mick Taylor's replacement, although his leaving was yet to be officially announced. And even though Spedding had plans of his own, he was intrigued enough to go and meet Mick and Keith.

"I soon realised the power struggle that was going on," Spedding remembers. "I realised both of them were playing games against the other one. Both had their own agendas and both had their own list of guitarists in mind, all of whom would have sided with one or the other.

"It wasn't a question of who was good enough to play with the Stones, but who could be easily controlled. It was all so obvious that I didn't even entertain the idea, and I wasn't surprised when I heard Ronnie got the job."

Ah, but he might have been had he witnessed the audition by a young Irish guitar whiz-kid called Rory Gallagher a couple of days before Ronnie showed up.

Gallagher had so impressed the band with his effortless brilliance that Keith reportedly said there was no need to look any further, telling Gallagher he was in.

"That's great, thanks but no thanks," came the reply in a soft Irish accent, "I don't like yer songs."

There would be no such insolence from Honest Ron. For while Spedding's comment above qualifies as one of the greatest backhanded compliments of all time, it was actually extremely close to the truth - but for reasons that Spedding didn't properly appreciate.

First, while Ronnie and Keith were as alike as to be the bookends Art Wood had originally noticed, Ronnie's first mate in the Stones had in fact been Mick. If Ronnie has one great quality, it's a sense of personal loyalty - if he decides that you're worthy of it. But having made that decision, he rarely changes his mind. Unfortunately, if he does change his mind he usually neglects to tell you, but you soon find out. Phone calls go unanswered, meetings are not kept, the back-stage passes dry-up and you become a non-person muttering, "Where did Ronnie go?" For Ronnie doesn't handle confrontation well, and would just as soon you worked out for yourself that you're no longer a mate, and why.

So enter Honest Ron, otherwise known as Mediator Man. The deal was never spelt out, but everyone understood the rules. Ronnie was to keep the peace between Mick and Keith: "I gave myself the title of Diplomatic Liaison Officer."

Ostensibly, he could be seen as Keith's mate - and accurately so, for the two were and are genuinely close. But his first loyalty had to be to the band itself. If push came to shove, friendship couldn't be allowed to get in the way of the band's business. If it ever did, Jagger for one would cut him off at the knees. In a sense he became Keith's minder, the man who would keep Keith relatively straight... yet in the end, with supreme irony, it would be a newly-straight Keith who would bring Ronnie back, kicking and screaming, from the wilder excesses of his own personal hell.

Of course in 1975 that was all in the future. Meanwhile, Ronnie had another role to perform, and one that no one in the Stones organisation had even realised.

Ronnie Wood was going to have to get The Rolling Stones back on track, whilst coincidentally, justifying his existence as the new boy in the band.

CHAPTER SIXTEEN
"I LOVE THE RISK."

Back in 1997, when this book was first mooted, Ronnie decided that his years with the Stones warranted their own appraisal, separate from his earlier career. He reasoned quite rightly that the Rolling Stones are a phenomenon, and one of the few rock and cultural icons that the world will remember well into the next millennium. They've lasted longer than any other band. Their impact, not just on music, but also on the social fabric has been immense. For sure, he'd played with many other great musicians. But no matter how good or revolutionary The Birds, The Creation, The Jeff Beck Group or The Faces were, only one other band besides the Stones will be remembered as much for their effect on society as for their music, although arguably, the Beatles were far more musically innovative than the Stones, who have mostly remained true to their R&B roots.

Nearly thirty years as a Rolling Stone, Ronnie decided, was a book in itself.

Well, no. For the truth is, he hasn't done a great deal in those years. At least, not in terms of his own music, which was once the be-all and end-all of Ronnie's existence. On the other hand, it's also true that, as with mathematicians, rock musicians tend to do all their best work in their twenties. There are exceptions in both professions, like Ronnie's old pal Bob Dylan or genius physicist, Richard Feynman, but generally speaking the innovation and drive begins to lessen from the early thirties onwards. Interestingly, it's not always the same with classical, Blues, Jazz or C&W musicians, or with full-time artists and writers.

But the fact remains that Ronnie Wood joined the Rolling Stones when he was possibly one of the top twenty best guitar players in Britain. He was an inordinately talented musician, with the ability to master any instrument that captured his interest. As Keith Richard says: "Woody's got the same ability as Brian (Jones) had to pick up on any instrument."

Which is praise indeed - but unlike Brian Jones, Ronnie appears to have quite happily given all that talent to the band he'd admired so much since his teens, while asking very little artistically in return. It's popularly assumed that once he'd joined the Rolling Stones, his ambition had semi-deflated, like a party balloon on the morning after the night-before. In terms of his own personal and musical development, and compared to his Faces output and his Stewart collaboration, the past twenty-odd years have led to allegations that Ronnie has simply been coasting.

Friends close to Ronnie are quick to deny such a comment, but all eventually agree with Art: "If he's got to where he wanted to be, why worry? He reached the top and achieved his goal and that was good enough for Ronnie."

True, he's managed to survive a bad case of drug and drink addiction - but then, so have many other musicians. More than a few haven't survived, of course, but either way there's no longer anything new or even surprising about the music industry and drugs. It's what happens, is all. Musicians and record company executives and music journalists either use or they don't, and no one in the business seems to care either way. And why should they?

The public made them into gods, so it's hardly surprising when they exhibit a certain disdain for mere mortal concerns. Besides, this is the industry that spawned music-to-take drugs-by, specifically Ecstasy and cocaine - try listening to techno, house, or jungle sober or straight: pained boredom arrives after ten seconds, unless you're a user and those drug-trained brain synapses kick in, flashing you back to last weekend's sweaty clubbing. There's a strong suspicion that certain record company executives prefer mindless consumers, anyway. The trouble with real bands, playing real music, is that they're just so, well, independent - and expensive. But when was the last time a computer generated rhythm track went on strike? Or couldn't make a rehearsal because of a hangover?

It's also true that Ronnie went from being relatively broke, to a fortune in excess of £50 million in a relatively short time. Okay, it didn't happen overnight; in fact, it wasn't until Bill Wyman left that he became a shareholder, as it were. But he's not the only wealthy musician, and to be honest, is hardly as conspicuous a spender as some of his peers.

The 1998-purchased private jet has to be seen as a business expense. He does own two exceptionally beautiful homes, in England and Ireland, the latter housing his art and recording studios - and oh yes, his own pub. He does own racehorses, but so do many other people, not all of them multi-millionaires. Aside from racing, his favourite form of non-musical relaxation is snooker. Once you can afford the room for the table and the table itself, there's not exactly a huge overhead required. It would be nice to report about cues made from the rarest of woods, inlaid with gold and platinum - or a chalk holder fashioned from a single emerald. Nothing so extravagant. He does quaff a fair amount of vintage Dom Perignon, but who wouldn't? He also has a private members drinking club in southwest London, but that's a business venture rather than a luxury.

"An ice cold can of Guinness in the morning sorts you out."

He still cares about his art, and art in general. In fact, during his early salaried days with the Stones, his art had helped him survive financially. But while his studies of various musicians do have an obvious interest and are professionally done, there is a sameness and a commercial slickness about them that emphasises his ability to toss them off with ease. Perhaps that wouldn't matter very much - except for the line drawings he can also produce, more for himself and his family or close friends than for sale. Drawings which demonstrate a natural talent that can be achingly good - and actually tell you something about Ronnie himself. In fact, it doesn't take long before Ronnie will start sketching on anything he finds; old envelopes, scraps of paper, empty cigarette packets - invariably ending up with your likeness scribbled down and always signed 'Ron'.

Perhaps Rolling Stones have lived for so long in the media spotlight that they've become very, very reluctant to expose their private emotions except to their immediate family. And maybe, Ronnie is still too much in awe of the Glimmer Twins.

True, his marriage to Krissie didn't survive. But that was neither surprising nor unique - people who've lived together for many years often do divorce soon after they finally marry. It's as if the marriage itself was a last ditch attempt to paper over the cracks, a magical ceremony that will make everything okay again, and let's face it, the seeds of that particular divorce had been sown long before.

They'd met as adolescents and while they might have matured as individuals - well to some extent - the relationship had remained stuck in the everything's-groovy, wow-man atmosphere of the sixties.

Yet Krissie's open affairs with Jimmy Page and George Harrison had actually hurt Ronnie far more than he'd admitted at the time. Of course, Krissie always came back to him, nor was the fault all hers: Ronnie always gave the impression of putting his music above everything else, while their marriage was, if not exactly open, fairly relaxed. Nonetheless, the general view was that Krissie always left Ronnie for someone more famous... her return home when he joined the Stones could almost be seen as the final affirmation that Ronnie had really made the big-time. It might well have been emotionally satisfying for Ronnie to see that he was now ranked above Jimmy Page in the fame game, but it was no way to restart the relationship.

All of which totally passed over Krissie's head, of course. For her, she was simply pursuing the great love of her life. But their closest and oldest friends knew, and privately wondered how long the latest new beginning would last. Most of them gave it no more than a year, perhaps eighteen months tops. Some were even less charitable.

Anyway, Ronnie had something far more important to do than mend a broken relationship. In his mind, he had to once again mend a broken rock 'n' roll band... and in the process, willingly sacrifice his own musical individuality for the good of the group. He has spent the last twenty-nine years becoming a Rolling Stone - always in the celebrity shadow of Jagger and Richards and even the long-dead Brian Jones, whose ghostly presence still hovers malignantly above them all.

"I have the rare distinction of having left the Rolling Stones and lived," Mick Taylor was to say later (but before Bill Wyman's exit put a stop to that little after-dinner number). The truth was that Taylor leaving allowed Ronnie to help shape the band's recovery with two key ingredients missing for some years: reappraisal and youth.

Never seen as good a player as Mick Taylor - who according to Richards has to rank as one of rock's great lead guitarists - Ronnie nonetheless rejuvenated the band in a way that the self-effacing Taylor never could:

"When I joined the Stones they weren't interested in playing "Satisfaction", "Paint It Black" or all the old classics. They didn't want to be bothered with them. But that's what I knew the Stones to be; I knew all those songs and that's what I wanted to be up there playing. I already knew all their back catalogue note for note - I'd grown up listening to them. They were the sound track to my life and I wanted to play those great, great songs and I got them to listen to a lot of that stuff again with fresh ears. Then we started to play it and it was different and new again."

Or as Keith also said: "With Ronnie it's dirtier, and rougher, not slick and a lot more exciting."

Ronnie was twenty-eight years old when he joined the Stones, slightly strung out, a bit sycophantic, but well-connected and unmistakably, rock and fucking roll. He'd actually travelled to Paris to audition for the Stones with legendary soul man Bobby Womack, so sure of landing the job that he asked Womack how much money he should demand for the upcoming tour. "Half a million," Womack replied, talking US dollars. Ronnie got two hundred and fifty thousand - pounds sterling.

The pairing of Ronnie and Keith allowed the band to return to the dual, lead and rhythm approach to live performances, missing from the Stones' live sound since Brian Jones had died.

Just as importantly, Keith had a new buddy to tour with: someone who thought like him, drank like him and was soon to take drugs like him. He'd found another little Keith.

Ronnie also supplied an energy on-stage that had also been lacking for some time. Keith Richards was now as famous for nodding off on stage as for his playing, while Mick Taylor had been the quintessentially laid-back and uninterested looking guitarist.

Nothing wrong in that, but this was a band that already had two members performing that detached, ultra-cool role: Bill Wyman and Charlie Watts. Three had been one too many.

Ronnie brought his own brand of cool to what Keith Richards dubbed 'The Rolling Stones Mark 3'. It was a high-energy, Faces style of boisterousness; a feeling of fun that hadn't been seen in the Stones camp for many a long year.

And while Ronnie is still an inconsistent guitar player, he was always an extremely imaginative one. He worked hard with Keith to develop two-guitar parts that beautifully fitted the songs and allowed Keith to do what he does best: keep up the steady, driving rhythm that was the heart of the Stones' live sound. It was obvious that the band was at last enjoying playing live again. So much so that within twelve months of Ronnie joining, the band decided to issue a double album, "Love You Live", recorded mainly in Paris and a testimony to the fact that demand for the Stones' live work had increased dramatically following Ronnie's first tour with them (the one when he was still nominally a Face). From the very first, he'd meshed perfectly into the Stones' live sound.

"It's natural," he was to say. "I still don't practise anything. I don't want to remember the new songs exactly. I love the risk; that's what keeps it interesting and different each night - although that approach can backfire. That's why I'm still getting better each time we go out on the road, that's my practise - that and recording a live album. So there!"

Or as Keith said in 1977: "Woody and I can start playing together until we don't know who played the last lick. It's as close as that. He has the right feel and spirit for the Stones even though he's still the new boy; he's the one I communicate with the most."

And perhaps behind the heartfelt compliment lay the automatic assumption that everything Ronnie had ever done before was merely to prepare him for life as a Rolling Stone.

New band, new life, new wife?

If Krissie thought that Ronnie achieving the pinnacle of rock success would be both a new beginning for them and a fitting climax to their early years together, she was sadly mistaken. Perhaps part of the problem was that she hadn't been around when Ronnie had become a Stone. It was something he'd done by himself - well, okay, she'd been truly supportive in the early years, and responsible for introducing him to Keith, but this was now and he'd become a world-class celebrity, whilst she was still living her fairytale existence with Jimmy Page.

From the beginning of her reunion with Ronnie, Krissie seemed to make a point of emphasising that she was her own woman and not just another rock-wife. That she knew Ronnie when he hadn't two plectrums to rub together. That his success was somehow also hers. That Ronnie owed her more loyalty than he did to the Stones themselves. That she had her own career to consider; her own career being not just the wife of a Rolling Stone - although it wasn't a bad one - but something better: Ronnie's partner in every sense of the word. And everything was back the way it had been, the way it always would be.

Well, no. Ronnie won't talk about why he got back together with Krissie again. To her, that meeting in Jamaica had been intensely romantic, the moment they both finally accepted that they belonged to each other. Other people have pointed out that she always was - and still is - an extremely attractive woman, and perhaps - just perhaps - Ronnie had nothing more in mind than a brief fling, typical of his easy come, easy go approach to life. For one thing was sure: they couldn't go back to being the way they were.

Both were older and the wife of a Rolling Stone does carry certain responsibilities. That might sound totally unfair, even - whisper the word - sexist, given the individual band members' own personal behaviour, but the principle is nonetheless plain. The wife of a Rolling Stone has to be strong and above suspicion. There are too many other pressures on the band to allow for a freewheeling spouse. For every fan looking to worship the Stones, there is at least one person who would delight in the band's destruction. Women must never, ever get in the way of Stones business, which as Ronnie knows was a lesson never learned in The Faces.

Whether or not Ronnie planned a permanent reconciliation, or was just content to see what happened, was actually beside the point, for Krissie soon became pregnant. Family is all for Ronnie, and now they were to be three. Sadly, this time it wouldn't be enough to save them.

"Krissie was always a flirt," remembers close friend and Keith Moon minder Dougal Butler. "I'm not saying she was easy, but she often gave that impression - probably because she can be so bloody dizzy at times, It's like she's not really aware of the signals she's sending. Or she is aware, but is a bit of a tease. And suddenly she's in LA, and the guys and gals there are predators. Like, no one plays games - it's all bloody business; you screw for power and the wife of a Rolling Stone is one hell of a scalp. Especially this beautiful, blonde, typical English girl, because all the local girls were either bimbos or would be actresses, often both, and as hard as fucking nails. Krissie was the quintessential English blonde and there was no way that marriage could have survived. In fact, LA was such a lunatic asylum in the mid seventies that I can't think of any relationship that survived."

The move to Los Angeles signalled the end of Kris and Ron. It almost signalled his own end, too: "America almost killed me," Ronnie was to admit years later. "Drugs and fucking celebrity worship aren't good for you. Everyone wants to fuck a celebrity. And the hangers-on are everywhere."

Yet at the time, moving to Los Angeles seemed such a good idea for two main reasons: Ronnie needed a tax-holiday; and he was convinced the British police were itching to arrest him for possession of drugs. Which wouldn't have been a problem if he wasn't using drugs - but he was; mostly hash, grass and cocaine, as was Krissie who'd been instrumental in spotlighting Ronnie as a potential police target.

A few months before Krissie and Ronnie had been reconciled in Jamaica, Krissie's arrest for possession of drugs (a slight trace of cocaine in a kitchen mixing bowl) and a gun (actually an antique firearm owned by Sir John Mills) at the Wick had finally reached its pulsating climax at the High Court. Ronnie was, as usual, conspicuous by his absence when Krissie and her co-defendant Audrey, also known as Lorraine to her friends (and the then-wife of Richard Barnes, the man who re-named The High Numbers The Who and all-round good bloke), were found not guilty.

However, they were still ordered to pay costs amounting to £12,000 by a sceptical judge who commented: "If I were to believe you were telling the truth, then in turn you must expect me to believe that fifteen police officers were lying."

Well, yes, actually she did.

The overall point being that Krissie had been using and everyone knew it. Even if the police had all been lying through their teeth, Krissie Wood did drugs. She was marked as a user and now, she was also marked as the wife of a Rolling Stone.

The police did not like The Rolling Stones. It was almost an English tradition. Nothing to do with their music, but a great deal with the belief that the Stones in general, and Keith Richards (since Brian Jones) in particular, were somehow encouraging the public to use drugs.

Also, there was intense frustration that even when caught, they somehow managed to wriggle out of it. Why, even the 'Times' had once warned against "breaking a butterfly on a wheel", with reference to Mick and Keith's bust for possession of marijuana in 1967. Overall, the police revelled in high-profile drug busts and the Stones were still good game.

Ronnie was becoming used to a Stones-style massive media intrusion into his life. But with that came the increasing police interest, which was another matter entirely. Earlier on that year he'd publicly announced that he and Krissie had reunited and were thinking of moving to Los Angeles: "I love Britain but I haven't lived there for nearly a year," he said, adding with an obvious reference to Krissie's arrest at The Wick, "mainly because I don't feel safe in my own bed."

Following his announcement, Ronnie and Krissie had been stopped by Customs when returning to England from a holiday in France. A pregnant Krissie had been strip searched for drugs, watched by an outraged Ronnie. Both Customs and the police had been wrongly tipped that Krissie always carried Ronnie's stash through Customs; on the naive basis that no one would search a pregnant woman.

"Aren't you something to do with the Rolling Stones?" they'd asked her, displaying either a surprising naiveté of their own, or heavy-handed sarcasm. Either way, the result was intense humiliation for both Krissie and Ronnie, and a pay-off - or possibly a news story - for the original informant. Still, the lesson had been plain: Ronnie was now a target, like all the rest of the Rolling Stones.

He needed a place that understood celebrities and drug use, and Los Angeles had her arms wide open.

Ronnie also explains the move on the fact that he'd started receiving hate mail: "Yeah, I got some. Well, one actually, and it wasn't just about me, it was about all the pop stars who were leaving the country at that time, for tax reasons, and it said at the bottom 'I wish you'd fuck off with them!'"

Tame by today's standards, but it was enough to make the idea of Los Angeles more and more seductive, especially Malibu - that luxurious Los Angeles suburb-by-the-sea that understood people like the Stones and which by the mid seventies, was overrun by drink and drug crazed, tax exiled British rockers.

It had more sand than Brighton and there was no need to search out the local, neighbourhood pusher anymore: drugs were delivered to your door with as much fuss as a pizza.

LA was full of all kinds of decadence, which if nothing else meant some great parties and Ronnie still liked a party. In fact, he could probably have carved out a respectable movie-career as 'interesting face in party crowd', an actual role he played in the film "Nine And A Half Weeks".

Another reason for escaping to the sun was the tax-bill left over from his years with The Faces. The Stones might well have just signed with Atlantic Records for a whopping $21 million, making them the then-highest paid recording artistes in the world - but Ronnie wouldn't see a lot of it.

He had to sell The Wick for £300,000, but kept the cottage as his London base, and together with Krissie, settled into a beachfront property next door to The Band's Rick Danko and a few houses down from Keith Moon, David Bowie and Ringo Starr.

"He hated to sell The Wick," Richard Barnes remembers. "They'd bought it before they could really afford it because he'd fallen in love with the place. They couldn't even afford to furnish it for ages. It was really funny because you'd go round there and it was a beautiful place, fantastic big rooms, and Ronnie and Krissie would be sitting in deck chairs and packing crates. They didn't get it together for ages, because Ronnie was building his studio."

Some men put up shelves on moving into a new home. Rock musicians build a recording studio. In fact, Surrey and the Home Counties are littered with neglected home-recording studios. It's what musicians do.

Ronnie may have lost his beloved Wick but he still had a little part of it, the cottage.

A place that at various times had housed both Ronnie Lane and Keith Richards, living happily at the bottom of his garden. Ronnie Lane had even painted the cottage stairs and floorboards alternate black and white, much admired by those who were drunk or stoned. Even Keith had tried his hand with the paintbrush, but the results were apparently not to everyone's taste. Well, to no-one's taste, really, as people still remember with a shudder. The Wick had been the dream house in the dream location, still close enough to his West London roots for his mother to pop over every day to make him a cup of tea.

Yet Ronnie knew a thing or two about moving on and that time had come again. So it was goodbye childhood dream, hello Los Angeles - another dream, but without the innocence, some even say nightmare.

Jessie James Wood - the names courtesy of Ronnie's fascination with the Wild West - was born in October 1976, after a madcap dash to Cedars Sinai Hospital by Krissie and Ronnie plus their houseguests - Mick Jagger, Linda Ronstadt, Governor Jerry Brown and Warren Beatty, all aboard a converted ambulance complete with siren that belonged to one of Neil Young's roadies: "His name was Sandie and he just happened to knock on the door as Krissie went into labour. He said he was driving by and thought he'd stop and see if we needed anything. I said "Yeah, a lift to the fucking hospital!"."

While Beatty was dropped off halfway there (he hated hospitals and had a girlfriend to visit), Jagger played the traditional role of expectant father's friend, even having to help a nervous Ronnie fill out the papers authorising a Caesarean section. For a short time Ronnie was as proud and excited as any new father. The baby was a stabilising influence on the marriage as the Wood family settled down to what Krissie felt was married bliss. She had her man and her baby. She was the wife of a Rolling Stone, living in Malibu and mixing daily with the stars. Paradise regained.

"I lost touch with both Krissie and Ronnie when they went to LA," says Sandy Serjeant, "except she used to call me up and say, "Don't you wish you were out here with me?" which was a stupid thing to ask, and of course I used to say yes. She tried to paint a rosy picture of their life out there, but it was obvious that things were going wrong between them, despite the baby. I saw the second split coming long before Krissie did. I think she straightened herself out - almost - after Jesse's birth. But I don't think Ronnie did, he wanted to party as much as he always did and LA was one big party; it was the John Lennon lost weekend era."

On 24th February 1977, Keith mistook the people rifling through his and Anita Pallenberg's luggage at Toronto International Airport for Stones roadies... only to discover to his horror they were in fact Customs who reportedly declared it was Christmas all over again when they discovered ten grammes of hashish, a blackened spoon that revealed heroin traces and a packet of Tic-Tacs that were taken away for analysis - along with the spoon - and never returned. Three days later, on 28th February, the Mounties themselves came looking for more when a search party blitzed through the Harbour Castle Hotel and arrested Keith for possessing enough heroin to qualify for a trafficking offence. There were those who claimed the bust was Anita's fault; that she'd attracted the Mounties' attention by buying it locally herself. Whatever, Keith got the blame.

No one had ever beaten a heroin trafficking offence in Canada, a fact that didn't escape Ronnie - who immediately assumed the Macavity position and quietly disappeared a few days later... last seen by Keith waving goodbye as the lift doors closed behind him.

"That's the hardest memory in all our years of friendship." Ronnie was to later say, and you can just imagine how difficult it had been to leave Keith on his own (Jagger, by all accounts, merely phoned Keith's room to announce his departure).

Although to be fair again, Ronnie did have his own problems at the time, mainly concerned with nearly - but unwittingly - toppling the Canadian government.

God only knows what Ronnie had been thinking of when he slipped off from a party with Canadian Prime Minster Pierre Trudeau's much younger wife, Margaret. Let's re-phrase that. It's pretty obvious what he was thinking of, but how on earth did he think he'd ever get away with it?

Ronnie and Maggie had originally met on 4th March, when she'd gone backstage after a gig at the El Moccambo club. Maggie Trudeau was an early Diana, Princess of Wales-type figure, who was married to a man who'd been a world leader while she was still at school.

Two sons had quickly arrived, and soon Maggie was showing signs of boredom and of wanting a life of her own. She, too, longed to glitter on the world stage, but in her own right. She was beautiful, vivacious, a little self-obsessed and ambitious beyond her talents. The Rolling Stone had been mixing with women like Margaret Trudeau for most of his life.

On the evening of 6th March 1977, Ronnie was wining and dining Maggie T in the Harbour Castle restaurant. They were also seen walking around outside. Much later, he was to say that he'd hoped to persuade her to intercede with the Canadian authorities on Keith's behalf. That is, persuade her husband to order the Royal Canadian Mounted Police to drop the charges. One thing led to another, as it so often does with Ronnie, and they ended up in his room... via a brief detour to meet his good mate, Keith.

A few hours later, Maggie was discovered in the corridor where the Stones entourage had their rooms and suites. She was clad only in a hotel bathrobe, and alternating between euphoria and sheer bloody-mindedness. Pete Rudge, responsible for the Stones' security, asked her to get dressed and leave, but when she wouldn't, Rudge called Mick Jagger who repeated the request - although less politely. Meanwhile, the hotel management were desperate to find a diplomatic solution to a potentially explosive incident. Eventually it was decided to give Maggie her own suite and hope that a) she'd behave, and b) that no-one had noticed. She eventually left early the next morning.

When the news first broke - oh yes, people had noticed - the media jumped to the obvious assumption that she'd been visiting Mick Jagger. After all, she was the Prime Minister's wife, and Canadian honour demanded no less than the Stones' lead vocalist. When Mick proved it hadn't been him, suspicion fell on the other Glimmer Twin, partly because Keith had been mistaken for Ronnie when Maggie had been seen in the restaurant and partly because she'd also been seen going into Keith's room - but not, apparently, later seen going into Ronnie's room.

Whether she knew it or not, Margaret was under surveillance - as much to make sure she didn't embarrass her husband as for her own security. So, too, was Keith under surveillance - it was later announced that a tiny electronic bug had been found in his room. All in all, introducing the Prime Minister's wife to a man accused of drug trafficking had not been the smartest thing Ronnie had ever done. But he'd meant well.

In the wake of Keith's bust, Ronnie and the other Stones had eventually and quietly faded away in order to re-group in New York. But Keith's passport had been confiscated, so he had to remain in Toronto with only Anita and the faithful Ian Stewart for company. February in Toronto can be a deeply depressing experience, even without the possibility of a jail term hanging over one's head. The sky often remains grey and overcast for weeks on end and if the snow doesn't get you, the freezing rain will.

While Keith was stranded in his hotel room he taped songs that mirrored his somewhat bleak outlook: "Apartment Number Nine", an apt Tammy Winette number, and "Worried Life Blues", an old Blues standard into which Keith inserted the poignant line: 'My friends have all left me.' And so they had, to party with David Bowie and Iggy Pop in New York and show up at the Eagles' sell-out gig at Madison Square Garden, where Ronnie couldn't but help himself from joining the band on stage.

In the meantime, the Canadian media were busily figuring out the truth about Margaret Trudeau, who was now on the missing list. Or rather, editors and proprietors were wondering if they dared print the truth as seasoned journalists looked at each other open mouthed: "What? Not Jagger, not Richards, but Ronnie Wood? Isn't he in The Faces?" But no one wanted to be the first to publish the story that put cuckold's horns on the country's Prime Minister. There was the matter of national pride and besides - Trudeau had a long memory and could be totally ruthless.

So it suited everyone, including the Stones, to pretend that it was all an innocent misunderstanding. Mick simply dismissed the entire episode when he said, "Oh, Margaret, she just dropped by. Someone said she wanted to come to the gig, so we took her. I'd never met her before, but I guess she likes to go out to clubs and go rocking and rolling like anyone else."

The New York Daily News finally broke the story when it announced that Ronnie was the true object of Margaret Trudeau's affections, ending with the comment that: "Ronnie Wood could probably tell you more about where Margaret Trudeau is staying than her husband."

In fact, two years later Keith would - much to everyone's intense surprise - avoid prison, instead sentenced to play a concert for charity. The feeling at the time amongst a few more cynical Canadian journalists was that a deal had been struck: no gaol, no raking up the Margaret Trudeau affair. So in that sense, Ronnie's attempts at mediation had somehow worked. Although the idea that he'd deliberately slept with the prime minister's wife in order to try and blackmail the Canadian authorities into being lenient with his best mate is, of course, utterly absurd. Why, that's the kind of scheme that only a stoned... irresponsible... crazy... person would come up with. Which is not like Ronnie at all. Well at least, not now.

The Harbour Castle episode, by the way, was widely held responsible for causing a knee-jerk run on the Canadian dollar. True, it was only a very small run that didn't last very long... but how many other rock-stars can claim to have blipped the economy of a major industrial nation?

Rock on, Woody.

"Love You Live" was released in 1977 and showed that the Stones had recovered all their old confidence, reaching number three in the US and number five in the UK. Few bands like live albums, since they never really recapture the atmosphere, but faithfully record every bum or missed note. In this instance, the album also captured Ronnie's own virtuoso performance: "That spell on bass with Jeff Beck had given me a different understanding of the guitar by the time I went to The Faces, even more so when I joined the Stones. I'd got in a rut and the bass gave me a new ground to build on. I learned to understand how important what you don't play is as important as what you do.

"My son Jesse has only just re-introduced me to those old Beck albums and I honestly can't believe it's me playing. With Beck I got that driving rhythm going and I still look at the guitar with the same driving idea. Hearing the guitarist on Aretha Franklin's "The Weight" got me into bottleneck and I never looked back. George Harrison is one of the greatest slide-guitar players ever, I love his playing, in the same way I rate the Burrito Brothers' Sneaky Pete's pedal steel playing. Duane Allman, too; as soon as I heard him I went Yeah! I've got to get one and I got a double-necked, pedal steel guitar, which I just plonked in my lap one day and worked it out for myself. I once went through a sax phase, which I really enjoyed and I think I could go a long way with it. I now mainly use it for sticking my paint-brushes in. You have to be careful and make sure you don't wander too far, because that's what happened to Brian Jones; that was a big part of his demise. He started playing everything, bar the kitchen sink - recorders, flutes, the sitar - and he lost his focus. Mick Taylor was also into experimenting with different instruments. But I'll always be a guitar-player at heart."

Ronnie first met twenty-two year old Josephine Howard, nee Karslake, the daughter of an architectural model-maker from Billericay in Essex, in late 1977. It was at a party at Sheffield Terrace, Kensington, in a flat that Jo was thinking of sharing with her roommate. It was also while Krissie was at home in Los Angeles with baby, Jesse James. Ronnie, who'd gone to the party with Bill Wyman, recounts the meeting in much the same way as he describes the transition from one band to another: "It came exactly at the right time."

Jo was a successful model with a two year-old son and an unhelpful ex-husband and by his own account, Ronnie fell in love the moment he first saw her.

Jo on the other hand was less impressed - she wasn't a Stones fan, but a typical twenty-two year old of the times, unaware of Ronnie and Wyman's musical legacy and into The Bay City Rollers. Faced with such indifference, Ronnie behaved like an infatuated schoolboy, and tried to impress her by shoving a copy of the Stones' "Black And Blue" album under her nose and excitedly pointing to his own picture profile and shouting, "Look, that's me!"

But she wasn't interested and said that while she had seen the Stones play at Earls Court, she hadn't noticed Ronnie on stage. She then added that she worked on the Pick n' Mix sweets counter at the big Woolworth's in Oxford Street... which wasn't exactly true, but was intended to put him off.

Ronnie told her that he was having marriage problems. Problems that for Krissie at least were about to become insurmountable. For Jo was soon to become Ronnie's constant companion until recently.

The day after he'd met Jo, Ronnie patiently waited for two hours outside Woolworth's for her to finish work, asking each and every departing employee in turn when Jo Howard would be finished... before realising that she'd had been winding him up and rushing back to the Kensington flat to confront a giggling Jo: "He seemed so different from the night before, when he was showing off and trying to impress me. This time he was so normal and sheepish."

They spent a few weeks together before Ronnie decamped back to America, leaving Jo wondering if he'd only seen her as a passing flirtation.

"I think at first people saw it as such," says Art, "because everything was always so casual with Ronnie. George Harrison was the same. When Ronnie was seeing Patti Boyd it was all very casual, not a heavy scene and that's a lot to do with the sort of people they are. George's attitude was brilliant; he was very peace and love: "It's okay to screw my wife because you're my mate." And Ronnie was the same, "You're my mate, you can drink from my brandy bottle and you can drink from my wife"."

The more sceptical among us may rise a quizzical eyebrow, but the evidence seems to back up Art's assessment of them both, with Ronnie appearing in George's video for "This Song" dressed up as a woman, and George and Ronnie both appearing in Eric Idle's Beatles pastiche, The Rutles.

Rick Cunningham remembers Ronnie reacting to Jo like a shy adolescent: "He actually told me he had a girlfriend, which really surprised me because he'd never said anything like that before, never while he was with Kris or even about Kris, and now he was admitting he'd found a girlfriend in Jo. When he first met her, he said it was the first time he'd felt serious about anyone. It was the inevitable end for Kris and Ron, or as everyone said, they'd become as much like brother and sister as man and wife, but I for one thought they were an entity forever. God knows why, but I just couldn't see them any other way."

A month later Ronnie invited Jo to Paris for a weekend and told her to meet him at the PLM hotel in the afternoon. Jo bought herself a special weekend round trip ticket and arrived deliberately late. For although she'd also fallen in love, Jo had no intention of being seen as a groupie - as her estranged husband had begun taunting her.

However, Ronnie was about to arrive even later, a whole day later, for when she arrived at the hotel and asked for Mr Wood's room, she was shocked to discover that no one of that name was registered. Worried and tired after her journey, Jo had no choice but to book herself in, asking for the cheapest rate. They gave her a maid's room, where a hungry Jo finally managed to fall asleep, for room service was far too expensive and she had no intention of walking the streets of Paris at night looking for food.

When Ronnie finally did arrive at the hotel around 6.00am the following morning, he was to be told in turn that no one called Howard was staying there. It was only with the erratic assistance of a pidgin-speaking night porter that he finally figured out Jo had, for whatever reason, booked in under her maiden name of Karslake.

So it was that Jo Howard's first real introduction to her future life was when she opened the door to see Ronnie standing there with a strung out Keith in tow, who frustratingly stayed with the couple the entire weekend. Apparently their Concorde had developed engineering problems in-flight, shaking and vibrating so hard that Ronnie's dinner had fallen into Keith's lap - plus Keith had also forgotten the address of the flat he was renting.

If this wasn't introduction enough, it had been made all the more alarming by Keith injecting heroin within minutes of entering the room with the heartfelt sigh of "God! I needed that!"

He had started using again, but only injecting into a muscle, as he now believed that you could avoid total addiction as long as you stayed away from the veins. On the other hand, Keith was and is one of the very, very few people with enough mental toughness to eventually kick his heroin habit without too much trauma. Not that he was ever in control of it. Not even dealers control smack... it always kills or damages anyone who becomes in the least way involved. Although Ronnie reckons that: "Keith was an intelligent drug user, if there is such a thing, now he's totally clean. I saw so many people end up in trouble by trying to impress or keep up with Keith. I saved John Belushi's life more than once, then had to save my own. My biggest step in recovering was to book myself into a clinic. It was a decision that Jo and I made together."

Rick Cunningham - who'd witnessed those hedonistic days first hand for one, never felt that Ronnie was in any way following Keith Richards' downward lead: "I never thought that Ronnie had a problem. It certainly never seemed to affect his health. Cocaine didn't keep Ronnie up until six in the morning - he does that anyway, that's how he lives his life, even now. The booze he could consume and still remain standing was simply amazing! He's got the constitution of an ox for such a skinny bloke; he's not exactly a mass of muscle, is he?"

While Art puts it down to Ronnie's personality: "His character is too strong for drugs to whittle it down. He's still got youthfulness about him. He's never had that old lag thing about him, ever."

Jo's introduction to life with the Stones couldn't have been too disturbing. The weekend stretched into the following week and then the next month, when Ronnie insisted Jo accompany him to the Pathe Marconi studios where the band was recording the album "Some Girls". Jo called the model agency in London and cancelled all her bookings.

"I remember bursting into tears the first time I saw Ronnie walk out on stage," Jo remembers, "and I turned round to friends and asked "How can I be going out with that?" Girls were screaming at the man I loved and I knew he hadn't been able to find his socks in the morning."

On 16th February 1978, a speeding Mercedes sports car - with Krissie Wood inside - smashed through the plate glass window of a hairdressing salon at the corner of Paradise and Richmond High Streets. That's Richmond, Surrey, as opposed to Richmond, Virginia, for Krissie was back in the UK. She'd heard the rumours about Ronnie and Jo and seemed resigned to the inevitable as she was in the company of one Charlie Heckstall-Smith, en route to The Wick cottage.

"He was a musician," is all Art remembers. "Not greatly talented, but very good-looking. I'd stopped trying to understand what Ronnie and Krissie were doing by now. Anyway, Charlie was driving Krissie in her car back to the Wick Cottage. I suppose he was her boyfriend, but that whole thing was over very quickly after the accident. I don't know if he was related to Dick Heckstall Smith. But there can't be that many Heckstall Smiths that I know two of them. How many do you know?"

A week later, Krissie was still lying in bed in the London Clinic when the door to her private room opened and Ronnie appeared. An eyewitness remembers that he moved very slowly and seemed to have trouble concentrating as he talked of this and that. Krissie was in traction and plaster and had difficulty following Ronnie with her eyes as he moved around the room, and then he stopped and point blankly asked for a divorce.

A moment later the door opened again and one of the nurses walked in, saying to Ronnie: "The lady in the car outside wants to know if you're going to be much longer."

Krissie filed for divorce, citing Jo Howard, as soon as she left hospital.

When asked for a comment, Ronnie stated from Paris where the Stones were finishing recording that it was all being dealt with a very civilized manner. So civilized it was never mentioned again.

"We never spoke about it again." Krissie says now: "We've never spoken about it since, there's so much that we've never worked through. It was over and done without any scenes really, and it's taken me years to get it straight in my own head. It's something Ronnie and I have never confronted, I don't know if Ronnie worked it through in his mind, I've never asked. But he did leave me with the most beautiful gift and that was Jesse."

She still keeps a blurred colour Polaroid of a tearful-looking Ronnie holding a tiny Jess wearing baby dungarees on the day of the final parting: "That was it! He came to say goodbye to both of us and then flew straight to LA with Jo and her son, Jamie, and I never saw or heard from him for God knows how long. They eventually moved to one of those classic brownstones on New York's Upper West Side."

Jesse's childhood memories include a sad amount of waiting in hotel lobbies for a father who never showed up, a father who was sinking fast into addiction.

As part of the settlement, Krissie was given the cottage at the bottom of The Wick's garden. Which she unwisely sold several years later for less than its market value. She said at the time that she wanted to rid herself of her past... and hopefully start a new life away from rock and roll, which she felt had robbed her of everything, bar Jesse.

Except, ever since she was sixteen, her entire life had been rock and roll. She'd grown up on it and had been linked to members ands ex members of the biggest groups of all time. She'd bedded a Beatle, shared a castle with a rock god and ended up an ex-wife of a Rolling Stone. Who was she kidding - the music world was her life. It was all she knew.

And for that matter, nothing was to change. Soon after her divorce Krissie began dating Thin Lizzy guitar player Brian Robertson, in time to witness the band's leader, Phil Lynot, die of drug addiction when his body simply gave up, and whose reputed last words to a nurse were: "There's no chance of a wank, then?"

In retrospect, perhaps Krissie herself was hooked - not so much on drugs, but on musicians. Regardless, she was to devote the next phase of her life to bringing up her son, Jesse - who's turned out to be totally unaffected - unlike some, no, unlike most - by Child-Of-Rock-Star Syndrome. Instead, Jesse is a polite, well-mannered, level-headed and gifted young musician now to be heard on his uncle Art Wood's revamped Quiet Melon album, "Money Due Melon", on the track "Knee Deep In Nephews", which brings together Jesse and all three Wood Brothers for the first time.

For her part and from the very beginning, Jo Wood nee Howard seemed to see her role in life as staying as close to Ronnie as she possibly could. She'd gone to Paris to meet Ronnie that first time and never went home: "Ronnie talked me into staying on with him and I never really went back to my other life," Jo was to say recently. "In all our time together, Ronnie and I have only ever been apart from each other for no more than a few weeks."

CHAPTER SEVENTEEN

"NEVER TRUST A HIPPY."

As the seventies drew to a close, both London and New York were shuddering to a different musical wavelength: Punk rock had arrived. "No Beatles, Elvis or the Rolling Stones in 1977!" screamed The Clash and they had a point. Although in truth, all the seminal punk bands secretly held The Faces and the Stones in awe.

Those flippant punk slogans, 'Never Trust A Hippy' and 'Rock Dinosaurs' looked and sounded good. Johnny Rotten had even slammed the door of Malcolm MacLaren's King's Road 'Sex Shop' in Mick Jagger's face - how lésè majeste can you get, for gob's sake? And while that story was later dismissed by Jagger as pure fantasy, the fact that so many people took pleasure from it was enough to worry the Stones: new gunslingers were in town.

Of course, Jagger et al weren't to know that the Sex Pistols - with the exception of Sid Vicious - had all been in the Kilburn State audience of Ronnie's two solo shows. Nor that the Pistols' Steve Jones and Paul Cook were responsible for a series of break-ins at The Wick and its cottage. Each time, guitars were the only victims - either one of Ronnie's or Keith's and each time there was always a note saying, 'Thanks mate, Steve was here,' because as they later admitted, who better to 'borrow' from than your heroes?

Nowadays, Mick Jagger says - a trifle smugly - that punk had never fazed them. Oh really? Reprise back to 1977 and Keith's comment about a certain track called "Shattered": "Why the fuck did Mick want a punk-sounding guitar?" Keith had wailed, "Why not have a Stones-sounding fucking guitar sound?"

Punk was there to linger. In 1979, even Ian McLagan would seriously consider joining Glen Matlock's post-Pistols outfit, The Rich Kids, after disastrously re-treading the boards with a re-formed Small Faces that in Kenney Jones' words had, "Happened for no good reason at all."

The paradox was that punk had followed the identical path of British R&B groups in the fifties and sixties, including the Stones. For punk had really begun with the likes of Lou Reed and the Velvet Underground or even better, the New York Dolls or the MC5. And as with Black R&B twenty years beforehand, that sound had been seized by British, white working-class kids who changed it into something completely different. While in the States, punk became one way for angst-ridden, white, middle-class kids to establish their street-culture, anarchistic credentials... with the possible exception of the Ramones, blue-collar to a man, who somehow managed to invent bubble-gum punk, looking and talking as if they'd just walked out of that bastion of Middle America, a Marvel super-hero comic.

It was the American punk band's teeth. No one can be a true, suffering anarchist with thousands of dollars of expensive dentistry gleaming in the face that mouths obscenities.

American punk bands on the whole looked too clean and well-fed, and so unlike Britain's own, dear Sex Pistols - although The Clash were a little neater, the Damned theatrical, and the Jam, well, they were mods - British punk had an urgency and an energy not seen since the Stones' hey-day. Such a shame then that its main legacy appears to be that tuneless, emotionless drone emitted by all those hundreds of Third Wave band-wagon jumpers, that spawned picture postcards of smiling Mohicans in the King's Road, and a musical technique that owes a great deal to the Keith Moon School of Guitar Playing.

Nagging doubts over Keith's liberty had unsurprisingly led to his keeping a low profile while awaiting trial in Toronto and during the recording of "Some Girls". The album was predominantly conceived and written by Mick, but the sessions also provided a song-writing opportunity for Ronnie. He ended up with his first Stones co-writing credits on two tracks: the aforementioned "Black Limousine" and "Everything is Turning To Gold", both of which would later appear on the albums "Tattoo You" and the compilation "Sucking In The Seventies", respectively. "Some Girls" stands as probably Ronnie's seminal Stones album, and his heightened presence is heavily felt on each track... none more so than on the cod-Country effort, "Far Away Eyes", and the vaguely-punk sounding "Shattered". In addition to his lead guitar work on the album, Ronnie contributed bass, pedal-steel, rhythm, acoustic guitars; backing vocals; and the occasional wallop on the old bass drum.

Just as importantly, he encouraged Mick to play guitar on several tracks and tutored him daily. Ronnie might have been Keith's best mate, but there was no way he was going to be seen taking sides. Besides, there was another reason for teaching Mick how to play guitar: if Keith's trial went the wrong way in Toronto, the band would be minus a rhythm guitarist. It made more sense for Mick to learn the job, than for two newcomers to be in the Stones line-up - for that would have surely diluted the band's sense of exclusivity.

Ronnie's heightened status in the band also allowed him to bring in Ian McLagan who fleshed out Ian Stewart's keyboards. This, in itself, established that he was going to be his own man, and even if he wasn't on an equal financial footing, he was now an integral and vital member of the band. The press had even stopped referring to him as 'ex-Faces guitarist'. He was now known as 'Rolling Stone, Ronnie Wood'. Bill Wyman was even moved to comment how much he'd enjoyed making the album, mainly due to Ronnie's presence.

The album's first single release, the mildly disco-orientated "Miss You", went straight to number one in the States and then on to become one of the band's best-selling single of all time.

On 7th October 1978, the Stones played live on television for the first time in ten years. Naturally, the show had to be Saturday Night Live, America's hottest rated TV programme of the seventies. The Stones were booked to open the first show of the fourth season. Within the industry, it was billed as a meeting of the gods, the World's Greatest Rock and Roll Band and the World's Greatest Rock and Roll Comedy Programme. And not without reason, for Saturday Night Live's two principal players, John Belushi and Dan Ackroyd had only just completed nine triumphant nights in their "Blues Brothers" guise supporting Steve Martin at the Universal Amphitheatre in Los Angeles. Their first album, "A Briefcase Full Of Blues", was currently sitting at number one, and the show's ratings were going though the roof. The Stones were there to promote their return-to-form album, "Some Girls" and felt that all concerned were on a roll. Dressing rooms were repainted and furniture specially hired by the network in anticipation of the Stones' arrival...and Ronnie and Mick repaid their generosity by 'shocking and revolting' ABC's president, Fred Silverman, when the pair openly French-kissed live on air. If nothing else, that was a very punk statement. As was Keith and Ronnie's blatant snorting of coke in front of the Rockefeller Centre security guards - and then ordering several crates of their latest favourite tipple, Rebel Yell whisky, which they naturally signed for in Jagger's name.

Keith got so stoned and drunk that the two sketches specially written for him had to be dropped: in the first one, Keith only had one line to say, but nonetheless managed to forget it time after time. In the second, he missed his entrance altogether, prompting comedienne Loraine Newman to say live on air: "It's nice to be standing and working with a dead person."

Ronnie was in such a state that he was written out long before the show began.

It got even worse. The Reverend Jesse Jackson called the network to complain that the lyrics to "Some Girls" contained a degrading slur on black people as in the line: "Black girls want to get fucked all night." The Stones responded with the flippant, "Well, who hasn't at some time in their lives?"

But that point was lost on the Reverend who began campaigning to have the album banned. Finally, Ahmet Ergun, head of Atlantic, issued a fulsome apology that explained Mick owed everything he had in life to Black Music and Black People, and was deeply mortified. Jagger simply said sorry, but was privately heard bemoaning the fact that some people couldn't take a joke.

It was no surprise that the Stones' appearance on Saturday Night Live hadn't been quite the success that the band had hoped for. Their performance had been laboured and sluggish - for they had made the classic mistake of peaking too soon the night before at Ackroyd and Belushi's illegal drinking den, "The Blues Bar". Here, the band had played brilliantly well into the early hours, meaning that by the time of the show's transmission, Ronnie and Keith in particular were too strung out to perform well.

If Ronnie's work with the Stones was generally going well - Saturday Night Live excepted - his own work was decidedly not. He'd formed a side project, The New Barbarians at the beginning of 1978 with Ian McLagan, in order to promote his second solo album, "Now Look" and would continue to tour with them on and off over the next two years. The band's name was coined by Ronnie's neighbour, Neil Young, while the line-up included Bobby Keys, Stanley Clarke, Ziggy Modeliste and Keith Richards:

"It was easy to get Keith to back me up. The Stones weren't gearing up to do much, so I rung him and said "Are you going to sit around on your arse or do you want to come out and tour?"."

Most of the band's members also played on Ronnie's solo albums - yet even with musicians like these, "Now Look" and its follow-up "Gimme Some Neck", sounded almost ordinary. The verve and sheer creativity that Ronnie had shown earlier in his career seemed to have burned itself out. It was also the first time that Ronnie had put together a full blown tour, running from 26th April to 21st May: sixteen sell-out shows in as many cities. It failed ignominiously on all levels, not least financially.

Ronnie had become so cocooned by the Rolling Stones' way of life - as brother Art had originally stated that he hadn't realised New Wave was currently ruling America. Blondie was sitting on top of the charts with Heart of Glass. Talking Heads and XTC were the current college darlings, and there was even a new Elvis in town in the shape of a bespectacled intellectual called Costello. Against all this, Ronnie and his band of Barbarians looked anything but new.

There was another reason why Ronnie lost money on the road, one that was by now sadly inevitable. He had insisted on touring in true Rolling Stones style. Private jets, whole floors reserved in the best hotels and fleets of limos all cut deeply into the budget.

"Now Look" came out mid-tour and sold poorly. The fans had been less than impressed. There was even a riot at one show in Milwaukee (resulting in Ronnie being charged with incitement to do just that), when the advertised special guests failed to appear - following a rumour that the main guest was in fact Mick Jagger.

Even worse, perhaps, Ronnie's relationship with Keith Richards began to suffer, due to what Keith described as Ronnie's increasing reliance on hard drugs... which Ronnie quite justifiably thought a bit rich, even if it was true. Not that it would stop the New Barbarians supporting the Rolling Stones in April 1979, as part of Keith's legal history-making sentence - a charity concert of the Canadian National Institute for the Blind played in Ontario.

Even though the local critics were enthusiastic about both bands, the reviews of the NB shows elsewhere had been mostly lukewarm at best. Unless he was working directly with the Stones, Ronnie's confidence often seemed to desert him. As he said later: "People think my song-writing has been set back. The truth is, I just respect Mick and Keith's song writing so much."

The truth was that Ronnie was still in awe of the Stones and still a fan - at one gig in LA he'd gone to the mike and gushed at the audience: "Ain't this fucking great? I wished I played with them!"

From his first tour with the Stones in 1975, he'd found himself travelling to gigs aboard a private Boeing 707 named The Starship and emblazoned by the Stones' famous red-tongue logo. An aircraft that wasn't a million miles removed from Air Force One in its luxury. Phones constantly rang, TV screens flickered and naked groupies cavorted along the aisles and around a wondrously equipped bar that served booze from take-off to touch down. The lifestyle and attention to detail was an eye-opener for Ronnie, whose past response to journalists complaining that The Faces' stage show lacked theatrics had been: "Next time, we'll get some more light bulbs."

Ronnie was performing on a hydraulic stage in the shape of a lotus flower, designed by Mick and Charlie, which would slowly unfold to the strains of Aaron Copeland's Fanfare to the Common Man, revealing each Stone alone on a single petal. At the show's climax, a twenty-four foot long inflatable penis would erect from the flower's centre. After that, the thought of the odd candelabra, and a drinks trolley pushed by midgets, seemed a little understated.

The lotus-flower shaped stage, by the way, was eventually bought by Keith Moon who let it rot in his front garden.

On that first New Barbarians tour, the Los Angeles shows were compèred by John Belushi, who introduced the band by saying: "I'm only a sleazy actor from a TV show. These guys are the real thing!"

Ronnie had first met Belushi while living in LA, and the pair had often played the blues together in the comedian's sound-proof bunker he called 'The Vault', sessions that had so easily turned into all-night coke binges. So, naturally it would be Ronnie who the authorities would question, along with Robert De Niro and Robin Williams, when Belushi's dead body was discovered in the notorious Chateau Marmont Hotel. All four had been regularly seen in the days leading up to his death, and had been named as clients by celebrity drug dealer, Kathy Smith - later convicted of supplying and assisting John Belushi to inject the dose that killed him. Along with De Niro and Williams, Ronnie was cleared of any involvement in Belushi's death but was obviously enough involved with cocaine to warrant the police keeping him under mild surveillance.

And not just in America or the UK.

CHAPTER EIGHTEEN

"WHY WORRY?"

On 22nd February 1980, Ronnie and Jo were arrested on the Franco-Dutch island of St Maarten in the eastern Caribbean for possession of 260 grammes of cocaine found hidden in a tree in the garden of their rented house in Philipsburg.

It was during a period that Jo describes as their 'Try Anything' stage, although she's quick to stress that never included needles - aside from anything else, Ronnie's terrified of them.

"We'd met these two guys who said they had loads of coke," she says, "and we invited them back to the house we were renting and did the usual thing of staying up all night. In the morning they asked to borrow our car, which we did because we were going to get some sleep. What we didn't know was they had hung their stash of coke in a sock in a tree in the garden. There was about 250 grammes' worth. A neighbour saw them take the car and thought they were stealing it, so they noted down the number plates then called the police."

When the police arrived Ronnie and Jo naturally thought there'd been a complaint about the noise. But within minutes the police had miraculously found the sock hanging in the tree and happily charged Ronnie and Jo with trafficking in opium.

Ironically, Ronnie had first noticed the two characters immediately after the plane had first touched down: "I could tell they were eyeing us up. I was carrying this giant ghetto blaster through Customs and one of the Customs officers followed us all the way to the house - they definitely had it in for us. Then we saw one of the guys at a casino a couple of nights later, and he turned out he was also a croupier. They kept on trying to sell us some coke for thousands of dollars and eventually they came to the house. It was a set-up; they'd driven off leaving both their jackets behind with convenient traces of coke in them."

Both Jo and Ronnie were taken to the local police station leaving their nanny, Jayne, in charge of a crying Jamie with orders to call the Stones office and arrange for the Stones' lawyers to fly out immediately.

Ronnie remembers ruefully. "I was still stupid enough to think the authorities would realise we'd been set up, but they were all in it together. I was still saying I'd be happy to help them out, but they just took my shoe-laces and left me in me cut-down jeans and a shirt, marched me down a pitch-black corridor and shoved me into a stinking cell, slammed the door and that was that. And then the same Customs guy turns up grinning at the window of my cell."

The only small comfort was that having stayed up for several nights, both Ronnie and Jo needed their rest - although the cells were a far cry from the sheltered luxury that life with the Stones offered.

A single stone slab with no blanket or pillow and a putrid-smelling metal bucket.

It was the same for Jo, only with the added fear that comes with being the only woman in a black, male prison - and a white one at that: "I was convinced I was going to be raped because I was actually sharing a cell with men, until one of the inmates realised who they had arrested. This one guy asked if in fact I knew Ronnie Wood, so I said yes. Then he thought about it for a minute and said "and Keith Richards?" So I said yes again, and the guy's eyes lit up. "Well, I was with them on the Seventy Five tour!" Can you imagine how relived I was to hear that?"

Instant bonding. And since the inmate was not only big enough to protect her, he was also able to reach through the bars and by using a stick, pass messages between Ronnie's and Jo's cells, so at least neither felt totally isolated.

As Ronnie remembers: "I worked out that if I stood on tiptoe and looked through the bars at a certain time of day, and our new mate could lift Jo up, then we could wave to each other. It was the only way I knew she was still alive."

The Stones' lawyers had flown in on the first available flight, only to discover that Ronnie and Jo had been arrested on the Dutch side of the island, which meant they were subject to 'parish law ' and therefore needed to be represented by a Dutch official. A deal was finally struck with a local Dutch firm of lawyers who arranged a hearing before a judge.

Ronnie and Jo were interviewed separately... luckily their stories matched up; the judge concluded they were innocent and ordered them released. It had taken six long, boring and for Jo, terrifying, days.

"I saw the croupier before I got out," Ronnie says sourly. "He'd obviously fucked up because he was in a cell. One of the officials turned to me and said: "Did this man try to sell you drugs?" And I looked him right in the eye and said, "fucking right he did!"."

Ronnie and Jo fled paradise and within twelve hours were back in America, where a relieved Jo told Ronnie: "That's it, I'll never touch anything again!" Although as equally shocked by the ordeal, Ronnie was not about to offer the same promise.

The Stones were due to go back on the road to promote their new album, "Emotional Rescue" - an apt title, considering the recent problems plaguing Ronnie and Keith, nor one wasted on Mick who when asked about promoting the album, wearily replied, "I don't know, there might not be a Rolling Stones to promote anything."

The band felt that Ronnie was now the one letting them down - even Keith, who could recognise the signs of self-destruction better than most   especially as he was trying to reorganise his own life. The fact that Ronnie was innocent-ish in terms of the latest bust was beside the point. He was seen as still taking too many risks. Didn't he realise that the Stones weren't just a band, or a way of life, but a major, multi-national business?

Actually, this wasn't the first time that Ronnie had been busted. Way back in 1975, during his first tour with the Stones, he and Keith had decided to drive between dates at Memphis and Dallas. En route, their limo had been pulled over by a motorcycle cop on the grounds that the car - with Keith driving - was swerving wildly across the road. A search then revealed a concealed penknife on Keith and a small quantity of cocaine in the limo boot. Both Ronnie and Keith were taken to Fordyce Jail, where they waited for Stones lawyer, Bill Canter, who duly arrived with $50,000 in a suitcase, somewhat less than the law required for bail. A few weeks later the charges were mysteriously dropped.

The mainly financial failure of The New Barbarian's tour promoting Ronnie's second solo album, "Now Look", had a knock-on effect on his third album, "Gimme Some Neck". Ronnie's finances were beginning to look strained. Aside from the wage he got from the Stones, his only other sources of income were the royalties from The Faces albums and the songs he'd co-written with Rod Stewart. Not bad - but not enough to support his lavish life-style. For although he wasn't making anywhere near the money the rest of the Stones were, he was determined to live in exactly the same way as his closest mates, Keith and Mick.

Despite the early eighties being the beginning of the band's most profitable period - a US and UK number one in 1980 with "Emotional Rescue"; a US number one, and a UK number two with "Tattoo You" in 1981; a top five live album with "Still Life" in 1982 - Ronnie rarely managed more than one song-writing credit per album, and saw precious little of the band's net profit. Aside from touring, his Stones income derived from air-play royalties (PRS), for these were pre-CD days when back-catalogues weren't anywhere near as vigorously marketed as they are to day.

In fact, when the CDs happened, the re-issued back-catalogue boom undoubtedly saved the industry - or at least helped keep record company executives carry on enjoying the lifestyles to which they'd become accustomed.

In 1983, "Undercover" was another hit album for the band, making number three in the US and number four in the UK. But a major blow to Ronnie's bank-balance occurred in 1984 when Mick Jagger announced he wasn't prepared to promote "Undercover" by touring, as he wished to "devote time to his solo pursuits." As if to confirm Ronnie's junior-partner status, he was excluded from a band meeting in June 1984 held at Munroe Terrace, Chelsea, where the group's future was discussed. It was reluctantly agreed to allow Mick freedom to spend time with his and Jerry Hall's new baby, Elizabeth, while promoting all his extra-curricular work - commencing with his first solo album and a single, "State Of Shock", a duet with Michael Jackson. This meant postponing all Stones work for the foreseeable future. Naturally enough, the press announcement of Jagger's plans sparked off more 'Stones To Quit' rumours, all of which Jagger vehemently denied. However, the rumours were fuelled by a disgruntled Keith Richards and Bill Wyman, with the latter quoted as saying: "I've lost touch with who Mick is now. He's just a business associate who has his share of five votes."

Note the use of the word 'five'. Wyman was far too scrupulous to make a mistake: as far as the outside world was concerned, Ronnie was a full member of the band. Later on, Wyman let his true feelings about Ronnie show for the first time, including his frustration at Ronnie's errant behaviour.

"Woody is difficult because he's so shallow... great for a laugh, but you can't talk to him."

Considering Ronnie's true status within the band, the comment was more than unfair. The only way he could keep his position was by remaining distinctly neutral, the hired foil between Mick and Keith. This was Stones business, the real Stones that is, the guys who'd been together for nearly twenty years - and in their eyes, Ronnie was still paying his dues.

Keith, although privately furious at what he saw as Mick's selfishness, restrained himself to the occasional muted comment until finally losing his temper openly in May: "If Mick tours without the band I'll slit his throat!"

Jagger was also busy with another solo pursuit outside music: his autobiography, for which he was paid a reputed £3million, but eventually had to return the advance, since Bill Wyman who kept the Stones diary refused to help him with the dates, or anything else very much. Wyman was planning his own book, the excellent "Stone Alone". He was not about to collaborate with the man who'd stopped the Stones touring.

Ronnie can be forgiven for feeling impotent. He hadn't been consulted about the band's future, nor involved with a recent settlement with Alan Klein, the band's old manager, that added considerably to the others' personal fortune - even the estate of Brian Jones. No reason why Ronnie should have been involved, of course, but it all emphasised how much of a new boy he was. He was beginning to feel distinctly superfluous to the band's needs, whatever they were. Wyman's jibe did little to cheer him up, especially in the light of a looming cash crisis: "They're all financially secure," he was heard to bemoan, talking of his colleagues, "they're content with the accomplishments they've made at their ages. But I'm younger; I've still got lots to do. I don't want to sit around the house when we could be on the road."

Ronnie soon discovered that the game was played strictly to the Stones' rules, and that his future included an lengthy and unpaid lay-off: To an extent, he was on his own.

"I knew I had to get busy. I needed to know the boundaries I was expected to work with."

Unable to tour, Ronnie admirably returned to school - actually an art workshop in San Francisco where he studied every day for three weeks from 10am to 5pm.

"I went to San Francisco to learn about woodcuts and monotypes which gave my art a new lease of life. I completely committed myself to working hard; it became my other definite priority. With no Stones work coming in for the foreseeable future, I had to seriously think about making my art work for me."

The results of Ronnie's return to school were seen when he held his first exhibition in Dallas on 28th November 1984 at the Foster Goldstrum Gallery. It was entitled "Portraits" and in addition to silk-screen prints of the Stones, it also featured John Belushi, John Lennon, Chuck Berry and oddly enough, Sid Vicious. The show was a success and ran until January 1985.

But there'd been another reason (besides financial) for immersing himself in his art: it also acted as therapy. Despite the happy arrival of baby Tyrone on 20th August 1983, Ronnie's personal decline had continued, with cocaine being the drug of choice. Even though his musical intentions were as strong as ever, his behaviour had seriously worried even Keith... who couldn't help but notice as far back as the Winter tour of 1981 (which netted £50 million) that his best friend had a serious habit. Keith eventually tried in his own inimitable way to counsel Ronnie, otherwise known as a good smack, which led to several violent punch-ups.

"That's one boy who hasn't got much longer the way he's going," Keith was heard to say about his best friend.

By early 1984, Ronnie found himself being marginalized. Not only excluded from Stones business meetings, he'd also been billeted separately from the rest of the band during the tour of '82, after Jagger added an ominous clause to the Stones tour contract, which read: "Anyone found in possession of drugs in any part of the backstage area will immediately be banished from vicinity whatever his capacity."

Jagger was even widely rumoured to be looking for Ronnie's replacement in the shape of the American guitarist, George Thorogood.

It finally dawned on Ronnie that if even Jagger wasn't taking the Stones' future for granted then what chance did he have.

"I saw the way things were heading" Ronnie said, "I was wondering how long I was going to have a job. It was fucking awful for a while; you had these two guys that had been mates since childhood, who'd started the world's greatest rock and roll band and written some of the greatest songs ever. Yet here they were drifting apart and I was in the middle - suddenly I was another problem. I'd landed the best job in my life and it was all slipping away. It was obvious that neither one wanted to be the one who said "ok that's it, let's split the band." It was a case of Mick thinking Keith hated him and vice versa."

What Ronnie hadn't realised was the fact that he really was out of control. He was addicted, strung out and facing the prospect of a Stones free existence. No tours were scheduled and a question mark was hovering morbidly over his and the group's musical future. "I had to get out of LA" Ronnie admitted years later. "LA lacked momentum and inspiration. It was also too spread out. In London you don't need a car to go and visit friends. I felt like one of those early convicts sent to Australia! On the other hand, if I hadn't moved there I'd never have got to hang out with people like my great buddy Jim Keltner who introduced me to Bob Dylan. Ringo was there and so was George a lot of the time, Jack Nicholson, and Dennis Hopper and Jimmy Caan. It had that thing whereby actors and musicians mingled. Sly Stone was my neighbour for a while and there were never any complaints about the noise. The biggest problem about LA was all the really slimy people that latched on to you. The pushers; you could have all the security in the world and they'd still find a way to crawl into your home. They would get in and slide open your bedroom door and wake you up, saying "I've got some more for you". One time Jo and me had been up for about five days before we managed to rid the house of all the crazy people and hit the sack. Only to be woke by the chauffeur who said to me "Mr Wood the canyon's on fire". We were living in Mandelville Canyon then, and I was going "Wha? Wha? Go away!" And all the time he was shouting "No, no, listen to me - you must get out now." We only had time to take enough possessions to fill a jeep - a couple of paintings and guitars. And run for it. I looked back as we went and the sky was black except for one patch of light above our house. Then the fire came down the hill really fast, turned left at the garden, went along a bit and then turned right. Ours was the only house saved. I found out later that people had been killed right where the bedroom was in a mudslide. That's when I found out we had bought a house smack in the earthquake epicentre. I mean, up until that point I'd always thought the epicentre was a fucking supermarket. It's funny, even now I look back at those times and I still think I was never out of control, I've always known what I was doing - but no one else did! Plus I had Jo, who I wouldn't exactly say saved my life, but she certainly brightened it up. It was living in America and LA that nearly did me in."

He finally faced up to his problem and checked himself into a rehab clinic, managing to straighten himself out in time for his exhibition in early 1984 and for the Stones' album "Dirty Work". It was also in time for the now legendary and long-expected open falling out between Mick and Keith that was to last on and off for years… leaving Mick and Keith to play Live Aid separately; Mick with David Bowie in London, and Keith joining Ronnie and his old LA neighbour, Bob Dylan, in Philadelphia: "Dylan changed the set list just as we were walking up the ramp on stage," Ronnie remembers, "and played all these fucking songs that Keith and me hadn't rehearsed."

A straightened-out Ronnie finally married Jo on 2nd January 1985 at St Mary's Church in Denham, Buckinghamshire. Keith Richard and Charlie Watts were the two best men and guests included Ronnie Wood look-alike, Gary Holton - star of Channel Four's Auf Weidersehn Pet, who was later to die of heroin; Rod Stewart; Jeff Beck; Ringo Starr; Peter Frampton; Peter Cook, who'd become one of Ronnie's closest friends; and the family: Lizzy, Archie, Art and Ted and including Jessie. Archie was in a wheelchair, having had a leg amputated because of thrombosis in 1980. When Archie had been told that his leg would have to go because of old age, he'd responded: "The other one's just as old, isn't it?"

Naturally enough, no Ronnie Wood wedding could pass off without some sort incident... in this case, the vicar, the Reverend Peter Crick, so overcome by the array of rock stars facing him that he launched into a diatribe about their overall godlessness to such an extent that Peter Cook began haranguing him back as an outraged EL Wisty. Meanwhile, the congregation could also hear Eric Clapton and Patti Boyd screaming at each other outside the church. But the wedding was doubly memorable for Ronnie, and indeed his mother and older brothers, for it also marked his father's last stage appearance, telling jokes and playing his harmonica.

"He had the whole reception in the palm of his hand," Ronnie remembers, "everyone was mesmerised by him; you could have heard a pin drop - except when they were laughing and cheering."

Archie was to die almost two years to the day later in 1987.

When the Stones did resume work in 1986 to promote the album "Dirty Work", the atmosphere was still somewhat tense. Keith was as annoyed with Mick as ever for releasing a solo album during sessions for the current Stones one and publicly said as much: "It was a totally inappropriate time to release a solo effort."

Mick's energies had been almost totally directed towards promoting himself. Which had left the preparation for "Dirty Work" solely up to Ronnie and Keith: who'd worked up the songs without a singer; chose the session musicians; and arranged the studio. It all reminded Ronnie of his early days with the singer-less Faces. But it did enable him to claim a co-writing credit on the B side (Had It With You) of the Stones' obvious filler single, a cover of "Harlem Shuffle".

By tradition, the Stones (normally) followed every new release with a tour. However, "Dirty Work", despite reaching number three in the British charts, was such a below-par release that it was panned by critics as the worst Stones album to date.

Jagger, for one, had no intention of promoting it beyond shooting a video for their next single: appropriately named "One Hit To The Body". And why would he? He had just signed a huge solo recording contract with CBS, and had the title track on the forthcoming Disney hit film, "Ruthless People". He also had a very lucrative sell-out tour of Japan booked.

So charged was the atmosphere between Mick and Keith at the Elstree shooting that the video's mock hostility and fighting scenes needed no rehearsal - least of all Keith's repeated attempts at kicking Mick at every passing opportunity.

Rumours were now rife that this was officially the end of the road for the Stones, and the "One Hit" video did little to dispel them. Neither did the news that Keith was about to sign his own solo deal with Richard Branson at Virgin Records.

To be fair, it wasn't just Jagger and Richards who pressed on with solo plans: Bill and Charlie were also adding their own tuppence-worth to the rumour mill by busying themselves with extra-curricular Stones activities.

Wyman was in the process of setting up his A.I.M.S. charity (Ambition. Ideas. Motivation. Success) - a project that was to give up-and-coming musicians the chance to play and record with established artists. Wyman organised a Europe-wide series of battle-of-the-bands contests, whose finalists were to be invited to play the Royal Albert Hall at an A.I.M.S. gala night.

Charlie put together his Charlie Watts' Orchestra and began touring, starting with a three-week engagement at the London Jazz landmark, Ronnie Scott's, and more dates up and down the U.S. East Coast. Keith went States-side too and joined Bob Dylan for dates at New York's Madison Square Gardens.

Just how close the Stones came to actually calling it a day at this time would be made evident by the fact that after Mick broke with the Record/Tour tradition, the group wouldn't share a stage together for almost nine years.

None of this bothered Mick back then. Instead he, along with David Bowie, Elton John, Eric Clapton and Tina Turner, took part in a fundraiser at The Albert Hall in aid of The Prince's Trust. He then began working on his next solo album with Dave Stewart of The Eurythmics in Los Angeles and Holland.

Mick's decision to seemingly go it alone and mothball the Stones was particularly disastrous for Ronnie as he was dangerously close to financial collapse and the only band member who was totally reliant on the band's touring income. He had worked with Keith in producing a version of the Stones' classic, "Jumping Jack Flash" for Tina Turner, but the release of a one-off Jagger/Richards cover would do nothing to swell his severely-depleted coffers. It was glaringly apparent that if he was to stay afloat, the much needed funds had to be generated elsewhere.

Plans were made to move back to England, concentrate on his artwork, and hopefully put together a band in order to get some live work of his own. However, the move back home was delayed when Phil Carson, a seasoned live-music road manager, suggested Ronnie pair up with the legendary Bo Diddley and tour together!

Ronnie had first met Diddley whilst struggling with The Birds and had sought the great man's advice regarding the lack of support the band was receiving from Decca Records. According to Ronnie, Bo had said "Go tell 'em to shit, or get off the pot!"

Carson got financial backing from the Japanese giant, Panasonic, and the resulting "Gunslingers" tour took to the road. The basic set up was for Bo to open the show with his four-piece band and for Ronnie to replace him mid-way through. The two would then unite for half a dozen numbers and encore at the end.

Thankfully, the stripped down back-to-basics tour (Ronnie travelled in a Winnebago with Jo and the kids) was a critical and financial success. Ronnie had at least learned one lesson from the extravagant New Barbarians tour which had left him $200,000 in debt. This time he hadn't had to carry the burden of forming and paying a band of his own, and the resultant album "Live At The Ritz" turned in a reasonable run of sales figures. Unfortunately, the tour's jovial atmosphere was slightly marred by Jo's insistence that Ronnie sever any financial dealings with Carson as soon as the tour ended.

So, with a well-received album and tour completed, and with no signs of the Jagger/Richards rift healing, Ronnie once again needed another source of income. As luck would have it, Ronnie's manager Nick Cowan (more about him later) had been approached by the British American Chamber of Commerce in Miami to see if Ronnie would be interested in getting involved with a live music venue planned for Miami's South Beach.

Of course he was! The result was 'Woody's on the Beach'.

The nightclub idea had been the dream of ex-pat, David Giles, a Stones fan living in Miami who'd bought a couple of derelict hotels along the seafront: The Arlington and The Savoy. Both were uninhabitable but, with a little bit of imagination and a relatively small investment from Ronnie (he was required to appear a mere twice a year), not only would he have his own bar and party central, he would also acquire a permanent art gallery for his paintings. The reception area made for a perfect venue and sound stage, which when renovated, could accommodate around eight hundred punters.

It couldn't fail! Jo threw herself into designing the interior of the club with the help of Biba founder, Barbara Hulanicki, who decked the place out in the beautiful art-deco style she was renowned for (apart from the very rock and roll touch of a guitar-shaped swimming pool). In addition to a private bar, there were two VIP areas depending on the level of VIP you were and what Ronnie described as an 'inner-inner, sanctum inside your 'ole run-of-the-mill inner sanctum'.

When completed, Ronnie played two press nights on 19th and 20th of December reprising The Gunslingers' live show with Bo Diddley, before closing until the club's official opening on New Year's Eve. During the day there was an opening ceremony for the art gallery, where Ronnie and Jo were somewhat surprised by Alex Daoud, the local Mayor, who presented Ronnie with the keys to the city. This was in honour of what Daoud described as the club's contribution to the expansion and re-development of what was at the time, a rundown neighbourhood of Miami. He went on to hail 'Woody's on the Beach' as a pioneer of Miami's club scene. Don Johnson, star of the hippest cop show at the time, performed the ribbon-cutting ceremony and somewhat bizarrely presented Ronnie with a Magnum .44 handgun.

If Ronnie was ever at all worried about what Miami's Mayor thought of him taking possession of a unlicensed firearm, he needn't have: Daoud was later indicted for forty-one counts of bribery, and served eighteen months in a federal prison. Whilst incarcerated he wrote a book "Sins Of South Beach" in which he recounted his tales of going on vigilante patrols where they routinely kidnapped and beat criminal suspects.

The opening night turned into a two-week long party with music supplied by a house band Ronnie christened "Woody's Orphans" that incorporated Ian McLagan and Stones side man, sax player Bobby Keys. Throughout the run, they backed stars like Jerry Lee Lewis, Ray Charles, Buddy Guy and ex-Stone, Mick Taylor. Art Wood even polished up his rocking shoes and fronted the band for his trademark renditions of "Hoochie-Coochie Man" and "Bright Lights, Big City".

The club was an instant success; the trouble was that it was too much of a success. It was too popular for its own good and attracted far more people than the club could accommodate. This led to large, noisy crowds aimlessly milling around nightly in the surrounding streets. Miami licensing laws allowed clubs to stay open until five am and this caused huge problems at closing time when eight hundred or so drunken revellers poured out en-mass. Miami at the time was predominantly a town for geriatrics, a retirement destination (think "The Golden Girls") and the club's lack of a parking area led to hundreds of cars parked in every available spot in the surrounding streets. This in turn led to much door-slamming, stereo-playing and engine-revving in the early hours.

For two years local residents complained in their droves. Pensioners set up committees and the Fire Department was repeatedly called to check on over-crowding. Eventually, a delegation stormed the Mayor's office and demanded he withdrew the club's licence on the undeniable grounds of noise pollution. 'Woody's on the Beach' closed two months later.

Ronnie tried to relocate the family and club to New York, but the same noise issue forced this short-lived venture to close before really taking flight. Once again, Ronnie found himself low on funds and pondering his next move.

His financial situation still seemed to have scant hope of rejuvenation from any immediate Rolling Stones activity as the continued ill-feeling between Mick and Keith looked set to run and run, fuelled in the press by petty schoolboy insults mainly emanating from Richards' camp.

The spat kept the inevitable Stones break-up stories circulating and even led to the speculation of a Faces reunion. This stemmed from a brief get-together at the end of a Rod Stewart show at Wembley in July, in aid of M.S. stricken Ronnie Lane, for whom Bill Wyman covered on bass.

The reunion never materialised, but those rumours still persist today. There have been the odd Faces sightings here and there (the Brit Awards in 1996 and two more Rod Stewart encores in Ireland in 1997), with Wyman standing in once again. The last appearance prompting Ronnie's comment; "Bill mate, you've done it all back to front! I left The Faces to join the Stones - I did it the right way round."

It's possible that until this point Ronnie had probably believed his entire life was pre-ordained. However, after several years of enduring earthquakes; mud-slides and forest fires that destroyed half his LA neighbourhood (one stopping just feet from Ian McLagan's front door); garbage strikes; brown-outs; freeze-ups and muggers in New York, America had lost its shine, and with the beach-less, New York version of 'Woody's' gone, a return to England, family and friends seemed the Woods' best move. So, Ronnie and family flew back and after a short spell as guests of ex- Free and Bad Company drummer, Simon Kirke, they found a modest house in Wimbledon and moved in.

With no musical projects to occupy him Ronnie fell back on his art for creative stimulation. He converted a large shed at the bottom of his garden into a studio and began a series of oil paintings depicting his fellow Stones. This renewed enthusiasm was greatly encouraged by his manager, Nick Cowan, who convinced Ronnie to venture back to the States once again. This time to San Francisco and to a studio that specialized in woodcuts and mono-types. "I never really lost touch with my drawing and painting. It was a talent I was born with, so I thought: right, I might as well exploit it. Music and art both go pretty much hand in hand."

Cowan also approached Christie's Contemporary Arts and negotiated a deal to start producing limited edition print runs of Ronnie's work. This led to Ronnie's first full-scale exhibition, and the beginning of a successful string of art shows in major cities around the world.

OK, it wasn't quite the same as carousing around the world's stages with the Stones, but it did enable Ronnie to maintain a more than reasonable lifestyle, albeit on an obviously unassuming level.

It was during this demure, yet relatively fruitful and artistic period, that Ronnie got to indulge in another of his great passions: drinking! He, along with a mixed bunch of quaffing connoisseurs that included Sir Tim Rice (then just plain Tim Rice), satirist Willie Rushton, cricketer Denis Crompton, model Sophie Dahl and Ronnie's snooker playing pal, Jimmy White, was let loose around London to judge the CAMRA London Pub of the Year competition. It was during these rounds of good-natured carousing that Ronnie received the shattering news of Arthur, his father's death!

Ronnie, by his own admission, is not a griever! It's an emotion he simply won't allow himself! Ever since the death of Stephanie de Court in 1964, Ronnie has stuck with a pact he made with himself never to let death get to him. Not because he's uncaring, but because he sees the bitterness and anger that so often accompanies the loss of loved ones as a waste of emotion.

However, losing his dad was different and Ronnie allowed himself a small concession - seeking a little comfort by listening to some taped interviews he'd made with his dad some years earlier in which Arthur recalled his own experiences as a young musician and father. I had no idea Ronnie had had the foresight to do such an interview whilst writing the first edition of this book, but I was happy to hear of it recently, and I also hope I was able to provide Ronnie with a modicum of comfort myself when following his mother's passing some years later, all the videoed interviews I did with Lizzie for this book were passed on to Ron.

The beginning of 1988 saw Ronnie back in live action, albeit for only two numbers at the finale of Bill Wyman's A.I.M.S. gala night at the Royal Albert Hall. Ronnie joined singers Ian Dury, Terrence Trent D'Arby and an all-star band that included Kenney Jones, for a work out of the Stones' and live Faces' classic, "It's All Over Now", followed by a version of "Honky Tonk Woman".

It was a welcome but momentary distraction from the fact that once again he was hurting for money. Thankfully, Cowan had a plan!

Cowan had decided to up the stakes with Ronnie's art and arranged an ambitious art tour of Japan with exhibitions in every city. Each show would have a lavish reception where buyers (predominantly moneyed business men and fanatic Stones fans) could be photographed shaking hands with Ronnie, or receiving a peck on the cheek. In addition to the extended showings, there were several one-off TV appearances and press interviews. All of which helped bring in the much needed yen. Midway through the tour, Ronnie got an additional and most welcome bonus: the chance to get together with Mick Jagger.

Coincidently, the head Stone was on his own tour of Japan. The contrast between his and Ronnie's outings couldn't have been greater, as Ronnie discovered when the pair met in Jagger's Osaka hotel suite and found out the singer was receiving a staggering £1,000,000 per show. Nevertheless, Ronnie seized the opportunity to start acting as an arbitrator in the bitter feud between Mick and Keith.

The seed may have been planted that night in Japan, but it would take all Ronnie's intermediary skills the rest of the year to convince not just Jagger, but Richards too that they both needed each other and that The Stones were still as relevant as ever.

The ploy may have been a tad mercenary on Ronnie's part, but who could blame him? Plus, as time would prove, he was more than right! In the meantime, however, he had other worries to deal with: extremely irate neighbours and the alarming accusation by The Daily Mirror that Ronnie had been cheating on Jo.

It seems the good people of Wimbledon were less than enamoured with Ronnie's twenty-four hour, rock and roll party lifestyle. An organised campaign reminiscent of the Miami objective had resulted in hundreds of persistent (yet probably justified) complaints from residents to the local authorities, which eventually forced the family out of the borough.

The story of their eviction made a light-hearted feature in The News of the World, with a picture of Ronnie and Jo, sitting on the steps of the house like two little homeless waifs. "I told them to buy a place far enough away from people so that they wouldn't annoy anyone," Ron's mum offered.

Less humorous was the erroneous Daily Mirror reports that Ronnie had been playing away from home. These allegations were eventually put to rest when Ronnie won undisclosed damages in the resultant libel case.

Ronnie had always been drawn to Richmond and so a move back to the south London suburb was a welcome one. They found an irresistible Georgian town house on the green a short walk from The Wick and moved in. Both Ronnie and Jo thought it was perfect. All that was needed was a method of paying for it!

Once again, Ronnie's Romany luck and timing stayed true to form. Thanks to his tireless mediating skills, he had at last manoeuvred Mick and Keith into talking again. Using the old adage that the whole was greater than any individual part, he had even managed to get them to discuss the possibility of some live work in 1989. For Ronnie (and to a lesser extent, Bill and Charlie), this couldn't come a moment too soon. Unfortunately, a return to duty wouldn't be that simple.

Keith declared that any Stones undertakings couldn't be resumed until after he'd completed the promotion of his own solo album, "Talk Is Cheap". It was now Keith's turn to call the shots, and he delighted in the critics hailing his effort as a brilliant piece of work, whilst comparing it favourably to Mick's "Primitive Cool" (which they said wasn't!). Keith was savouring his victory and took to the road in celebration with a band he called "Organized Crime" before he changed it to "The X-Pensive Winos" for the opening night of a sold-out tour of the States.

The first signs that the Stones looked set to roll again came in January 1989 when the band was inducted into the Rock and Roll Hall of Fame in New York. Ronnie joined Mick, Keith and Mick Taylor for the ceremony at The Waldorf Hotel (Charlie and Bill both had commitments and stayed in England) to hear Pete Townshend introduce the group "Whatever you do, don't try and grow old gracefully. It wouldn't suit you!"

Following Mick and Keith's speeches, Ronnie took the podium and thanked both Brian Jones and Mick Taylor for his own position in the band. They were then joined by Bruce Springsteen, Tina Turner and Little Richard for the usual jam session that saw Mick and Keith play together for the first time in almost nine years. Ronnie described the moment as "The Stones' second coming" and must have sighed with relief in the knowledge that his mortgage looked guaranteed.

Charlie met up with Mick, Keith and Ronnie the very next day and, together with the group's financial and legal teams, flew on to Barbados (Bill was still busy with a charity concert) where The Rolling Stones finalised their plans for a new album and a one hundred and fifteen date tour - both of which were to be called "Steel Wheels".

The band flew to New York to announce to the world that they were back. They held a press conference at Grand Central Station where Mick played a short preview of the band's new single "Mixed Emotions" on a ghetto blaster to hundreds of reporters and a few thousand screaming fans.

It was to be a show business come-back, like no other show business come-back ever seen. A solid, continued and record-breaking touring schedule; a mind-boggling string of multi-mega deals; film releases and tie-ins that would see the world's greatest Rock and Roll band become one of the world's greatest, exclusive and most lucrative entertainment business brands s ever.

And finally, Ronnie was in line for a near-equal slice of the profits!

Nick Cowan had been fighting Ronnie's corner, against the Stones' financial adviser Rupert Lowenstein (who went by an old Bavarian title of Prince) since just before the start of the "Tattoo You" tour in 1981. Unfortunately, Lowenstein would hear none of it and had consistently refused to award Ronnie anything like a fair share of the considerable incomes generated by the Stones' live earnings.

The shrewd money man had always argued the point that profit sharers must also be in a position to cover potential losses and, as Ronnie was only a salaried member of the band, he was therefore not able to carry the same risk as the other group members!

A convenient Catch 22, I think you'll agree!

It took Cowan up until the start of the behemoth two-part "Steel Wheels" and "Urban Jungle" junket (which kicked off in 1989) a full eight years later to finally negotiate a profit-sharing contract which would increase in a percentage value over the ensuing years until it was only a fraction below a full and equal share.

Bill was naturally an equal member of the band right up to his resignation in January 1994 and therefore he had to be bought out by Mick, Keith and Charlie. He settled for his usual equal split of the group's next world tour without having to set foot on a stage or play a single note! Only then did he surrender his share of the Stones' name, famous tongue logo and likeness!

So, let's pause for a moment to try and get an idea of what kind of man Ronnie Wood was at this (arguably) life-changing time and maybe we can work out just where he's currently at today!

First off, he's generous to a fault and craves company. That said, his past path is littered with so many people wondering where their new best friend disappeared to. He doesn't do it deliberately, but his natural charm which makes a person feel they're the most important person in the world - RONNIE'S WORLD - inevitably leads to feelings of hurt.

"Ronnie finds it hard to pin himself down, he likes too many people," says family friend Richard Barnes. "That's tough on the people close to him. He's not the kind of man to sit and watch TV on his own - he needs to have loads of people over to share it with him. He's certainly not someone who'd go to the cinema on his own; he's got to have someone to share his humour. He never wants to neglect anyone and sometimes that means he neglects himself! He's a bit of a butterfly that flits around and can be comfortable with almost anybody - certainly more so than most people I've met in that business."

Ronnie was still as wild as ever, perhaps more! Even when cosseted by the ever-watchful Jo, Ronnie always found a way of living on the edge. In many ways his approach to life reminds me of the stereotypical Japanese or American tourists who only have forty eight hours to see Europe. It's as if Ronnie has always known that time began running out on him from the moment he was born. He approaches all his passions be it music, art or... drinking, with the same level of intensity! And now he was about to became a multi-millionaire!! What could go wrong?

Well, let's just jump ahead a little.

By the end of 1990, The Rolling Stones were literally on a roll and back to their full commercial power. In addition to the $260,000,000 success of the 1989 "Steel Wheels" and "Urban Jungle" outings, there was a tour-related movie; a two-hour TV special; and a pay-per-view TV rights tie-up worth between $6,000,000 and $7,000,000. There was also a $6,000,000 sponsorship deal with Anheuser-Bush and Budweiser Beer, plus merchandise deals with department stores such as Macy's, J.C. Penney's and Marshall Field, who sold official band and tour-related material ranging from bandanas, T-shirts and baseball caps to $450 bomber jackets. Oh, and two lines of Converse high top sneakers featuring the famous tongue logo.

1991 also saw the release of the band's fifth live album, "Flashpoint", and the group were honoured at the Ivor Novello Awards Ceremony in London for their outstanding contribution to British music. Honours also came from Rolling Stone magazine who nominated them the best artists of 1989; "Steel Wheels" the best album, and "Mixed Emotions" the best single. Personal recognition also went to Mick for best singer and Bill and Charlie for best bass player and drummer.

If that wasn't enough to be getting by on, Lowenstein next negotiated a further mega-bucks deal with Virgin Records for three new albums and the rights to the Stones' impressive and substantial back catalogue.

Forbes magazine ran a front cover feature on the top forty richest entertainers in the world with a full page photo of Mick and Keith, and asked the question, "What'll They Do with All That Money?"

Well... Ronnie recorded another solo album, "Slide On This" at his newly bought and lavishly refurbished country pile Sandymount (complete with recording studio), in County Kildare, Ireland.

He and Jo embarked on a frenzied and extravagant spending spree, converting an old stable block into their own personal pub, christened 'Yer Father's Yacht' coined after one of Ronnie's dad's favourite sayings (as in "Where do you think you are? On yer father's yacht?"). He turned a cow byre into an art studio and another into a beautiful indoor pool that was bigger than the actual house. This came with hot tub and a fully-functioning bar with draught Guinness on tap. He also had a 'granny flat' built for his mum between the art studio and the pub, which came complete with Marie Antoinette's bed. Art and Ted were treated to houses each in Teddington and Twickenham, respectively and Krissie a flat in Richmond.

In addition to that little lot, Nick Cowan managed to talk a local farmer into selling off 60 acres of land surrounding the house, and thus overnight turned the property into arguably one of the finest small Georgian estates within an hour's drive from Dublin. Ronnie would fly to Ireland at every opportunity, drinking and partying in the endless pubs between Sandymount and Dublin.

Inevitably, Ronnie was a magnet for every local girl and naturally he was more than a good host on many occasions; however, word eventually reached Jo's ears and his visits to Ireland became a huge bone of contention.

With Cowan's encouragement, horses became another passion for Ronnie whilst in Ireland. He bought a dozen of them and with the help of the renowned trainer, Jessica Harrington, became so embroiled in the breeding and racing scene that he was eventually named the Irish Thoroughbred Breeder of 1998.

Keith also released a solo album, his second, "Main Offender". Not one to be out-done, and still hankering after a bit of solo appreciation, Mick put out his third "Wandering Spirit". Both sold poorly, as did Ronnie's.

At the beginning of 1993, Ronnie took off to promote his new album "Slide On This" by flying to Japan, where he combined a handful of solo gigs (with Ian McLagan on keyboards) with a prestigious opening of an exhibition of his paintings. He returned to England with Mac in time for the aforementioned Faces reunion at the annual Brit Awards.

Keith too set out for a bit more solo action and after a short European tour, he became the first of the band to ever play down South America way, when he and his solo outfit The X-Pensive Winos sold out a 40,000 seat stadium in Argentina.

In late 1993, the four remaining Stones re-grouped at Ronnie's Sandymount estate in order to record their next album, "Voodoo Lounge" and plot their next money-spinning tour of the world.

Also on the agenda (although never announced, and away from the media's prying eyes), was the opportunity to break in the group's new bass player, Darryl Jones - aka The Munch. There was to be no press statement, or any mention of Jones being named as Bill Wyman's replacement - and there would certainly be no talk of the black American ever becoming a Rolling Stone!

Although Jones had already recorded with the band, his (as in the manner of other tour and recording sidemen, such as keyboard player, Chuck Leavell and long-time sax player, Bobby Keys) involvement, stage movement and audience interaction was expected to be kept low-key and at all times understated. He, like Ronnie for so many years, was to be a salaried musician only, and was therefore nowhere to be seen when the four-man Stones roared up to Pier 60 in New York in a motor launch to announce they were hitting the road once again.

But not before more honours were bestowed upon them. Whilst in New York the band picked up an MTV award and a Billboard Lifetime Achievement Gong for Artistic Excellence.

The sold out tour kicked off in Washington DC and went on to cover the entire United States, Canada, Japan, Mexico and Australia, plus a first for the band as a whole, South America.

They also somewhat triumphantly announced to the world on 18th November that the Stones were about to make music history by becoming the first band to broadcast a concert live on the internet! However, the Stones were forced to retract the boast when it came to light they'd been pipped to the post a whole year earlier by four computer geeks from California calling themselves Severe Tyre Damage.

The Stones' performance broadcast from The Cotton Bowl Arena in Dallas, Texas suffered another humiliating setback, when the same band took full advantage of the open-to-everyone site and popped up right before and after the Stones' 20 minute set segment, thus rightfully laying claim once and for all, to the title of first band in Cyberspace.

Drummer Mark Weiser was interviewed from the group's base in the Xerox Parc building saying "We didn't want to stamp on the Stones' performance, but we did want to play in front of an appreciative audience."

If any of the Stones were at all pissed off by being up-staged on such a momentous occasion it would have been soon forgotten, especially as they later heard that sales of their "Voodoo Lounge" album had topped the 4 million sales mark and the tour was another record breaker - grossing $300,000,000.

The hysteria that now surrounded the Stones was of Beatlemania proportions.

It was hugely evident that the group's popularity was at an all-time high. They had a top ten live album "Stripped" on both sides of the Atlantic, 27 different countries had been covered and over 7 million gig-goers impressed by a newly rejuvenated Stones!

The opportunity to capitalise on such renewed, or rekindled, interest in the band was not lost on the astute Jagger and Loewenstein and no sooner had the tour finished, when plans were made for the group to do it all over again.

And this time it was going to be bigger and better. Fortunately, there was to be a little time out before kick-off and with no money problems, Jo decided it was time to start spending. After all, Ronnie was now a proper Rolling Stone and that made her a Rolling Stone wife (second only to a Beatle wife in rock hierarchy); so it was only right she started living like one.

They moved from Richmond to a massive gated pile on Kingston Hill, appropriately named Holmwood. Built around 1840, Holmwood was a beautiful twenty-room turreted Gothic masterpiece that had originally been a gift from the nation to Queen Victoria on her engagement to Prince Albert, who used it as a hunting lodge when out hunting deer in Richmond Park.

Yet as extravagant and historical as it was, it wasn't as lavish as Jo knew it could be. Never mind that it was fit for royalty, Hell No! This had to be fit for a Rolling Stone - THE NEW ROYALTY.

So she set herself the task of transforming the house and grounds into the most opulent and sumptuous residence imaginable. She also convinced Ronnie to have another studio built in a hugely-expensive engineering project that required the complete excavation of an underground level.

Although Ronnie took little persuading in going ahead with the ridiculously costly and somewhat superfluous studio plan, he secretly knew it was more of a ploy on Jo's part to stop him disappearing to Ireland at a moment's notice. There was more than a little truth to this, and friends agree that Jo made no bones about the fact that she hated Ronnie spending so much time out of sight on the Emerald Isle. And to be fair, who could blame her? The tales of Ronnie and his Irish antics are legendary, as are the dozens of rock and roll icons who partied with him there!

Bob Dylan dropped in to record demos for his "Time Out Of Mind" and Ronnie worked on tracks with Elvis's right hand man, guitarist Scotty Moore and drummer DJ Fontana. There were also collaborations with Jeff Beck, Bobby Womack, Willie Weeks, U2's The Edge, Ian McLagan, and George Harrison.

CHAPTER NINETEEN
"BRIDGES TO BEYOND."

Ever since The Stones announced their 1975 tour by playing on the back of a flatbed truck riding down 5th Avenue, the group have strived to come up with a gimmick with which to greet the press. The "Bridges To Babylon" tour would be no different. This time the four members were filmed by helicopter for live TV driving over The Brooklyn Bridge in a 1955 Red Cadillac Convertible. Mick driving while Ronnie, Keith and Charlie threw copies of the new 'Bridges to Babylon' CD to the crowds lining the route.

The tour would prove to be yet another record breaker, raking in an incredible $87 million over 108 shows. This was also the first tour the band used an A and B stage set up, with a bridge connecting the main stage to a smaller round island in the middle of the crowd.

The group had tried it on the Voodoo Lounge tour, but only at one gig. This time it would be a regular nightly highlight. The B stage, which was only big enough to accommodate the four-man Stones, would rise up out of the floor giving the huge stadium a club like atmosphere.

Some live dates were recorded for a live album and DVD called "No Security", which was released towards the end of the Bridges tour. This prompted the band's decision to promote both by repeating the entire road trek all over again as the "No Security" tour. They also decided to perform in smaller venues like the Brixton academy and the Shepherd's Bush Empire, where they overran and were fined £50,000 for breaching council regulations.

It was the longest tour the Stones had ever undertaken, and it was almost Ronnie's last. During a break from playing, he and his party took a trip to Pig Island off the coast of Copacabana, where the boat they had rented exploded and sank. Ronnie and all aboard were luckily rescued by the flotilla of following paparazzi. There was news footage around the world of Ronnie being helped aboard a speed boat - beer in hand - just as the stricken boat's captain leapt into the sea seconds before the final explosion.

The almost two year-long tour and near death experience had become a journey of discovery for Ronnie, or should that be recovery? Ronnie's battle with drugs has been a well documented and hard fought one. It's also been, for the most part, a victorious one. Unfortunately, Ronnie never stopped long enough to take stock of the compensatory measures he'd relied on in kicking his habit. This was to basically drink and smoke more heavily.

Both had become his steady substitutes throughout the seventies and eighties in his determination to stay off the hard stuff, but by the new Millennium, they had both got way out of hand. Ronnie has always been a regular smoker and drinker; he'd be the first to admit that his entire family were hardened in both categories, but with millions in the bank and unlimited access to these so-called life's little luxuries, they too can take on a frightening new meaning.

He was now drinking around a dozen pints of Guinness a day. Not overly excessive sure, but he was backing this up with at least two bottles of Vodka mixed with Cranberry juice, bottles of Champagne and a hefty quantity of Jack Daniels. Add to that several packs of cigarettes and Houston, we have a problem. The problem reached a new height in 2002 when the Stones announced their "Licks" tour and the papers reported yet another stay in rehab for Ronnie, who'd failed the insurance medical and looked unlikely to be joining them.

"I've never known anything different," he said of his amazing capacity to sup. "It's always been a very natural thing to always be drinking. It really took off in The Faces - we'd never eat breakfast before meeting up for rehearsals, and it would be straight down the pub at twelve. Then we'd get stuck in: several pints and bottles of Blue Nun. We even gave crates of Mateus Rosé to the audiences at the gigs so they could get as drunk as us. Apparently, I should have died around the time Keith Moon did because Keith and me were hitting it all pretty hard, but even when people like Jimi Hendrix, John Belushi, Harry Nilsson and Peter Cook were dropping like flies, it didn't bother me because I've been around it all my life.

"Everyone I knew or met were big drinkers, so it was normal behaviour. Alcoholism runs in my family; it's in my blood, from my grandparents, to my parents and my brothers, everyone I knew were alcoholics." Ronnie has spent several well-publicised stints in and out of rehab, working with a life coach and councillor and to his credit even managed to play the entire "Licks" tour without a drink or a cigarette. Unfortunately, he's fallen off the wagon every time. "I had got used to feeling sick all the time, but it's funny I never thought I was ever out of control; everyone else did of course, but I always felt I knew exactly what I was doing."

This, it seems, is only partly true, as the most recent of Ronnie's adventures have proved. However, to borrow a phrase from one of his predecessors, Brian Jones, let's not judge him too harshly. Instead, let's try to trace back to exactly where the wheels began to fly off Ronnie's Rock and Roller coaster.

Elvis had a motto that went "taking care of business". He even had a logo drawn up with the letters TCB emblazoned on the tail fin of his personal 747 jet the 'Lisa Marie'. Ronnie's dictum should have read "who's taking care of business?" with a logo of the big eared boy (Alfred E Newman) from the Mad Comics, whose slogan was "what, me worry?"

Now to be fair, creativeness and financial aptitude have never made for good bedfellows, and the history of music and the arts bears this out. There are literally thousands of tales of horror and tragedy involving unscrupulous managers and record companies that have preyed on the naivety of the gifted. It's almost like an unwritten rite of passage for those poor souls whose only interest is playing their music, writing their screenplay or creating their art, to be right royally ripped off.

Ok, some bring it on themselves, either through total arrogance, over-indulgence or sheer stooopidness. I'm not saying just who fell foul of such underhandedness, or which category they fall into; neither for that matter, which scoundrel took advantage of them. But, it's a cautionary tale all the same and in Ronnie's case, a relevant one.

Look at Steve Marriott, a mere five years after the demise of Humble Pie he was living down and out in Los Angeles and collecting beer bottles for their deposit money. He eventually perished in a blaze at his rented cottage in the Essex village of Arkesden in 1991, aged just forty four. Ronnie Lane suffered from MS and died far from well-off after being framed in a deceitful million dollar charity scam. He died in Colorado at a house paid for by Ronnie and Rod Stewart in 1997. He was fifty one. Both men passed away without ever receiving a penny in royalties from the Small Faces. Micky Waller died of liver failure at his home in Barnes, South West London in 2008 aged 66, His local pub had a whip round, and mourners held a collection at his funeral to pay for it.

Ronnie is, of course, in far better shape financially and physically than Marriott, Lane or Waller were, but it could be said that despite being a undisputed natural talent, he owes most of this to the incredible earning power of the Rolling Stones. Oh, and maybe a little to the Romany blood that has had to share a body with enough booze and drugs coursing through its veins to kill ten men.

It certainly can't be said he owes much of his success to his attention to business matters.

His personal manager of some 22 years, Nick Cowan, came into Ronnie's orbit in the early eighties, via a recommendation from a potential investor in a Roller Skating Disco venture that he was managing in Los Angeles. Cowan, an Old Etonian, started his working life at a London law-firm of divorce lawyers before switching to another one that specialised in representing clients working in the entertainment industry.

However, he didn't stay there long, preferring instead to pursue a far more colourful and eclectic career as a movie producer, a record company president, a proprietor in an escort agency and a manager of the aforementioned roller disco. There was also a foray into the endorsement business and pre-paid phone cards that crashed and burned after he produced hundreds of thousands of cards featuring OJ Simpson days before 'The Juice' was charged with murder.

Now all these endeavours are honourable enough, but they all came with an element of risk, and were more often than not liable to have a short shelf life. This was due to a certain trait of Cowan's: his uncontrollable tendency to gamble. And sometimes he was really good at it, as his nomination in the Guinness book of records attests to. Cowan's entry is for winning the biggest jackpot in the history of horse racing. He scooped over two million dollars.

I asked Ronnie about the win and whether he thought it was a good idea to have someone who was more known as an entrepreneur and a gambler than a straight-laced business manager. Ronnie just looked at me and said, "I fucking hope it is!" To give credit where credit's due, when Cowan was appointed manager and given full control of Ronnie's affairs, he inherited a total nightmare situation, even by Ronnie's admission.

When Cowan got down to familiarizing himself with the running of Ronnie Wood's world he could have been forgiven in thinking that maybe he'd bitten off a little more than he could chew. During his very first visit to the Wood's LA home, he was confronted by a mountain of unopened letters, bills and papers dating back years. Such was Ronnie's aversion to business matters, he'd never read any.

Cowan soon realized that his new client was far from being a wealthy rock star - in fact, Ronnie was on the verge of bankruptcy. Not a single tax return had ever been filed since joining The Stones and the mountain of unpaid solicitor's bills filled a small cupboard. He was £200,000 in debt from the lavish 'New Barbarians' tour alone, plus he'd sold his future share of royalties from the Stones' "Emotional Rescue" album back to Mick and Keith. There also happened to be the decidedly dodgy matter of several LA drug dealers who apparently hadn't been paid.

The fact that Cowan eventually managed to straighten out Ronnie's precarious financial ill-health is a small miracle in itself. But to wrestle a near full-membership deal out of the economical Prince Rupert Loewenstein is a testament to his negotiating and management skills, big time.

Unfortunately, there were two monetary black spots that Cowan just couldn't manage.

First, was the difficult task of curbing Ronnie's well-known generosity; he naturally supported both his and Jo's family and extended families, but he also lent large sums of cash to people indiscriminately. These loans would very rarely be paid back and were a nightmare for Cowan to keep track of.

Second, and more importantly, was the fact that he was powerless to stem the flow of money that Jo was well-known to haemorrhage. Especially once a new project got underway, like designing the houses in Ireland, on Kingston Hill, and another on Chelsea's Cheyne Walk. However, no matter how expensive they became, not one of them came close to the amount of money that was poured into the ultra-exclusive and expensive private members' club called the Harrington.

The Harrington Club on Harrington Street, South Kensington was Jo's most wildly-spectacular design project to date, and by all accounts one that she threw herself into with more than just her customary lavishness. Fitting it out with a spa with six massage rooms, fountain centre pieces, an organic restaurant and members' bar. It took several years of construction to completely gut and re-fit the five floors and for Jo to fill it from top to bottom with Ronnie's paintings and classic guitars lining the walls alongside fine art and furniture, both antique and designer.

When it was finished it was arguably the finest club (outside the House of Lords) in London. There was one little problem: Cowan was unable to secure a late night liquor licence. This didn't affect the club's initial attraction, but after a year of closing at 12am, the allure to star members that included Mick Jagger, Rod Stewart, Bob Dylan and Angelina Jolie, wore thin. Ronnie appointed (at an exuberant cost) a manager to start running the place, which should have started alarm bells ringing: the guy in question already owned the building's freehold, leaving Ronnie with a 25-year lease at around half a million pound a year rent.

Unsurprisingly, the combined problem of costly membership and no late licence meant the club continued to flounder, yet Ronnie continued to sink a fortune into it for the next three years. Eventually it became clear that the club was not going to survive without regular cash injections, so Ronnie consulted lawyers and considered his options. The result was Ronnie had two choices; he could tough it out and risk watching the club slowly bleed him dry, or at a considerable cost, buy himself out, walk away and lose everything.

The choice was obvious; the club had to go and with it went Nick Cowan, who Ronnie blamed for misguiding him. Jo replaced Cowan as Ronnie's manager with the surprising choice of her son, Jamie, who instantly began legal proceedings against the Harrington management team. They in turn counter-claimed, saying Ronnie owed around £17,000 in unpaid rent.

Ronnie applied to the high court to get some of the £1,000,000 plus worth of his belongings back, including his artwork and several guitars, which he rightly claimed were lent to the club and were an extension of his own home. He said the argument had got so bitter he and his entire family were even barred from the premises.

Friends jumped to Ronnie's defence and told of his affable nature, and how he'd be the first to admit that he was a guitarist and not a business man. One tellingly said that Ronnie has had to trust people all his life, adding he's a naturally kind and generous man and he genuinely feels the items belong to him. The whole sorry saga would drag on and suck yet more money out of Ronnie's bank account. It probably came as some relief when Ronnie returned to rehab in preparation for the next Stones outing: the celebratory 40th anniversary "Licks" world tour.

Oh, but then his Mum died! She had taken a fall at her home in West Drayton, but passed away in hospital some weeks later of undetected cancer. On a positive note, Ronnie completed his treatment in rehab and was declared fit enough to join Mick, Keith and Charlie for the band's usual attention-grabbing stunt that signalled the tour's start. This time floating down from the sky to land at Van Cortlandt Park in the Bronx, New York onboard a giant yellow blimp, emblazoned with their ever-enduring logo.

Ronnie was relieved to leave the unresolved Harrington club debacle behind and get back to earning on the road. He knew the tour would ultimately save his situation, but he knew the whole episode had cost him dearly: so much so that he was forced to take an advance on his tour takings and, unbelievably, re-mortgage his homes. The tour would roll on for a year, and continue the group's practice of mixing up the venues between theatre, arena and stadium shows. For example, in July they headlined at the Molson Canadian Rocks for Toronto concert - an aid benefit to help the city recover financially and psychologically from the effect of the SARS epidemic which was attended by around 490,000 people. Then they did the same for the city of Hong Kong in November. They then returned to London and performed at the 1,000-people capacity Astoria Theatre on Charing Cross Road.

Ronnie came off the tour clean and sober, and fit enough to begin putting his house (or houses) in order. He was not completely debt free, but another tour was already in the planning and only a year away. If he could stick to his painting, keep out of trouble and avoid any business propositions, then another tour would set him up once AGAIN! Yet a lot can happen to Ronnie in twelve months of down time, and luckily it did. He received a very nice commission from Sir Andrew Lloyd Webber to paint thirty regular/famous diners from the Ivy restaurant in London. And he had a year to complete it! Perfect!

Well, it would have been if tragedy hadn't struck twice, and in quick succession, with first his brother Ted dying, and then his old Birds and Creation band mate, Kim Gardiner. Yet again the spectre of cancer had come perilously close to home and claimed two more of Ronnie's loved ones.

He could have well been forgiven at this point for thinking that the only safe place for him was back in the pampered cocoon of a Rolling Stones road-show. No good seemed to come of living in the real world.

There was a boost to Ronnie's morale at the start of 2004 when he was chosen as the subject of Melvyn Bragg's arty "The South Bank Show". Screened in February, the hour-long programme took an insightful and appreciative look at not only the origins of Ronnie's musical career, but his work as an artist too. It also touchingly brought Ronnie together with Art, in a poignant display of mutual love and affection. It was a nice touch, made all the more moving following the recent passing of their brother Ted.

The programme was a fantastic platform for Ronnie to re-establish his standing as a serious painter, and it led to a showing at the Royal Academy where his 'Ivy' canvas was unveiled and a permanent exhibition at Sir Lloyd Webber's Theatre Royal in Drury Lane. With things on the up, Ronnie decided to take the family on holiday to Africa which seemed a great way to sit out the short wait until the imminent tour. Only it wasn't; with a relaxed and laid back family atmosphere around him it seemed so natural to have a drink. The truly shocking news that Krissie had seemingly committed suicide in June 2005 hardly helped his recovery. Krissie was found dead from a suspected valium overdose at a friend's flat in Barnes, South West London. Krissie had been suffering from severe depression for several years, and at the time of her death was allegedly in dire financial trouble. She was being forced into selling her flat and several prized processions, including some of Ronnie's paintings and a classic Gibson guitar. The coroner latterly concluded that her death was misadventure due to the misuse of drugs. Ronnie arranged her funeral and 150 guests attended a memorial at a restaurant in Richmond Park with a view overlooking the River Thames almost identical to that of 'The Wick.'

Luckily, being back on the bottle didn't affect Ronnie's re-joining the Stones for the opening night press mini-gig at a school in New York to announce the beginning of the two-year "Bigger Bang" all-time record-breaking assault on the world. Stretching from August 2005 through to August 2007, the "Bigger Bang" excursion became the highest grossing rock and roll tour of all time, taking over $558,000,000. The outstanding scale of the tour was realised on 18th February 2006 when the Stones played a free concert on the Copacabana beach in Rio de Janeiro, Brazil. Two million people attended, making it the largest rock music crowd to ever gather for a concert.

Rod Stewart ironically claims the nomination for himself. The Guinness Book of Records states Rod pulled over three million people to his gig on 31st December 1994, but that was on New Year's Eve and the beach attracts around a million people every year to watch the fireworks. So, make of that what you will.

Ronnie struggled with the bottle throughout the tour, a mammoth task considering the totally excessive environment that accompanies any rock and roll tour, let alone a Stones tour. But mid way through, Ronnie got the news that I consider changed him forever. Art had been diagnosed with prostate cancer. Ronnie instantly organised a private medical centre and specialist treatment, and flew back and forth to check on Art's condition. But despite his every effort, it was all to no avail.

When Art died on Friday, 3rd November 2006, Ronnie was by his side. A beautiful memorial was held in a huge marquee in Ronnie's garden at Kingston Hill, where he, Mick and Charlie jammed long into the night with a band made up of Art's friends. It was a send-off fit for a king! 'King Arthur'.

Coming down from the "Bigger Bang" experience was most probably an even bigger bang to Ronnie.

Back on Civvie Street, the cold harsh realisation that in the space of four years, he had lost his Mum; both his brothers; and his ex-wife was startling. He was now managed by Jamie and, to all intents and purposes, Jo and by all accounts this mother and son team was not an ideal situation. Everyone knows living and working with family twenty-four/seven can only lead to tension, but one can only speculate as to what led Ronnie to finally call a halt to the personal life he'd known for over twenty years and so publicly leave Jo for another woman?

It was probably a combination (or should that be culmination?) of too many factors in Ronnie's life to ever analyse it correctly. Close friends all have their theories: from Jo and Jamie's lavish spending habits, to a simple mid-life crisis. Certainly, Jamie being quoted in 'The Sunday Observer' as saying "I love money" wouldn't have been something Ronnie would have wanted to read. Or, when talking about how he now runs the 'Wood Family Business', I doubt he'd have been happy with the very un-PC remark "I remember going in those Paki shops, you know? Where they all work together and thinking I'd like us to be a Paki family." No, I'm sure that didn't do him any favours. Did he just get tired of Jo's overbearing, ever presence (she was the only Stones wife who accompanied them on every tour), or did he just fall out of love? Certainly the £1,000,000 a year loss her Organics beauty products range was making would start to cool your passion.

Whatever the reason for Ronnie calling time on his marriage and disappearing to Ireland with a twenty year-old cocktail waitress can only be known by Ronnie himself. But that's what he did! Ronnie met Muscovite, Ekaterina Ivanova (Kat for short) at the 'Capricorn' lap dancing club in Goodge St., Soho after joining Mick, Keith and Charlie for the Leicester Square premiere of Martin Scorsese's, Rolling Stones docu-movie, "Shine A Light".

The story was headline news around the world, and the lurid details filled the tabloids for months. Some reports said that Ronnie had unbelievably taken Kat home to meet Jo, (although Jo denied this), where according to some sources, Jo begged the Russian to not steal Ronnie away. Kat was supposed to have sneered "I'm not taking him - he's leaving."

Whether true or not, leave he did - holing up at Sandymount for what he called a 'painting holiday' with the twenty year-old as his model. Jo (it was reported) was understandably sick with worry at the news that Ronnie had hit the sauce hard and was drinking over two bottles of vodka a day. "She is mad, she's a terrible alcoholic who's wormed her way into becoming Ronnie's drinking buddy. Ronnie told me she was staying with him, and I said OK get on with it! Drink and go mad, drink your guts up!"

Kat used the social networking site 'Facebook' to tell friends she was quickly falling in love, to which Jo replied, "They're not boyfriend and girlfriend! Not in that way." Kat, however, told a different story, according to one friend who said, "She is besotted with him. Whether he knows it or not she plans a future with him. She has told everyone Ronnie has left his wife for her, and they are a full on item."

When finally questioned personally, Kat told reporters, "You can't choose who you fall in love with, I fancy him because of the person he is. I don't care about his age or the fact he is a Rolling Stone."

Of course, close friends of Ronnie's predicted it wouldn't last and after a much publicised year which included romantic holidays in Hawaii and California, watching 'Prince' and partying with Rod, it didn't.

The couple split after a very public bust up in the street near the mock castle that Ronnie was renting for £4,000 a week in Claygate, Surrey. Ronnie ended up getting arrested on suspicion of assault and spent the night in the cells at Staines police station. According to friends of Ronnie's, the argument had flared up at a local Indian restaurant after Kat repeatedly nagged a drunken Ronnie to put Sandymount in her name in order to show he loved her.

Ronnie was bailed and subsequently let off with a caution after Kat refused to press charges. Jo said, "I knew it would end in tears."

Kat went on to have her brief (Ronnie- related) fifteen minutes of fame as a reality show contestant in 'Celebrity Big Brother' and then sold her story to 'Hello' magazine. Jamie no longer manages Ronnie and Jo settled for an out of court divorce settlement of reportedly six and a half million pounds.

Ronnie went on a string of high profile dates that included a three-day fling with another Russian girl, Hannah Kamelmacher, before falling for thirty year-old Brazilian Polo coach, Ana Araujo, who he met at the Royal Opera House in Covent Garden. Ronnie had one last successful stint in rehab and left to re-form a version of The Faces with Kenney, Mac, and Simply Red singer, Mick Hucknall replacing Rod, with Sex Pistol Glen Matlock as bass player.

As for Ronnie? "I have Ana to thank for my sobriety, and I have strength in the fellowship. I do a meeting every day but it's a hell of a thing: I go all over London, to A.A. and N.A. and I just keep going. I have to pat myself on the back for it because it's been a long, long journey."

Ain't that the truth?

FINIS

WHERE ARE THEY NOW?

THE BIRDS:

TONY MUNROE - Rhythm guitar player Tony Munroe runs a successful sheet-metal business in Yorkshire, he occasionally plays in a local pub band. He hasn't seen or spoken to Ronnie since his dismissal from 'The Birds'. Ronnie: "Did we replace him?" No! "Probably just as well then!"

ALI McKENZIE - Ali McKenzie still lives in West Drayton and fronts a new 'Birds' who are playing regularly. He collects VW Camper Van's too! Ronnie: "Ali's lovely – he used to always go round and visit my mum, bless him"

KIM GARDINER - Kim Gardiner is sadly no longer with us, but after his stint in 'The Creation' he went on to form 'Ashton, Gardiner and Dyke' with Tony Ashton and Greg Dyke, who had the monster hit "Resurrection Shuffle". He then opened the English pub 'The Cat and Fiddle' in Los Angeles which he ran until he succumbed to cancer.

THE CREATION:

EDDIE PHILLIPS - Eddie Phillips is still playing regularly on the club and pub scene, and has reformed various versions of 'The Creation'. Still can't play the violin!

BOB GARNER - Bob Garner, has joined Eddie in every re-formation of 'The Creation' whilst earning a credible reputation as stand up comic. He lives in Wales.

JACK JONES - Jack Jones owns a newsagents' in West London he also joins Eddie in the odd 'Creation' re-formations when he, Eddie and Bob can agree on it (which is mostly never!)

KENNY PICKETT - Kenny Pickett went on to roadie for 'Led Zeppelin' and most famously wrote the hit 'Grandad' for 'Dad's Army' hero Clive Dunn! He mysteriously dropped dead at the bar of his local pub!

KIM GARDINER - See above.

THE JEFF BECK GROUP:

JEFF BECK - Jeff Beck is successfully still being Jeff Beck!
Ronnie, "In all the years I've known him, I've never mentioned his spots!"

ROD STEWART - Rod is equally successful (if not more so) at just being Rod!

MICKY WALLER - Micky (Sticky Wallet) Waller was a regular on the South West London pub scene but sadly passed on following liver problems.

THE FACES:

ROD! - See above.

KENNEY JONES (now with an extra e!) - Kenney Jones owns the hugely successful Hurtwood Polo Club in Surrey and heads-up his solo band 'The Jones Gang'. He is also back in the fold of the re-formed version of 'The Faces' which features Sex Pistol and major Faces fan Glen Matlock who replaces Ronnie Lane. The band also features ex 'Simply Red' leader Mick Hucknall in the place of Rod who is too busy being Rod!

IAN McLAGAN - Ian McLagan lives in Austin Texas where he is a regular fixture on the town's renowned music scene. He too has joined Kenney and Ron in the re-modelled 'Faces' line up. He also has his own 'Bump Band' back in The States.

TETSU - Tetsu has long since vanished in to the Rock and Roll ether! Although Kenney apparently came across him some years back and came to the conclusion he had probably lied about his age when joining 'The Faces' back in the Seventies. Make of that what you will...

RONNIE LANE - Ronnie Lane tragically died from M.S. related symptoms in the U.S.